LINCOLN AT PEORIA

Ambrotype by Samuel G. Alschuler, Urbana, Illinois, April 25, 1858

Courtesy of the Abraham Lincoln Presidential Library and Museum

LINCOLN AT PEORIA

THE TURNING POINT

Getting Right with the Declaration of Independence

*"an abstract truth, applicable to
all men and all times"*

ABRAHAM LINCOLN, APRIL 6, 1859

*"Stand with anybody that stands RIGHT.
Stand with him while he is right
and PART with him when he goes wrong."*

ABRAHAM LINCOLN, OCTOBER 16, 1854

STACKPOLE
BOOKS

Published by
STACKPOLE BOOKS
5067 Ritter Road
Mechanicsburg, PA 17055
www.stackpolebooks.com

Printed in the United States

First edition

10 9 8 7 6 5 4 3 2 1

Library of Congress Cataloging-in-Publication Data

Lehrman, Lewis E.
  Lincoln at Peoria : the turning point / Lewis E. Lehrman. — 1st ed.
    p. cm.
  Includes bibliographical references and index.
  ISBN-13: 978-0-8117-0361-1 (hardcover)
  ISBN-10: 0-8117-0361-4 (hardcover)
  1. Lincoln, Abraham, 1809–1865—Political career before 1861. 2. Lincoln, Abraham, 1809–1865—Oratory. 3. Lincoln, Abraham, 1809–1865—Political and social views. 4. Slavery—Political aspects—United States—History—19th century. 5. United States. Kansas-Nebraska Act. 6. Douglas, Stephen Arnold, 1813–1861—Political and social views. 7. Speeches, addresses, etc., American—Illinois—Peoria. 8. Lincoln, Abraham, 1809–1865—Travel—Illinois—Peoria. 9. Peoria (Ill.)—History—19th century. I. Title.
  E457.4.L44 2008
  973.7092—dc22
                    2007050200

For my dearly beloved, Louise, turning point of my life.
For my children—Leland, John, Thomas,
Eliza, Peter and their spouses.
For my grandchildren and their children,
may Lincoln be a trusted guide.
For my countrymen, this testimony to
the promise of America.

"Every man is said to have his peculiar ambition.
Whether it be true or not, I can say for one that I have no
other so great as that of being truly esteemed of my fellow
men, by rendering myself worthy of their esteem. How far
I shall succeed in gratifying this ambition, is yet to be
developed. I am young and unknown to many of you.
I was born and have ever remained in the most humble
walks of life. I have no wealthy or popular relations to
recommend me. My case is thrown exclusively upon the
independent voters of this county, and if elected they will
have conferred a favor upon me, for which I shall be
unremitting in my labors to compensate. But if the good
people in their wisdom shall see fit to keep me in the
background, I have been too familiar with
disappointments to be very much chagrined."

ABRAHAM LINCOLN, AGE 23
MARCH 9, 1832

". . . measuring him by the sentiment of his country,
a sentiment he was bound as a statesman to consult,
[Lincoln] was swift, zealous, radical, and determined."

FREDERICK DOUGLASS
APRIL 14, 1876

CONTENTS

ILLUSTRATIONS AND MAPS

"*Slavery is founded in the selfishness of man's nature—opposition to it in his love of justice. These principles are an eternal antagonism; and when brought into collision so fiercely, as slavery extension brings them, shocks, and throes, and convulsions must ceaselessly follow. Repeal the Missouri Compromise—repeal all compromises— repeal the declaration of independence—repeal all past history, you still can not repeal human nature. It still will be the abundance of man's heart that slavery extension is wrong; and out of the abundance of his heart, his mouth will continue to speak.*"

ABRAHAM LINCOLN,
OCTOBER 16, 1854

Introduction

*L*incoln at Peoria tells the tale of a hardworking lawyer in Springfield, Illinois, at a political turning point in 1854. Admitted to the Illinois Bar in 1836, having served four terms in the state legislature and a single term in Congress (1847–1849), Abraham Lincoln had substantially withdrawn from politics between 1849 and 1854. During these five years, his Springfield law practice prospered. Traveling often by horse and buggy, he became a well-respected litigator on the Eighth Judicial Circuit of Illinois. Then in 1854, the Kansas-Nebraska Act, one of the most explosive congressional statutes of American history, burst upon the Illinois prairie. This congressional statute repealed the 1820 prohibition of slavery in the Kansas-Nebraska territory. The repeal inaugurated a new stage in the slavery debates of the early American Republic. In response to the Kansas-Nebraska Act, Lincoln launched his antislavery campaign with crucial speeches at Springfield and Peoria, Illinois, in October. These speeches and their consequences are the subjects of this book.

In 1854 Lincoln was little known. Now a vast library records the words and actions of Lincoln's life. More has been written of the sixteenth president, perhaps, than any historical figure but Jesus of Nazareth. The narrative of this Lincoln volume has only a limited scope, taking its place in the vast world of Lincoln scholarship. Thus, there is no claim here to consider more of the Lincoln story than the period suggested by the title of this book. The crucial issue of black slavery in America is considered primarily as it bears on Lincoln at the turning point in 1854. There is little space to note the remarkable extent to which black Americans, living here as slaves ten generations before the Civil War, resisted slavery and created their own freedom—even before emancipation. Mr. Lincoln believed black Americans were entitled to the inalienable right to liberty, and to the fruit of their own labor. He also came to believe they would fight for their freedom. Of this he was confident, earnestly believing that "all men are created equal" and wished to be free. And Lincoln was right. That stalwart African Americans joined the Civil War armies to free themselves might not have surprised the Lincoln who appeared in Peoria to give his speech on October 16, 1854—seven years before the Civil War.

Students of Abraham Lincoln know the canon of his major speeches—from his Lyceum Speech of 1838 to his "Final Remarks" delivered from a White House window, days before he was assassinated in 1865. The Gettysburg Address and the Second Inaugural are brief and timeless. Some works are nostalgic such as the eulogy for Henry Clay in 1852. Before them in the 1830s and 1840s, there are speeches of the younger Lincoln on the high road and some on the low road. Later came monumental masterpieces, such as the "House Divided" speech of 1858 and the Cooper Union address of 1860. There are the extraordinary debates of 1858 with Senator Stephen A. Douglas. In contrast, there are the short, impromptu speeches of modest substance given on his way to Washington in 1861. The president's public letters in mid-1863 to James C. Conkling and Erastus Corning read like well-crafted speeches. The First and Second Inaugurals spell out President Lincoln's interpretations of the causes and consequences of the Civil War.

Less well known are the speeches given at Springfield and Peoria two weeks apart in 1854. They mark Lincoln's reentry into the politics of Illinois and, as he could not know, his preparation for the presidency in 1861. Historians and biographers have noted their importance, but they have not received the full study they merit. These Lincoln addresses catapulted him into the debates over slavery which dominated Illinois and national politics for the rest of the decade. Lincoln delivered the substance of these arguments several times—certainly in Springfield on October 4, 1854, for which there are only press reports. A longer version came twelve days later in Peoria. The Springfield remarks did not survive, but by preparing them meticulously for publication, Lincoln made sure the text from Peoria endured.

By his research and editorial care Lincoln made clear his respect for the historian's record. I, too, respect the historian's record. Scholars and teachers have taught me what I know of the American saga. I am deeply in debt to them. Still, I am not a scholar. My full-time vocation has allowed me irregular hours to research, study, and write, but I have tried to adhere to the traditional standards of historical scholarship. Thus, this book—a labor of love, in the works for more than two decades—has taken needed inspiration from dedicated teachers of our history. In this study I try to let the exact words of Lincoln himself, of his contemporaries, and of six generations of scholars tell the tale. They speak very well for themselves. The admonition of my graduate school teacher still rings in my ears—let readers make up their own minds from the evidence on the record, and from different interpretations presented by witnesses and scholars. I have tried to apply this principle, especially in the straightforward historical narrative of chapters I through III. My own judgments—of the momentous issues at stake, of the rival ideas and leaders of the 1850s—are more transparent in chapters IV through IX.

Lincoln himself was suspicious of biography and history, according to William Herndon, his law partner of sixteen years. Herndon reported that Lincoln, perusing a biography of Edmund Burke, observed: "Biographies as generally written are not only misleading, but false." Lincoln pondered a while and added: "Billy, I've wondered why book-publishers and merchants don't have blank biographies on their shelves, always ready for an emergency; so that, if a man happens to die, his heirs or his friends, if they wish to perpetuate his memory, can purchase one already written, but with blanks. These blanks they can at their pleasure fill up with rosy sentences full of high-sounding praise."[1] Though difficult to uphold, I try in this book to follow Mr. Lincoln's admonition and to introduce a balanced view, not only of Lincoln at the turning point, but of his chief adversary, Stephen A. Douglas. Both were ambitious, both patriots, both endowed with great talent. Neither needs hagiography, nor has either earned demonization. In matters of character, principle, and policy, I do make comparisons, but I try to avoid invidious distinctions.

Of Lincoln I do not shirk my own judgments. I confess that I have little doubt that the mature Lincoln at Peoria in 1854 is of a piece with the man who would be recognized as a great American statesman. There is, I believe, an unmistakable wholeness of character, genius, and enterprise to his public life from 1854 to 1865. But in 1854, the future President could not know what awaited him and his countrymen. Given the benefit of hindsight, every historian must be careful to avoid presumption. Historical interpretation should acknowledge how little of the future can be foreseen by men and women of affairs; how intractable are the circumstances facing political leaders; how unpredictable are historical outcomes; how varied are the motives that drive each contingent human decision; how, nonetheless, leadership can influence what might otherwise be improbable outcomes. Lincoln's antislavery campaign was an exercise in leadership.

To understand President Abraham Lincoln, one must understand the Peoria speech of October 16, 1854. It forms the foundation of his politics and principles, in the 1850s and in his presidency. The Peoria speech, delivered in three hours and ten minutes and composed of more than 17,000 words, is reprinted in full in an appendix. It is a rhetorical and literary masterpiece. This speech is the primary statement by Abraham Lincoln about the nature of early American history and its "peculiar institution" of slavery. Lincoln's arguments at Peoria were a comprehensive repudiation of the Kansas-Nebraska Act of May 1854. Sponsored by Illinois Senator Stephen A. Douglas, this legislation voided the congressional prohibition on slavery in that section of the Louisiana Territory north of the 36° 30' parallel, a restriction on the spread of slavery agreed to in the Missouri Compromise of 1820. Lincoln was appalled by this reversal of three decades of settled policy. He was opposed to any further spread of slavery in the American republic, founded as it was upon the Declaration of Independence. That "all men are created equal," with the "inalienable right to liberty," was, for Lincoln, a universal principle that Americans must not ignore.

With research and study conducted in the State Capitol, the forty-five-year-old attorney carefully prepared a counterattack on the Kansas-Nebraska Act. Years of studying Sir William Blackstone's *Commentaries on the Laws of England*, preparing for jury trials, litigating in the courts of Illinois, and researching American political history had prepared Lincoln's mind and speech to argue the issues raised by the new legislation. To his natural aptitude for learning Lincoln now joined a mature intellect, a driving instinct for political organization, and a masterful grasp of the facts and logic of the case against Kansas-Nebraska.

- Chapter I opens the book with a narrative of Lincoln's many visits to Peoria, Illinois, and the events of the summer and fall of 1854 during which Lincoln contested the Kansas-Nebraska Act.
- Chapter II considers Lincoln's antislavery campaign in October when he delivered speeches in Springfield, Peoria, and several other locations in central and northern Illinois.
- Chapter III reviews the tortuous journey of Senator Stephen Douglas's Kansas-Nebraska legislation as it moved through Congress—providing the essential backdrop and the occasion for Lincoln's reentry into politics.
- Chapter IV analyzes the logic by which Lincoln attacked the Kansas-Nebraska legislation in his Springfield-Peoria speeches. This analysis considers Lincoln's views on the history of slavery.
- Chapters V, VI, and VII chronicle how Mr. Lincoln built upon the arguments of the Peoria speech during the six years before the presidency and then in the presidency itself.
- Chapter VIII, the Coda, winds up the story of the Peoria speech and its influence.
- Chapter IX, the Historians' Record, analyzes how Lincoln's contemporaries and historians have evaluated the Peoria Speech since 1854.
- The full text of the Peoria Speech follows.
- The Acknowledgments record the debts the author owes to teachers, historians, and to his own contemporaries.
- Milestones in the lives of Abraham Lincoln and Stephen A. Douglas chronicle the parallel, intertwined events of the two men and their families.

- The original orthography and punctuation of these quotations are retained; for readability "[sic]" is inserted infrequently only if necessary to preserve the intelligibility of the quote.

At Peoria, Lincoln developed the mature model that would guide his principal writings for the last decade of his life. Parts of his antislavery case at Peoria, its spirit, and even exact phrases can be found at the center of almost every subsequent major speech, public letter, and state paper. Indeed, understanding Lincoln's conduct in 1854 and thereafter suggests that the great divide between the statecraft of his presidential years and his early legislative years comes with the speech at Peoria on October 16. Shorn of grandiloquence and jokes, the address was earnest, rigorous, logical, and grounded in thorough historical research. The Peoria speech—together with similar speeches he gave in the summer and fall of 1854—dramatically altered the political career of the speaker and, as a result, the history of America.

The Kansas-Nebraska Act had intensified the historic national dispute about slavery, a controversy born with America at the Founding. Lincoln brought formidable intellectual and political skills to the task of leading the antislavery opposition to Senator Douglas in Illinois. Master of himself and master of his political and economic philosophy, the forty-five-year-old lawyer became a master of men. At Peoria, Lincoln took his stand on slavery; and, as Archimedes suggested, with a place to stand one might move the world. The Kansas-Nebraska Act, with its potential to extend slavery, had created conditions that led Lincoln to assert his interpretation of the fundamental principles of the American Founding and the proper application of those principles as announced in the Declaration of Independence. In Lincoln's antislavery statecraft, abstract principles were joined to a bold but prudential wisdom, expressed in unforgettable argument and action. These principles would later inform the letter and spirit of the Emancipation Proclamation in 1863 and the abolition of slavery in the Thirteenth Amendment that followed in 1865.

After delivering the Peoria speech on October 16, Lincoln submitted his text, carefully edited, for serial publication in the Illinois *State Journal,* inaugurating the practice of editing carefully his important speeches for subsequent publication. He applied this editorial technique to the Peoria speech, just as he would later prepare for publication his 1858 debates with Stephen A. Douglas. Thus, Lincoln's October 4, 1854, speech in Springfield—and perhaps even earlier versions given at Winchester and Bloomington—became known generically as the "Peoria speech." The Peoria text is surely the most comprehensive version—as Lincoln signaled there when he said, "At Springfield, twelve days ago, where I had spoken substantially as I have here, Judge Douglas replied to me—and as he is to reply to me here, I shall attempt to anticipate him, by noticing some of the points he made there."[2] At both places, Senator Douglas spoke before Lincoln and then responded to him. By the time the Peoria speech was published, it was too late for the printed text to have additional impact on the November elections in Illinois—but not too late to influence the course of American history.

These less famous Lincoln-Douglas debates of 1854 marked a clear dividing line in the political career of Abraham Lincoln. The Kansas-Nebraska Act of May 1854 had opened up the possibility that slavery could be extended into the vast northern portion of the Louisiana Purchase, suggesting even that slavery could spread nationwide. This dramatic shift in national legislative policy drew Lincoln from private life into the incendiary struggle over the future of slavery in America. The year 1854 became a turning point for the country; as it became the political turning point for Mr. Lincoln. The antislavery speeches Lincoln gave in the political campaign of 1854 separated him from a lifetime of commentary almost exclusively on national economic policy. During the 1830s and 1840s, Lincoln had concentrated on tariff, tax, banking, and public works policies—the essential issues of Whig Party politics. In 1854, however, Lincoln turned his full attention to slavery, the preeminent issue of the decade. His view of American history, his command of the intricacies of the slavery debate, and his mature political philosophy were all spelled out at Peoria. The case he made there would inform his important public comments until his death on April 15, 1865.

Lewis E. Lehrman
August 15, 2007

"In order to [get] a clear understanding of what the Missouri Compromise is, a short history of the preceding kindred subjects will perhaps be proper."

ABRAHAM LINCOLN,
OCTOBER 16, 1854

I.

On the Road to
the Springfield Speech

The political activities of Abraham Lincoln in Illinois were well noted by his father-in-law in Lexington, Kentucky. Less than two years after the Lincoln-Todd marriage in November 1842, Robert Todd wrote to one of his sons-in-law: "Mr. Lincoln I discover is using his influence & talents for the Whig Cause. I think he is right; for a good government should be first in the mind of every patriot. I can use influence here if Mr [Henry] Clay is elected (of which there can be no doubt) to procure some appointment for him, which will keep him out of Congress until his Situation in a monied point of view, will enable him to take a stand in Congress, creditable both to himself and Country. Such as *District Attorney or Judge.*"[3] Even after eight years of legal practice and four terms as a state legislator, success eluded the thirty-five-year-old Lincoln. His wealthy father-in-law thought financial independence necessary for Lincoln "to take a stand in Congress."

Lincoln also needed to build his political base. He anticipated a try for the Whig Party nomination to Congress that he had abandoned in 1843 when it became clear he would lose at the Whig convention. The 1844 nomination would go to the Whig runner-up from 1843; Lincoln aimed for the Whig slot in the 1846 election. Lacking legislative office in 1844, Lincoln did not lack political ambition. The presidential candidacy

1

of fellow Kentuckian Henry Clay provided the opportunity for Lincoln to hone his speechmaking in support of the Whig ticket. As a candidate for the Electoral College in Illinois, it was natural for him to do so.

Such was the setting for Lincoln to speak at Peoria, Illinois.[4] Although it numbered less than 2,000 residents, Peoria was an ambitious American community. It had begun to develop a manufacturing base of flour milling, pork packing, and constructing farm implements. Peoria's political status would soon rise to that of a "city." A debate had been scheduled there between Lincoln and former Congressman William L. May, a Jacksonian Democrat who had twice left the Whig Party over the previous decade. As a Democrat, he had deserted President Martin Van Buren over economic policy. May had lost renomination to a rising young Democrat, Stephen A. Douglas, who then himself lost the 1838 election.[5]

It was a hot and humid night in 1844 when ex-Whig May opened the debate inside the Presbyterian church on Peoria's Main Street.[6] May concluded his political remarks, according to a newspaper editor in attendance, by ridiculing "the pole raised by the zealous Whigs of the town near the public square. He explained the three kinds of wood of which it was constructed, and informed the audience that the main or lower stick, like the Whig Party, was hollow and without heart! The Democrats applauded, the Whigs looked serious and Colonel May took his seat." Like former Congressman May, future Congressman Lincoln spoke in earnest. He concluded by responding wryly to May's comment about the Whig pole: "The Whigs of Peoria had no cause to be especially proud of their pole," said Lincoln. After all, "it was not made of the best timber and was not straight, but there was one thing about it he could explain, account for and admire. The hollow place at the butt of the pole was where Colonel May had crawled out of the Whig Party, and his party friends now propose to close it up so that the colonel never could return."[7]

Lincoln's sardonic comments were made in good humor and so they were taken by the audience. They were not so well received by the Kentucky-born May. The fifty-one-year-old attorney was incensed, denouncing Lincoln's audience as they left the church: "Leave you blank infernal coons! Blank you, you are such blank cowards you won't stay till I skin your blank champion, blank him to blanknation." May was no fool, however. He knew that Lincoln was formidable, physically and intellectu-

ally. According to Thomas J. Pickett, a Lincoln friend and longtime political ally, May "knew that if he carried his indignation too far there was
danger that Lincoln would throw him over the pulpit rails."[8] Standing just
a bit under 6'4", muscular and lean, Lincoln could intimidate a potential
adversary. That year, while on the way to a Whig convention in Peoria, he
helped to lift a railroad car off the tracks so that a freight train could pass
in the opposite direction.[9]

When May had cooled down the next day, he asked Lincoln why he
had introduced "personalities" into the debate. "Colonel, I was like the
little boy who kissed the girl at school. When the teacher asked him why
he had acted so rudely, [he] replied, 'She stood so fair I couldn't help
it!'"[10] Thomas Pickett, who edited the local Whig newspaper, remembered: "May threatened for a day or two to bring the matter within the
range of the *code duello*. But as Lincoln was an ugly customer, whose cool
and dauntless courage no man doubted, his antagonist concluded that
'the better part of valor was discretion,' and took his revenge by swearing
violently every time the pleasantry was alluded to in his presence."[11]

Some recollections, such as those of the May-Lincoln confrontation,
cannot be confirmed by contemporary documents, only later testimony.
Nevertheless, as historian James M. McPherson has observed, if historians
confined themselves only to incontrovertible evidence, it "would . . . leave
large gaps in the Lincoln story, both in Lincoln's early life and in his presidential years."[12] Don E. and Virginia Fehrenbacher have done yeoman
work in *The Recollected Words of Abraham Lincoln* by classifying the reliability
of various quotations attributed to Lincoln by his contemporaries, but it is
impossible to verify all the recollections of what Lincoln did and said,
especially in his early life.

Memories of Lincoln on the stump during the 1830s and 1840s
demonstrate Lincoln could be harsh—so much so that his impersonation
of Jesse B. Thomas Jr. was known for years as the "skinning of Thomas." In
the winter of 1839–1840, leading Springfield Democrats were debating
their Whig counterparts in a series of meetings. When Lincoln heard
Democrat Thomas was ridiculing him and his Whig colleagues, he rushed
to the church where the meeting was being held. Lincoln the storyteller
became Lincoln the mimic. William H. Herndon recalled the crowd's
reaction to Lincoln's devastating caricature of the way Thomas walked

and talked: "Encouraged by these demonstrations, the ludicrous features of the speaker's performance gave way to intense and scathing ridicule." But according to Herndon, Lincoln also felt bad that he had driven Thomas weeping from the scene. So Lincoln sought out Thomas to apologize. "The incident and its sequel proved that Lincoln could not only be vindictive but manly as well," wrote the loyal Herndon, Lincoln's third and last law partner.[13]

Lincoln's confrontation with May had come when he was campaigning on behalf of the Whig cause in Illinois. He delivered at least two more speeches in Peoria during 1844. The first came on a Saturday night in April, when Lincoln answered John Calhoun, a Democrat and friend who had once been his surveying boss in Sangamon County. Herndon wrote that "Calhoun was polite, affable, and an honest debater, never dodging any question. This made him a formidable antagonist in argumentative controversy."[14] This Saturday night, Calhoun talked for several hours, trying the patience of his listeners and hoping they would not stay around for his Whig rival. It was almost midnight when Lincoln got his chance to rebut Calhoun. Editor Pickett reported that "for thirty minutes poor Calhoun was first skinned and then drawn and quartered, and the operation was performed with the utmost good nature." The Peoria *Democratic Press* was less impressed. It reported: "Mr. Lincoln, the opposing candidate of Mr. Calhoun, followed in reply. He set out by stating that Mr C.'s great complaint against the tarif[f] was that it taxed the people. This was enough for us on that occasion—We did not stay to hear him out."[15]

In June 1844 Lincoln spoke again in Peoria, this time at the Whig Party convention. As he stood to speak, he "did not on rising show his full height; stood rather in a stooping posture, his long-tailed coat hanging loosely around his body, descending round and over an ill-fitting pair of pantaloons that covered his not very symmetrical legs," reported one witness. "He commenced his speech in a rather diffident manner[,] even seemed for a while at a loss for words; his voice was irregular, a little tremulous, as at first he began his argument by laying down his propositions. As he proceeded, he seemed to gain more confidence, his body straightened up, his countenance brightened, his language became free and animated, as, during this time he had illustrated his argument by two or three well-told stories, that drew the attention of the thousands of his audience to every word he uttered. Then he became eloquent, carrying the swaying crowd at his will, who, at every point he made in his forcible argument, were tumultuous in their applause." Whig editor Jeriah Bonham remembered Lincoln's speech on the protective tariff "showed to the people that he had thoroughly mastered all the great questions of the day, and brought to their discussion closeness and soundness of logic, with numerous facts, clinched by the most elaborate and powerful arguments."[16]

Lincoln and Douglas—the Early Years

In the decade between his appearances at Peoria in 1844 and October 16, 1854, Lincoln matured as a lawyer, politician, and speaker. He returned regularly to Peoria on legal and political business. By the time the fierce storm over the Kansas-Nebraska Act blew across Illinois in 1854, Lincoln had become a successful attorney, a formidable litigator, and a powerful debating opponent. Few thought Lincoln a match for the self-confident and accomplished "Little Giant" of Illinois, the Democratic senator who had masterminded the Kansas-Nebraska Act through Congress. Vermont-born Stephen A. Douglas had been a fixture in Illinois political life for most of Lincoln's adult life. They first met in the Illinois State Legislature in 1834—Lincoln then twenty-five, Douglas only twenty-one. In December 1837, Douglas replaced May as the Democratic congressional nominee at a Peoria convention where May was urged to resign. Douglas then lost the 1838 congressional campaign to Lincoln's senior law partner, John Todd Stuart, in the district that included Peoria. After a series of vigorous debates around the district, the low point of the race occurred in Springfield. Stuart reportedly picked up the smaller Douglas by the scruff of his neck; Douglas then bit Stuart's thumb nearly in half.[17] Lincoln was mindful of Douglas, later writing: "We were both young then; he a trifle younger than I. Even then, we were both ambitious; I, perhaps, quite as much so as he."[18] Lincoln did not minimize his ambition, nor Douglas's national success.

John G. Nicolay and John Hay, both a generation younger than Lincoln, knew him in Illinois before accompanying him in 1861 to Washington as his White House secretaries. Decades later as biographers, they wrote that "while Lincoln knew all Douglas's strong points he was no less familiar with his weak ones. They had come to central Illinois about the same time, and had in a measure grown up together. Socially they were on friendly terms; politically they had been opponents for twenty years. At the bar, in the Legislature, and on the stump they had often met and measured strength. Each therefore knew the temper of the other's steel no less than every joint in his armor."[19] Size, character, personality, and party set them apart. Douglas "always had a crowd around him, which he entertained," wrote Gustave Koerner, who was the state's lieutenant governor in 1854. "Yet he was no story-teller, and would have spoiled the best story in telling it,—in fact, he had very little imaginative power. But he would speak of his travels, of the resources of the different States, of the prospects of this or that city, or the greatness of the country, giving statistics, and occasionally talking of the prominent men whom he had seen. He would at the same time, without lowering himself, take a drink when invited to do so, and shake hands and laugh at a joke, good or bad. Lincoln delighted his crowds and kept them in [a] perfect roar of laughter; Douglas interested his hearers by his impressive, almost enthusiastic, conversation."[20]

Isaac N. Arnold, a contemporary Illinois politician and later a historian, knew both men. Douglas, he wrote, "was a man of an iron constitution and a strong and acute intellect. Possessed of a wonderful memory, without being a scholar, his mind was well stored with practical and accurate information. He never forgot anything he had ever read, or seen, or heard; and he had that happy faculty of a politician, of always remembering names and faces. His resources were always at his command, and he needed little preparation. Of a kind and genial disposition, with a frank, open, and cordial manner, endowed with remarkable conversational powers, bold, dashing, and somewhat reckless, he had all the qualities which go to make up a great popular leader, in a degree equal to any man of American history. As a speaker and debater, either in the Senate or on the stump, he had few equals. He spoke, always with great fluency and power. He seized the strong points of his case, and enforced them with great vigor. Quick and ready to seize the weak points of his antagonist, he would drive them home with strong and well-applied blows, never being disposed to yield an advantage which he had once obtained."[21] Douglas was a formidable political leader. Princeton Professor Woodrow Wilson wrote of Douglas: "His short and massive figure, his square head, steady, deep-set eyes, and mouth cut straight and firm, in lines unsensitive and full of will, bespoke him the man he was: a man to make and have his way, fearless, sincere, compact of force; commanding others, but not to be commanded himself; coarse-fibred, daring, ready witted, loud, and yet prepossessing withal, winning friends and receiving homage."[22]

It has been argued that in 1854 Lincoln seized upon the Kansas-Nebraska Act primarily to advance his ambition, but the odds were stacked against him in the coming contest with America's gifted, popular, and powerful senator. By the early 1850s Douglas had become the supreme arbiter of Illinois politics and the well-placed chairman of the Senate Committee on Territories. By contrast, Lincoln in 1849 had withdrawn to the parochial stage of a Springfield law office. Lincoln biographer Benjamin Thomas emphasized that Douglas was "often inscrutable, incessantly active in politics, business, and Washington social life, a brilliant improviser rather than a reflective, far-seeing planner. . . . Well versed in governmental and political lore, scornful of opposition, he was an overpowering orator when in the right, and a skillful and sometimes unscrupulous dissembler when arguing a bad cause."[23]

Douglas, not more than five feet, four inches in height, had become a giant of American politics. Denied the Democratic presidential nomination at age thirty-nine in 1852, he had become the de facto leader of his party in the Senate. William O. Stoddard, an Illinois newspaper editor who became familiar with Douglas in the 1850s, later wrote: "His experience in debate, his easy audacity and assurance, his great ability, his strong will, his unconquerable ambition, and his untiring industry, made him a most formidable antagonist. . . . Mr. Douglas entered into an exposition and defense of his principles and policy with the bearing of a man who had already conquered. His long and uninterrupted success had made him restive under inquisition, impatient of dispute, and defiant of opposition."[24]

In 1854 Lincoln paled in conventional public comparisons to Douglas. Effectively out of politics for the past five years, he held no public office. His Whig party was disintegrating. In 1852, its national leaders—Henry Clay and Daniel Webster—had died. It seemed an inauspicious

time to renew political activities against a national Democratic leader in a
state dominated by the Democratic Party. But Illinois also offered a
respectful audience. While spirited and rough, Illinois politics featured
policy debates often conducted at a high intellectual level, focused on the
major issues facing the country. Historian Allan Nevins noted that "the
inhabitants of the Old Northwest, from Ohio to Iowa, were then a folk of
superior character and intelligence."[25] Nevins quoted German immigrant
Carl Schurz who observed: "A universal struggle of opinion among a free
people has about it something unbelievably imposing, and never does
one see with more clarity what a comprehensive influence political freedom exercises upon the development of the masses."[26]

Lincoln had returned to his Springfield law practice after a single term
in Congress from 1847 to 1849. Having campaigned vigorously for the
Whig presidential victory in 1848, he had been frustrated in an unsuccessful bid to be appointed in 1849 by President Zachary Taylor as the new
commissioner of the General Land Office. Lincoln had been disappointed
by politics, by his party, and perhaps by his own performance in Washington. He again embraced the practice of law. As Lincoln would observe in
1860, "Work, work, work, is the main thing."[27] From 1849 to 1854, Lincoln
did work long hours, traveling the vast Eighth Judicial Circuit in Illinois.
Allan Nevins concluded that "for five years he had devoted himself to self-
improvement in general culture, the law, and thought by sustained study
and hard desk work. In 1854, when he rose to the challenge of the
Nebraska Act, some fruits of that discipline had appeared."[28]

Helping Congressman Yates

Antislavery principle, public ambition, and political opportunity drove
Lincoln to select an immediate and practical target in 1854—the need for
central Illinois to reelect its anti-Nebraska congressman. Richard Yates,
the Springfield area representative, was one of the first Illinois Whigs to
speak out against the Kansas-Nebraska Act of 1854. The legislation, sponsored and managed by Senator Douglas, had repealed the historic Missouri Compromise of 1820, which had barred slavery north of the 36° 30'
parallel in the enormous Louisiana territory purchased from France in
1803. Yates in 1854 had criticized "the opening of this dangerous agita-

tion, fraught with such imminent peril to the existence of the Union itself."[29] The Whig congressman advocated the position Lincoln himself held: "All that we claim for the Missouri Compromise is, that there were great conflicting interests and that there was a settlement, in which both parties conceded something; and that though in strict law it is repealable, yet, in honor, good faith and morals, it is as much a compact as drawn on parchment, under the hand and seals of the people of the North and South. . . ."[30] (The "North" was used to describe the free states while the "South" referred to slave states. This division had historically threatened the "Union" sealed by the Continental Congress on July 4, 1776.)

The Kansas-Nebraska Act became law on May 30, 1854. Prior to its passage, Yates had warned the South from the House floor: "If you pass this bill, your friends in the North, who have considered the Abolitionists the aggressors and have vindicated your cause, will consider you the aggressors. They will laugh at your flimsy apology that you take the forbidden fruit because it is offered you by a Northern hand. They will consider it a vandal march on territory which, by your own hands, by universal consent and long acquiescence, by patriot sons, by solemn contract and plighted faith, has been consecrated to freedom" by the Missouri Compromise of 1820.[31] In addition to these sentiments, Lincoln and Congressman Yates had much else in common. Yates, too, was a native of Kentucky and a four-term state legislator. He knew and admired Lincoln. But Yates was more fashionable. One contemporary described Yates as "a splendid looking man, well made, erect, easy and graceful in form with mild brown eyes, long wavy brown hair and always dressed in the height of fashion." Inspired by Lincoln, Yates told a friend that Lincoln's speech on August 26, 1854, at Winchester, Illinois, was "the strongest speech I ever heard on the subject" of Kansas-Nebraska. Lincoln reportedly had "got up a speech on the Kansas-Nebraska bill which he has never made before and he has come down here to 'try it on the dog' before he delivers it to larger audiences."[32] One observer at Winchester noted that Lincoln had been called from the crowd to address the Nebraska issue, which he did in an "ingenious, logical, and at the same time fair and candid manner. . . ." Writing to the *Illinois Journal*, this eyewitness concluded that Lincoln's "was [a] masterly effort—said to be equal to any upon the same subject in Congress . . . replete with unanswerable arguments, which must and will effectually tell at the coming election."[33] Another witness at Winchester noted that Lincoln "impressed me with the feeling that the country was on the brink of a great disaster."[34]

Lincoln's antislavery arguments had matured as the Kansas-Nebraska bill moved through Congress and roused indignation across the North. Law partner William H. Herndon wrote that Lincoln quickly understood that the Kansas-Nebraska Act's passage presented more than a "live issue." Herndon recalled: "In the office discussions he grew bolder in his utterances. He insisted that the social and political difference between slavery and freedom was becoming more marked; that one must overcome the other; and that postponing the struggle between them would only make it more deadly in the end."[35] Friends remembered that such ideas kept Lincoln up at night, thinking them over before the fire at hotels where he slept on the Eighth Judicial Circuit. Fellow Whig lawyer T. Lyle Dickey wrote that he discussed the Kansas-Nebraska legislation with Lincoln when news of its enactment reached them on the Illinois court circuit. As Dickey remembered, they talked in their hotel room late into the night. In the morning when Judge Dickey awoke, he saw Lincoln sitting on the bed. "I tell you, Dickey, this nation cannot exist half slave and half free."[36] Dickey reportedly replied: "Oh, Lincoln, go to sleep."[37]

Many plausible recollections by contemporary observers cannot be authenticated, but some who recorded them accompanied Lincoln at the time. What cannot be questioned is that Lincoln's revulsion at the Kansas-Nebraska Act pushed him from the judicial circuit to the political circuit. The two circuits were linked, and Lincoln shifted his focus in 1854. "I was losing interest in politics, when the repeal of the Missouri Compromise aroused me again," he acknowledged later.[38] After completing his semiannual court circuit through the Central Illinois county seats of Jacksonville, Lincoln, Bloomington, Metamora, Pekin, Urbana, and Danville, Lincoln returned to Springfield in the late spring. There, he had ready access on the first floor of the Capitol to the State Library where he gathered his political thoughts before the fall legal circuit would begin. On many other occasions Lincoln and his friends collected here or in the club-like State Law Library for political discussions, chess, and smoking.[39] But as historians Paul M. Angle and Earl Schenck Miers observed: "Characteristically, Lincoln said little and did nothing until the approach of the fall elections. The ballot, in his creed, was the instrument by which a citizen registered his protest."[40] Experience taught him that the electorate generally focused on political issues before elections. He would need to be ready.

Conventional party politics in Illinois had become unstable by 1854, presenting peculiar challenges for Lincoln, a loyal conservative Whig. The repeal of the Missouri Compromise intensified the instability. The Know-Nothing movement, opposed to unchecked immigration, had stirred in Illinois, where the Democratic Party's dominance was under challenge. The Kansas-Nebraska legislation and the nativist Know-Nothings put party loyalties to the test, even undermining the ascendancy of the Democratic Party. Some free-soil Democrats, who opposed the expansion of slavery into new territories, broke with their party, rejecting Douglas and his Kansas-Nebraska Act. Some Whigs moved to support Douglas, embracing his doctrine of popular sovereignty which held that residents of new territories (rather than Congress) should decide whether to permit or prohibit slavery. Wrote Nicolay and Hay:

> In the northern counties, where the antislavery sentiment was general, there were a few successful efforts to disband the old parties and create a combined opposition under the new name of Republicans. This, it was soon apparent, would make serious inroads on the existing Democratic majority. But an alarming counter-movement in the central counties, which formed the Whig stronghold, soon began to show itself. Douglas's violent denunciation of "abolitionists" and "abolitionism" appealed with singular power to Whigs from slave States. The party was without a national leader; Clay had died two years before, and Douglas made skillful quotations from the great statesman's speeches to bolster up his new propagandism. In Congress only a little handful of Southern Whigs opposed the repeal [of the Missouri Compromise], and even these did not dare place their opposition on antislavery grounds. And especially the familiar voice and example of the neighboring Missouri Whigs were given unhesitatingly to the support of the Douglas scheme.[41]

Preparation to Fight Kansas-Nebraska

It was a daunting moment for an Illinois Whig to reenter political combat. Tensions had built to the breaking point in Washington. National and Illinois politicians focused on the Kansas-Nebraska legislation as it was debated in Congress in 1854. With antislavery Whigs and free-soil Democrats, Lincoln believed the Douglas bill would open the door to the spread, perhaps the eventual nationalization, of slavery. William Herndon recalled that Kansas-Nebraska, freedom, and slavery stirred Lincoln's powers of political metaphor: "The day of compromise has passed. These two great ideas have been kept apart only by the most artful means. They are like two wild beasts in sight of each other, but chained and held apart. Some day these deadly antagonists will open or the other break their bonds, and then the question will be settled."[42] With Euclidean logic, Lincoln laid out his analysis of the problems of slavery in a private memorandum to himself:

> If A. can prove, however conclusively, that he may, of right, enslave B.- why may not B. snatch the same argument, and prove equally, that he may enslave A?- You say A. is white, and B. is black. It is color, then; the lighter, having the right to enslave the darker? Take care. By this rule, you are to be slave to the first man you meet, with a fairer skin than your own.
>
> You do not mean *color* exactly?—You mean the whites are *intellectually* the superiors of the blacks, and, therefore have the right to enslave them? Take care again. By this rule, you are to be slave to the first man you meet, with an intellect superior to your own.
>
> But, say you, it is a question of *interest*; and, if you can make it your *interest*, you have the right to enslave another. Very well. And if he can make it his interest, he has the right to enslave you.[43]

Just as Lincoln girded for the coming political battle, Congressman Yates made ready to lay down his sword. Yates intended to announce his retirement from Congress when he returned to Springfield on August 9. Rumors of alcoholism shadowed Yates's entire political career, but Lincoln wrote to a friend of Yates that he believed such charges "incorrect." He stated that he had never seen or heard of such unseemly behavior:

You perhaps know how anxious I am for Yates' reelection in this District. I understand his enemies are getting up a charge against him, that while he passes for a temperate man, he is in the habit of drinking secretly—and that they calculate on proving an instance of the charge by you. If, indeed, you have told them any thing, I can not help thinking they have misunderstood what you did tell them. Other things being equal, I would much prefer a temperate man, to an intemperate one; still I do not make my vote depend absolutely upon the question of whether a candidate does or does not *taste* liquor.[44]

Lincoln began to make ready in other ways. Lincoln biographer Michael Burlingame wrote: "In the Springfield courthouse that summer, he attended a meeting to discuss the slavery issue and nominate candidates for office. Most of the thirty attendees, although angry about 'the encroachments of slavery,' hesitated to take action to combat them. Lincoln, however, purportedly said 'if we hold these opinions in regard to the outrages upon the black man why should we fear to avow them and say what we think and do what we can in behalf of right and justice.'"[45]

Whig Lincoln had focused on political organization as well as political ideas. He had determined that stalwarts opposed to the Kansas-Nebraska Act like Congressman Yates should be persuaded to run for reelection. Yates recalled that

on my return home at the close of the long session of 1854, having published a card that I would not be a candidate for reelection, I was met at the depot in Springfield by Lincoln. He said I had taken the right course on this question, and though he could not promise me success in a district so largely against us, yet he hoped for the sake of the principle, I would run, . . . and if I would, he would take the stump in my behalf. I remember his earnestness, and so deeply did he impress me that the question was one worthy of our noblest efforts whether in victory or defeat, that I consented. From the circumstances I believe that the only consideration with Lincoln was a disinterested and patriotic desire for the success of correct principle.[46]

Earlier in 1854, it appeared that Yates might actually benefit from passage of the Kansas-Nebraska Act.[47] Supporters wrote him that anti-Nebraska feeling would assure his reelection. The Democratic candidate, however, was formidable—erstwhile Congressman Thomas L. Harris. Major Harris had gained military fame at the Battle of Cero Gordo in the Mexican-American War. He gained his political acclaim in 1848 by defeating Lincoln's former law partner Stephen T. Logan in the race to succeed then-Congressman Lincoln, who had opposed the war. Harris was a particularly close ally of Senator Douglas, who wrote that "I have no secrets from him. I have implicit confidence in his discretion, firmness & fidelity."[48] Harris had a supposed link to the Mormon movement in Utah. His Whig critics labeled him "Polygamy Harris"—a stigma he was largely able to shake during the campaign.[49]

Meanwhile, Lincoln pushed Yates to run for reelection. Douglas had started a political war with his Kansas-Nebraska Act, and Lincoln wanted every opposing recruit to take the field. He wrote Yates in mid-August: "I am disappointed at not having seen or heard from you since I met you more than a week ago at the railroad depot here. I wish to have the matter we spoke of settled and working to its consummation." He asked Yates to allow himself to be drafted for reelection by fellow Whigs—by placing a political notice in the *Illinois State Journal*.[50] In order to assist Yates, Lincoln in September reluctantly agreed to join Judge Logan as a Sangamon County candidate for the Illinois State Legislature. Slowly, Lincoln was drawn into the campaign maelstrom. First, he had to overcome a formidable domestic opponent—his wife. According to Dr. William Jayne, "I took the names of Judge Logan & Abrm Lincoln to the *Sangamon Journal* Office and had them published" as candidates for the Illinois House of Representatives. However, "Mrs. Lincoln saw [Simeon] Francis the Editor and had Lincoln[']s name taken out. Lincoln was absent. When L[incoln]. came home[,] I went to see him in order to get him to consent to run. This was at his house. He was then the saddest man I Ever Saw—the gloomiest: he walked up and down the floor—almost crying and to all my persuasions to let his name stand in the papers—he said 'No—I can't—you don't Know all—I Say you don't begin to Know one half and that's Enough.'" Lincoln apparently dealt persuasively with his strong-willed spouse. Jayne put his name back on the Whig list at the *Journal*.[51]

Historians have debated how much Lincoln thought ahead to the looming election for the U.S. Senate—to be decided in early 1855 by the state legislature. Lincoln biographer David Herbert Donald attributed to legal grounds Lincoln's reluctance to be a legislative candidate, concluding: "Neither then nor later did Lincoln explain his misgivings, but in all probability he had his own political future in mind."[52] Lincoln doubtless knew that the state constitution prohibited a member of the state legislature from being elected to the U.S. Senate. Historian Richard J. Carwardine argued: "To run for the legislature, which was imminently to choose a successor to the incumbent Democratic senator [Shields], would rule him [Lincoln] out of consideration. But to decline to run would be an act of disloyalty to the party, costing him the very support he needed for his grander objective."[53] Lincoln made the race for the state legislature, even if the statute presented a potential roadblock to the "grander objective" of the U. S. Senate.

Lincoln forged ahead, cultivating anti-Nebraska sentiment in the Yates-Harris contest. He intervened with Democrat John M. Palmer of Macoupin County, who sought reelection from a State Senate district encompassed by Yates's congressional district. In January 1854, Palmer had opposed a state legislative resolution endorsing Douglas's proposed Kansas-Nebraska Act. Democrats loyal to Douglas had nominated a pro-Nebraska Democrat for Palmer's seat, but Palmer had stayed in the race as an independent. Palmer thus became an early Democratic opponent of the Kansas-Nebraska Act. He "repelled with scorn the attempt to foist this bastard plan into the democratic creed." In early May 1854, Palmer proposed a resolution: "That the provisions of the bill for the organization of Kansas and Nebraska, now pending in the congress of the United States, so far as the same proposes to tolerate the introduction or existence of slavery in said territory, or weakens or impairs the restrictions imposed thereon by the Missouri Compromise, meet the unqualified condemnation and opposition of this general assembly, as directly exciting the elements of agitation and strife so happily allayed by the Compromise aforesaid."[54] Instead of Palmer's anti-Nebraska resolution, the Illinois legislature endorsed another supporting the Douglas bill.

Beset by the allies of Douglas, Palmer worried about not only the fate of the Democratic Party, but also his own scruples: "I supposed that the

Democratic party would again unite upon other issues, and I was mainly anxious to preserve my personal independence and the right, inside of the party lines, to act according to the dictates of my own sense of personal duty." Palmer had been invited to speak at a July 4 celebration near the border of Sangamon and Macoupin counties.

> I indulged in the usual glorification of our revolutionary fathers and quoted from the Declaration of Independence, as I had often done on like occasions, that "All men are created equal, and are endowed with certain inalienable rights, among which are life, liberty and the pursuit of happiness," words which Mr. John C. Calhoun [from South Carolina] had characterized as "glittering generalities," and Mr. Douglas said meant "no more than our fathers intended to claim by those words that British subjects born on this continent had the same rights that British subjects had who were born in Great Britain." I attacked Mr. Calhoun, but spoke of Mr. Douglas with the respect I really felt for him, but my remarks stirred up a storm. Before I left the ground I was convinced that the Democratic party was hopelessly divided, and that the repeal of the Missouri compromise had stirred up passions that could not be allayed, and that the country was about entering upon a struggle which would probably result in very serious consequences. My first conclusion was to avoid all participation in the approaching controversy, and I did, in a letter dated August 14, 1854, decline to be a candidate for nomination for reelection to the state senate by any convention which made adhesion to the Nebraska bill a test of party orthodoxy.[55]

In early September Lincoln wrote to stiffen Palmer's resolve. Lincoln urged Palmer, though still a loyal Democrat, to avoid helping Douglas Democrats supporting the Kansas-Nebraska Act:

> You know how anxious I am that this Nebraska measure shall be rebuked and condemned every where. Of course I hope something from your position; yet I do not expect you to do any thing which may be wrong in your own judgment; nor would I have you

Pro-Lincoln Journalists

Thomas J. Pickett

Courtesy of the Abraham Lincoln Presidential Library, reference number I-13423

Horace White

Courtesy of the Abraham Lincoln Presidential Library, reference number I-17867

Noah Brooks

Courtesy of the Abraham Lincoln Presidential Library

William O. Stoddard

Courtesy of The Lincoln Museum, Fort Wayne, Indiana, reference number 4282

do anything personally injurious to yourself. You are, and always
have been, *honestly,* and *sincerely* a democrat; and I know how
painful it must be to an honest sincere man, to be urged by his
party to the support of a measure, which on his conscience he
believes to be wrong. You have had a severe struggle with yourself,
and you have determined *not* to swallow the *wrong.* Is it not just to
yourself that you should, in a few public speeches, state your reasons, and thus justify yourself? I wish you would; and yet I say
"don't do it, if you think it will injure you." You may have given
your word to vote for Major Harris, and if so, of course you will
stick to it. But allow me to suggest that you should avoid speaking
of this; for it probably would induce some of your friends, in like
manner, to cast their votes. You understand. And now let me beg
your pardon for obtruding this letter upon you, to whom I have
ever been opposed in politics. Had your party omitted to make
Nebraska a test of party fidelity; you probably would have been
the Democratic candidate for congress in the district. You
deserved it, and I believe it would have been given you. In that
case I should have been qui[e]t, happy that Nebraska was to be
rebuked at all events. I still should have voted for the whig candidate; but I should have made no speeches, written no letters; and
you would have been elected by at least a thousand majority.[56]

Such subtle and decorous prose characterized much of Lincoln's correspondence, especially when intended to persuade political opponents.
In this case Lincoln sought to retain a Democratic ally in the anti-
Nebraska fight. There is no record of a Palmer reply, nor is there any
record of Palmer undermining Yates or supporting Harris. In 1860
Palmer would be an important Lincoln advocate at the Republican presidential nominating convention.

Senator Douglas Returns to Illinois

Legislative races such as Palmer's would determine the fate of U.S. Senator James Shields, who had been a loyal supporter of Douglas and Kansas-
Nebraska. A former state auditor, Shields was no friend of Lincoln, having

challenged him in 1842 to a duel which friends succeeded in averting at the last minute. Shields's former law partner, Gustave Koerner, recalled: "Both I and Governor [William H.] Bissell, who was then a member of Congress, tried our best to prevent him [Shields] from voting for the ill-omened bill, and I prophesied that it would defeat his election; I also told him from the start that I could not support him unless he severed his political connections with Douglas." Koerner wrote that Shields "had been at the start unfriendly to the measure, but had yielded to Douglas, his life-long friend. Besides, the last Legislature had endorsed Douglas, and had instructed the Senator to vote for the bill. An effort in this session to instruct him otherwise had failed, and would have come too late anyway, because the bill had passed."[57]

The political fate of Shields would be determined in early 1855 by the new Illinois legislature. The election would be a referendum on the popularity of Stephen Douglas. In this contest Lincoln was not ruled by his past personal conflict with Senator Shields but by his political antipathy to the Kansas-Nebraska Act. As historian Allen C. Guelzo observed: "Much as Shields had given Lincoln political offense by supporting Kansas-Nebraska in Congress, the real political enemy for Lincoln was the man behind Shields, Stephen Douglas, and the great object in obstructing Shields's re-election was the damage it could do to Douglas's political standing"— especially if Lincoln himself were elected.[58] Douglas had created other political problems for himself. He made Democratic unity on Kansas-Nebraska a party-line stand from which no deviation would be tolerated. In so doing, he effectively read out of the party such loyal Democrats as Palmer, former Judge Lyman Trumbull and Chicago Congressman John Wentworth.[59] Instead of uniting the Democratic Party, Douglas helped to divide it. Most free-soil Democrats would not support the repeal of the Missouri Compromise restriction on slavery.

Whigs and antislavery Know-Nothings rallied against Douglas, a favorite of Irish Catholic immigrants in Illinois. When Kentucky abolitionist Cassius Clay spoke in Springfield on July 10, Lincoln stretched out on the grass, knife in hand, whittling his way through the speech. Douglas meanwhile had been put on the defensive, having been required to explain his actions in Congress during the summer. Douglas chose to attack the Know-Nothing movement across the North; he needed a

demon, and the secretive apparatus of the nativists in the American Party
provided a convenient devil. "The Know-Nothings are suspected of being
about, but no one knows anything of them or what they design," contended the senator's journalistic mouthpiece, the Illinois *State Register*.[60]

The Democratic defensive strategy had limited success. Burning effi-
gies of Douglas marked his train ride back to Illinois in late August. Even
his hometown, Chicago, turned unfriendly. Both the antislavery clergy
and journalists of Chicago attacked his role in the Kansas-Nebraska Act.
Douglas had written a group of Chicago ministers "that I differ with you
widely, radically, and fundamentally, in respect to the nature and extent
of your rights, duties, and powers, as ministers of the Gospel." He added:
"If your 'divinely-appointed institution' has the power to prescribe the
mode and terms for the organization of Nebraska, I see no reason why
your authority may not be extended over the entire continent, not only to
the country which we now possess, but to all which may hereafter be
acquired."[61]

Having taken on the Chicago ministers by mail, Douglas took on the
Chicago mob in person. "I speak to the people of Chicago on Friday next
Sept 1st on Nebraska. They threaten a mob but I have no fears. All will be
right," Douglas wrote *State Register* editor Charles H. Lanphier in Springfield. "Please give the notice in your paper as I have received many letters
asking to be informed of the time of the meeting. Come up if you can &
bring our friends with you."[62] Douglas embraced the confrontation. His
combative nature relished a fight. Many newspapers and clergymen had
rallied to his opponents. Even though his denunciations of Know-Nothings
had guaranteed the support of the immigrant Irish in Chicago, his rhetoric
had mobilized nativists against him.

The Saturday night event was strategically located in an Irish strong-
hold of the city. Thus, a clash loomed between anti-immigrant Know-
Nothings, opposed to Kansas-Nebraska, and immigrant Irish supporting
Douglas.[63] But too few Irish-Americans showed up to counter Douglas's
impassioned opponents. "On the afternoon of his coming many flags in
the city and on the shipping in the river and harbor were hung at half-
mast," John G. Nicolay and John Hay wrote in their Lincoln biography.
"At sunset sundry city bells were tolled for an hour to signify the public
mourning at his downfall. When he mounted the platform at night to

address a crowd of some five thousand listeners he was surrounded by a little knot of personal friends, but the audience before him was evidently cold if not actively hostile."[64]

Confronting the unfriendly crowd gathered outside North Market Hall, Douglas vigorously defended the Kansas-Nebraska bill. "The spirit of a dictator flashed out from his eye, curled upon his lip, and mingled its cold irony in every tone of his voice and every gesture of his body," reported the anti-Douglas Chicago *Daily Democratic Press*.[65] Douglas "began his speech, defending his course as well as he could," wrote Nicolay and Hay.

> He claimed that the slavery question was forever settled by his great principle of "popular sovereignty," which took it out of Congress and gave it to the people of the territories to decide as they pleased. The crowd heard him in sullen silence for three-quarters of an hour, when their patience gave out, and they began to ply him with questions. He endured their fire of interrogatory for a little while till he lost his own temper. . . . Douglas, of short, sturdy build and imperious and controversial nature, stood his ground courageously, with flushed and lowering countenance hurling defiance at his interrupters, calling them a mob, and shaking his fist in their faces; in reply the crowd groaned, hooted, yelled, and made the din of Pandemonium.[66]

"Meows" and "boos" from the mob did not deter Douglas.[67] A brave man with a stout heart and a big ego, he rose to such occasions. The Little Giant tried to shout down his rowdy opponents. He damned critics such as the *Chicago Tribune* and the Know-Nothings, believing that they had incited the crowd against him. But the noise and heckling were too much, even for Douglas. The crowd's opposition to him was so vociferous that he could not complete his speech. Hecklers chanted: "We won't go till morning, till morning, till morning, till morning, till daylight doth appear."[68] Chicago journalist Horace White recalled: "I was on the platform as a reporter, and my recollection of what happened is still vivid. There was nothing like violence at any time, but there was disorder growing out of the fact that the people had come prepared to dispute Douglas's sophisms and that Douglas himself was far from conciliatory when he found himself facing an unfriendly audience."[69] Hay and Nicolay wrote: "The tumultuous proceeding continued until half-past ten o'clock at night, when the baffled orator was finally but very reluctantly persuaded by his friends to give up the contest and leave the stand."[70]

According to one amusing but doubtful version of the night's events, Douglas concluded with one last outburst. Looking at his watch to assure himself that it was now past midnight, he yelled: "Abolitionists of Chicago! It is now Sunday morning. I'll go to church and you may go to hell!" Douglas probably quit speaking long before midnight.[71] The event was not a complete disaster for Douglas, noted Hay and Nicolay: "It was trumpeted abroad by the Democratic newspapers that 'in the order-loving, law-abiding, abolition-ridden city of Chicago, Illinois's great statesman and representative in the United States Senate was cried down and refused the privilege of speaking'; and as usual the intolerance produced its natural reaction."[72] Douglas himself remained confident of a Democratic victory. He wrote to Kentucky Senator John C. Breckinridge: "*We shall carry the State with a majority in the Legislature . . . for Nebraska.* The Chicago mob has done us much good & we know what use to make of it."[73]

Douglas rested, and then embarked on a speaking tour of Illinois. He warmed up in the northern part of the state where he could expect the most heat. When confronted by hecklers, the senator appealed to his constituents' sense of fair play. One Douglas biographer observed: "His audiences were openly hostile, and his speeches were frequently interrupted by expressions of displeasure.'"[74] Another wrote: "On every hand there were symptoms of disaffection. Personal friends turned their backs upon him; lifelong associates refused to follow his lead; even the rank and file of his followers seemed infected with the prevailing epidemic of distrust."[75] The indomitable Douglas could not help but be unsettled by the incensed opposition. "At Geneva he was compelled to leave off speaking until his opponent, Ichabod Codding, responding to calls of the audience, graciously urged that Douglas be heard through," wrote Illinois historian Arthur Charles Cole. "Undaunted, he continued on his canvass, dashing from point to point in the country of the enemy and in the more favorable territory in central Illinois."[76] There, Douglas had always been strong, but anti-Nebraska sentiment had advanced to the heartland of Illinois.

Senator Douglas appeared bold, brazen, persistent, even refractory. "Always his speech was the same," Lincoln biographer Albert J. Beveridge wrote admiringly. His rhetoric focused on "the development of the West; the sectional nature of the Missouri Compromise and yet the refusal of Northern Whigs, Free-Soilers, and Abolitionists to observe even the line of that measure; his own attempts, as a matter of good faith to stop slavery agitation, to extend the Missouri line to the Pacific, and the defeat of his efforts; the abandonment of a sectional and adoption of a national principle [popular sovereignty] of the Great Compromise [of 1850]; the logical, natural, and necessary application of that principle to Kansas and Nebraska; the impossibility, as a practical matter, that slavery could long exist in Kansas or Nebraska because of soil, climate, and the resultant products of agriculture."[77] Emboldened on the attack, Douglas remained upbeat, writing in mid-September: "We have had glorious meetings at Joliet, Morris, and Ottawa. I speak here [LaSalle] today. The party are all right everywhere. We will gain more votes than we will lose on Nebraska and No Nothingism."[78] Douglas insisted that popular sovereignty—permitting people to choose for or against slavery—was sound national policy. He argued that the Compromise of 1850 had applied popular sovereignty to the previously unorganized territories of New Mexico and Utah. Douglas used this precedent to justify popular sovereignty for Kansas-Nebraska, and to repeal the slavery restriction of the Missouri Compromise.

The farther he traveled away from Chicago, the more favorably Douglas and his positions were received. In southern Illinois, Douglas was received as a visiting celebrity, according to biographer George Fort Milton. "In each place party leaders made elaborate plans for his coming, he would be greeted by an enthusiastic committee, the faithful would stream to his hotel quarters and party workers would bring those who were not quite so faithful," wrote Milton. "In such a campaign as this, Douglas was incomparable. He knew the people throughout the State, many thousands by name and circumstance. His memory of incidents was uncanny and his stock of stories full and pertinent. His willingness to laugh, even at himself, endeared him to the people."[79]

Speeches and Debates

During the summer of 1854, Lincoln worked the central part of the state, so familiar to him from his legal practice throughout the Eighth Judicial Circuit. He appeared several times in August and early September, either with Congressman Yates or in his stead. At Winchester on August 26, Lincoln foreshadowed the arguments he would make against Kansas-Nebraska at Peoria on October 16. "The rural population always welcomed his oratory, and he never lacked invitations to address the public," wrote Nicolay and Hay. "When he went, however, he distinctly announced that he did not purpose to take up his time with this personal and congressional controversy [the Yates-Harris congressional race]. His intention was to discuss the principles of the Nebraska bill."[80] With this stated purpose, Lincoln grounded his campaign on antislavery principle.

Lincoln's first serious debate on the Kansas-Nebraska Act came on September 9 at the Springfield court house. He squared off against fellow lawyer John Calhoun, now an ardent Douglas supporter, and always a very skilled debater.[81] Herndon claimed Lincoln once said that "Calhoun gave him more trouble in his debates than Douglas ever did, because he was more captivating in his manner, a more learned man than Douglas."[82] Robert Browne, a young contemporary, later recalling the Lincoln-Calhoun debate, wrote that Lincoln campaigned

> with such continuing interest and increase of power that all realized something unusual and wonderful in the man, his control of himself, his subject, and his influence over his hearers. Not then, but later in his work, we called this marvelous power "Lincoln's inspiration." Such meetings to that day no man ever held. People came from far and near, and waited all day, stood in the wind, the sun, and the rain, uncovered, to hear him, and remained to his close. . . . His was the strong and convincing appeal of a very serious, earnest man, calling the people to their senses in reason and righteousness and fair treatment of our fellow-men of whatever color, condition, race, or creed, and to an observance and enforcement of the great principles of human liberty, upon which our Government was founded.[83]

Browne's remarks suggest something new in Lincoln had emerged. Familiar with Lincoln the story-teller, his listeners may have expected entertainment and conventional politics. Instead, they got a rigorous education in American history and political philosophy. "They heard from his lips fewer anecdotes and more history," Nicolay and Hay wrote. "Careless listeners who came to laugh at his jokes were held by the strong current of his reasoning and the flashes of his earnest eloquence, and were lifted up by the range and tenor of his argument into a fresher and purer political atmosphere." Antislavery rhetoric "furnished material for the inborn gifts of the speaker, his intuitive logic, his impulsive patriotism, his pure and poetical conception of legal and moral justice."[84] Lincoln had long been among the state's leading speakers. He was "a standout stump speaker," noted Lincoln scholar Douglas L. Wilson. "His eventual prominence and leadership in his political party was squarely based on such abilities, not only to speak extemporaneously on the stump but also to put down live opponents in debate on the floor of the legislature and elsewhere."[85] But his intellectual skills had become more focused. Lincoln historian David C. Mearns wrote that his speeches "contained a new cogency, directness, shrewd analysis, which differed conspicuously from the broad humor and oratorical flourish which formerly had characterized them."[86] Gone was the extensive use of biting, partisan rhetoric and the demeaning sarcasm of Lincoln's earlier political career. Gone too were insults which might lead to implacable enmities, if not duels.

Campaigning for Free-Soil

Lincoln's detailed itinerary for the 1854 campaign remains unknown. Most of what he said in his public appearances has been lost, but some important evidence remains. In early September, Lincoln wrote an unsigned editorial for the *Illinois State Journal*, one of several which he may have written anonymously for the newspaper during the spring and summer. Lincoln also made two campaign speeches in Bloomington in which he laid out many of the arguments to be used at Springfield on October 4 and at Peoria on October 16.[87] In his *Journal* editorial, Lincoln spoke of himself in the third person, presenting an analogy to the Kansas-

Nebraska crisis, caused by the repeal of the Missouri Compromise. He wrote that the Kansas-Nebraska territory had been opened to slavery by the Douglas legislation, just as "Mississippi or Arkansas were when they were territories." The editorial continued the arguments of his debate two days earlier with John Calhoun:

> To illustrate the case: Abraham Lincoln has a fine meadow, containing beautiful springs of water, and well fenced, which John Calhoun had agreed with Abraham (originally owning the land in common) should be his, and the agreement had been consummated in the most solemn manner, regarded by both as sacred. John Calhoun, however, in the course of time, had become owner of an extensive herd of cattle—the prairie grass had become dried up and there was no convenient water to be had. John Calhoun then looks with a longing eye on Lincoln's meadow, and goes to it and throws down the fences, and exposes it to the ravages of his starving and famishing cattle. "You rascal," says Lincoln, "what have you done? what do you do this for?" "Oh," replied Calhoun, "everything is right, I have taken down your fence, but nothing more. It is my true intent and meaning not to drive my cattle into your meadow, nor to exclude them therefrom, but to leave them perfectly free to form their own notions of the feed, and to direct their movements in their own way."
>
> Now would not the man who committed this outrage be deemed both a knave and a fool,—a knave in removing the restrictive fence, which he had solemnly pledged himself to sustain;—and a fool in supposing that there could be one man found in the country to believe that he had not pulled down the fence for the purpose of opening the meadow for his cattle?[88]

Lincoln believed Senator Douglas had torn down the agreed-upon fence of the Missouri Compromise, thus opening the Kansas-Nebraska pasture to slavery. On September 12, the day after the editorial appeared, Lincoln spoke at the county court house in Bloomington, about sixty miles northeast of Springfield, to an anti-Nebraska meeting organized by

German-Americans. He talked about the Compromise of 1850, a set of measures designed to admit California as a free state and to organize the territory in the Southwest that had been acquired from Mexico as a result of war. The status of slavery in the organized New Mexico and Utah territories would be decided by popular sovereignty. That is, the settlers in these two territories would decide for or against slavery when they applied for statehood.[89] Southern demands for tougher sanctions against runaway slaves gave rise to a new and harsh Fugitive Slave Act as part of the Compromise of 1850. Another section of the 1850 Compromise granted northern demands that the slave trade be abolished in the nation's capital. Likewise, the Missouri Compromise of 1820 had been a series of laws that provided for the admission of Missouri as a slave state and Maine as a free state. The Compromise of 1820 established a dividing line at 36° 30', north of which slavery in the Louisiana Territory would be prohibited. The 1850 Compromise followed the pattern established by the Missouri Compromise; both compromises sought to quiet sectional discord on the slavery issue. In 1852, both the Democratic and Whig campaign platforms endorsed these compromises as settled agreements on the contentious issue of the spread of slavery. In this political context, the Kansas-Nebraska legislation slowly advanced from 1853 into 1854.

Lincoln told his Bloomington audience that with the Compromise of 1850, the "matter with regard to slavery was now settled, and no disturbance could be raised except by tearing up some of the Compromises with regard to the territory where it was already settled. The South had got all they claimed, and all the territory south of the compromise line [of 1820] had been appropriated to slavery; they had gotten and eaten their half of the loaf of bread; but all the other half had not been eaten yet; there was the extensive territory of Nebraska secured to freedom, that had not been settled yet. And the slaveholding power attempted to snatch that away." Lincoln continued: "So on Jan. 4, 1854, Douglas introduced the famous Nebraska Bill, which was so constructed before its passage as to repeal the Missouri Compromise, and open all of the territory to the introduction of slavery. It was done without the consent of the people, and against their wishes, for if the matter had been put to [a] vote before the people directly, whether that [Kansas-Nebraska] should be made a slave territory, they would have indignantly voted it down. But it was got up unexpectedly by the people, hurried through, and now they were called upon to sanction it."

Unsanctioned by a popular vote, the repeal of the bipartisan Missouri Compromise was now law. Lincoln believed it to be illegitimate, and he called for voters to revolt against the Kansas-Nebraska Act:

> They ought to make a strong expression against the imposition; that would prevent the consummation of the scheme. The people were the sovereigns, and the representatives their servants, and it was time to make them sensible of this truly democratic principle. They could get the Compromise restored. They were told that they could not because the Senate was [controlled by advocates of] Nebraska [legislation], and would be for years. Then fill the lower House with true Anti-Nebraska members, and that would be an expression of the sentiment of the people. And further- more that expression would be heeded by the Senate. If this State should instruct Douglas to vote for the repeal of the Nebraska Bill, he must do it, for "the doctrine of instructions" was a part of his political creed. And he was not certain he would not be glad to vote its repeal anyhow, if it would help him fairly out of the scrape. It was so with other Senators; they will be sure to improve the first opportunity to vote its repeal. The people could get it repealed, if they resolved to do it.[90]

The Bloomington *Pantagraph* reported that "Lincoln's speech was clearly unanswerable, for it was a plain statement of facts, and of sound, strong argument; it was eloquent, for he spoke the deep convictions of truth from a heart warmed with the love of his country, and the love of freedom. The address was not only instructive, and his argument against the Nebraska outrage unanswerable, but it was spiced with remarks that were diverting, and at the same time gave a deeper felt conviction of the weight of sober argument."[91] Illinois contemporaries long remembered the force and logic of Lincoln's speeches that fall. "I heard his speech in the old court house in 1854, on the Kansas and Nebraska bill, in answer to the speech of Mr. Douglas on the same subject, made a few days before," reported James S. Ewing, a local lawyer who witnessed the Bloomington speech.

> In this speech, what impressed me most was that same wonderful power of statement to which I have before referred. I can never forget the manner in which he stated the causes and events which led up to the enactment of the Missouri Compromise; just what that compromise was, and how it affected the question of slavery; the history of the events and causes which led to the passage of the compromise of 1850; its constitutional elements; just what the South got and just what the North got by it, and how it was affected by the repeal of the other compromise bill. It seems to me I could almost repeat those statements to-day, after a half century, so vivid was the impression.[92]

Much of the October 16 speech at Peoria was rehearsed at Bloomington. On September 26, Senator Douglas and Lincoln again appeared together at Bloomington. Douglas talked in the afternoon; Mr. Lincoln spoke in the evening. Prior to the speeches, Bloomington businessman Jesse W. Fell proposed a series of Lincoln-Douglas debates, but the senator demurred. Fell came to Douglas "with a proposition that Mr. Lincoln and Mr. Douglas have a discussion, remarking that there were a great many people in the city, that the question was of great importance, and that it would afford the crowd the luxury of listening to the acknowledged champions of both sides. As soon as the proposition was made it could be seen that the Judge was irritated. He inquired of Mr. Fell, with some majesty of manner: 'Whom does Mr. Lincoln represent in this campaign—is he an Abolitionist or an Old Line Whig?'" Attorney Lawrence Weldon also recalled the meeting: "Mr. Fell replied that he was an Old Line Whig."

> "Yes," said Douglas, "I am now in the region of the Old Line Whig. When I am in Northern Illinois I am assailed by an Abolitionist, when I get to the center I am attacked by an Old Line Whig, and when I go to Southern Illinois I am beset by an Anti-Nebraska Democrat. I can't hold the Whig responsible for any-

thing the Abolitionist says, and can't hold the Anti-Nebraska
Democrat responsible for the positions of either. It looks to me
like dogging a man all over the State. If Mr. Lincoln wants to
make a speech he had better get a crowd of his own; for I most
respectfully decline to hold a discussion with him."[93]

Fell claimed to have already invited Lincoln to speak that day in
Bloomington. He remembered:

After conferring with our Anti-Nebraska friends—as we were then
commonly called—I opened a correspondence with Mr. Lincoln,
resulting in his coming to Bloomington on that day, in order to
take notes and reply to Mr. Douglas, if the way opened, on the
same day, and if not, in the evening. This fact became pretty
widely known, and a very large meeting, composed of quite as
many Anti-Nebraska men as Democrats, met in the grove near
town—no hall we then had being sufficient to hold the crowd. In
order that the country people should have the benefit of the discussion, there was a universal desire, on the part of our friends,
that Lincoln as well as Douglas should be heard in the day-time,
and I had been requested to see Lincoln on his arrival and get his
approval that we propose to, and *urge* upon the Judge to divide
time, so as to have a joint discussion.

Lincoln had a sense of fair play, however, and told his Bloomington
friend:

Fell, this is not our meeting; it is Judge Douglas's meeting; he
called it, and he and his friends have a right to control it. Notwithstanding all you say about our country people, and the great
desire I have to talk to them, we must do nothing to defeat his
object in calling it. He has heard of the great racket the passage
of his Bill has kicked up, and he wants to set himself right with his
people, a job not very easily done, you and I being the judges.
Partly on this ground and partly to keep me from speaking, he
will no doubt consume so much of the time that I'll have no

chance till in the evening. I fully appreciate all you say about our country friends and would like mighty well to talk to them on this subject. If Judge Douglas will give me a chance I will follow him out in the grove, but as he won't do this, I guess you may give it out, after he is done, that I will reply to him after candle lighting in the courthouse.[94]

Lincoln had visited Douglas in his hotel room and there declined a different kind of invitation. The teetotaling Whig demurred when Douglas offered him a drink. "Why! Are you a member of the temperance society?" inquired the senator. Replied Lincoln: "I do not in theory, but I do in fact, belong to the temperance society, in this, to wit that I do not drink anything, and have not done so for a very many years."[95] Lawrence Weldon recalled that Judge Douglas introduced him to Lincoln, apparently at this meeting: "The impression he made when I was introduced was as to his unaffected and sincere manner, and the precise, cautious and accurate mode in which he stated his thoughts even when talking about commonplace things."[96]

At Bloomington when Mr. Lincoln did speak in reply to Douglas, he was not cautious but direct. After reviewing the history of slavery and territorial expansion, Lincoln analyzed the fundamental flaw in the popular sovereignty doctrine of Senator Douglas. As reported in the Bloomington *Weekly Pantagraph*, Lincoln insisted that the people of Illinois would not have approved the Kansas-Nebraska Act, the senator's pretensions to the contrary notwithstanding:

Judge Douglas has said that the Illinois Legislation [Legislature] passed resolutions instructing him to repeal the Missouri Compromise. But said Mr. L[incoln], the Judge, when he refers to resolutions of instruction, always gets those which never passed both houses of the Legislature. The Legislature [passed] a resolution, upon this subject which the Judge either forgot or didn't choose to read. No man who voted to pull down the Missouri Compromise represented the people, and [the Legislature] of this State never instructed Douglas or any one else to commit that act. And yet the Judge had told the people that they *were* in favor of repealing the Missouri Compromise, and all must acquiesce in his assumption or be denounced as abolitionists. What sophistry is this, said Mr. L, to contend and insist that you did instruct him to effect the repeal of the Missouri Compromise, when you know you never thought of such a thought of it [Cries of "No! No!!"]— that all the people of Illinois [according to Douglas] have always been opposed to that Compromise when no man will say that he ever thought of its repeal previous to the introduction of the Nebraska bill.[97]

Despite this forceful criticism, the *Pantagraph* reported that Lincoln "spoke of Judge Douglas in a less denunciatory manner than is the custom on such occasions."[98] Lincoln's return to the political stump was marked not only by a rhetoric grounded in logic and history, but also by generosity to his opponents. Years later, Bloomington resident James S. Ewing recalled: "In my judgment it was the most remarkable speech I ever heard."[99] The report of the Bloomington Weekly *Pantagraph* was similarly effusive. Lincoln's address was "clear and unanswerable for it was a plain statement of facts, and of sound, strong argument. It was eloquent, for he spoke the deep convictions of truth from a heart warmed with the love of his country and the love of freedom."[100]

Writing in the third person six years later, Lincoln himself recalled his campaign of 1854: "In the autumn of that year [Lincoln] took the stump with no broader practical aim or object . . . [than] to secure, if possible, the reelection of Hon[.] Richard Yates to congress. His speeches at once attracted a more marked attention than they had ever before done. As the canvass proceeded, he was drawn to different parts of the state, outside of Mr. Yates' district. He did not abandon the law, but gave his attention, by turns, to that and politics."[101] Lincoln sought the reelection of Yates, but principally he aimed to block the extension of slavery. Increasingly, he sensed the importance of his own leadership to the antislavery campaign.

Nicolay and Hay noted that other anti-Nebraska politicians had begun to make speaking tours around the state. "Later in the summer Joshua R. Giddings and Salmon P. Chase, of Ohio, made a political tour through the State, and at Springfield the future Secretary [of the Treasury] and Chief-Justice [of the Supreme Court] addressed an unsympathetic audience of a few hundreds in the dingy little court-house, almost unheralded, save by the epithets of the Democratic newspapers. A few local speakers of this class, of superior address and force, now also began to signalize themselves by a new-born zeal and an attractive eloquence. Conspicuous among these was Owen Lovejoy, of northern Illinois, brother of the man who, for opinion's sake, had been murdered at Alton [in November 1837]."[102] Meanwhile, Kansas-Nebraska had fueled a Democratic family feud. Numerous Democratic newspapers in Illinois were lukewarm or antagonistic to Douglas's legislation. Undeterred, Douglas in February wrote to the editor of the Illinois *State Register:* "The principles of this bill will form the test of Parties, and the only alternative is to stand with the Democracy [the Democratic Party] or to rally under [New Yorkers William H.] Seward, John Van Buren & Co."[103] Lincoln's Whig Party, already weak, would crack under the pressure of the Kansas-Nebraska dispute.

For Lincoln, the facts and circumstances in which he applied his antislavery rhetoric in 1854 were substantially new. He had touched on slavery in previous speeches as a state legislator, congressman, and Whig campaigner. In 1837, State Representative Lincoln had coauthored with one colleague a minority legislative resolution which in part stated "that the institution of slavery is founded on both injustice and bad policy."[104] In Congress he voted repeatedly for the Wilmot Proviso to prohibit slavery in the new territories acquired from Mexico. In 1849, Congressman Lincoln announced his intention to introduce legislation for compensated emancipation in the nation's capital. Neither his state legislative nor congressional effort prevailed. Nor did they then preoccupy him.

Lincoln's 1854 antislavery speeches were the first major dissertations on a subject which would dominate the rest of his life. He had done research in the State Library to gather evidence from primary sources to make his case against the Kansas-Nebraska Act. Lincoln "had prepared with uncommon thoroughness, even for him," wrote Albert J. Beveridge. "He had studied the debates in Congress, and as we have seen, Douglas's speech in the Senate had been printed in pamphlet form as well as published in the newspapers. For weeks, Lincoln had spent toilsome hours in the State Library, searching trustworthy histories, analyzing the Census, mastering the facts, reviewing the literature of the subject. In his office he had written fragments on government and scraps of arguments against

slavery, obviously trying to clarify his reasoning."[105] Lincoln rarely studied
for the sake of pure learning. "Study with Mr[.] Lincoln was a business
not a pleasure," wrote friend Joseph Gillespie. "He was extremely diligent
when he had anything to do in preparing himself but when his task was
done he betook himself to recreation. The information he gathered up
was in reference to special questions and not with a view of laying in a
general store of knowledge expecting that he would have occasion to use
it and yet his natural tastes and aptitudes led him to explore most of those
departments of study which bore mainly on the practical affairs of life."[106]

Lincoln had done some hard thinking about slavery and the consequences of the Kansas-Nebraska Act. Perhaps in July 1854, probably later,
he jotted down a few thoughts about the injustice of slavery: "The ant,
who has toiled and dragged a crumb to his nest, will furiously defend the
fruit of his labor, against whatever robber assails him. So plain, that the
most dumb and stupid slave that ever toiled for a master, does constantly
know that he is wronged. So plain that no one, high or low, ever does mistake it, except in a plainly *selfish* way; for although volume upon volume is
written to prove slavery a very good thing, we never hear of the man who
wishes to take the good of it, *by being a slave himself.*" Lincoln then mused
about the Declaration of Independence, noting that the United States
was founded on principles inimical to slavery: "*Most governments* have been
based, practically, on the denial of equal rights of men, as I have, in part,
stated them; *ours* began, by *affirming* those rights. *They* said, some men are
too *ignorant*, and *vicious*, to share in government. Possibly so, said we; and,
by your system, you would always keep them ignorant, and vicious. We
proposed to give *all* a chance; and we expected the weak to grow stronger,
the ignorant, wiser; and all better, and happier together."[107]

This was not a new train of thought for Lincoln—freedom and economic opportunity having long been his focus. But his thinking had taken
an important new direction. The increasingly permanent plight of the
slave had been highlighted by the repeal of the Missouri Compromise
restriction on slavery. Fellow lawyer Samuel C. Parks subsequently recalled:

> In politics Mr[.] Lincoln told the truth when he said he had
> "always hated slavery as much as any Abolitionist" but I do not
> know that he deserved a great deal of credit for that for his hatred

of oppression & wrong in all its forms was constitutional—he could not help it[.] The occasion of his becoming a great anti-slavery leader was the agitation of the Repeal of the Missouri Compromise[.] His first great speech in opposition to that measure & in reply to Mr[.] Douglas in Spring field [sic] was one of the ablest & most effective of his life[.] Pending the Repeal I was in Springfield & urged upon Mr[. Simeon] Francis the necessity of the leaders of the Whig Party coming out at once against it[.] I remember well his reply 'I will see Lincoln & get him to make a speech' against it[.] And Lincoln did make a speech & rallied the Whig Party of Central Illinois almost to a man against "Nebraska Bill[.]"[108]

Lincoln's Springfield speech of October 4 would follow the Lincoln-Douglas speeches at Bloomington. At the Springfield confrontation, the senator would be a reluctant combatant.

"*Threats of breaking up the Union were freely made; and the ablest public men of the day became seriously alarmed. At length a compromise was made, in which, like all compromises, both sides yielded something. It was a law passed on the 6th day of March, 1820, providing that Missouri might come into the Union* with *slavery, but that in all the remaining part of the territory purchased of France, which lies north of 36 degrees and 30 minutes north latitude, slavery should never be permitted. This provision of law,* is the Missouri Compromise. *In excluding slavery North of the line, the same language is employed as in the Ordinance of '87.*"

ABRAHAM LINCOLN,
OCTOBER 16, 1864

II.

Springfield, Peoria, and Beyond

On October 2, 1854, Senator Douglas arrived in Springfield. He settled down at the Chenery House on the corner of Adams and Sixth Street—just west of the State Capitol near Lincoln's law office. That night, Democrats gathered to greet the most powerful citizen of Illinois. Douglas delivered a short prelude to the main event scheduled for the following day: "I have come home, as I have done so many times before, to give an account of my stewardship. I know the Democrats of Illinois. I know they always do their duty. I know, Democrats, that you will stand by me as you have always done. I am not afraid that you will be led off by those renegades from the party, Trumbull, Palmer, Judd, and Cook, who have formed an unholy alliance to turn the glorious old Democratic party over to the black Abolitionists."[109] The senator continued: "I tell you the time has not yet come when a handful of traitors in our camp can turn the great State of Illinois, with all her glorious history and traditions, into a negro-worshiping, negro-equality community. Illinois has always been, and always will be, true to the Constitution and the Union."[110]

It was on the afternoon of the next day, October 3, that the Little Giant delivered his long defense of the Kansas-Nebraska Act. Originally, the speech had been scheduled for the site of the State Fair near Spring-

37

field, where a very large audience could be assembled. For residents of the capital area the State Fair was the "annual Jubilee and School of Life," according to historian James G. Randall.[111] Lincoln biographer Carl Sandburg noted that 1854 was a boom year, with thousands of easterners moving through Springfield on their way west. It was a boom year too for fair participants, according to Sandburg: "There were sows, boars, stallions, mares, rams, ewes, hens, roosters, geese, ganders, ducks, drakes, turkeys, gobblers; peaches, apples, crab apples, pears, picked from sunny orchards and canned by farmers' wives; also jellies, jams, apple butter, peach marmalade; and wheat, oats, rye, each with its ticket naming the farmer who had raised the grain."[112]

The politics of the Kansas-Nebraska controversy accentuated the fair's appeal. The hopeful farmers brought their produce; the opposing politicians brought arguments for free-soil and popular sovereignty. Journalist John L. Scripps described the fair in an 1860 campaign biography of Lincoln: "Hundreds of politicians had also assembled, among whom were many of the ablest men of the State. Much time was devoted to political speaking; but the great event of the occasion was the debate between Lincoln and Douglas." Scripps wrote that it was in some ways a rematch for the two men—noting their competing speeches in the presidential election of 1840. Lincoln was then but thirty-one; Douglas was even younger, only twenty-seven.[113] Politically, Douglas had far surpassed Lincoln by 1854. Senator "Douglas's speech was doubtless intended by him and expected by his friends to be the principal and the conclusive argument of the occasion," wrote Nicolay and Hay. "But by this time the Whig party of the central counties, though shaken by the disturbing features of the Nebraska question, had nevertheless reformed its lines, and assumed the offensive . . ."[114]

Heavy rain forced Douglas and his audience from the fairgrounds to the State Capitol in downtown Springfield. The Greek Revival State House stood a stone's throw from the law office of Lincoln and Herndon on the south side of the square—in the same building where Lincoln had practiced law with Stephen T. Logan. Nearby were the offices where Lincoln had practiced law with John Todd Stuart, later as the senior partner with

"Billy" Herndon. The Illinois *State Journal*, originally the *Sangamon Journal*, occupied offices near the square. There, Lincoln read newspapers and contributed editorials. There too, he immersed himself in politics and public policy. In an adjoining alley, he became famous for his game of handball. Anchoring the square was the State Capitol, housing the library where Lincoln did much of his legal and historical research. Most of the elected state officials had offices in the Capitol, and there the State Supreme Court held its sessions. Only a short walk to the southeast of the State House was the Lincoln family home on Jackson Street. In 1856 while Lincoln was away practicing law, his wife Mary would add a second story to the original cottage—transforming it into a substantial home with four bedrooms and two parlors.

On the afternoon of October 3, 1854, Lincoln awaited the Douglas speech in a front row of the semicircular House chamber on the second floor of the Capitol. The House chamber took up the north half of the building. On the south side was the smaller Senate chamber. Nearby was the governor's office.[115] Visitors packed the main floor and the smaller gallery of the House. The ornate Corinthian columns supporting the gallery signalled the increasing urbanity of Springfield. Senator Douglas would talk from the speaker's dais, overshadowed by a full-length portrait of President George Washington. With polished eloquence, Douglas ranged over the usual ground of Kansas-Nebraska, but without his usual vigor. The Little Giant's "voice was hoarse, and he seemed fatigued and not well," wrote Douglas biographer Robert W. Johannsen. "Even so, much of the old fire remained. One member in the audience later wrote that he could understand why the Chicagoans had not allowed Douglas to speak, 'for he would most assuredly have turned the Current against them.'"[116] Lincoln biographer Noah Brooks, no Douglas partisan, later noted that Douglas's arguments were "ingenious, plausible, and as effective as it could have been in the hands of any living man."[117]

Douglas's "justification of the [Kansas-Nebraska] bill was that it established the principle of popular sovereignty in the Territories as it already existed in the States," recalled journalist Horace White. "Why, he asked, should not the people of the Territories have the right to form and regulate their own domestic institutions in their own way? Did they lose any of their rights or capabilities of self-government by migrating from their old homes to new ones? By ringing the changes on popular sovereignty and the 'sacred right of self-government,' he was able to raise a good deal of dust and to obscure the real issue. The fallacy lay in assuming that property in slaves did not differ in character from other kinds of property, and that taking negroes to the new Territories and holding them there as slaves was to be regarded in the same way as taking cattle, sheep and swine."[118]

Douglas stated at the outset "that it is understood by some gentlemen that Mr. Lincoln, of this city, is expected to answer me," wrote Lincoln biographers John G. Nicolay and John Hay. "If this is the understanding, I wish that Mr. Lincoln would step forward and let us arrange some plan upon which to carry out this discussion. Mr. Lincoln was not there at the moment, and the arrangement could not then be made."[119] Douglas biographer George Fort Milton described Lincoln as anxiously pacing in the Capitol's lobby around the central circular staircase.[120] This disputed description is one of several controversies about the Lincoln-Douglas encounters of 1854. After Douglas finished, Lincoln informed the crowd that the next day they would hear from him or Lyman Trumbull, a prominent anti-Nebraska Democrat, then a candidate for Congress. Springfield businessman-banker John W. Bunn recalled that after the Douglas speech, Lincoln asked Bunn his opinion of it. "Hard to answer & hard to beat," replied Bunn. Lincoln responded: "I will answer that speech without any trouble; because Judge Douglas made two misstatements of fact, and upon these two misstatements he built his whole argument. I can show that his facts are not facts, and that will refute his speech."[121] Upon the facts, Lincoln had learned to build his court cases. In his speeches he believed his arguments were based on the evidence and the logic of the law. Douglas, he thought, lacked a sound moral and historical foundation for his arguments.

Lincoln answered Douglas on October 4. He set forth the historical background of his antislavery arguments—disputing Douglas' interpretation of the American Founding. Speaking without notes for three hours, Lincoln dissected the Little Giant's well-known doctrine of Popular Sovereignty.[122] Compared to the expansiveness of the fairgrounds west of

Springfield, the House chamber of the Capitol was cramped. Set against the ever-dapper, ever-confident Douglas, Lincoln seemed ill-dressed, even ill-at-ease.[123] On October 3 the audience had seen the Douglas they knew well—earnest, angry, vengeful, forceful, robust, short. Lincoln on October 4 was ironic, easy, relentless, logical, lank, tall. Horace White, a Lincoln partisan, recalled the historic moment:

> At the appointed time Douglas and Lincoln entered the hall, the former taking a seat on the front row of benches and the latter advancing to the platform. The two men presented a wide contrast in personal appearance, Lincoln being 6 feet 3 inches high, lean, angular, raw boned, with a complexion of leather, unkempt, and with clothes that seemed to have dropped on him and might drop off; Douglas, almost a dwarf, only 5 feet 4 inches high, but rotund, portly, smooth faced, with ruddy complexion and a lionlike mane, and dressed in clothes of faultless fit. When speaking he seldom moved from his first position, but notwithstanding his diminutive size he always seemed to fill the platform.
>
> Mr. Lincoln began his speech with a historical sketch of the events leading up to the repeal of the Missouri Compromise, and then took up the fallacy of Douglas's "sacred right of self-government," which he showed to mean in the last analysis that if A wished to make a slave of B, no third person had a right to object.[124]

White, just twenty years old at the time, later wrote: "I heard the whole of that speech. It was a warmish day in early October, and Mr. Lincoln was in his shirt sleeves when he stepped on the platform. I observed that, although awkward, he was not in the least embarrassed. He began in a slow and hesitating manner, but without any mistakes of language, dates, or facts. It was evident that he had mastered his subject, that he knew what he was going to say, and that he knew he was right. He had a thin, high-pitched falsetto voice of much carrying power, that could be heard a long distance in spite of the bustle and tumult of a crowd. He had the accent and pronunciation peculiar to his native State, Kentucky. Gradually he warmed up with his subject. His angularity disappeared, and he passed into that attitude of unconscious majesty that is so conspicuous in Saint-Gaudens's statue at the entrance of Lincoln Park in Chicago."[125] William H. Herndon agreed; Lincoln "always stood squarely on his feet, toe even with toe; that is, he never put one foot before the other. He neither touched nor leaned on anything for support. He made but few changes in his positions and attitudes. He never ranted, never walked backward and forward on the platform. To ease his arms he frequently caught hold, with his left hand, of the lapel of his coat, keeping his thumb upright and leaving his right hand free to gesticulate. . . . As he proceeded with his speech the exercise of his vocal organs altered somewhat the tone of his voice. It lost in a measure its former acute and shrilling pitch, and mellowed into a more harmonious and pleasant sound. His form expanded, and, notwithstanding the sunken breast, he rose up a splendid and imposing figure. In his defense of the Declaration of Independence—his greatest inspiration—he was 'tremendous in the directness of his utterances; he rose to impassioned eloquence.'"[126]

There was drama in Lincoln's manner, but it was minimal compared to the political histrionics of his day. His case was based primarily on facts, logic, and history. Reporter White recalled the speech: "Progressing with his theme, his words began to come faster and his face to light up with the rays of genius and his body to move in unison with his thoughts. His gestures were made with his body and head rather than with his arms. They were the natural expression of the man, and so perfectly adapted to what he was saying that anything different from it would have been quite inconceivable. Sometimes his manner was very impassioned, and he seemed transfigured with his subject. Perspiration would stream from his face, and each particular hair would stand on end. . . . His speaking went to the heart because it came from the heart. I have heard celebrated orators who could start thunders of applause without changing any man's opinion. Mr. Lincoln's eloquence was of the higher type, which produced conviction in others because of the conviction of the speaker himself."[127] William Herndon also described Lincoln "on the stump." He wrote:

. . . his body inclined forward to a slight degree. At first he was very awkward, and it seemed a real labor to adjust himself to his surroundings. He struggled for a time under a feeling of apparent diffidence. . . . When he began speaking, his voice was shrill, piping, and unpleasant. His manner, his attitude, his dark yellow face, wrinkled and dry, his oddity of pose, his diffident movements, everything seemed to be against him, but only for a short time. After having arisen, he generally placed his hands behind him, the back of his left hand in the palm of his right, the thumb and fingers of his right hand clasped around the left arm at the wrist. For a few moments he displayed the combination of awkwardness, sensitiveness, and diffidence. As he proceeded he became somewhat animated, and to keep in harmony with this growing warmth his hands relaxed their grasp and fell to his side. Presently he clasped them in front of him, interlocking his fingers, one thumb meanwhile chasing another. His speech now requiring more emphatic utterance, his fingers unlocked and his hands fell apart. His left arm was thrown behind, the back of his hand resting against this body, his right hand seeking his side. By this time he had gained sufficient composure, and his real speech began. He did not gesticulate as much with his hands as with his head. . . . He never sawed the air nor rent space into tatters and rags as some orators do. He never acted for stage effect. . . . His style was clear, terse, and compact. In argument he was logical, demonstrative, and fair. He was careless of his dress, and his clothes, instead of fitting neatly as did the garments of Douglas on the latter's well-rounded form, hung loosely on his giant frame. As he moved along in his speech he became freer and less uneasy in his movements; to that extent he was graceful. He had a perfect naturalness, a strong individuality; and to that extent he was dignified. He despised glitter, show, set forms and shams. He spoke with effectiveness and to move the judgment as well as the emotions of men. . . . If the sentiment was one of detestation— denunciation of slavery, for example—both arms, thrown upward and fists clenched, swept through the air, and he expressed an execration that was truly sublime.[128]

Lincoln's Springfield "remarks about Union saving were sound and patriotic, and his appeal to the Southern States for moderation and forbearance, fraternal and eloquent," reported the *Illinois State Journal.* "He did not set so much store on the restoration of the Missouri Compromise by act of legislation, as he did on the immediate and effectual restoration of it by popular sentiment."[129] The Union could be safe, Lincoln believed, if the institution of slavery could be put, as the Founders intended, in the course of ultimate extinction. It was a powerful presentation. Even the Democratic *Register* reported on the "grace" and the "wonderful labors" of Lincoln's speech:

Mr. Lincoln had been selected as the Goliath of the anti-Nebraska black republican fusionists. He had been nosing for weeks in the state library, and pumping his brains and his imagination for points and arguments with which to demolish the champion of popular sovereignty. It is our duty to record the result of his wonderful labors and exertions. He commenced by a number of jokes and witticisms, the character of which will be understood by all who know him, by simply saying they were Lincolnisms. He declared he was a national man—that he was for letting the institution of slavery alone when it existed in the states—that he was for sustaining the fugitive slave law—that there was a clear grant of power in the constitution to enable the south to recover their fugitive slaves, and he was for an efficient law to effect the object intended. He then branched off upon the ordinance of 1787, and worked his way down to the Kansas and Nebraska act. Leaving out the declarations we have spoken of, his speech was one that would have come from [Congressman Joshua] Giddings or [Senator Charles] Sumner, and that class of abolitionists, with more grace than from any men we know of. He quoted the speech of Judge Douglas in 1849 [against repeal of the Missouri Compromise], and endeavored to show that he stood now where Judge D. stood then. He attempted to show that the Kansas-Nebraska bill was inconsistent with the legislation of 1850, and maintained that it was as much the duty of congress to prohibit slavery in the territories as to prohibit the slave trade— made what some of his hearers seemed to consider good hits, and called forth the cheers of his friends.[130]

Invited to do so, Douglas repeatedly interrupted Lincoln during his speech. Lincoln biographer Noah Brooks, who began his journalism career in Illinois in 1854, described the confrontation:

With his customary fairness, he [Lincoln] said that he did not wish to present anything but the truth, the whole truth, and that if Mr. Douglas, who was present should detect him making any error he would be glad to be corrected on the spot. Douglas availed himself of this invitation to interrupt Lincoln frequently, to ask him impertinent questions, and endeavor to break him down by distracting his thought from the matter in hand. Finally Lincoln lost patience, severely tried, by these unfair tactics, and said: "Gentlemen, I cannot afford to spend my time in quibbles. I take the responsibility of asserting the truth myself, relieving Judge Douglas from the necessity of his impertinent corrections." From this point he was allowed to speak without interruption to the end of his speech, which occupied three hours and ten minutes in delivery. The sensation produced by this speech, so convincing, so powerful in its logic, and so tremendous in its array of facts and arguments was indescribable.[131]

In an editorial, probably written by Herndon, the *Journal* noted: "Mr. Lincoln's argument was clear and logical, his arrangement of facts methodical, his deductions self-evident, and his applications striking and most effective. We venture to say that Judge Douglas never in the Senate chamber or before the people, listened to just such a powerful analysis of his Nebraska sophisms, or saw such a remorseless tearing of his flimsy arguments and scattering them to the winds, as he endured yesterday from Mr. Lincoln."[132] William O. Stoddard, a Lincoln presidential aide and biographer, wrote: "The enthusiasm of the party press was unbounded, and was manifestly genuine. The Kansas-Nebraska bill was the subject of debate; and his exposure of its fallacies and iniquities was declared to be overwhelming. His whole heart was in his words."[133]

One may discount the encomiums of Lincoln's friends, but it seems clear that Judge Douglas was stunned. Though Douglas partisans did not admit that the Little Giant had been beaten, he gave every evidence of feeling the pressure. The senator's rejoinder to Lincoln lasted an hour and a half. The pro-Douglas *State Register* reported that Douglas's speech was greeted by "deep, heartfelt and heart-reaching concurrence." Douglas "went over every one of Mr. Lincoln's points, and when he concluded, there was nothing left of his arguments—as we heard it remarked, he seemed not content to butcher his antagonist with tomahawk and scalping knife, but he pounded him to pumice with his terrible war club of retort and argument." The Democratic *Register* concluded: "We hope that the effect of this discussion will be to make Mr. Lincoln a wiser man, and will teach him that no talent he may possess, no industry he may see, no art he can invent can stay the power of truth that supports the friends of the Nebraska measure."[134] The pro-Lincoln *Journal*, by contrast, acknowledged that Douglas's speech was "adroit and plausible, but had not the marble of logic in it."[135]

The immediate impact of the confrontation would be disputed by contemporaries and historians. Lincoln contemporary Isaac N. Arnold wrote: "Douglas himself felt that he was crushed. At the close of Lincoln's speech he attempted a reply, but he was excited, angry, loud, and furious, and after a short time closed by saying that he would continue his reply in the evening, but he did not return to the State House, and left the city without resuming his discourse."[136] Lincoln biographer Albert J. Beveridge was skeptical that Douglas so reacted: "For a man thus 'crushed,' Douglas displayed surprising vitality; for he instantly took the platform and spoke for an hour and a half in reply."[137] Douglas biographer George

Fort Milton likewise wrote: "But if Douglas had been 'crushed,' they had forgotten to tell him of it, for he leaped to the platform and spoke for an hour and a half. Lincoln had not forced him off his foundations."[138]

While Beveridge and Milton were respected historians, they were not present for the event. Horace White was there. He believed "Douglas was somewhat intimidated by Lincoln's unexpected strength at the Springfield meeting. . . ."[139] Nicolay and Hay wrote: "The occasion greatly equalized the relative standing of the champions. The familiar surroundings, the presence and hearty encouragement of his friends, put Lincoln in his best vein. His bubbling humor, his perfect temper, and above all the overwhelming current of his historical arraignment extorted the admiration of even his political enemies." The two Lincoln presidential aides concluded in their Lincoln biography: "All reports plainly indicate that Douglas was astonished and disconcerted at this unexpected strength of argument, and that he struggled vainly through a two hours' rejoinder to break the force of Lincoln's victory in the debate."[140] Already wary of Lincoln, Douglas worried anew.

Lincoln's anti-Nebraska friends enthusiastically embraced Lincoln's Springfield case, believing it a sword with which to challenge Douglas and the Kansas-Nebraska Act. They urged Lincoln to wield it—wherever and whenever possible. Lincoln friend Benjamin F. Irwin recalled that after Lincoln's speech, several other Springfield listeners "filled out and signed a Written request to Lincoln to follow Douglas untill he run him into his hole or made him holler Enough. . . ."[141] Among the signers were such close Lincoln associates as Dr. William Jayne, brother-in-law of Lyman Trumbull, and William Butler, a Springfield Whig leader who supposedly authored the petition.[142]

Later that day, prominent anti-Nebraska Democrats Lyman Trumbull, Colonel E. D. Taylor, and Judge Sidney Breese delivered speeches, but the Lincoln-Douglas debate dominated political discussion in Springfield. Trumbull himself had arrived too late to join Lincoln at the podium. "By a sort of common consent his party looked to [Lincoln] to answer Douglas's speech," wrote Nicolay and Hay. "This was no light task, and no one knew it better than Lincoln. Douglas's real ability was, and remains, unquestioned."[143] When Trumbull did speak later, it came perhaps as an anticlimax to Lincoln's performance. The *State Register* reported that Trumbull "closed his speech in an argument against slavery in the usual abolition style and was greatly cheered by the members of the fusion [anti-Nebraska] convention, all of whom are present."[144]

On to Peoria

Lincoln did not linger in Springfield to bask in the praise of supporters. William Herndon worried about the abolitionist enthusiasm generated by the Springfield speech. Lincoln's law partner contended that he tried to insulate Lincoln from more radical Nebraska opponents with whom Herndon himself sympathized ideologically. Congregational ministers Owen Lovejoy and Ichabod Codding sought Lincoln to speak under their auspices. Lovejoy and his allies had issued a convention call one month earlier "for the organization of a party which shall put the government upon a Republican tack and to secure to non-slave holders throughout the Union their just and constitutional weight and influence in the councils of the nation."[145]

Herndon himself held some abolitionist opinions, but he claimed that the political ambitions of his senior partner would have collapsed in antiblack Illinois were Lincoln to have been identified with abolitionism. In an account that has been questioned by leading Lincoln historians, Herndon contended:

> As soon therefore as Lincoln finished his speech in the hall of the House of Representatives, Lovejoy, moving forward from the crowd, announced a meeting in the same place that evening of all the friends of Freedom. That of course meant the Abolitionists with whom I had been in conference all the day. Their plan had been to induce Mr. Lincoln to speak for them at their meeting. Strong as I was in the faith, yet I doubted the propriety of Lincoln's taking any stand yet. As I viewed it, he was ambitious to climb to the United States Senate, and on grounds of policy it

Anti-Nebraska Leaders in Illinois

John M. Palmer

The Gilder Lehrman Collection, courtesy of the Gilder Lehrman Institute of American History, on deposit at the New-York Historical Society, New York, reference number GLC 5111.02.0633

William H. Herndon

Courtesy of The Lincoln Museum, Fort Wayne, Indiana, reference number 1638

Richard Yates

The Gilder Lehrman Collection, courtesy of the Gilder Lehrman Institute of American History, on deposit at the New-York Historical Society, New York, reference number GLC 5596.22

Lyman Trumbull

Library of Congress Prints and Photographs Division, reference number LC-BH83-296

would not do for him to occupy at that time such advanced ground as we were taking. On the other hand, it was equally as dangerous to refuse a speech for the Abolitionists. I did not know how he felt on the subject, but on learning that Lovejoy intended to approach him with an invitation, I hunted up Lincoln and urged him to avoid meeting the enthusiastic champion of Abolitionism.[146]

As Lincoln was the "leading Whig of Illinois," noted one Lincoln biographer, "it would have been a great catch if Codding could have drawn Lincoln into his [abolitionist] net. He was unable to do so."[147] The disputed Herndon story nevertheless illustrates how difficult it was to navigate antislavery politics amid the racism of Illinois. It also shows how hard it is to sift through the recollections of Lincoln's contemporaries for historical truth.

Whatever the cause, Lincoln departed Springfield before the Lovejoy platform was discussed. With his horse and rig he set off to attend court in Tazewell County.[148] Four years later in yet another debate with Douglas at Ottawa, Lincoln recalled what happened in 1854: "There was a call for a Convention to form a Republican party at Springfield, and I think that my friend Mr. Lovejoy, who is here upon this stand, had a hand in it. I think this is true, and I think if he will remember accurately he will be able to recollect that he tried to get me into it, and I would not go in."[149] Thus did Lincoln discreetly deflect the charge that he was an abolitionist.

The Republican organizing meeting at Springfield turned out to be less radical than Herndon expected. It was also smaller; only twenty-six delegates attended. "Committed antislavery men, led by Lovejoy and Ichabod Codding, dominated its deliberations; yet, contrary to the expectations of those Whigs and Democrats who declined to participate, the convention adopted a moderate statement of principles. Lovejoy, whose antislavery principles were tinctured with a large measure of political pragmatism, was probably influential in formulating this broad appeal. The resolutions declared it the 'right and the duty of the general government' to prohibit slavery in all territories, including any acquired in the future,'" wrote historian William E. Gienapp.[150] They did not, however, propose repealing the federal fugitive slave law. Nor did they endorse abolitionist policies toward slavery in the South. Lovejoy understood that no candidate nor any party in Illinois could have prevailed statewide on such a platform. Contemporary Illinois journalist Paul Selby maintained that a large and representative cross section of anti-Nebraska politicians were present. Selby wrote that "someone raised the question whether Lincoln was in harmony with the views of the convention, and I remember it was Owen Lovejoy who responded with an earnest endorsement of Lincoln's position on the slavery question. . . ."[151] Selby later contended that "it is a poor tribute to [Lincoln's] memory to picture him as resenting the act of a body of men . . . which he joined with patriotic zeal and enthusiasm two years later, and which finally resulted in his election to the Presidency."[152]

For almost two weeks following his Springfield speech, Lincoln concentrated on his legal work. Meanwhile, the Lovejoy-Codding group had nominated him as a member of the new Republican State Central Committee. Invited to a committee meeting, Lincoln declined—writing to Codding in late November: "I was not consulted on the subject; nor was I apprized of the appointment, until I discovered it by accident two or three weeks afterwards. I suppose my opposition to the principle of slavery is as strong as that of any member of the Republican party; but I had also supposed that the *extent* to which I feel authorized to carry that opposition, practically; was not at all satisfactory to that party. The leading men who organized that party, were present on the 4th. of Oct. at the discussion between Douglas and myself at Springfield, and had full oppertunity [*sic*] to not misunderstand my position. Do I misunderstand theirs?"[153] In 1858 Lincoln would remember: "It is true they did place my name, though without authority, upon the committee, and afterward wrote me to attend the meeting of the Committee; but I refused to do so, and I never had anything to do with that organization."[154] Douglas's house organ, the *State Register*, nevertheless connected Lincoln to the abolitionists: "It was impossible for this black republican concern to carry on its proceedings without a decided expression in some way of the feelings . . . resulting from Mr. Lincoln's [Springfield] speech," reported the paper. It said "all indorsed the sentiments of that speech."[155] But the *Register* could not truthfully say Lincoln's speech was explicitly abolitionist, though it was certainly antislavery.

Peoria Speech

Senator Douglas had been scheduled to speak at Peoria on Monday, October 16. By then the state's second largest city, Peoria had grown up on the west bank of the Illinois River, about sixty-five miles north of Springfield. The city would become an important railroad hub for the Midwest, though the first train would not reach it until November 1855. Often on horseback, sometimes with a buggy, Lincoln went to Peoria frequently on political and legal business. He first visited the town in 1832 when he bought a canoe there on his way home to New Salem after service in the Black Hawk War. Lincoln gave his first campaign speech at Peoria in February 1840—at a Whig meeting to celebrate the nomination of William Henry Harrison for president. "Lincoln here rose and made just such a speech as would be expected from a gentlemen [*sic*] of his high reputation for argument and eloquence. No sketch from memory of his remarks," reported a local newspaper, "could do them justice."[156]

Byron C. Bryner was a small boy and a strong "Douglas man" when he heard Douglas and Lincoln speak in Peoria in October 1854. He described the village of Peoria with "bluffs covered with oak and hickory—undergrowth of hazel brush and wild blackberry—ravines in which the wolf still lingered. At the narrows butternuts, wild grapes, plums pecans, persimmons and pawpaws. Rope ferries at opposite ends of the lake—wild ducks floating upon the river's bosom. Clouds of black birds darkened the skies. The honk of the wild geese winging their way north or south in endless file the whole day long foretold the seasons's change. Morning and evening heard the drumming of partridges, or the call of the quail in back yards and streets." Bryner remembered "music of bands—of drum and fife with drummers and fifers garbed in colonial costume—the 'Spirit of "76."' Campaign songs—flags mounted on saplings with bunches of leaves at the top. Only thirty-four stars then. Floats with pretty girls in white representing Columbia and the several states . . . tallow candles for illumination—butter, eggs and milk lowered into the cistern to keep fresh."[157]

Peoria's Democratic welcoming committee had decreed that those wishing to greet "Judge Douglas" gather on horseback on the Farmington Road at 9 A.M. "Mr. Douglas rode into our city yesterday at the head of a triumphal procession, seated in a carriage drawn by four beautiful white palfreys and preceded by a band of music," reported the *Peoria Republican*. "Cannon boomed in welcome to the distinguished visitors and the cheers of his friends resounded through our quiet streets. He was waited upon by a committee of the faithful and escorted to the place of speaking. . . ."[158] It was a festive affair. According to one local history, "a procession, preceded by a brass band, was made up of footmen, horsemen and citizens in carriages, all under direction of Smith Frye, former Sheriff, as chief marshal. By the time it had reached the public square it numbered fully five hundred persons."[159] The crowd included hundreds of farmers who traveled to Peoria for the entertainment and education of democratic politics. The event chairman "seemed to assume that the Judge was the great man of the age—the greatest man of any age in the past, and greater than any man that may flourish in any age in the future," reported the *Peoria Republican*.[160] No one yet made such assumptions about the lawyer from Springfield. "Mr Lincoln was attending court at Pekin[.] Myself and other friends induced Mr Lincoln to come here and make a reply[.] He did so," recalled Benjamin F. Irwin.[161] Another Lincoln friend, Abner Y. Ellis, recalled that Lincoln slipped into town about 2 A.M. "unbeknown to any one." Ellis recalled that the next morning Douglas's friends at the hotel were "having a good time in his Company, & thinking what a clear field he was to have that day all to himself" until the proprietor informed them that Lincoln had checked in.[162] Douglas and Lincoln probably stayed at Peoria House, a large four-story establishment built in 1841 at the corner of Adams and Hamilton streets. Originally called Planter's House, it was then the largest hotel in Illinois.[163]

The supporters of Judge Douglas should not have been surprised at Lincoln's arrival. A group of twenty Peoria residents had sent Lincoln an invitation on September 28: "Understanding that Judge Douglas is expected to address our citizens on the 16th of next month on the principles of the Nebraska-Kansas Bill . . . the undersigned, on behalf of themselves and the Whigs of Peoria, are exceedingly desirous that (if not too gr[e]at a tax upon your time and strength) you will consent to be present and take a convenient opportunity, after the speech of Judge Douglas, to reply to it, and give us your own views upon the subject."[164] Abner Ellis recalled that after learning of his rival's presence, Douglas went immediately to Lincoln's room to express his chagrin "that you have Come as I well Know you[r] business. . . ."[165] Elihu N. Powell recalled: "As the meeting was called for Mr Douglas alone we had no right to claim to have Mr Lincoln to participate in the discussion of the questions which then agitated the country but at all events it was so arranged, that Mr Douglas should open the debate and speak as long as he desired when Mr Lincoln should reply as long as he might wish when Mr Douglas was to have 40 Minutes to reply. Mr Douglas commenced and spoke for near three hours[.]"[166]

By agreement, the rivals debated in front of the eight-year-old Greek Revival court house on Adams Street. Built of brick and stone, flanked by trees and surmounted by a handsome lantern, the building had been completed in 1846. Half of the first floor was rented as offices, the other half housing the county sheriff and court clerks.[167] Amidst four Corinthian pillars on the front portico, two sets of external stairs led to an open-air balcony, itself the entrance to the second floor where the county court was held.[168] At least one witness claimed that the speeches were delivered from a platform below. Another said they were made from a "veranda or porch."[169]

Stretched out in front of the court house was the large square where the audience would gather. Byron C. Bryner recalled: "From the north corner of the square, extending to the foot of the bluff and running through where now stands the Woman's Club House, was an avenue of locust trees fragrant in bloom time. Around the square were hitching racks to which were tied horses and mules attached to vehicles of every description."[170] The Douglas appearance was managed by an impressive contingent of "officers." The event chairman was State Senator Washington Cockle, a wealthy local businessman who was a key Democratic supporter of Senator Douglas. Cockle would become a strong Republican supporter of President Lincoln.

When Douglas rose to speak on the afternoon of October 16, he complained that it was his lot to confront anti-Nebraska speakers with inconsistent viewpoints, each conveniently tailored to the region in which he was making his presentation. According to the Peoria *Union*: "In an abolition settlement an abolitionist was deputed as the organ of denunciation and abuse. In another place where the Whigs were not wholly abolitionized, a half Whig was selected. In a Democratic locality, the duty was assigned to any disaffected Democrat who was willing to unite with the opponents of the Nebraska Bill and denounce its author. It would only be fair that his antagonist should be one who would proclaim the same sentiments in Knoxville that were uttered in Peoria. If this were done, every true Whig in Peoria would turn his back upon the 'fusion' advocates."[171] Douglas cast himself as a martyr beset by a host of persecutors. James M. Rice, a Peoria resident, remembered: "I was then a young man, and not much inclined to political life, but having been brought up a democrat, I was disposed to side with Senator Douglas. I listened with much interest to his speech in defense of the repeal of the 'Missouri Compromise,' but was not altogether satisfied with it."[172] According to the *Illinois Journal*, "When he closed he was greeted with six hearty cheers; and the band in attendance played a stirring air. The crowd then began to call for LINCOLN, who, as Judge Douglas had announced was, by agreement, to answer him."[173]

Lincoln shrewdly suggested that the tired and hungry crowd—having listened to Senator Douglas for three hours—get something to eat and return at 7 P.M. to hear his reply. Lincoln added: "The Judge has already informed you that he is to have an hour to reply to me. I doubt but you have been a little surprised to learn that I have consented to give one of his high reputation and known ability, this advantage of me. Indeed, my consenting to it, though reluctant, was not wholly unselfish; for I suspected if it were understood, that the Judge was entirely done, you democrats would leave, and not hear me; but by giving him the close, I felt confident you would stay for the fun of hearing him skin me."[174] Rice remembered that Lincoln asked: "'What do you say?' Immediately a cheer went up from his friends all over the vast audience, accompanied by throwing of hats in the air, and other demonstrations of approval."[175] The meeting adjourned. Dr. Robert Boal, an anti-Nebraska activist and long-time Lincoln friend from nearby Lacon, recalled: "The people . . . were tired from standing so long, but they came back in increased number, and with increased interest."[176] Rice noted that the delay "gave Mr. Lincoln the advantage of a much larger night audience, and an opportunity of arranging his thoughts beforehand."[177]

It was dark when Lincoln began to speak. Light came from candles in windows of houses that lined the court house square—and from lanterns around the square. Gas streetlights would not arrive in Peoria until at least 1855.[178] There in the dim illumination and cool autumn air, Lincoln delivered his "Peoria speech" from the portico of the court house below the upper balcony. Access to this makeshift dais was reportedly gained through a window from one of the first floor offices, easier for the compact Douglas than the lanky Lincoln. According to Dr. Boal, "Mr. Lincoln slowly arose, and, after surveying the large audience, commenced his speech by saying: "He thought he could appreciate an argument, and at times, believed he could make one, but when one denied the settled and plainest facts of history, you could not argue with him; the only thing you could do would be to stop his mouth with a corn cob."[179] He carefully reviewed the Douglas speech, his conception of popular sovereignty, and the history of slavery in the United States, emphasizing its inconsistency with the principles of the Declaration of Independence:

> Judge Douglas frequently, with bitter irony and sarcasm, paraphrases our argument by saying "The white people of Nebraska are good enough to govern themselves, *but they are not good enough to govern a few miserable negroes!!*"
>
> Well I doubt not that the people of Nebraska are, and will continue to be as good as the average of people elsewhere. I do not say the contrary. What I do say is, that no man is good enough to

govern another man, *without that other's consent.* I say this is the leading principle—the sheet anchor of American republicanism. Our Declaration of Independence says:

"We hold these truths to be self evident: that all men are created equal; that they are endowed by their Creator with certain inalienable rights; that among these are life, liberty and the pursuit of happiness. That to secure these rights, governments are instituted among men, DERIVING THEIR JUST POWERS FROM THE CONSENT OF THE GOVERNED."

I have quoted so much at this time merely to show that according to our ancient faith, the just powers of governments are derived from the consent of the governed. Now the relation of masters and slaves is, PRO TANTO, a total violation of this principle. The master not only governs the slave without his consent; but he governs him by a set of rules altogether different from those which he prescribes for himself. Allow ALL the governed an equal voice in the government, and that, and that only is self government.[180]

In principle, Lincoln argued here that the "consent of the governed" included black as well as white Americans. Few American politicians in 1854 ventured so boldly. As at Springfield, Lincoln's supporters at Peoria took heart from his presentation. Decades later, William H. Pierce wrote that Lincoln "stood up straight on the back side of the veranda; his hands hanging by his sides. I don't think he raised either hand while he was speaking. . . . There was no cheering while he was speaking. Perfect silence prevailed. His articulation was good and his voice loud so I heard every word he said. I think I was about 50 feet from him. His speech was full of facts and argument. He was not the humorous, story telling Lincoln sometimes pictured in the newspapers. His speech was highly didactic."[181] According to Pierce, "Empty tar barrels had been piled 20' high; as soon as Lincoln ceased speaking they were blazing higher than the top of the court house and the booming of cannon and cheering by the people showed that Lincoln had plenty of friends and that they knew how best to let him know the fact."[182]

William O. Stoddard, a Lincoln partisan, later wrote: "At Peoria, Lincoln's triumph was even more marked than at Springfield, for his antagonist had lost something of his assurance. He was a wounded and weakened man, indeed. He had become conscious that he was not invulnerable. He had been a witness of Mr. Lincoln's power over the people; and it is quite possible that his faith in his own position had been broken."[183] Attorney Elihu N. Powell recalled the impact of the speech: "I need only say that the friends of Mr L were well satisfied with the result." Powell concluded that "Douglas had the worse of the debate—and was not anxious at that time to speak when Lincoln was to reply. . . ."[184] Lincoln himself made sure his remarks found wide distribution by publishing the edited speech in the *Illinois State Journal,* for which he regularly wrote anonymous editorials. Lincoln the speaker became Lincoln the editor, and he was meticulous. The *Journal* reproduced the Peoria speech in seven installments—along with the notation that "Mr. Lincoln spoke substantially as follows . . ."[185]

After Lincoln had spoken for three hours, Douglas responded with remarks that were estimated to last between thirty and ninety minutes. Lincoln had driven "Mr. Douglas into some very close quarters," remembered James Rice. "When the latter arose to reply, he manifested strong symptoms of anger, and continued to speak in that strain until the close of his hour."[186] One historian of Peoria wrote: "When the time came for Mr. Douglas to reply he seemed to be much worried and spoke in angry tones, sometimes in a manner not excessively courteous."[187] The Democratic senator may also have lost his voice. According to the Peoria *Republican*, Douglas "was entitled, according to the terms of the discussion, to an hour after Mr. Lincoln had concluded. He arose to reply, but he had very little to say. He had talked himself hoarse in the afternoon and with his voice had gone his arguments. He made a feeble effort to collect them, but soon became conscious that the route [*sic*] was complete."[188]

The End of the 1854 Debates

The following day, October 17, the speakers prepared to leave town. It was reported that Senator Douglas told Lincoln that he "understood the

Territorial Question from the organization of the Government Better
than all the opposition in the Senate of the U.S. and he did not see that
he could make any thing by debating it with him." Douglas, according to
a witness, said that Lincoln had provided "[m]ore trouble than all the
opposition in t[he Senate com]bined and followed up w[ith the pro-
pos]ition that he would [go home and] Speak no more [during the] campaign if Lincoln would [do the sam]e to which proposition Lincoln
acceded."[189] These events after the Peoria speeches remain surrounded
by historical disputes, but the controversy reflected the intensity of the
battle between Lincoln and Douglas that persisted until 1861.

Dr. Boal, one of the founders of the Illinois State Medical Society,
recalled: "The late Judge Silas Ramsey and myself went to Peoria to hear
the speeches and to induce Mr. Lincoln to go to Lacon the next day to
answer Senator Douglas. He agreed to go." Dr. Boal, himself a candidate
for the state legislature, recalled: "When we arrived about 1 o'clock at
Lacon, we found Senator Douglas at the hotel. Mr. Lincoln went in to see
him, and, after a few minutes, came out and told his friends that Mr.
Douglas said he was sick and worn out and would not speak."[190] Douglas
claimed he had almost lost his voice. Some of Lincoln's friends thought
Douglas had lost his nerve. Judge Powell confirmed that Douglas "was in
a poor condition to speak being hoarse and not otherwise very well and
did not wish to speak."[191] Douglas, however, had not tried to conserve his
voice on the trip to Lacon, having engaged Powell in an extensive conversation about Douglas's visit to Russia in 1853.

The Peoria *Republican* reported at the time: "The large crowd assembled in this city [Lacon] on yesterday [October 17], to hear the celebrated champions discuss great questions of the day were doomed to
disappointment. Douglas arrived from Peoria on the morning train; but
was too unwell—in consequence of long speaking during the cool
weather of Monday—to address the people. Hon. Abram Lincoln was also
in town, but declined to speak unless in answer to Douglas. Thus there
was no speaking at the time appointed, to the great disappointment of
many who had come from a distance to the discussion, and the infinite
annoyance of the court, which had adjourned to accommodate the speakers. Messrs. Lincoln and Douglas left the city this morning for their

respective homes."[192] In 1860 Lincoln campaign biographer John L. Scripps wrote: "It was Mr. Lincoln's purpose and desire to continue the discussion with Mr. Douglas during the remainder of the canvass, but that gentleman shrank from a repetition of the discomfiture he had suffered at Springfield and Peoria. He gave Mr. Lincoln no further opportunity of meeting him."[193]

Albert J. Beveridge contended: "If [Douglas] did say that he would stop speaking during the last two weeks of the campaign if Lincoln would agree not to speak again, it was the only time in his life that Douglas ever asked quarter of any man or combination; and it was the most uncharacteristic thing that fearless and combative man ever did."[194] Beveridge notwithstanding, the reports suggest that Douglas did indeed ask for quarter from Lincoln, perhaps because he was genuinely too sick to muster his full strength.

Lincoln had probably intended to debate with Douglas after Peoria because Lacon led him away from home. Otherwise, he could have gone straight to Springfield after Peoria—as he promptly did after Lacon. Whatever the explanation, Douglas did have trouble pacing himself during his political campaigns. His powerful voice was often weakened by overuse, sickness, tobacco, and alcohol. His strength had been gravely diminished by the tragic loss of his wife and daughter in 1853. Perhaps too, he recognized Abraham Lincoln to be as formidable an opponent as he had met. Whatever his ailment, Douglas recovered quickly. He spoke at Princeton on October 18, just two days after Peoria. There, Owen Lovejoy delivered a half-hour rejoinder. Douglas then "talked till dark against time. Giving no opportunity for reply."[195]

William H. Herndon reported that the confrontation at Princeton annoyed his law partner: "Lincoln was much displeased at this action of Douglas, which tended to convince him that the latter was really a man devoid of fixed political morals." Herndon recalled that Lincoln's "friends in Springfield and elsewhere, who had urged him to push after Douglas till he cried 'enough,' were surprised a few days after the Peoria debate to find him [Lincoln] at home, with the information that by an agreement with the latter [Douglas] they were both to return home and speak no more during the campaign."[196] Herndon attributed Lincoln's decision to his inability to "refuse a polite request—one in which no principle was involved. I have heard him say, 'It's a fortunate thing I wasn't born a woman, for I cannot refuse anything, it seems.'"[197]

Paul M. Angle maintained that "contemporary evidence indicates that at Lacon, on Oct. 17, 1854, and for some time afterward, Douglas was really ill."[198] But, at Princeton on October 18, Douglas was able to speak until dark, thus suggesting that the degree of his infirmity might have fluctuated in proportion to his proximity to Mr. Lincoln. "By the time Douglas reached Princeton, his voice had recovered sufficiently to enable him to debate with Owen Lovejoy, but a scheduled appearance the following day in Aurora, where the Negro abolitionist Frederick Douglass was prepared to answer him, was canceled," wrote Douglas biographer Robert W. Johannsen.[199] According to the Aurora *Guardian*: "On Wednesday the word came that Senator Douglas was to be met by Frederick Douglass, the Fugitive Slave, at Aurora. No one knew of it until announced in Chicago papers—and no one at Chicago as far as we can learn, until he informed the editor of the Western Citizen that he had come West to canvass Northern Illinois with the Senator. Well, Thursday [October 19] came, and hundreds of people from abroad. The two Douglasses came. As soon as they arrived, both were taken sick. Frederick got well enough to speak, but Stephen did not. The Congregational church was crowded to overflowing with ladies and gentlemen. Frederick did not speak long . . ."[200]

The *Guardian* noted: "We saw Stephen A. Douglas as he got into the Cars—he really looked sick. He looked as though he had no money, no friends, no home." Biographer Johannsen wrote: "On October 19, Douglas returned to Chicago, unwell and tired. Except for a few speeches in the hostile First Congressional District later in the month, his campaign had closed."[201] One Lincoln ally in Chicago wrote on October 20 that "Douglas came to town last night pretending to have the ague, & probably cannot be induced to speak here again."[202] The pro-Douglas *Chicago Times* reported: "Judge Douglas—This gentlemen returned to Chicago last evening; he was met at the cars by a committee appointed for that purpose by the Cook county convention, and escorted to his rooms at the Tremont

House. He left this city four weeks ago, and since then has made over twenty speeches [in] as many different places; and has traveled on his route more than a thousand miles. We regret to say that his health in consequence of the great physical exertion he has made is not as good as it was. He returns as undaunted in spirit and buoyant in hope as a man confident of the rectitude of his course can only be. A few days rest will, we hope, restore him to his wonted health."[203] Time and distance from the Lincoln-Douglas debate at Peoria may have proved a tonic for Douglas.

The competitive relationship of the two men persisted from 1834 until the death of Douglas in 1861.

The End of the Campaign

Although he left Douglas alone, Lincoln did not entirely leave the campaign trail. After attending court in Champaign on October 24, he spoke there against Kansas-Nebraska. Lincoln delivered at least three more campaign speeches against the Nebraska Act—one in Urbana on October 24, one in Chicago on October 27, and one in Quincy on November 1. Lawyer Henry Clay Whitney, a Lincoln friend who sometimes exaggerated his own importance and embellished his accounts of events, recalled that he met Lincoln on the court circuit in Urbana a few days after the Peoria Speech: "I saw him as he drove into town behind his own horse, which was an indifferent, raw-boned specimen in his own blacksmith-made buggy—a most ordinary looking one. He was entirely alone; and might have passed for an ordinary farmer, so far as appearances were concerned."[204]

Whitney wrote that he "called at the Old Pennsylvania House, on the east side of the public square, in Urbana, where [I] found Mr. Lincoln and Judge [David] Davis in their plainly furnished bedroom, upon the hearth of which was a comfortable wood fire. It was my first interview with either of those distinguished men, but I was put at complete ease, at once, by the cordiality of my welcome by both; ostentatiously and effusively by the latter: heartily and laconically by the former. I at once mentioned to Lincoln the fact which had just appeared in the papers, that he and

Douglas had had an encounter the preceding week at Peoria, to which he answered, 'Yes, the Judge and I locked horns there.'"[205]

Whitney in his memoirs presented Lincoln's speech at Urbana as almost identical to the Peoria speech. He declared the Urbana speech was notable for "the simplicity of its style, clearness of its diction and the force and completeness of its argument."[206] Paul M. Angle contended that "it is possible—even probable—that at Urbana Lincoln repeated what he had said earlier in the month at Springfield and Peoria. But would he have repeated these speeches verbatim? Only the novice at public speaking feels so insecure as to stick absolutely to a prepared text. . . . One is forced to the conclusion that Whitney adapted the well known text of Lincoln's Peoria address to fit a slightly different situation and published it as his own discovery."[207] Angle may have been right, but a very close repetition at Urbana of the Peoria text may have been a self-conscious decision on the part of Lincoln. By late October, Lincoln had researched the facts, transcribed his thoughts, and rehearsed the Peoria themes in several places. He had even reduced the Peoria speech to a formal written text. An experienced trial lawyer and politician, he knew the value of repeating a successful speech at different places. Whitney recalled that Judge "Davis and I were with him from the adjournment of court till we went to the court house; he regaled us with stories—then made this great speech; then resumed his story-telling where he left off as if the making of such a speech as this was pastime."[208]

Meanwhile, Lincoln's friend Abraham Jonas had invited him to Quincy—saying that all Whigs "would be much gratified if you could make it convenient and pay us a visit while the little giant is here[.] It is believed by all who know you, that a reply from you, would be more effective, than from any other —I trust you may be able to pay us the visit and thereby create a debt of gratitude on the part of Whigs here, which they may at some time, have it in their power, to repay with pleasure and with interest." Chicago *Tribune* editor Richard Wilson echoed the Quincy invitation: "Our folks want you to come & I think it would have a most excellent effect not only upon the present canvas, but for future action consequent on the result."[209] Horace White wrote Lincoln a few days later that the "idea is to have you go to Chicago and make a speech. You will have a crowd of from eight to ten or fifteen thousand and the result will be that the people will demand of their Representatives to elect a Whig Senator."[210] At Quincy, Lincoln's avowed purpose was to promote anti-Nebraska congressional candidate Archibald Williams, who opposed incumbent William A. Richardson, a strong Douglas ally. "Dick" Richardson was a slovenly contrast to the stylish Douglas. Historian Allan G. Bogue wrote that Richardson "was accused of sometimes wearing shirts 'absolutely black,' except where stained from the tobacco juice that ran from each corner of his mouth in a 'steady drizzle,' and was derided by the Chicago *Tribune* in 1864 as one of the two 'habitual drunkards of the Senate,'" where Richardson served at the end of the Civil War.[211] Richardson, however, possessed one quality Lincoln admired—loyalty. Lincoln said of Richardson: "I regard him as one of the truest men that ever lived; he sticks to Judge Douglas through thick and thin—never deserted him, and never will. I admire such a man!"[212]

The anti-Nebraska coalition in Illinois was more divided than the pro-Nebraska forces of Douglas and Richardson. Some former Whigs had become adherents of the American Party, a nativist group popularly known as Know-Nothings, which opposed immigrants, especially Irish and German Catholics. Lincoln reflected on the strain when he wrote Yates from Jacksonville in late October: "I am here now going to Quincy, to try to give Mr. Williams a little life. I expect to be back in time to speak at Car-linville on Saturday, if thought expedient. What induces me to write now is that at Jacksonville as I came down to-day, I learned that the English in Morgan county have become dissatisfied about No-Nothingism. Our friends, however, think they have got the difficulty arrested. Nevertheless, it would be safer, I think, to do something on the subject, which you alone can do." Lincoln then lectured Yates on political tactics, but with the restraint he would exercise in writing to Union generals a decade later: "The inclosed letter, or draft of a letter, I have drawn up, of which I think it would be well to make several copies, and have one placed in the hands of a safe friend, at each precinct where any considerable number of the foreign citizens, german as well as english—vote. Not knowing exactly where a letter will reach you soonest I fear this can not be very promptly attended to; but if the copies get into the proper hands the day before the election, it will be time enough. The whole of this is, of course, subject to your own judgment."[213] Lincoln was at work behind the scenes. He had been opposed to the anti-Catholic, anti-immigrant movement to which some Whig allies had been attracted. Lincoln worked to separate the Yates campaign from the Know-Nothing movement.

Lincoln's speech at Quincy on November 1 drew the praise of his admirers. The Quincy *Whig* spared few words: "The large company present listened with unwearied attention and an approbation emphasised by the repeated outbursts of enthusiastic applause. The address was one of the clearest, most logical, argumentative and convincing discourses on the Nebraska question to which we have listened. Commencing with the history of its earliest events which led to the Compromise of 1820, he traced that Compromise up to the present time, showing that it had ever remained in the hearts of the people a sacred thing which no ruthless hand should have dared to destroy."[214] At every turn of his travels during the fall of 1854, Lincoln created new friendships while renewing relationships with old allies. Longtime Lincoln friend Orville H. Browning described the personal moments of the Quincy event in his diary: "Attending Court. Beautiful day. A. Lincoln Esqr of Springfield arrived in Town last night. Dined & took tea with me, and at night addressed the people at Kendall's Hall on the Nebraska question."[215] The evening speech in Kendall's Hall did not end Lincoln's day. Before retiring to Quincy House, Lincoln joined attorney Abraham Jonas at an "oyster saloon." Lincoln paced himself, but his were long days. Before he went to bed, he had to locate a stagecoach driver for his transportation the next morning.[216]

On October 27, Lincoln closed his anti-Nebraska campaign at Chicago. His remarks there provided a geographical symmetry to the opening speech Douglas had made at Chicago on September 1. After Lincoln's address the *Chicago Daily Journal* reported that "his speech of last evening was as thorough an exposition of the Nebraska iniquity as has ever been made, and his eloquence greatly impressed all his hearers, but it was manifest, as he frequently remarked that 'he could not help feeling foolish in answering arguments which were no arguments at all.' He could not help feeling silly in beating the air before an intelligent audience. It is a fruitless job to pound dry sand, under the delusion that it is a rock. The laborer may get his eyes full, but the sand is just as sandy as it was before."[217] The newspaper reported: "The impression created by Mr. Lincoln on all men, of all parties, was first, that he was an honest man, and second, that he was a powerful speaker."[218] The Chicago *Journal* concentrated on the man as well as his speech: "Born of parents who could only give him faith in rectitude and virtue, he has become what he is through the trials of poverty and by the sweat of his brow. How he guided a flatboat over the Ohio, or how he afterwards had his last article of property consisting of a chain and compass, sold under the sheriff's hammer, are matters of small interest now. How he became the most powerful speaker and one of the ablest lawyers in the West are of more moment."[219] He was not yet well known in the East, but Lincoln's reputation in Illinois had now been established. The smear of Whig elitism, with which he had been charged in the 1830s and 1840s, had been wiped clean.

Like Congressman May a decade earlier, Senator Douglas had learned that Lincoln had an instinct for finding holes in a politician's argument and that he did not give his opponent much room to crawl out. The Little Giant increasingly respected the trial lawyer and appeals court litigator. Lincoln and Douglas would meet again in 1858 for the most famous debates in American history. The format of these meetings would again favor Douglas, but in 1858 the senator committed himself to seven joint appearances, enough to assure sustained public debate on America's "peculiar institution"—slavery.[220]

The lawyer-politician from Springfield could be bold on the offense, but he was not reckless. Neither was he an impulsive stage-seeker. Lincoln adjusted his tactics to fit the circumstances. In the 1860 presidential campaign, it was Lincoln who deliberately remained mute during the campaign. He stayed quiet from the time he returned to Springfield from the East in March 1860 until he departed Springfield for Washington, D.C., in February 1861. It was then traditional for presidential candidates to be circumspect, but Senator Douglas criss-crossed the country in the 1860 election—defying precedent. Lincoln maintained that the policy positions of the four presidential standard-bearers were printed and well known. The 1858 Lincoln-Douglas debates had been reported in newspapers throughout the nation and widely distributed in a pamphlet edited by Lincoln himself. No public or private pressure could, during the 1860 campaign, goad him into additional public commentary. His chosen words, from Peoria to Cooper Union, had been printed for any who cared to read them. For what he had said and done, Lincoln was severely criticized. Even his obscurity and humble origins were the object of scorn. Still, he maintained his self-discipline and his silence.

As President, Lincoln's self-mastery enabled him to endure invective far worse than the "blanknation" William May had directed at him in 1844. The tone Lincoln set at Peoria in 1854 became the even-tempered standard by which he guided his public life. His informed logic and magnanimous disposition became sheet anchors of his political rhetoric. His consistency of principle and prudent tactics, joined to tireless public and private labors, would forge an antislavery party which dominated American political history for generations. Although his antislavery arguments may have unnerved the South as it moved toward secession, they readied the North to fight the Civil War and eventually to accept the justice of emancipation.

The Peoria speech had set Lincoln on the road to the Emancipation Proclamation. At Peoria, he had established himself, in the words of the Quincy *Whig*, as "one of the 'truly great men' of Illinois."[221]

"On January 4th, 1854, Judge Douglas introduces a new bill to give Nebraska a territorial government. He accompanies this bill with a report, in which last, he expressly recommends that the Missouri Compromise shall neither be affirmed nor repealed."

ABRAHAM LINCOLN,
OCTOBER 16, 1854

III.

The Kansas-Nebraska Act: The Context

In his First Annual Message to Congress of December 1853, President Franklin Pierce embraced peace and slavery: "That this repose is to suffer no shock during my official term if I have power to avert it, those who placed me here may be assured."[222] In his Inaugural Address the previous March, Pierce had stated: "I believe that involuntary servitude, as it exists in different States of this Confederacy, is recognized by the Constitution. I believe that it stands like any other admitted right, and that the States where it exists are entitled to efficient remedies to enforce the constitutional provision. I hold that the laws of 1850, commonly called the 'compromise measures,' are strictly constitutional and to be unhesitatingly carried into effect."[223]

The New York *Tribune*'s capital correspondent, James S. Pike, predicted that President Pierce would "give us a quiet, moderate, conservative, unexceptionable, good-for-nothing kind of an Administration, to which nobody will think of making any especial objection or opposition; and that by the close of his term there will be a pretty general fusion of all the parties."[224] As Pierce steered complacently into the storm of 1854, the nation's political parties had been breaking apart. No unifying leader had appeared to command the disparate elements. Pierce himself was essentially an accidental President—a dark horse chosen by the Democratic

Party in 1852 because he was not totally objectionable to party leaders, North or South. Not a bad man, neither was Pierce a brave man. Weak-willed, he lacked the strength to manage the warring factions of the Democratic Party. Perhaps no national Democrat might have unified the Democratic Party, much less the nation. The customary clamor for patronage, joined to divisions over slavery, split President Pierce's party.

Even though the Compromise of 1850 had been designed to settle sectional differences, the disputes persisted. The 1850 settlement had begun as the work of Kentucky Senator Henry Clay, also the central figure of the Missouri Compromise of 1820. But, it was Illinois Senator Stephen A. Douglas who created the legislative majorities for each part of the complex bill in 1850. By 1853, without effective leadership from President Pierce, the strong-willed Douglas had emerged the party's *de facto* head. (Both Pierce and Douglas suffered devastating losses during 1853. Pierce's 11-year-old son died in a train accident. Douglas lost his wife Martha and shortly thereafter their baby daughter. Alcohol abuse exacerbated these personal tragedies, affecting the health of both Democratic leaders.)

Ambition and territorial policy gradually moved Douglas to believe that the slavery restriction in the 1820 Missouri Compromise was expendable, not least because its demise would assure southern support for congressional organization of the Nebraska territory. But the ambition of Douglas was not merely personal, for it was linked to his vision of continental integration. As chairman of the Committee on Territories, Douglas had the power to shape the Kansas-Nebraska legislation—just as the Missouri Compromise of 1820 had been shaped by Illinois Senator Jesse B. Thomas. Thomas had sponsored legislation to prohibit slavery in the former Louisiana Territory north of the southern boundary of Missouri at 36° 30'. When the legislation stalled in the House of Representatives, House Speaker Henry Clay took charge. As Stephen Douglas would later do with the Compromise of 1850, Clay had divided the 1820 bill into parts for which there might exist separate majorities. Using his power as speaker to appoint pliable members to a House-Senate conference, Clay then called for *separate* votes on the three parts of the legislation: free statehood for Maine, slave statehood for Missouri, and a ban on slavery north of 36° 30'. When all the parts passed the House, Clay immediately sent the bills back to the Senate where they also passed. President James

Monroe signed them immediately. The number of slave and free states remained in balance at twelve each.

Senator Thomas understood that the early residents of Illinois were divided on slavery, especially since so many had come from slave-holding states such as Kentucky. Historian Walter A. McDougall observed that residents of Illinois had differed on slavery from the moment the state had joined the union in 1818. "Illinoisans were tempted by slavery—just one or two bondsmen could be a big help on a pioneer farm. They especially resented being denied choice in the matter by an old national fiat [the Northwest Ordinance of 1787]." A state referendum on the issue was held in 1824 and by a 6,640–4,972 margin, Illinois rejected opening the state to slavery.[225] The pro-slavery advocates of choice in Illinois did not disappear.

Douglas's Motives

Three decades later, the adroit Senator Douglas straddled the issue—declaring his indifference toward slavery while arguing that slavery was impractical in northern climates, including the Great Plains. Some contemporaries and subsequently many historians have tended to accept the Douglas hypothesis about climate and soil.[226] However, economists Robert W. Fogel and Stanley L. Engerman have shown that slavery in mid-nineteenth-century America was an economically profitable system for both agricultural and industrial pursuits: "Economies of large-scale operation, effective management, and intensive utilization of labor and capital made southern slave agriculture 35 percent more efficient than the northern system of family farming." It was not only plantations which were suited for slave labor: "Slaves employed in industry compared favorably with free workers in diligence and efficiency. Far from declining, the demand for slaves was actually increasing more rapidly in urban areas than in countryside."[227] That slavery could go wherever slaveholders were at liberty to take it grounded the case Lincoln would make at Peoria.

The power of Senator Douglas had peaked with the Compromise of 1850, even as his national platform broadened. The ensuing years frustrated his immense ambition and political talent. He had sought and lost the Democratic nomination for President in 1852—coming in third at the national convention. By early 1853, Douglas was a widower responsible for two young sons and the Mississippi plantation they had inherited from their grandfather. Physically and mentally, he was exhausted. Hoping to restore his health, Douglas took an extended trip through Europe from May until October of 1853. On his return, the senator reasserted his political influence and power—limited by the jealous princes of the U.S. Senate.[228] Having built his political platform on America's manifest destiny, western expansion, and continental integration, Douglas's ambitions now moved him to take risks that would diminish his presidential prospects. Douglas in 1854 seemed an indomitable political force, but he still had to clear formidable roadblocks to his territorial legislation. Only Congress could act to open the West promptly for economic development. The senator's national goals could be attained only by peopling the territory between Missouri and California. The vast Kansas-Nebraska territory must first be organized by federal law. Then it could be linked to both the Atlantic and Pacific coasts by a transcontinental railroad. A bill to organize the "Nebraska" territory, encompassing both Kansas and Nebraska, had failed to pass the Senate in 1853. Even though Douglas chaired the Senate Committee on Territories, he did not have unquestioned authority to lead it.[229] As Congress reconvened at the end of the year, Iowa Senator Augustus C. Dodge reintroduced the failed legislation on December 14, 1853. The Douglas committee took jurisdiction. At that moment Douglas was under intense pressure from Senate President Pro Tempore David Rice Atchison of Missouri. According to Atchison's biographer, the proslavery Missouri senator claimed "that he approached Douglas soon after the Senate had committed the Dodge bill to the Committee on Territories. He asked his Illinois colleague at that time to relinquish the chairmanship of the committee in order that he himself might be appointed to that position and bring in a Nebraska bill allowing slavery in the new territory."[230] Douglas did not yield the chairmanship, but he would eventually yield to the slave lobby.

Publicly, Douglas played down his presidential ambitions. Arthur Charles Cole emphasized that in the senator's "letter of November 11 [1853] to the editors of the Illinois *State Register* . . . he first disposed of rumors concerning his presidential candidacy. Stressing the obligations that were due to the party in its 'distracted condition,' in order to secure the consolidation of its strength and the perpetuity of its principles he waived aside all talk of the coming contest and declared his intention of remaining entirely noncommittal."[231] But the evidence suggests his letter was a charade. Gustave Koerner, a close political colleague, remembered: "Douglas had his eye fixed on the Presidency. This idea had taken such a hold of him as to obscure his mind, otherwise so clear. He had received at the last national convention in 1852 a very flattering vote for President. He expected to get the nomination in 1856, but of course he must get the South, and they gave him to understand that if, in organizing the Territories, he should exclude slavery under the Missouri Compromise, he would not get any Southern support."[232] Douglas did understand he was playing a game of presidential poker, one which would determine not only his prospects for 1856, but also the economic opportunities for Illinois. "The role that he played in shaping the Kansas-Nebraska Act," observed Don E. Fehrenbacher, "clearly enhanced his reputation in the South, where restriction of slavery north of the line of 36° 30' rankled as a continued symbol of congressional interference with that section's most significant domestic institution. But Douglas's southward-looking political motivations did not primarily determine his course. More important was his desire to develop economic opportunities for his Illinois constituents."[233]

Douglas did aim to develop the potential of the Kansas-Nebraska territory. The economic integration of the nation could then be completed by a transcontinental railroad on a northern route that would favor rapidly expanding Illinois. Settlement of this territory was important to many national constituencies but crucial to Douglas in his home base. To populate and possess land in the new territories appealed to westward-looking Illinois workers, farmers, and businessmen. The first step was to settle the area west of Iowa and Missouri.[234] Douglas "had worked for the organization of Nebraska ever since coming to Congress in 1843," wrote historian Ludwell H. Johnson. "It was a matter affecting his own political career and the future of the Democracy in his section. It was the essential prelude to the coming of age of the great American heartland, which was fated, said Douglas, to rule the national destiny."[235] As to the governance of the new territories, Douglas came to believe his principle of popular sovereignty should prevail, even in territory where slavery had been prohibited by the legislation of 1820. To let the first settlers of the Kansas-Nebraska territory decide for or against slavery meant destruction of the Missouri Compromise line (36° 30'). Douglas embraced popular sovereignty as a political doctrine, not least because it was one by which to advance the new territorial legislation he wanted. Enshrining popular sovereignty in federal legislation, he argued, would take the issue out of Washington politics and shift it to the residents of the newly organized territories.[236] However, under Article IV, Section III of the Constitution, Congress had the authority to make all necessary rules for the territories. Thus Douglas aimed to substitute popular sovereignty in place of congressional authority over slavery in the territories.

The Illinois senator was also determined to forestall a southern plan for a transcontinental railway through Texas to southern California. Secretary of War Jefferson Davis of Mississippi and many fellow southerners favored this route, which possessed a compelling advantage over a rail line through the Kansas or Nebraska plains. Louisiana, Texas, and New Mexico had already been organized politically. Douglas had supported a transcontinental railroad for a decade, but the northern route he backed must traverse territories yet unorganized by Congress. And so, until the Kansas-Nebraska territory could be organized under federal legislation, the transcontinental designs of Douglas would be stymied. According to biographer Robert W. Johannsen, Douglas's plan had three major pieces: "The first of these was the extension of territorial government to the growing settlements on the Pacific and to the vast intervening country between Missouri and the Rockies. Second, a railroad route from Illinois to the Pacific should be selected and surveyed. Finally, in order to encourage the settlement of the country through which the railroad would run, Douglas asked that western lands be donated in 160-acre tracts 'to the actual settler.'"[237] Settlers needed homesteads and Douglas needed settlers in Kansas-Nebraska to occupy the land. The strategy designed by the chairman of the Senate Committee on Territories could assure a transcontinental line from Chicago to San Francisco.

Populating the territories and connecting the country by a transcontinental railroad were thus indissolubly linked for Douglas. But the precise site of the railroad would be determined by where people were settling. As a Chicago resident and an investor, Douglas had a clear interest in the location of the railroad. The economic interests of the nation, the state, and the senator were intertwined. "While he was negotiating the details of the Compromise of 1850, Douglas managed to push through Congress a bill that granted the Illinois Central Railroad 2,595,000 acres of land along its surveyed route south," wrote historian John Niven. "Railroad land grants, which took their form from the Northwest Ordinance, allocated alternate sections of land to railroads with the assumption that these sections would help finance construction and at the same time stimulate settlement along the route. The Illinois Central precedent inaugurated a frenzy of special interest groups that besieged the Congress and made Douglas's Senate Committee on Territories one of the most important instruments of government."[238] The Illinois legislature had chartered the Illinois Central in 1851, commencing five years of intense construction. Lincoln would become one of the railroad's attorneys.

Douglas was a nationalist and an expansionist by political conviction. He aimed to fulfill not only America's "manifest destiny" but also to profit by that fulfillment. Because he had substantial real estate interests in northern Illinois and northern Wisconsin, the northern route could enhance his investments. Historian Louis Filler wrote that Senator Douglas possessed "a national perspective. He could even be seen as a western leader who was 'progressive' in wishing to augment his section's economic status and build its industrial potential. His Democracy was typical of his section, as was his indifference to Negroes."[239] The Kansas-Nebraska legislation provided Douglas with an opportunity to broaden the appeal of his presidential candidacy in the South while strengthening the potential for a northern railroad route to the Pacific. Moreover, he held the view that the Kansas-Nebraska Act, if approved by both North and South, would mitigate sectional and Democratic Party division. Such statesmanship might pave the way to a Douglas presidency.

Douglas erred, however, in his judgment that the Kansas-Nebraska Act would relieve sectional strife and reinvigorate the Democratic Party. Many leaders foresaw more sectional conflict. Historian Henry H. Simms noted that "there were some factors which still kept sectional feeling alive. *Uncle Tom's Cabin*, resistance in parts of the North to the Fugitive Slave Law of 1850, proposals for the annexation of Cuba and for the granting of free homesteads in the public land domains, all provoked controversy. But the most controversial of all sectional issues, that of the status of slavery in the territories, seemed to have been settled, until it was revived by the introduction of the Kansas-Nebraska Act of 1854."[240] When Senator Douglas introduced his territorial legislation in early January 1854, he ignited sectional strife anew. Lincoln's favorite Springfield newspaper recognized the threat of discord. "We had hoped to gain a short respite from that old din of 'Slavery Agitation,' and 'Slavery Extension' that has been warring in our country so often for the last twenty years, but it seems that it is about to be let in upon us again, more repulsive and disgusting than ever from having been so many times kicked out of doors," editorialized the *Illinois State Journal*. "We can't conceive of a greater piece of mischief than is here set on foot by our Senator."[241]

"The Southern Senators did not show any haste to follow Douglas at first," recalled Horace White. "They generally spoke of the measure as a free-will offering of the North, both Douglas and Pierce being Northern men, and both being indispensable to secure its passage. Francis P. Blair, Jr., of Missouri, a competent witness, expressed the opinion that a majority of the Southern senators were opposed to the measure at first and were coerced into backing it by the fear that they would not be sustained at home if they refused an advantage offered to them by the North."[242] White put the blame on Douglas for repealing the Missouri Compromise of 1820, but historians have disputed this analysis.[243]

It can be argued that Douglas was simply fulfilling his congressional obligations as a committee chairman charged with territorial oversight. Douglas was "chairman of the Committee on Territories," noted historian Elbert B. Smith. "It was his duty to get territories organized, and lying in the path of his proposed railroad route to California was the vast area to become Kansas and Nebraska. A railroad through these virgin regions would require liquidation of Indian titles, new territorial governments and occupation by the usual horde of frontiersmen waiting for new lands."[244] To attain these goals, Douglas gave up legislative ground to his proslavery colleagues during January 1854.[245] His primary goal was to organize the huge Kansas-Nebraska territory. In the 1850 debate in Congress, Douglas had declared: "We have a vast territory, stretching from the Mississippi to the Pacific, which is rapidly filling up with a hardy, enterprising, and industrious population, large enough to form at least seventeen new free states, one-half of which we may expect to be represented in this body during our day. . . . I think I am safe in assuming that each of these will be free territories and free states, whether Congress shall prohibit slavery or not."[246] Climate and soil, Douglas argued, would make these territories inhospitable to slavery.

The Kansas-Nebraska Act encompassed a number of objectives—some of them partisan, some of them economic, some of them personal, some of them national. Douglas knew that southern Democrats had an effective veto over both the territorial legislation and the presidency he coveted. The implied price to neutralize the veto was high: repeal the Missouri Compromise and open up the Kansas-Nebraska to slavery. It was a price Douglas proved willing to pay. However, the political opportunity seized by Douglas and southern slaveholders turned out to be a decisive opening for Lincoln. Douglas had declared himself indifferent to slavery and its consequences. With popular sovereignty, Douglas may have thought he was satisfying the slave states with a meaningless gesture because he believed the Kansas-Nebraska territory did not have the climate for slavery. But Douglas certainly underestimated the consequences of his decision. "Stephen A. Douglas was not a systematic thinker in an abstract sense," observed biographer Robert W. Johannsen. "He was a pragmatic, professional politician, frequently bumptious and full of bluster, subject to outbursts of oratory that were not always designed to clarify the issues under discussion."[247]

Insertion of "Inoperative and Void"

Douglas first tried to finesse the Missouri Compromise line by ignoring it in the territorial bill he revised and introduced on January 4, 1854. This draft split the Kansas-Nebraska territory in two—a relatively small Kansas and a larger Nebraska, inclusive of current South and North Dakota. Douglas's report, which accompanied the bill, rationalized the potential controversy: "The principal amendments which your committee deem it their duty to commend to the favorable action of the Senate, in a special report, are those in which the principles established by the compromise measures of 1850, so far as they are applicable to territorial organizations, are proposed to be affirmed and carried into practical operation within the limits of the new Territory."[248] In this draft Douglas hid the repeal of the Missouri Compromise by artfully using the language of the

Compromise of 1850, drafted for the territories of New Mexico and Utah, which stated "when admitted as a State or States, the said territory, or any portion of the same, shall be received into the Union, with or without slavery, as their constitution may prescribe at the time of their admission."[249]

Douglas contended: "A proper sense of patriotic duty . . . enjoins the propriety and necessity of a strict adherence to the principles, and even a literal adoption of the enactments, of the adjustment of 1850."[250] Thus did Douglas argue that the "adjustment of 1850" implied the repeal of the 36° 30' slavery restriction of 1820. But he misjudged the irreconcilable mood of some southern members of Congress. His initial language was not sufficiently radical for southerners such as Georgia Senator Robert Toombs, who insisted the Missouri Compromise of 1820 had already been supplanted by the Compromise of 1850. Senator Douglas then put in a new section which ruled that the status of slavery in the Kansas-Nebraska territory would be determined by popular sovereignty. But this change still did not satisfy the slavery expansion goals of some southern Democrats.[251]

On January 16, 1854, Kentucky Senator Archibald Dixon introduced an amendment to repeal explicitly the Missouri Compromise. Douglas had been boxed in. Since he did not want a fight on Dixon's amendment, Douglas acquiesced, telling a fellow senator that "I will incorporate it in my bill, though I know it will raise a hell of a storm."[252] Rather than explicitly state that the 1820 legislation was repealed, Douglas drafted language that the Missouri Compromise was "inconsistent with the principles of the legislation of 1850, commonly called the compromise measures, and is hereby declared inoperative."[253] Later, to satisfy slaveowners, the legislation was revised to read "inoperative and void." The words meant "repealed." Douglas steered into the storm.

Senator Douglas now needed political cover for this change—which he sought on Sunday, January 22, through the intervention of Secretary of War Jefferson Davis. Douglas went to Davis's home, accompanied by the "F Street Mess," a group of powerful southern senators who boarded together. They included Senate Finance Chairman Robert M. T. Hunter of Virginia, Foreign Relations Chairman James M. Mason of Virginia, Judiciary Chairman Andrew P. Butler of South Carolina, and Senate Presi-

Pro-Nebraska National Leaders

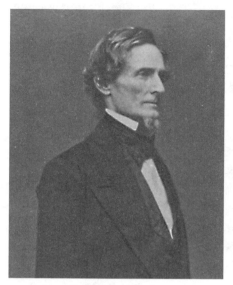

Jefferson Davis

*The Gilder Lehrman Collection, courtesy of the
Gilder Lehrman Institute of American History, on
deposit at the New-York Historical Society, New
York, reference number GLC 8485*

Alexander H. Stephens

*Courtesy of the Kentucky Historical Society,
reference number 1987PH29.alb1.p37n109*

David Rice Atchison

Courtesy of the U.S. Senate Historical Office

Franklin Pierce

*The Gilder Lehrman Collection, courtesy of the
Gilder Lehrman Institute of American History, on
deposit at the New-York Historical Society, New
York, reference number GLC 5247*

dent Pro Tempore David Rice Atchison. Their failure to support Kansas-Nebraska had doomed the legislation in 1853. Douglas believed their backing was indispensable. Even while aspiring to control the national Democratic Party, the senators had the seniority and power to promote their regional interests. With Douglas, they now sought to enlist Secretary Davis and President Pierce.[254]

Southern senators had a receptive but passive audience in the Pierce Administration. John Niven wrote that the members of the Pierce cabinet all thought the Missouri Compromise to be unconstitutional. Still, "they differed on the means for removing it from the statute books," noted Niven. "Their differences reflected sectional sympathies. The president and the northern members of his cabinet favored Douglas's original bill that ignored the Compromise. They were certain if the matter were left to the Supreme Court, the Missouri Act would be declared unconstitutional."[255] Indeed, the day before he met with the F Street Mess, President Pierce had indicated his desire not to resolve the issue explicitly, but rather to avoid it by simply reaffirming the Compromise of 1850, and by implication its use of popular sovereignty. Secretary of War Davis, a Mississippi slaveholder, later recalled that Douglas

> . . . fully explained the proposed bill, and stated their purpose to be, through my aid, to obtain an interview on that day with the President, to ascertain whether the bill would meet his approbation. The President was known to be rigidly opposed to the reception of visits on Sunday for the discussion of any political subject; but in this case it was urged as necessary, in order to enable the Committee to make their report the next day. I went with them to the Executive mansion, and, leaving them in the reception-room, sought the President in his private apartments, and explained to him the occasion of the visit. He thereupon met the gentlemen, patiently listened to the reading of the bill and their explanations of it, decided that it rested upon sound constitutional principles, and recognized in it only a return to that rule which had been infringed by the compromise of 1820, and the restoration of which had been foreshadowed by the legislation of 1850.[256]

Secretary Davis favored repeal, but he had taken no active role on Kansas-Nebraska until that morning at the White House. Nevertheless, his participation was crucial. According to biographer William C. Davis, "if he had not backed the plan, if he had not enjoyed a relationship with Pierce that allowed him to call on him that day, and if he had not argued the repealers' case with Pierce in their behalf, the Kansas-Nebraska bill might never have become an administration measure, with what consequences no one can know."[257] And so, the Douglas bill became the president's bill, too. Reluctantly, Pierce agreed to sign a repeal of the Missouri Compromise restriction on slavery. President Pierce claimed he sought national peace even as the Kansas-Nebraska Act brought increased conflict. Fierce political combat broke out in the Senate—seven years before the bombardment of Fort Sumter. Douglas and the F Street Mess had set loose the demon of American politics—sectional battle over slavery. A new Kansas-Nebraska bill was introduced by Douglas on Monday, January 23. Kentucky Senator Dixon declared triumphantly: "Upon the question of slavery I know no Whiggery and I know no Democracy. I am a proslavery man."[258]

The Chase Appeal

Ohio Senator Salmon P. Chase had shrewdly secured an agreement with Douglas to delay debate on the Kansas-Nebraska bill so he could review the legislation. Chase himself was a lame duck, having been elected in 1849 by a one-vote majority of free-soil Democrats and their antislavery allies in the Ohio Legislature. He had failed to make a major mark as an effective, antislavery advocate of "Free Democracy," and his Democratic successor had already been chosen. The Douglas bill presented an opportunity for the ambitious Ohioan. Earlier in January, Chase and his free-soil Democratic allies had begun work on a plan to defeat or delay the Douglas bill in the Senate. They intended to make their case at both the state and national levels. Chase biographer John Niven wrote that Chase was chosen to lead the assault on Kansas-Nebraska because of his "composure under strain, his powers of logical analysis, and his reputation."[259] The Douglas revisions to the Kansas-Nebraska bill had allowed time for Chase to organize his arguments. Key allies were Massachusetts Senator Charles Sumner and abolitionist Congressman Gerrit Smith of New York.

They carefully prepared their counterattack while Douglas was revising the bill to include the Missouri repeal.

By January 19 Senator Chase and Ohio Congressman Joshua R. Giddings had written the "Appeal of the Independent Democrats in Congress to the people of the United States." The Appeal was published in the Washington-based *National Era* and the *New York Times* on January 24, just one day after the filing of Douglas's repeal legislation. One Chase biographer called the Appeal "one of the most effective pieces of political propaganda ever produced."[260] Historian Richard H. Sewell wrote that "Chase and his fellow signators developed a case against the Kansas-Nebraska 'crime' calculated to attract the cooperation of groups hitherto outside the free-soil movement. Former Whigs, for instance, were assured that Henry Clay would have been the first to denounce Douglas's pretense that the Compromise of 1850 had implicitly nullified the prohibition of 1820."[261] The Chase-Giddings strategy aimed to galvanize an antislavery coalition from disparate factions in the North. Lincoln in Illinois would adopt a similar strategy. The Chase Appeal directly attacked the fundamental Douglas arguments:

> The pretenses . . . that the territory covered by the positive prohibition of slavery in 1820 sustains a similar relation to slavery with that acquired from Mexico, covered by no prohibition except that of disputed constitutional or Mexican law, and that the Compromises of 1850 require the incorporation of the pro-slavery clauses of the Utah and New Mexico Bill in Nebraska act, are mere inventions, designed to cover up from public reprehension meditated bad faith. Were he living now, no one would be more forward, more eloquent, or more indignant in his denunciation of that bad faith than Henry Clay, the foremost champion of both compromises. . . . The interests of freedom and the Union are in imminent peril. Demagogues may tell you that the Union can be maintained only by submitting to the demands of slavery. We tell you that the Union can only be maintained by the full recognition of the just claims of freedom and man.[262]

If Douglas had thought the Kansas-Nebraska Act a railroad bill or a territorial compromise, he could do so no longer. The Chase Appeal repositioned it as proslavery legislation. As Chase predicted on the Senate floor, "This discussion will hasten the inevitable reorganization of parties upon the new issues. . . . It will light up a fire in the country which may, perhaps, consume those who kindle it."[263]

The delay of debate enabled Douglas to prepare a reply. On January 30, he delivered a withering attack on Chase and Sumner, whom he called the abolition confederates. Their Appeal was "an abolition manifesto." Douglas was indignant: "Our motives are arraigned and our characters calumniated—coarse epithets are applied to me by name." He charged: "This was done on the Sabbath day and by a set of politicians, to advance their own political purposes, in the name of our holy religion."[264] On the Senate floor, Chase remained cool and dignified, briefly buttressed by a speech from Senator Charles Sumner.[265] The Massachusetts senator indicted the Kansas-Nebraska bill as "a soulless, eyeless monster—horrid, unshapely, and vast."[266]

Rigorous consistency of argument characterized neither the proponents nor the opponents of this provocative legislation. "The debates on the Kansas-Nebraska bill ranged over the whole of the slavery controversy— its history, moral conflict, and constitutional theory. Southerners frequently justified their support of the measure by arguing that the Missouri Compromise restriction was unconstitutional," wrote Don E. Fehrenbacher. "These were in many cases the same men who, as recently as 1850, had urged extension of the 36° 30' line as the best means of resolving the sectional conflict. Yet perhaps even more anomalous was the spectacle of radical antislavery men appealing to the sanctity of the venerable Missouri Compromise, which they had consistently rejected as a basis for further conciliation."[267] Chase challenged Douglas and his allies to repeal the Missouri Compromise line "openly" and "boldly" rather than simply declaring it "inoperative." Chase now played to the gallery of public opinion, reversing his own earlier position on the Missouri Compromise, which he had thought too accommodating to slavery.[268] Douglas had also changed his policy of 1849, having said then in a speech at Springfield: "All the evidences of public opinion at that day seemed to indicate that this [Missouri] Compromise had become canonized in the hearts of the American people as a sacred thing, which no ruthless hand should attempt to disturb."[269]

On February 3, 1854, Chase took the Senate floor to offer an extended defense of the Appeal. Obliquely, he referred to President Pierce's 1853 inaugural statement by observing that "the country was at peace" before the Kansas-Nebraska bill was introduced. "And now we find ourself in the midst of an agitation, the end and issue of which no man can foresee." Chase blamed the turmoil on the South: "It is Slavery that renews the strife. It is Slavery that again wants room. It is Slavery with its insatiate demands for more slave territory and more slave states." Chase said the Kansas-Nebraska bill inaugurated a new era: "That will be the Era of Reaction. The introduction of this question here, and its discussion, will greatly hasten its advent. We, who insist upon the denationalization of slavery, and upon the absolute divorce of the General Government from all connection with it, will stand with the men who favored the compromise acts, and who yet wish to adhere to them, in their letter and in their spirit, against the repeal of the Missouri prohibition." Chase then prophesied that "you may pass [Kansas-Nebraska legislation] here. You may send it to the other House. It may become law. But its effect will be to satisfy all thinking men that no compromises with slavery will endure, except so long as they serve the interests of slavery and that there is no safe and honorable ground for non-slaveholders to stand upon, except that of restricting slavery within State limits, and excluding it absolutely from the whole sphere of Federal jurisdiction. The old questions between political parties are at rest. No great question so thoroughly possesses the public mind as this of slavery. This discussion will hasten the inevitable reorganization of parties upon the new issues which our circumstances suggest." He concluded: "We will assert the ancient doctrine, that no person shall be deprived of life, liberty, or property, by the legislation of Congress, without due process of law. Carrying out that principle into its practical applications, we will not cease our efforts until slavery shall cease to exist wherever it can be reached by the constitutional action of the Government."[270]

Ohio's other senator was a bold, irreverent, cantankerous, antislavery man. A pro-immigrant businessman, Benjamin F. Wade was less politic than his patrician colleague. "You may call me an Abolitionist, if you will," said Wade in his speech on February 6. "I care little for that; for, if an undying hatred to slavery constitutes an Abolitionist, I am that Abolitionist. If man's determination, at all times and at all hazards, to the last extremity, to resist the extension of slavery, or any other tyranny, constitutes an Abolitionist, I before God, believe myself to be that Abolitionist."[271] Wade in debate spoke of the Declaration of Independence: "I had supposed that the great principles touching upon the rights of human nature set forth in that immortal instrument, were universally acknowledged in this country. Judge my surprise when I heard them assailed, denounced, and repudiated, in the Senate of the United States as self-evident falsehoods."[272]

Senator Sumner had readied himself to attack. He took longer than Chase to prepare and practice his speeches. Vain and intellectual like Chase, Sumner was tall, dignified, didactic. Like Chase, Sumner had been elected by a fragile coalition of Democrats, free-soilers and rogue Whigs who had provided him with a single-vote victory in the Massachusetts Legislature three years earlier. The Harvard-educated lawyer's prickly, even pompous, demeanor attracted as many critics as supporters. His Massachusetts allies had been antislavery Conscience Whigs appalled by the pro-South sympathies of the commercially-focused Cotton Whigs. In his February 21 speech on the Senate floor Sumner proclaimed that the American Founding rested on an antislavery basis. Contemptuously, he referred to Senator Douglas as a doughface—"that human anomaly—a Northern man with Southern principles."[273] Sumner biographer Frederick J. Blue wrote:

> Using an Old Testament text, "Cursed be he that removeth his neighbor's landmark," [Deuteronomy 27:17] his major thrust was to prove that the Missouri Compromise ban against slavery north of 36° 30' was a sacred trust that Southerners had willingly supported at the time of its enactment in 1820. The Douglas bill was "an infraction of solemn obligations, assumed beyond recall by the South on the admission of Missouri into the Union as a Slave state." Listing prominent southern slaveholding legislators and cabinet members who, thirty-four years earlier had backed it, including William Crawford and John C. Calhoun, and concluding with President James Monroe, who had signed the measure, Sumner reminded the Senate that the Missouri Compromise "takes its life from the South." Now, the next generation of Southerners refused to accept the obligations of their fathers: "The Prohibition of slavery in the Territory of Kansas and Nebraska stands

on foundations of living rock, upheld by the early policy of the Fathers by constant precedent and time-honored compact."[274]

Sumner's "Landmark of Freedom" speech was reprinted by many newspapers nationwide. The aggressive debates in the Senate displayed a combative and heroic side to Sumner that rallied his constituents. Sumner's stock rose with Massachusetts Whigs, disappointed as they had become by the temporizing of their party's senator, Edward Everett—the man who in 1863 would give from memory the two-hour speech preceding President Lincoln's two-minute Gettysburg Address.

Senators Chase and Sumner set the antislavery tone for the national debate, but Douglas maintained his iron grip on Senate action. Legislators rejected all Chase amendments designed to limit the impact of the Nebraska bill. Douglas pressed his advantage, branding Chase a liar who had gratuitously slandered him. The Douglas assault made Chase seem moderate by contrast, especially when the Ohio senator rose on March 2–3 to criticize the bill in more temperate language. Both sides had raised the temperature of the debate, but Douglas had set the stage for the scorching attacks he would suffer later in the year.[275]

The Opposition

Within his own Democratic Party, attacks on Douglas mounted. The onslaught surprised the Illinois senator. Chase and his cohorts had done their work well. Through the distribution of their Appeal, northern newspaper editors had been aroused. So too were indignant northern clergymen, who compiled an enormous petition against the bill, signed by more than 3,000 northern ministers. They sent it to the Senate by way of Massachusetts Senator Everett. Everett's successor in the Senate, Henry Wilson, would write: "Perhaps no measure before Congress ever excited more thoroughly the moral and religious sentiments of the nation. The clergy took an unusual interest. Memorials and protests, numerously signed, were sent to Congress."[276] Douglas rose to the challenge of the bill's critics in the North. In February, he answered the editor of a New Hampshire newspaper: "The bill provides in words as specific and unequivocal as our language affords, that the *true intent and meaning* of the act is NOT to legislate slavery into any Territory or State. The bill, therefore, does not introduce slavery; does not revive it; does not establish it; does not contain any clause designed to produce that result or which by any possible construction can have that legal effect."[277] Indeed, wrote Douglas, "the true intent and meaning of this act [was] not to legislate slavery into any Territory or State, nor to exclude it therefrom, but to leave the inhabitants thereof perfectly free to form and regulate their domestic institution in their own way, subject only to the Constitution of the United States." Missouri Congressman Thomas Hart Benton called the printed letter a little "stump speech" and a Douglas biographer said it "proved a very effective stump speech indeed."[278] Still, no one could deny that the Kansas-Nebraska Act opened the unorganized Louisiana Territory north of 36° 30' to slavery.

The repeal of the Missouri Compromise line of 1820 signaled, in Lincoln's adroit analogy, that the Missouri fence had been dismantled by slave owners looking for more slave pasture. Legislatures in ten northern states condemned the Kansas-Nebraska legislation. Only the Illinois Legislature—with a majority loyal to Douglas—passed a resolution of support. To his intimate friend in Kentucky, Joshua F. Speed, Lincoln confided in 1855: "Douglas introduced the Nebraska bill in January. In February afterwards, there was a call session of the Illinois Legislature. Of the one hundred members composing the two branches of that body, about seventy were democrats. These latter held a caucus, in which the Nebraska bill was talked of, if not formally discussed. It was thereby discovered that just three, and no more, were in favor of the measure. In a day or two Douglas' orders came on to have resolutions passed approving the bill; and they were passed by large majorities!!! The truth of this is vouched for by a bolting democratic member. The masses too, democratic as well as whig, were even, nearer unanamous [sic] against it, but as soon as the party necessity of supporting it, became apparent, the way the democracy began to see the *wisdom* and *justice* of it, was perfectly astonishing."[279]

The Whigs

At stake was the future of the Whig Party. "To many Northern Whigs the popular outcry against repeal of the Missouri restriction came as a godsend, bringing hopes of resurrection to a party all but dead," wrote historian Richard H. Sewell. But old Whig loyalties had become fragile—even in the North. Sewell contended that "freesoil Whigs, their state organizations already in shambles, early showed a willingness—even eagerness—to fuse with anti-Nebraska elements in other parties. In part, this readiness to set aside old loyalties and join in the creation of a completely new political party stemmed from an awareness that free-soilers, antislavery Democrats, and even some radical Whigs would have nothing to do with the Whig organization on any terms."[280]

The New York *Tribune*, edited by the mercurial Horace Greeley, had a very wide impact through its weekly national edition. The *Tribune* launched a national campaign against the Kansas-Nebraska Act because "it proposes to disturb the Missouri Compromise, involves great perfidy, and is bolstered up by the most audacious false pretenses and frauds." Greeley insisted: "We regard this Nebraska movement of Douglas and his backers as one of measureless treachery and infamy. Founded on a gigantic and impudent falsehood—the assumption that the Adjustment of 1850 in spirit if not in letter repealed so much of the Compromise of 1820 as was favorable to freedom—it seeks to discomfit and humiliate the North by a surprise—a snap judgment—an ambuscade by a flag of truce."[281]

Douglas drove a stake into the heart of the Missouri Compromise. It penetrated to the heart of the Whig Party as well. Most southern Whigs rallied with southern Democrats rather than their northern counterparts. On February 15, the southern Whigs caucused in the House and Senate. They agreed to back the repeal of the Missouri Compromise slavery restriction. Meanwhile most northern Whigs united against the legislation. Rather than sharply defining the split between Whigs and Democrats, the Kansas-Nebraska legislation instead widened the division between North and South. But the dissolution of the Whig Party was delayed, according to Michael F. Holt, because the Kansas-Nebraska bill "forced together and kept intact the entire northern wing of the Whig party by stopping conservatives aligned with [former President Millard] Fillmore from bolting to a new Union party."[282]

Still, the minority Northern Whigs were a sideshow in Congress. In the Senate, Douglas fought renegade members of his own party. In the final debate on Kansas-Nebraska, Senator Douglas again denounced Chase and Sumner, saying, "You degrade your own States. . . . You have stimulated

Anti-Nebraska National Leaders

Salmon P. Chase

The Gilder Lehrman Collection, courtesy of the Gilder Lehrman Institute of American History, on deposit at the New-York Historical Society, New York, reference number GLC 5111.02.0077

William H. Seward

The Gilder Lehrman Collection, courtesy of the Gilder Lehrman Institute of American History, on deposit at the New-York Historical Society, New York, reference number GLC 5111.02.0094

Charles Sumner

The Gilder Lehrman Collection, courtesy of the Gilder Lehrman Institute of American History, on deposit at the New-York Historical Society, New York, reference number GLC 5597.23

Sam Houston

The Gilder Lehrman Collection, courtesy of the Gilder Lehrman Institute of American History, on deposit at the New-York Historical Society, New York, reference number GLC 4124

[the people] to these acts [of opposition to the Nebraska bill], which are disgraceful to your State, disgraceful to your party, and disgraceful to your cause."[283] Earlier, on February 17, in a speech of nearly three hours to packed galleries, New York's Seward defined the issue as one of fundamental moral principle: "A life of approval of compromises and of devotion to them only enhances the obligations to fulfill them; a life of disapprobation of the policy of compromises only renders one more earnest in exacting the fulfilment of them when good and cherished interests are secured by them." Seward then stipulated the moral issue: "Say what you will, do what you will here, the interests of the non-slaveholding and of the slaveholding States remain just the same; and they will remain just the same until you shall cease to defend and cherish slavery, or we shall cease to honor and defend freedom. The slavery agitation is an eternal struggle between conservatism and progress, between truth and error, between right and wrong."[284] Seward was pleased with his remarks. So too were others far away. "Mr Lincoln my partner and your friend," William Herndon wrote to Seward from Springfield, "thinks your speech most excellent."[285] In Seward's remarks are intimations of Lincoln's speeches at Peoria in 1854 and at Cooper Union in 1860.

Pushing Passage

Douglas rarely shied from a fight. Nor did he waver in his belief that in principle he was right and his opponents wrong. "I know the Bill is right & have full faith it will become a law this Session," he wrote to Lincoln's brother-in-law in Springfield.[286] Douglas was correct that it would become law, but wrong in his assessment of its political implications for Illinois. Among German-Americans in Douglas's home town of Chicago, the impact was profound. They protested against the Kansas-Nebraska legislation—through petitions presented to fellow German-American Gustave Koerner, the state's Democratic lieutenant governor, and State Senator Norman B. Judd, a prominent Democratic lawyer. At a rally in Chicago on March 16, Douglas was denounced as "an ambitious and dangerous demagogue."[287] The German-American community was especially affronted by a proposal to strip new immigrants of the right to vote and hold office in the Kansas-Nebraska territory. This amendment, authored by Delaware

Senator John M. Clayton, narrowly passed the Senate with southern support. It was stripped from the bill in the House in order to insure passage.[288] Southerners in the Senate contemplated making other changes in the bill, noted historian Robert R. Russell, but there was an "understanding that to do so would result in the defeat of the bill in the House, if not also in the Senate, and the disruption of the Democratic party."[289]

In his correspondence, as well as on the floor of Congress, Douglas aimed to unite his party and trample the opposition. To a Georgia politician, he wrote: "I am not detered or affected by the violence & insults of the Northern Whigs & abolitionists. The storm will soon spend its fury, and the people of the north will sustain the measure when they come to understand it. In the meantime our Southern friends have only to stand firm & leave us of the North to fight the great Battle."[290] In Congress nearly all southerners supported the bill. But in future political contests, Douglas would not receive the southern support he sought for his presidential ambitions. One distinguished southern dissenter clearly saw political danger in the repeal of the Missouri Compromise. "If this repeal takes place," Texas Senator Sam Houston prophesied, "I will have seen the commencement of the agitation, but the youngest child now born, will not live to witness its termination."[291] In his final speech against the legislation, Houston said: "The proud symbol (pointing to the eagle) above your head, remains enshrouded in black as if deploring the misfortune that has fallen upon us, or as a fearful omen of future calamities, which await our Nation in the event this bill should become a law. Above it, I behold the majestic figure of Washington, whose presence must forever inspire patriotic emotions, and command the admiration and love of every American heart. By these associations, I adjure you to regard the contract once made to harmonize and preserve this Union. Maintain the Missouri Compromise! Stir not up agitation! Give us peace!"[292]

During the late winter and early spring of 1854, Douglas worked tirelessly on and off the Senate floor as the legislative shepherd of his bill. "Douglas took little part in the actual debate, delivering only the opening speech and the final summation," wrote Robert W. Johannsen. "He played the role of floor manager for the bill, opposing distracting issues, objecting to delay, and moving postponement when it seemed in the best interest of the legislation."[293] Douglas pushed and pulled most northern Democratic senators into line.[294] He was an accomplished parliamentary tactician whom others underestimated at their peril. "For two days, March 2 and 3, there was a running fight, in which Douglas showed his immense powers, silencing his opponents right and left, and returning with the most furious language to his attack on Chase, unblushingly twisting his own record, and insisting over and over again that the Compromise of 1850, though in its terms applying to New Mexico and Utah, was intended to repeal the Missouri Compromise, which applied to the Louisiana purchase," wrote Chase biographer Albert Bushnell Hart. "Chase was no match in debate for this extraordinary man." [295] Douglas not only stonewalled his opponents, but also used racist vocabulary. In this he was rebuked by Senator Seward: "Douglas, no one who spells Negro with two gs will ever be elected President of the United States."[296]

At the close of debate on the bill, Douglas offered to yield his senatorial prerogative to give the final statement. But he acquiesced to pressure from his colleagues to close the debate. Casting himself as the besieged victim, Douglas appeared in full battle mode, giving his adversaries no quarter. Biographer Allen Johnson described the "characteristic performance. It abounded in repetitions, and it can hardly be said to have contributed much to the understanding of the issues. Yet it was a memorable effort, because it exhibited the magnificent fighting qualities of the man. . . . Knowing himself to be addressing a wider audience than the Senate chamber and its crowded galleries, he appealed with intuitive keenness to certain fundamental traits in his constituents. Americans admire self-reliance even in an opponent, and the spectacle of a man fighting against personal injustice is often likely to make them forget the principle for which he stands."[297] Senator Douglas regarded the attacks by Chase and Sumner as "personal injustice."

Douglas again defended popular sovereignty, arguing: "This was the principle upon which the colonies separated from the crown of Great Britain; the principle upon which the battles of the Revolution were fought, and the principle upon which our republican system was founded."[298] His performance was interrupted by Seward, who said: "'I hope the Senator will yield for a moment, because I have never had so much respect for him as I have tonight." Douglas was not so accommodating when Salmon P. Chase protested that he had never intended

Douglas any personal "injustice." Douglas retorted: "Sir, did he not say in the same document to which I have already alluded, that I was engaged, with others, 'in a criminal betrayal of precious rights,' 'in an atrocious plot'? . . . Did he not say everything calculated to produce and bring upon my head all the insults to which I have been subjected publicly and privately—not even excepting the insulting letters which I have received from his constituents, rejoicing at my domestic bereavements, and praying that other and similar calamities may befall me?" [299]

The marathon final session lasted seventeen hours. On March 4, the Kansas-Nebraska Act passed the Senate by a 37–14 vote. Democratic defections in the North were replaced by nine Whig votes from the South. The only southerner voting with the minority was Sam Houston of Texas. When it was all over, Chase said to Sumner: "They celebrate present victory but the echoes they awaken will never rest till slavery itself shall die."[300]

The bill's future was much more in doubt in the House of Representatives, where there were more northerners, more opposition, and more opportunity for legislative delay. Supporters of the bill suffered an early setback when opponents circumvented the Committee on Territories chaired by Douglas's Illinois ally, Congressman William A. Richardson. Instead, jurisdiction for the bill was given to the Committee of the Whole, where opponents could delay Kansas-Nebraska through the lengthy list of bills ahead of it and by intricate parliamentary rules that dictated how legislation should come to the House floor.[301] Lincoln ally Isaac N. Arnold later wrote that the Nebraska opponents "began what is called in Congressional phrase, 'fillibustering' by all the dilatory motions known to parliamentary law: motions to adjourn, to adjourn over, to lay on the table, to reconsider, to excuse members from voting, for a call of the House, and other motions; upon all of which, piled up, one after another, the ayes and noes were ordered, preventing any action upon the question. A call of the House is ordered, the doors of the House are closed, and no member can get in or out without the leave of the House."[302]

Richardson's chief lieutenant in managing the bill was an old congressional friend of Abraham Lincoln, Alexander H. Stephens of Georgia. He helped to corral southern Whig votes and determine legislative tactics. Stephens had "sprung from the depths of poverty, and was educated by charity," wrote Isaac N. Arnold. "Of a frail and feeble constitution, his mind was always too vigorous and active for his weak body. He was never married, and lived at home a life of isolation and solitude, devoting himself to the pursuits of politics and literature. Under the ordinary height, he was of a very slender form, and considerably stoop-shouldered. His weight was less than 100 pounds. His complexion was very sallow. His arms were of a disproportionate length, and his fingers long and skinny. He had the blackest and keenest eyes; his hair was long, and black, and came down on his forehead like a schoolboy's. His voice was boyish and squeaking, but he was one of the most interesting and eloquent of speakers, and he never addressed the House without commanding universal attention."[303] A decade later, Lincoln observed Stephens, then vice president of the Confederacy, taking off his topcoat at a meeting near the end of the Civil War. Lincoln remarked wryly that the Georgian was "the biggest shuck and the smallest nubbin I ever laid eyes on."[304]

Early in the congressional session, on February 17, Stephens arose to speak on the House floor. The future vice president of the Confederacy had been sick much of the winter with flu-like symptoms. He had been confined to bed until a week before his speech. Still weak, his emaciated body looked closer to the grave than usual.[305] While Stephens spoke in the House, Seward was delivering his major Kansas-Nebraska address in the Senate. The Georgian attracted greater attention, launching an attack on the sacrosanct position the Missouri Compromise was accorded by antislavery northerners. He demeaned the importance of the 1820 compromise, saying that it was "nothing but a law, with no other sanction than any statute."[306] For Stephens the Missouri Compromise was a dead issue. "Stephens ultimately defined the highest value, and therefore what was right, as what was lawful and constitutional," wrote biographer Thomas E. Schott. "Slavery was both; so was popular sovereignty. To question either on moral grounds could only be attributed to stupidity, malevolence, or madness."[307]

For Alexander Stephens the repeal of the 1820 restriction on slavery implied much more than a law to open the Kansas-Nebraska territory for slaveholders. To expand slave territory had been slaveholder strategy for a generation. Stephens anticipated the annexation of Cuba as a slave state even though he had previously opposed it. Future President James Buchanan was one of three Pierce Administration diplomats who would meet in Belgium in October 1854. There, they issued the "Ostend Manifesto" declaring that Americans should take Cuba by force if Spain declined to sell the colony.[308] Congressman Stephens wrote on May 9: "We took up the Nebraska [bill] yesterday by twenty-one majority, and will take a final vote on it this week. I think it will pass; but the vote will be closer on the final test than it was yesterday. We are on the eve of a great issue with Cuba. . . . We must and will have it . . ."[309]

Senator Douglas did not wholly entrust the fate of his legislation in the House to his friend Richardson. Douglas himself worked the House tirelessly, spending more time there whipping Democrats into line than he had done on the Senate side. He even appeared on the House floor in defiance of its rules. Historian David M. Potter wrote: "The contest lasted for fifteen days, and tension mounted as the final vote drew nearer."[310] There was talk of violence. Among the bill's more prominent opponents was Missouri's Thomas Hart Benton.[311] On April 25, Benton delivered an impassioned defense of the Missouri Compromise. Dismissing the validity of popular sovereignty, the well-respected Benton compared territories to children of the States and said Congress was obliged "to take care of these minors until they are of age." When Benton had used up his allotted time, Illinois Congressman "Long John" Wentworth, also a Democrat, yielded his so Benton could continue. Benton correctly prophesied that non-slaveowners would outnumber slaveowners in Kansas territory. More ominously, Benton predicted violence if the bill passed "and the destruction of the peace of the country."[312]

Congressman Stephens had little patience with Benton and the anti-Nebraska partisans. "We have had questions of peace, and questions of war taken after less debate than has already been permitted on this measure," he complained. As Richardson pushed the bill to the top of the House calendar, success was in doubt. Stephens, who understood the House rules better than his contemporaries, was willing to bet on a successful outcome. He knew that the amendment process offered endless possibilities to delay the final vote. But one motion could take precedence over all other amendments. If a motion were introduced to delete the "enacting clause" of the legislation, under House rules it must be given immediate precedence by the Committee of the Whole. Over the objections of Douglas ally Richardson, Stephens made his move on May 22.[313]

It was a complicated, even cynical act on Stephens's part, requiring at first the pro-Nebraska forces to vote against the bill in the Committee of the Whole. Then, having succeeded in reporting it negatively to the full House, Stephens wagered he could get the House to vote immediately to pass the bill. "The plan was consummate parliamentary tactics, and Stephens . . . had been 'more excited' for a week than ever before, understandably, for despite the soundness of his plan, he had not been able to sell it to Douglas and the other managers," wrote Thomas E. Schott.[314] Stephens ignored Douglas and put his plan into operation.

President Pierce and Douglas's allies then pressured wavering congressmen. After a final marathon session stretching over a day and a half, the act passed the House by a relatively narrow 113–100 margin. "Although the Administration had sought to make Douglas's measure 'a test of Democratic orthodoxy,' when it came to a decision in the House forty-four Northern Democrats voted for passage, forty-three against—a division that probably reflected rank-and-file sentiment as well," wrote historian Richard H. Sewell.[315] The margin of victory for Douglas was provided by southern Whigs. Congressman Stephens wrote: "Nebraska is through the House,—majority thirteen. Eight Southern men in the negative; all Whigs except Benton. I took the reins in my hand, applied whip and spur, and brought the 'wagon' out at eleven o'clock p.m. Glory enough for one day."[316]

The bill—stripped of the Clayton amendment barring immigrants from voting in the territories—was returned to the Senate where on May 26, it passed, 35–13. At the end of the debate Senator Seward announced: "We are on the eve of the consummation of a great national transaction— a transaction which will close a cycle in the history of our country . . . what has occurred here and in the country, during this contest, has compelled a conviction that Slavery will gain something, and Freedom will endure a severe, though I hope not an irretrievable loss."[317] Isaac N. Arnold invoked a metaphor of war to describe the scene: "On Capital [sic] Hill, outside, salvos of artillery announced the triumph of the slave power in Congress, over the cause of justice, honor and freedom; but the boom of the cannon awakened echoes in every valley and on every hill side in the free North."[318] Whig editor Thurlow Weed, a close ally of Seward, wrote: "The crime is committed. The work of Monroe, Madison, and Jefferson is undone. The wall they erected to guard the domain of liberty is flung down by the hands of an American Congress, and slavery crawls like a slimy reptile over the ruins." The New York political boss was furious: "It was fitting that the Kansas-Nebraska bill should be passed as it was. It was in accordance with its spirit that it should be conceived in treachery, sprung upon the House by fraud, and forced through by a parliamentary lie. It was appropriate that one member should be bribed, another bullied, and another bought, until the ranks of slavery were full. Had law, or order, or honesty, had aught to do with its passage, there would have been a strange incongruity between the means and the end."[319]

President Pierce signed the legislation on May 30, 1854. The Kansas-Nebraska Act declared the slavery restriction clause of the Missouri Compromise to be "inoperative and void" because of its supposed inconsistency with popular sovereignty and the Compromise of 1850. Senator Douglas exalted: "I passed the Kansas-Nebraska Act myself. I had the authority and power of a dictator throughout the whole controversy in both houses. The speeches were nothing. It was the marshalling and directing of men and guarding from attacks and with a ceaseless vigilance preventing surprise."[320]

Protesting Passage

The implications of the Kansas-Nebraska Act went far beyond the vainglory of the principals. Repeal of the Missouri Compromise ended the teetering equilibrium between proslavery and antislavery forces in the Union. "Douglas never desired and never intended to repeal the Missouri Compromise. But," wrote political scientist Harry V. Jaffa, "in 1854 Douglas came to the conviction that only the full and consistent application of the doctrine of popular sovereignty—the true principle of republican institutions as he understood them—could resolve the territorial question and provide a firm basis for future national development. These assertions are paradoxical in two respects: First, because Douglas, after the repeal, always insisted that he had always intended it. Second, because there is a manifest incongruity between the proposition that Douglas did not intend the repeal and that he did intend full recognition of popular sovereignty."[321] The deed was done. Resistance began. "In city after city, merchants and mechanics, lawyers and draymen, clergymen and architects—many of

EXPANSION OF SLAVERY PERMITTED UNDER THE KANSAS-NEBRASKA ACT OF 1854

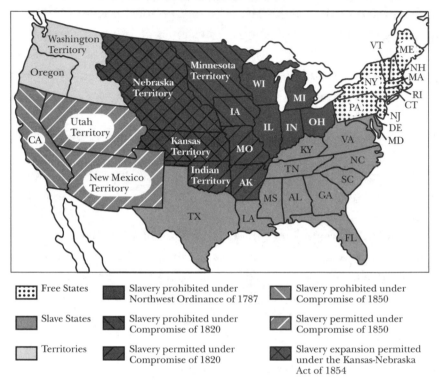

	Free States		Slavery prohibited under Northwest Ordinance of 1787		Slavery prohibited under Compromise of 1850
	Slave States		Slavery prohibited under Compromise of 1820		Slavery permitted under Compromise of 1850
	Territories		Slavery permitted under Compromise of 1820		Slavery expansion permitted under the Kansas-Nebraska Act of 1854

them old foes of antislavery agitation, men new to political action—joined in petition campaigns and mass rallies to denounce Douglas's 'treasonable scheme' and to swear war on doughfaces who voted for it," wrote Richard H. Sewell. "Conservative Whigs like Robert C. Winthrop, Hamilton Fish, and Thomas Ewing now stood shoulder to shoulder with Whiggish liberals and veteran Free Soilers in blistering the 'Nebraska infamy.'"[322]

Illinois contributed men from both major parties to the Kansas-Nebraska opposition. As early as March 2, 1854, a protest meeting had been organized in Peoria. A group of Whigs and Democrats had drafted a resolution lamenting the Kansas-Nebraska legislation. A week later a counter-meeting of Peoria Democrats endorsed Douglas and his legislation.[323] Across the Illinois prairie came the call for a free-soil coalition opposed to slavery extension. In Illinois, political reorganization happened gradually. Scholar David Zarefsky noted that the Kansas-Nebraska

Act "changed the terms of political discourse, making the slavery issue not an isolated local matter but an issue charged with emotion and symbolism."[324] Douglas had "reopened the struggle over the extension of slavery, and from that time on the contest between the North and South for control of the western territories dominated national politics," wrote Robert W. Johannsen. "Douglas had hoped that his act would ease sectional tensions by allowing the people in the new territories to decide the slavery question for themselves. In fact, the legislation had the opposite effect."[325]

Looking homeward, Douglas again challenged his critics in Illinois. In early April, Douglas had written twenty Chicago clergymen who had complained about his policy: "Thus, you see that the principle of the Nebraska bill is purely a question of self-government, involving the right and capacity of the people to make their own laws and manage their own local and domestic concerns. This is the only controverted principle involved in the bill. I am unwilling to believe that, upon mature reflection, and with all the advantages which your Christian character and experience may enable you to summon to your assistance, you will sanction the declaration that a proposition to carry this principle into effect is 'a great moral wrong, exposing us to the righteous judgments of the Almighty.'"[326]

Senator Douglas did not believe he would face the righteous judgments of the Almighty, but very soon, at Peoria, he would have to grapple with an inspired Abraham Lincoln.

"The doctrine of self government is right—absolutely and eternally right—but it has no just applications, as here attempted. Or perhaps I should say that whether it has such just application depends upon whether a negro is not *or* is *a man. . . . If the negro is* a *man, why then my ancient faith teaches me that 'all men are created equal;' and that there can be no moral right in connection with one man's making a slave of another."*

ABRAHAM LINCOLN,
OCTOBER 16, 1854

IV.

The Peoria Speech: The Ideas and Arguments

L incoln's speech at Peoria was carefully edited by him and then printed in the Illinois *State Journal.* This speech established the principles, the policies, and arguments whereby he made his way on an improbable pilgrimage to the presidency. During the 1850s, his political attention turned decisively from his economic program of the 1830s and 1840s to a concentrated focus on the restriction of slavery in the territories. In the turmoil occasioned by the repeal of the Missouri Compromise, Lincoln's historical and moral imagination fastened upon the principles of the Declaration of Independence, the policies of the American Founding, and the history of slavery. At Peoria his mastery of argument had matured into antislavery eloquence which allies and opponents would recognize as the stuff of national leadership.

Chicago Republican Isaac N. Arnold wrote in the 1880s: "When Lincoln made this Peoria speech he was an obscure man. Scarcely heard of out of Illinois, his audience was far inland, and away from the great cities, where reputation and fame are acquired. There were present no reporters of any great metropolitan papers, to take down the speech and spread it the next morning by the thousand, broadcast, on the breakfast tables of the voters. There were no admiring scholars, with wealth and appreciation, to put it in pamphlet form, and scatter it by the hundred thousand. There is a single copy of this speech in an obscure newspaper, and it would be difficult, if not impossible, to duplicate it."[327] Lincoln had surely found his political footing in Illinois. Biographer Nathaniel Wright Stephenson wrote that Lincoln "had discovered himself as a man of letters. . . . The oratory of 1854 was not statecraft in any ordinary sense."[328] Extraordinary too was the energy with which he would sustain the campaign for eleven years to come.

During the course of the Kansas-Nebraska debate, Lincoln had refined his antislavery ideas and arguments. These ideas had also been well-grounded in the logic of his political and economic philosophy of the 1830s and 1840s—what historian Gabor Boritt has called the "Economics of the American Dream."[329] During that early period, he had stressed free labor, free markets, and the positive economic benefits to a free people of a national bank, revenue-raising tariffs, public works, and the opportunities they created for individual Americans. Moreover, the first principle guiding the economics of free labor meant that no man should be a slave of another. Thus, after the Kansas-Nebraska Act threatened to extend slavery, Lincoln shifted his focus from the policies of free economics to the antislavery principles of free labor. During the late spring and early summer of 1854, he researched the historical narrative of American slavery and formulated the logic of his antislavery policy. Then later that summer and in the early fall, he replied directly to the Nebraska justifications of Senator Douglas. Although there is limited evidence of his speaking schedule for July and early August, Lincoln responded to one request to speak at the end of August: "I have promised to be at Mount Morris, in Ogle Co., on the 11th of August and on the 18th and 19th at other places in that vicinity, so that I could not be at at Pekin on the 20th."[330] Lincoln had begun to make the kind of political appearances which would culminate at Peoria on October 16. Don E. Fehrenbacher wrote: "Lincoln had already made several political speeches when his candidacy for the legislature was announced on September 4. Thereafter, he averaged about one a week until election day. . . . In each of his appearances Lincoln went over approximately the same general arguments. His presentation was well polished by the time he spoke at Peoria on October 16, and here for once his words were fully reported. Thus it was the 'Peoria Speech' that became famous."[331] The reporter and editor for the printed speech was also its author. He had perfected it for the stump and then for publication.

At Peoria and Springfield in 1854 many citizens—and later, numerous biographers—noted the dramatic change in Lincoln's demeanor, the evolution in the content and style of his rhetoric, and his mastery of the intricate history of slavery in America. "Lincoln's outrage and moral earnestness over the Nebraska issue surprised many in his audiences, who were expecting less seriousness and history, and more anecdotes," wrote Richard J. Carwardine. "This new-found authority has prompted historians to dramatize the change from the Lincoln of 1849, the clever but essentially provincial and 'self-centered' politician, to the powerful, broad-horizoned statesman of the anti-Nebraska struggles." In 1854 his well-formed conscience, joined to years of study and considerable ambition, seized the moral moment. Lincoln had gradually gained self-confidence between 1849 and 1854. He had also shed the partisan Whig rhetoric of the 1830s and 1840s. But he was recognizably the same man. From the moment of his arrival in 1832 at New Salem, at age twenty-three, Lincoln had unapologetically aspired to the esteem of his fellow Americans. In announcing his candidacy for the state legislature in 1832, Lincoln had written: "Every man is said to have his peculiar ambition. Whether it be true or not, I can say for one that I have no other so great as that of being truly esteemed of my fellow men, by rendering myself worthy of their esteem. How far I shall succeed in gratifying this ambition, is yet to be developed."[332]

The Founders and the Declaration of Independence

The force, the rigor, and the learning of Lincoln's intellect were much more evident at Peoria than ever before. Lincoln, the self-tutored historian of the American Founding, made his first dramatic appearance. Midway through the Peoria speech, Lincoln invoked the authority of the Founders: "In support of his application of the doctrine of self-government, Senator Douglas has sought to bring to his aid the opinions and examples of our revolutionary fathers. I am glad he has done this. I love the sentiments of those old-time men; and shall be most happy to abide by their opinions."[333] The sentiments of those old-time men of the Revolution resonated with Lincoln. It was their Declaration of Independence that now inspired his ideas and action. His study and mastery of the facts and circumstances of the Founding era had prepared him for the contest with Douglas over the extension of slavery. The three-hour Peoria speech was a magisterial tour of antislavery principles, their constitutional and legislative history, and the antislavery policies of the federal government from the Founding through the Kansas-Nebraska Act. At this turning point in American history, Lincoln queried whether America was destined to become a free-soil republic or a slaveholding nation. Throughout his remarks, he celebrated the intent of the Founders to put slavery in the course of ultimate extinction.

Lincoln was approximately correct when he argued, from 1854 onward, that the Founders, with some important exceptions, had hoped to put slavery in the course of ultimate extinction. The motives of the Founders were complex. Grounded by the Declaration of Independence, during the revolutionary fight for liberty, many slaveholders came to oppose slavery in principle. As allowed by the U.S. Constitution of 1787, Congress prohibited the international slave trade in 1808. By ending the importation of slaves, some Founders believed that slavery—under harsh conditions—would waste away. The inconsistency of slavery with republican institutions, and with the Declaration of Independence, led others to sense the hypocrisy. "So jarringly did the facts of the transatlantic slave trade conflict with American notions of righteous idealism that most whites in the North and the South were very willing to eliminate the practice in 1808, as soon as the Constitution allowed," wrote historian Orville Vernon Burton.[334] Many opposed slavery in the abstract, even as they continued to own slaves. A few Founders freed their slaves—as did George Washington in his will. Indeed Pennsylvania passed an Emancipation Act as early as 1780, other northern states doing the same in the ensuing founding years. In the flush of revolutionary victory, in the enthusiasm for liberty and equality, voluntary manumission by owners freed thousands of slaves, even in the southern states. Upper South slaveholders had economic motivations, too, such as the collapse of the southern tobacco economy in the late eighteenth century. A surplus of slaves in the Upper South developed, the value of which could be stabilized if the importation of new slaves was prohibited. Moreover, the revolutionary principles of liberty and equality held slavery to be a threat to the moral virtue and restraint necessary in free and self-reliant citizens. Slavery of blacks led to despotic dispositions in whites.

A prominent Founder and opponent of slavery was Pennsylvanian James Wilson, who signed both the Declaration of Independence and the Constitution before being appointed one of the original members of the U.S. Supreme Court by President George Washington. Wilson summarized the consensus of the 1787 Constitutional Convention at his state's ratifying convention in December. The constraints on slavery, in the new Constitution, lamented Wilson, represented "all that could be obtained. I am sorry it was no more; but from this I think there is reason to hope that yet a few years, and it will be prohibited altogether. And in the meantime, the new states which are to be formed will be under the control of Congress in this particular, and slaves will never be introduced amongst them."[335] A slaveholder and southern delegate to the Philadelphia convention, Charles Cotesworth Pinckney represented a different but complementary viewpoint to Wilson's. Pinckney told the South Carolina House of Representatives: "In short, considering all circumstances, we have made the best terms for the security of this species of property [slaves] it was in our power to make. We would have made better if we could; but on the whole, I do not think them bad."[336] Benjamin Franklin, who served on Pennsylvania's delegation to the Constitutional Convention, had once owned slaves. But in February 1790, shortly before he died, Franklin signed a strong petition to Congress from the Pennsylvania Society for Promoting the Abolition of Slavery. He provided in his will for the emancipation of a slave owned by his son-in-law.

There was, during the Founding era, a common sense, admittedly not universal, that slavery must be restricted, both for high-minded and self-interested motives. Thus arose during this period the hope for the ultimate extinction of slavery in America.[337] Mr. Lincoln campaigned to restore this hope, that the reality might eventually follow. "Let no one be deceived," argued Lincoln of the Declaration of Independence and the Kansas-Nebraska Act. "The spirit of seventy-six and the spirit of Nebraska [of 1854] are utter antagonisms; and the former is being rapidly displaced by the latter."[338] Biographers Nicolay and Hay remarked on the compelling moral dimension of Lincoln's argument: "The main, broad current of his reasoning was to vindicate and restore the policy of the fathers of the country in the restriction of slavery; but running through this like a thread of gold was the demonstration of the essential injustice and immorality of the system."[339] Lincoln could accept the temporary "necessity" of accommodating slavery in order to form the Union, as the Constitution of 1787 implicitly acknowledged, but he would neither accept the further extension of slavery nor its permanence in the American republic. At Peoria Lincoln brought irony, even pathos, to bear on the Founding:

> Near eighty years ago we began by declaring that all men are created equal; but now from that beginning we have run down to the other declaration, that for SOME men to enslave OTHERS is a "sacred right of self-government." These principles can not stand together. They are as opposite as God and mammon; and whoever holds to the one, must despise the other. When [Indiana Senator John] Pettit, in connection with his support of the Nebraska bill, called the Declaration of Independence "a self-evident lie" he only did what consistency and candor require all other Nebraska men to do. Of the forty odd [pro-]Nebraska Senators who sat present and heard him, no one rebuked him. Nor am I apprized that any Nebraska newspaper, or any Nebraska orator, in the whole nation, has ever yet rebuked him. If this had been said among [South Carolina Continental Army officer Francis] Marion's men, Southerners though they were, what would have become of the man who said it? If this had been said to the men who captured [British spy John] André, the man who said it, would probably have been hung sooner than André was. If it had been said in old Independence Hall, seventy-eight years ago, the

very door-keeper would have throttled the man, and thrust him into the street. [340]

The Lincoln target here was Senator Douglas, his doctrine of popular sovereignty, and its implied license for one man to make a slave of another.

Lincoln's Peoria speech opened with an analytical narrative of the history of the slavery policy of the federal government. As a Whig, Lincoln had long been opposed to the proslavery Democratic Party of Thomas Jefferson and Andrew Jackson. At Peoria and later, however, he singled out Jefferson's Declaration of Independence and the slavery restrictions of the Northwest Ordinance to support his arguments. Lincoln's Jeffersonian tactic was aimed in part at Democrats, who had dominated national politics during the entire first half of the nineteenth century. To hijack Jefferson from the Democrats was a sincere and shrewd maneuver to reawaken national reverence for the Declaration of Independence and the antislavery sentiments Jefferson had expressed in that document. Lincoln described Jefferson as "a chief actor in the revolution; then a delegate in Congress; afterwards twice President; who was, is, and perhaps will continue to be, the most distinguished politician of our history; a Virginian by birth and continued residence, and withal, a slave-holder; he [Jefferson] conceived the idea of taking that occasion, to prevent slavery ever going into the north-western territory. He prevailed on the Virginia Legislature to adopt his views, and to cede the territory, making the prohibition of slavery therein, a condition of the deed.[341] Congress accepted the cession, with the condition; and in the first Ordinance (which the acts of Congress were then called) for the government of the territory, provided that slavery should never be permitted therein. This is the famed ordinance of '87 so often spoken of. Thenceforward, for sixty-one years, and until in 1848, the last scrap of this territory came into the Union as the [free] State of Wisconsin, all parties acted in quiet obedience to this ordinance. It is now what Jefferson foresaw and intended—the happy home of teeming millions of free, white, prosperous people, and no slave amongst them." Lincoln concluded: "Thus, with the author of the declaration [*sic*] of Independence, the policy of prohibiting slavery in new territory originated."[342] (The usage of *free and white* was a commonplace of the time, not always naked racism. In this case it distinguished "free and white" from being black and slave. Depending upon the intent of the speaker, what was generally an invidious distinction might not be race-baiting. Lincoln understood the ambiguity. He also shrewdly enlisted Jefferson, a slave owner and a southerner, against the Kansas-Nebraska Act designed by Democratic Party leaders.)

The Declaration of Independence became the bedrock upon which Lincoln in 1854 built his philosophical and political reasoning. "Before the 1854 speeches, Lincoln had only twice made public reference to the Declaration, once in his 1838 Lyceum speech and again in 1852 in his eulogy for Henry Clay," wrote Lincoln scholar Allen C. Guelzo. "The Declaration, of course, was Thomas Jefferson's document, and throughout the 1780s and 1790s the Declaration was one of the public icons of Jefferson's party. But even before Jefferson's death in 1826, the Declaration was slowly becoming an embarrassment for the Democratic Party, especially in the South."[343] It was no longer politically convenient in the cotton-producing South, or in the commercial North, to endorse the principle of the Declaration of Independence that "all men are created equal." Still, Lincoln subtly modified the meaning of familiar words like equality. Guelzo wrote that there was a "harder edge to Lincoln's handling of the Declaration than the conventional Whig political script." For Lincoln, "the Declaration came to assume the role of a substitute scripture, and the [Founding] Fathers the role of political patriarchs in creating what Lincoln called in 1838 a 'civil religion.'"[344] That "all men are created equal" was elevated by Lincoln to the nation's Founding principle.

If one mark of the statesman is to clarify issues for fellow citizens, then Lincoln was becoming a statesman. He had, however, entered controversial historical territory. Lincoln's contemporaries debated, and scholars continue to debate, the attitudes of the Founders toward slavery. For example, Harvard historian William E. Gienapp wrote that "Lincoln simplified the Founders' record concerning slavery, which was much more mixed than he suggested. It was at this point in his career that the Declaration became a significant component of Lincoln's thought. Hailing it as the 'first precept of our ancient faith,' he henceforth designated it (rather than the Constitution) as the nation's founding charter."[345]

Abolitionists like William Lloyd Garrison considered the Constitution a pact with the devil. Legal historian Paul Finkelman argued that "the Garrisonians were correct in their analysis of the Constitution as a slaveholders' compact. I do not, however, believe that the Garrisonians' response to that analysis was correct. They withdrew from politics to avoid the stain of working within an imperfect and morally corrupt system. Fortunately, not all antebellum northern opponents of slavery withdrew from politics. Some, like Salmon P. Chase, Charles Sumner, and Abraham Lincoln, were willing to participate in politics and challenge the nation to live up to its ideals. Through political success, constitutional change, and military victory, the United States was eventually able to implement the important ideals encapsulated in the Declaration of Independence."[346]

Perhaps nowhere does Lincoln assert the equality precept, and its provenance, more confidently than in the Gettysburg Address of 1863. There, President Lincoln would emphasize that "our fathers brought forth upon this continent, a new nation" in 1776, the year of the Declaration of Independence, not in 1788, the year the Constitution was ratified. Such a rhetorical and political strategy Lincoln deemed true and necessary. If the republic itself had been founded upon the proposition of human equality, it must have been at its inception antislavery in principle. Lincoln also based his argument upon the fact that the Declaration was a formal congressional act of American Union and it carried the force of law. Thus did he ground the antislavery rhetoric of his Peoria speech in the 1776 act of the Founding. In 1854 Lincoln insisted that restoration of the Declaration's equality principle would set slavery in the course of ultimate extinction: "Our republican robe is soiled, and trailed in the dust," he lamented. "Let us repurify it. Let us turn and wash it white, in the spirit, if not the blood, of the Revolution. Let us turn slavery from its claims of 'moral right,' back upon its existing legal rights, and its arguments of 'necessity.' Let us return it to the position our fathers gave it; and there let it rest in peace. Let us re-adopt the Declaration of Independence, and with it, the practices, and policy, which harmonize with it. Let north and south—let all

Americans—let all lovers of liberty everywhere—join in the great and good work. If we do this, we shall not only have saved the Union; but we shall have so saved it, as to make, and to keep it, forever worthy of the saving. We shall have so saved it, that the succeeding millions of free happy people, the world over, shall rise up, and call us blessed, to the latest generations."[347] The Kansas-Nebraska Act had inaugurated a struggle to save the Union on the basis of the equality principle, but Lincoln still argued at Peoria that the legal rights of slaveholders in the Southern states had to be acknowledged under existing constitutional law.

Lincoln "was *not* proposing some altogether new departure," observed Lincoln scholar William Lee Miller. "On the contrary, he was calling for a *return* to what had been—the Founders' own spirit and principles."[348] Lincoln was neither radical by temperament nor revolutionary in policy. He often referred to his policy as conservative. However, Lincoln's struggle for restoration of an earlier order, though conservative in spirit, might entail unforeseen and radical means every bit as bloody as revolution. His strategy of restoration of the Missouri Compromise and the "Spirit of 1776" was a profound challenge to slaveholders and to the Douglas doctrine of popular sovereignty. Moreover, Lincoln was intimidated neither by slaveholder threats nor by southern domination of the federal government. His convictions were grounded in moral principles. Harry V. Jaffa wrote: "Lincoln did not appeal to the Declaration of Independence merely because it was our first and foremost founding document. It was, he said, the immortal emblem of man's humanity and the father of all moral principle because it incorporated a rational, nonarbitrary moral and political standard. The equality of man and man was a necessary inference from the inequality of man and beast—and of man and God."[349]

National Expansion and Compromise

The intellectual rigor and moral force of Lincoln's mature rhetoric ranks without peer among American presidents. He was not an academically trained intellectual on the model of James Madison, Thomas Jefferson, or John Adams. Nor was he a master of the ancient classics as were many of the Founders. Though Lincoln had less than a year of formal schooling, he became a master of economic, legal, and political ideas.[350] Rarely preoccupied by theories for their own sake, he grasped their relevance to those policies by which a prudent statesman adapts means and ends. "Lincoln had no constitutional theory as such," observed Allen C. Guelzo, "not because theory had no attractions for him, but because he believed the original intent of the Founders was actually quite easy to discover in the text of the Constitution and the historical context of the Founders."[351] Lincoln did begin political life as an untutored young man with no constitutional theory, but by 1854 and certainly by 1860 he had developed a studied and coherent constitutional framework.

Lincoln's intellectual process resembled that of a scientist. To first principles, he married empirical evidence. His research and study of primary sources permeated the Peoria speech. In it he set out a comprehensive analysis of the slavery question from the Northwest Ordinance of 1787 through the Louisiana Purchase of 1803, the Missouri Compromise of 1820, and the subsequent admission of new states to the Union. In one of the first substantial biographies of Lincoln after his death, Lincoln's political and scholarly contemporary, Isaac N. Arnold, made the case for Peoria's importance: "The speech is distinguished above all others by its full, accurate, and exhaustive knowledge of the history of the legislation relating to slavery. He demonstrates that under the policy of prohibition [of slavery extension] there had been peace, while the repeal of [this] prohibition [in the Kansas-Nebraska Act of 1854] had brought agitation."[352]

Lincoln showed that previous legislative restrictions on slavery had been the effective means to prohibit the spread of slavery in America. Of the Northwest Ordinance, Mr. Lincoln said: "If the ordinance of '87 did not keep slavery out of the north west territory, how happens it that the north west shore of the Ohio river is entirely free from it; while the south east shore, less than a mile distant, along nearly the whole length of the river, is entirely covered with it?" He compared the experiences of Illinois and Missouri: "If that ordinance did not keep it out of Illinois, what was it that made the difference between Illinois and Missouri? They lie side by side, the Mississippi river only dividing them; while their early settlements were within the same latitude. Between 1810 and 1820 the number of slaves in Missouri INCREASED 7,211; while in Illinois, in the same ten

years, they DECREASED 51. This appears by the census returns. During
nearly all of that ten years, both were territories—not States. During this
time, the ordinance forbid slavery to go into Illinois; and NOTHING forbid it to go into Missouri. It DID go into Missouri, and did NOT go into
Illinois. That is the fact. Can any one doubt as to the reason of it?"[353]

With modest irony, Lincoln then observed that Senator Douglas had
once supported the slavery restrictions of the Missouri Compromise.[354]
But the senator now dismissed the opponents of his Kansas-Nebraska legislation, arguing that slavery would not go where climate and soil were
unsuitable. On the contrary, Lincoln replied that slavery would go anywhere the slave owner could take it—into the mines, factories, farms, and
households of new territory—unless there were legal restrictions. He
recited the history of the Missouri Compromise in well-researched detail:

In 1803 we purchased what was then called Louisiana, of France.
It included the now states of Louisiana, Arkansas, Missouri, and
Iowa; also the territory of Minnesota, and the present bone of
contention, Kansas and Nebraska. Slavery already existed among
the French at New Orleans; and, to some extent, at St. Louis. In
1812 Louisiana came into the Union as a slave state, without controversy. In 1818 or '19, Missouri showed signs of a wish to come
in with slavery. This was resisted by northern members of Congress; and thus began the first great slavery agitation in the
nation. This controversy lasted several months, and became very
angry and exciting; the House of Representatives voting steadily
for the prohibition of slavery in Missouri, and the Senate voting as
steadily against it [prohibition]. Threats of breaking up the
Union were freely made; and the ablest public men of the day
became seriously alarmed. At length a compromise was made, in
which, like all compromises, both sides yielded something. It was
a law passed on the 6th day of March, 1820, providing that Missouri might come into the Union *with* slavery, but that in all the
remaining part of the territory purchased of France, which lies
north of 36 degrees and 30 minutes north latitude, slavery should
never be permitted. This provision of law, *is the Missouri Compro-*

mise. In excluding slavery North of the line, the same language is employed as in the Ordinance of '87. It directly applied to Iowa, Minnesota, and to the present bone of contention, Kansas and Nebraska.[355]

Lincoln held the Missouri Compromise line of 1820 to be "settled" national policy, not least because it had already been applied in what became the slave states of Arkansas and Texas as well as on behalf of free-soil in Iowa and Minnesota.

This settled policy of restricting slavery, based upon statutes developed by the Founders and their successors, grounded the legitimacy of Lincoln's Peoria argument to restore the Missouri Compromise line. To make his case, he presented the chronology of these congressional decisions subsequent to the Constitution of 1787:

In 1794, they prohibited an out-going slave-trade—that is, the taking of slaves FROM the United States to sell.

In 1798, they prohibited the bringing of slaves from Africa, INTO the Mississippi Territory—this territory then comprising what are now the States of Mississippi and Alabama. This was TEN YEARS before they had the authority to do the same thing as to the States existing at the adoption of the constitution.

In 1800 they prohibited AMERICAN CITIZENS from trading in slaves between foreign countries—as, for instance, from Africa to Brazil.

In 1803 they passed a law in aid of one or two State laws, in restraint of the internal slave trade.

In 1807, in apparent hot haste, they passed the law, nearly a year in advance, to take effect the first day of 1808—the very first day the constitution would permit—prohibiting the African slave trade by heavy pecuniary and corporal penalties.

In 1820, finding these provisions ineffectual, they declared the trade piracy, and annexed to it, the extreme penalty of death. While all this was passing in the general government, five or six of the original slave States had adopted systems of gradual emancipation; and by which the institution was rapidly becoming extinct within these limits.

Thus we see, the plain unmistakable spirit of that age, towards slavery, was hostility to the PRINCIPLE, and toleration, ONLY BY NECESSITY.[356]

By "necessity," Lincoln meant that slavery already existed in the colonies at the creation of the American nation in 1776, and moreover, that the United States Constitution would not have been ratified by slave states without acceptance of slavery in those states. Most of the Founders, Lincoln said, rejected slavery in principle. (In Lincoln's Cooper Union speech of February 1860, he would provide the detailed evidence that most of the Founders wanted to put slavery in the course of ultimate extinction.) Even as they embraced the Declaration of Independence, they did yield to "necessity" in order to forge the Union. Lincoln was further drawn to the Missouri Compromise because its architect was Lincoln's "beau ideal of a statesman"—Henry Clay of Kentucky, who was House speaker at the time of its passage in 1820.[357] At Peoria Lincoln quoted verbatim from a speech made by Senator Douglas in 1849 in which Douglas expressed admiration for Clay's work: "The Missouri Compromise had been in practical operation for about a quarter of a century, and had received the sanction and approbation of men of all parties in every section of the Union. It had allayed all sectional jealousies and irritations growing out of this vexed question, and harmonized and tranquilized the whole country. It had given to Henry Clay, as its prominent champion, the proud sobriquet of the '*Great Pacificator*' and by that title and for that service, his political friends had repeatedly appealed to the people to rally under his standard, as a presidential candidate, as the man who had exhibited the patriotism and the power to suppress an unholy and treasonable agitation, and preserve the Union." In 1849 Senator Douglas had said the Missouri Compromise was "conceived in the same spirit of fraternal affection, and calculated to remove forever, the only danger, which seemed to threaten, at some distant day, to sever the social bond of union. All the evidences of public opinion at that day, seemed to indicate that this Compromise had been canonized in the hearts of the

American people, as a sacred thing which no ruthless hand would ever be reckless enough to disturb."[358] The Douglas of 1854 would never adequately rationalize the Douglas of 1849.

The Kansas-Nebraska legislation had again stirred the demon of slavery, which Clay had sought to exorcize, and for which Douglas had awarded Clay great praise in 1849. Despite the best efforts of Congress, the Missouri Compromise of 1820 and the Compromise of 1850 failed to settle the historic controversy between pro- and antislavery Americans. The conflict had intensified, not least because Douglas in 1854 had amended his own bill so "as to declare the Missouri Compromise inoperative and void; and, substantially, that the People who go and settle there [the Kansas-Nebraska territory] may establish slavery, or exclude it, as they may see fit. In this shape the bill passed both branches of congress, and became a law."[359] Lincoln contended: "This is the *repeal* of the Missouri Compromise. The foregoing history may not be precisely accurate in every particular; but I am sure it is sufficiently so, for all the uses I shall attempt to make of it, and in it, we have before us, the chief material enabling us to correctly judge whether the repeal of the Missouri Compromise is right or wrong."[360]

The right or wrong of the Douglas repeal, Lincoln believed, was both a moral and a practical question. The Kansas-Nebraska Act of 1854 reignited the slavery debate which Lincoln argued had been resolved prudently and permanently by the legislation of 1820 and 1850. Speaking of the Compromise of 1850, Lincoln said: "Preceding the Presidential election of 1852, each of the great political parties, democrats and whigs, met in convention, and adopted resolutions endorsing the compromise of '50; as a 'finality,' a final settlement, so far as these parties could make it so, of all slavery agitation. Previous to this, in 1851, the Illinois Legislature had indorsed it."[361]

In a Socratic dialectic Lincoln denied the arguments Douglas and his partisans used to justify "repeal of the Missouri Compromise." Only Lincoln's exact words can do justice to his comprehensive antislavery case at Peoria, which inspired much that he would say and do during the next decade. He rejected the commonplace assertion of the legislation's advocates that the Kansas-Nebraska Act was needed or wanted: "First, then, if that country was in need of a territorial organization, could it not have had it as well without as with the repeal? Iowa and Minnesota, to both of which the Missouri restriction applied, had, without its repeal, each in succession, territorial organizations. And even, the year before, a bill for Nebraska itself, was within an ace of passing, without the repealing clause; and this in the hands of the same men who are now the champions of repeal. Why no necessity then for the repeal? But still later, when this very bill was first brought in, it contained no repeal. But, say they, because the public had demanded, or rather commanded the repeal, the repeal was to accompany the organization, whenever that should occur."[362]

After denying that "the public . . . ever repudiated the Missouri Compromise—ever commanded its repeal," Lincoln went on to discuss his own experience in Congress.[363] As a one-term U.S. congressman in 1847–49, he had joined northern Democrats and Whigs in voting repeatedly for a legislative amendment first proposed by a Pennsylvania Democrat, David Wilmot. The "Wilmot Proviso" had been rejected several times before Lincoln arrived in Washington. Congressman Lincoln participated in subsequent votes over the proviso, which stated "neither slavery nor involuntary servitude shall ever exist in any part of said territory [obtained from Mexico], except for crime, whereof the party shall first be duly convicted."[364] The Wilmot Proviso was repeatedly blocked in the Senate after receiving House approval. At Peoria, Lincoln reminded his audience of the history of the Proviso. In 1847 "President Polk asked [Congress] to place two millions of dollars under his control, to be used by him in the recess, if found practicable and expedient, in negotiating a treaty of peace with Mexico, and acquiring some part of her territory. A bill was duly got up, for the purpose . . . in the House of Representatives, when a member by the name of David Wilmot, a democrat of Pennsylvania, moved as an amendment 'Provided that in any territory thus acquired, there shall never be slavery.'" Lincoln said:

> The "Wilmot Proviso" or the principle of it, was constantly coming up in some shape or other, and I think I may venture to say I voted for it at least forty times; during the short term I was there. The Senate, however, held it in check, and it never became law. In

the spring of 1848 a treaty of peace was made with Mexico; by which we obtained that portion of her country which now constitutes the territories of New Mexico and Utah, and the now state of California. By this treaty the Wilmot Proviso was defeated, as so far as it was intended to be, a condition of the acquisition of territory. Its friends however, were still determined to find some way to restrain slavery from getting into the new country. This new acquisition lay directly West of our old purchase from France, and extended west to the Pacific ocean—and was so situated that if the Missouri line should be extended straight West, the new country would be divided by such extended line, leaving some North and some South of it. On Judge Douglas' motion a bill, or provision of a bill, passed the Senate to so extend the Missouri line. The Proviso men in the House, including myself, voted it down, because by implication, it gave up the Southern part to slavery, while we were bent on having it *all* free.[365]

Lincoln's votes for the Wilmot Proviso were in fact consistent with the Missouri Compromise, which applied to the Louisiana purchase, whereas his votes for the Wilmot Proviso were to prevent the extension of slavery in all the new territory acquired from Mexico: "When we voted for the Wilmot Proviso, we were voting to keep slavery *out* of the whole [Mexican] acquisition; and little did we think we were thereby voting, to let it *into* Nebraska, laying several hundred miles distant."[366] Don. E. Fehrenbacher noted that "the Nebraska matter, while raising the same old question of slavery in the territories, put it in new and explosive terms. The proponents of the Wilmot Proviso had been on the offensive, attempting to bar slavery from all newly conquered land. In resisting the reality of the Missouri compromise, however, antislavery forces were fighting a desperate defensive battle to preserve gains long since won and regarded as sacrosanct."[367] Lincoln argued it was not inconsistent to support the Missouri Compromise and the Wilmot Proviso: "It is not contended [by Douglas], I believe, that any such command [to repeal the Missouri Compromise] has ever been given in express terms. It is only said that it was done *in principle*." Lincoln's intricate explanation continued:

The support of the Wilmot Proviso, is the first fact mentioned, to prove that the Missouri restriction was repudiated in *principle*, and the second is, the refusal to extend the Missouri line over the country acquired from Mexico. These are near enough alike to be treated together. The one was to exclude the chances of slavery from the *whole* new acquisition by the lump; and the other was to reject a division of it, by which one *half* was to be given up to those chances. Now whether this was a repudiation of the Missouri line, in *principle*, depends upon whether the Missouri law contained any *principle* requiring the line to be extended over the country acquired from Mexico. I contend it did not. I insist that it contained no general principle, but that it was, in every sense, specific. That its terms limit it to the country purchased from France, is undenied and undeniable. It could have no principle beyond the intention of those who made it. They did not intend to extend the line to country which they did not own.[368]

In emphasizing that the Wilmot Proviso applied only to the Mexican territory but that the Missouri Compromise applied to the Louisiana Purchase, Lincoln further pointed out that the state of Missouri itself was north of the 36°30': "If that law contained any prospective *principle*, the whole law must be looked to in order to ascertain what the *principle* was. And by this rule, the south could fairly contend that inasmuch as they got one slave state north of the line at the inception of the law, they have the right to have another given them *north* of it occasionally—now and then in the indefinite westward extension of the line. This demonstrates the absurdity of attempting to deduce a prospective *principle* from the Missouri Compromise line."[369] It was an absurd construction because no legislator in 1820 had any such "principle" in mind. Instead, it was practical legislation to be applied strictly to the Louisiana Purchase.

So, to support the Wilmot Proviso, prohibiting slavery in the Mexican territory, did not mean to reject the Missouri Compromise line of 1820. "When we voted against extending the Missouri line, little did we think we were voting to destroy the only line, then of near thirty years standing. To argue that we thus repudiated the Missouri Compromise is no less absurd than it would be to argue that because we have, so far, forborne to acquire Cuba, we have thereby, in principle, repudiated our former acquisitions, and determined to throw them out of the Union!"[370] The truth that "we never thought of disturbing the original Missouri Compromise, is found in the facts, that there was then, and still is, an unorganized tract of fine country, nearly as large as the state of Missouri, lying immediately west of Arkansas, and south of the Missouri compromise line, by its northern boundary; and consequently is part of the country, in which, by implication, slavery was permitted to go, by that compromise. There it has lain open ever since, and there it still lies."[371] The Wilmot Proviso, had it been passed, would not have disturbed the 1820 Missouri line, which applied to the Louisiana Purchase.

One by one, sometimes with a touch of irony, Lincoln took up each of the complicated arguments of his adversary: "Senator Douglas sometimes says the Missouri line itself was, *in principle*, only an extension of the line of the ordinance of '87 . . . that is to say, an extension of the Ohio river. I think this is weak enough on its face. I will remark, however that, as a glance at the map will show, the Missouri line is a long way farther South than the Ohio; and that if our Senator, in proposing his extension, had stuck to the *principle* of jogging southward, perhaps it might not have been voted down so readily."[372] Lincoln the lawyer could dispute the fine points of the law with humor and the same rigor with which he contested high principle.

The Compromise of 1850

In 1854 another dispute arose over whether the Kansas-Nebraska Act conformed with the Compromise of 1850. Senator Douglas insisted at Peoria: "The Nebraska Bill was made to conform to the compromise of 1850, and was taken word for word from these measures. Was not every Democrat pledged to sustain the compromise of 1850?"[373] In his reply, Lincoln dismissed the Douglas position that the Compromise of 1850 "established a *new principle*, which required the repeal of the Missouri Compromise. This again I deny. I deny it, and demand the proof. I have already stated fully what the compromises of '50 are. The particular part of those measures, for which the virtual repeal of the Missouri compromise is sought to be inferred (for it is admitted they contain nothing about it, in express terms) is the provision in the Utah and New Mexico laws, which permits them when they seek admission into the Union as States, to come in with or without slavery as they shall then see fit. Now I insist this provision was made for Utah and New Mexico, and for no other place whatever. It had no more direct reference to Nebraska than it had to the territories of the moon. But, say they, it had reference to Nebraska, *in principle.*"[374] The North agreed to the Utah and New Mexico provisions, Lincoln said, because "California [came] into the Union as a free State. This was far the best part of all they had struggled for by the Wilmot Proviso. They also got the area of slavery somewhat narrowed in the settlement of the boundary of Texas. Also, they got the slave trade abolished in the District of Columbia. For all these desirable objects the North could afford to yield something; and they did yield to the South the Utah and New Mexico provision."[375]

Three weeks earlier, in Bloomington on September 26, Lincoln had said: "Now what was there in the Compromise Measure of '50 that repudiated the Missouri Compromise? The North secured that portion of the Louisiana purchase north of 36.30 [36° 30'] to freedom, by giving the South what they demanded as an equivalent therefor, namely, Missouri. We got it fairly and honestly, by paying for it: then what reason was there in endeavoring to make the stipulation upon which we purchased it apply as a principle to other and all future territories? The Missouri Compromise was a contract made between the North and the South, by which the former got all the Louisiana purchase north, and the latter all south, of the line of 36° 30' *within that territory.* There was no show of sense in endeavoring to make this bargain apply to any future territory acquired by the United States."[376] The territory of California, for example, had become part of the United States after the Missouri compromise without any reference to it.

At Peoria, Lincoln further detailed the history of California: "In the fall of 1848 the gold mines were discovered in California. This attracted people to it with unprecedented rapidity, so that on, or soon after, the meeting of the new congress in Dec., 1849, she already had a population of nearly a hundred thousand, had called a convention, formed a state constitution, excluding slavery, and was knocking for admission into the Union. The Proviso men, of course were for letting her in, but the Senate, always true to the other side would not consent to her admission. And there California stood, kept *out* of the Union, because she would not let slavery *into* her borders. Under all the circumstances perhaps this was not wrong. There were other points of dispute, connected with the general question of slavery, which equally needed adjustment."[377]

At mid-century, a free California tipped the balance of political power between slave states and free states in the U.S. Senate. As historian Michael Holt wrote, "In the early 1850s many Deep South Democrats still fumed that California's admission as a free state had upset the precious sectional balance of power in the Senate, even though California's two Democratic senators usually voted with the South. These Southerners knew that Minnesota and Oregon might soon become additional free states. With slavery prohibited from the remainder of the Louisiana Territory, where, they wondered, could new slave states be obtained to offset this growth of northern political power."[378] This was a crucial question because the South, operating through the Democratic Party, had generally dominated federal institutions from the birth of the republic.[379] Without continued dominance of the national government, the future of the South's slave-based economy, especially the cotton kingdom, might be threatened by an antislavery North.

Lincoln referred to other points of disagreement in 1850, among which he included the fugitive slave law, the slave trade in the nation's capital, territorial governments for Utah and New Mexico, and the western boundary of Texas. "These points all needed adjustment; and they were all held up, perhaps wisely to make them help to adjust one another. The Union, now, as in 1820, was thought to be in danger; and devotion to the Union rightfully inclined men to yield somewhat, in points where nothing else, could have so inclined them. A compromise was finally effected. The south got their new fugitive-slave law; and the North got California, (the far best part of our acquisition from Mexico,) as a free State. The south got a provision that New Mexico and Utah, *when admitted as States* may come in *with* or *without* slavery as they may then choose; and the north got the slave-trade abolished in the District of Columbia. The north got the western boundary of Texas, thence further back eastward than the south desired; but, in turn, they gave Texas ten millions of dollars, with which to pay her old debts. This is the Compromise of 1850."[380] But that was not all. In devotion to the Union, Lincoln added, both the Democratic and Whig parties ratified the permanence of the Compromise of 1850 at their 1852 presidential conventions. Compromise between North and South on the slavery question had thus become both a national and a party compact.

After reviewing the provisions of the Compromise of 1850, Lincoln put to Douglas a series of withering interrogatories: "If by any, or all these matters, the repeal of the Missouri Compromise was commanded, why was not the command sooner obeyed? Why was the repeal omitted in the Nebraska bill of 1853? Why was it omitted in the original bill of 1854? Why, in the accompanying report, was such a repeal characterized as a *departure* from the course pursued in 1850? and its continued omission recommended?"[381] The final Kansas-Nebraska Act of 1854, Lincoln argued, had brazenly broken up the ground upon which the Missouri Compromise of 1820 and the Compromise of 1850 had been constructed.

As to the meaning of the Compromise of 1850, Lincoln asked "if Congress, at that time, intended that all future territories should, when admitted as States, come in with or without slavery, at their own opinion, why did it not say so? With such an universal provision, all know the bills could not have passed. Did they, then—could they—establish a *principle* contrary to their own intention? Still further, if they intended to establish the principle that wherever Congress had control, it should be left to the people to do as they thought fit with slavery why did they not authorize the people of the District of Columbia at their adoption to abolish slavery within these limits. I personally know that this has not been left undone, because it was unthought of. It was frequently spoken of by members of Congress and by citizens of Washington six years ago; and I heard no one express a doubt that a system of gradual emancipation, with compensation to the owners, would meet the approbation of a large majority of the white people of the District."[382] As a congressman, Lincoln himself had supported compensated emancipation of slaves in the capital. Only Congress had the constitutional power to enact such a law for Washington or for the territories.

Lincoln challenged every spurious assertion by Senator Douglas, including one "that by the Resolutions of the Illinois Legislature, passed in 1851, the repeal of the Missouri compromise was demanded. This I deny also. Whatever may be worked out by a criticism of the language of those resolutions, the people have never understood them as being any more than an endorsement of the compromises of 1850; and a release of our [Illinois] Senators from voting for the Wilmot Proviso."[383] As was his habit in the courtroom, Lincoln applied Euclidean logic to the established facts and circumstances. By endorsing the Compromise of 1850, "I meant not to ask for the abolition of slavery in the District of Colombia. I meant not to resist the admission of Utah and New Mexico, even should they ask to come in as slave States. I meant nothing about additional territories, because, as I understood, we then had no territory whose character as to slavery was not already settled. As to Nebraska, I regarded its character as being fixed, by the Missouri compromise, for thirty years—as unalterably fixed as that of my own home in Illinois. As to new acquisitions I said 'sufficient unto the day is the evil thereof.' When we make new [acquisitions] we will, as heretofore, try to manage them some how. That is my answer. That is what I meant and said; and I appeal to the people to say, each for himself, whether that was not also the universal meaning of the free States."[384]

Lincoln then questioned the senator's arguments on a decisive point: "I am aware Judge Douglas now argues that the subsequent express repeal is no substantial alteration of the bill. This argument seems wonderful to me. It is as if one should argue that white and black are not different. He admits, however, that there is a literal change in the bill; and that he made the change in deference to other Senators, who would not support the bill without. This proves that those Senators thought the change a substantial one; and that the Judge thought their opinions worth deferring to. His own opinions, therefore, seem not to rest on a very firm basis even in his own mind—and I suppose the world believes, and will continue to believe, that precisely on the substance of that change this whole

agitation has arisen."[385] Having rejected all arguments that the public
"demanded the repeal of the Missouri compromise," Lincoln then proceeded to the fundamental political issue at hand:

> I now come to consider whether the repeal, with its avowed prin-
> ciple, is intrinsically right. I insist that it is not. Take the particular
> case. A controversy had arisen between the advocates and oppo-
> nents of slavery, in relation to its establishment within the country
> we had purchased of France. The southern, and the best of the
> [Louisiana] purchase, was already in as a slave State. The contro-
> versy was settled by also letting Missouri in as a slave State; but
> with the agreement that within all the remaining part south of the
> line, nothing was said; but perhaps the fair implication was, that it
> should come in with slavery if it should so choose. The southern
> part, except a portion heretofore mentioned, afterwards did
> come in with slavery, as the State of Arkansas. All these many years
> since 1820, the Northern part had remained a wilderness. At
> length settlements began in it also. In due course, Iowa, came in
> as a free State, and Minnesota was given a territorial government,
> without removing the slavery restriction. Finally the sole remain-
> ing part, North of the line, Kansas and Nebraska, was to be organ-
> ized; and it is proposed, and carried, to blot out the old dividing
> line of thirty-four years standing, and to open the whole of that
> country to the introduction of slavery. Now, this, to my mind, is
> manifestly unjust. After an angry and dangerous controversy, the
> parties made friends by dividing the bone of contention. The one
> party first appropriates her own share, beyond all power to be dis-
> turbed in the possession of it; and then seizes the share of the
> other party. It is as if starving men had divided their only loaf; the
> one had hastily swallowed his half, and then grabbed the other
> half just as he was putting it to his mouth![386]

The issue, Lincoln believed, could be resolved only by new political action, not by abstract debate: "The Missouri Compromise ought to be restored. For the sake of the Union, it ought to be restored. We ought to elect

Lincoln and Douglas

Abraham Lincoln

*The Gilder Lehrman Collection,
courtesy of the Gilder Lehrman Institute
of American History, on deposit at the
New-York Historical Society, New York,
reference number GLC 590*

Stephen Douglas

*The Gilder Lehrman Collection,
courtesy of the Gilder Lehrman Institute
of American History, on deposit at the
New-York Historical Society, New York,
reference number GLC 5111.01.0286*

a House of Representatives which will vote its restoration. If by any means, we omit to do this, what follows? Slavery may or may not be established in Nebraska. But whether it be or not, we shall have repudiated—discarded from the councils of the Nation—the SPIRIT of COMPROMISE; for who after this will ever trust in a national compromise? The spirit of mutual concession—that spirit which first gave us the constitution, and which has thrice saved the Union—we shall have strangled and cast from us forever. And what shall we have in lieu of it? The South flushed with triumph and tempted to excesses; the North, betrayed, as they believe, brooding on wrong and burning for revenge. One side will provoke; the other resent."[387] Lines of conflict had now been drawn on both sides: "Already a few in the North, defy all constitutional restraints, resist the execution of the fugitive slave law, and even menace the institution of slavery in the states where it exists."[388]

Popular Sovereignty and Slavery

To organize the vast territory of the Great Plains required congressional legislation. Although Lincoln deplored repeal of the Missouri line, he celebrated the settlement of new territories. Until 1850, "Nebraska had remained, substantially an uninhabited country, but now emigration to, and settlement within it began to take place. It is about one third as large as the present United States, and its importance so long overlooked, begins to come into view. The restriction of slavery by the Missouri Compromise directly applies to it; in fact, was first made, and has since been maintained, expressly for it. In 1853, a bill to give it a territorial government passed the House of Representatives, and in the hands of Justice Douglas, failed of passing the Senate only for want of time. This bill contained no repeal of the Missouri Compromise. Indeed, when it was assailed because it did not contain such repeal, Judge Douglas defended it in its existing form."[389]

Into the Kansas-Nebraska Act Douglas had insinuated a definition of "popular sovereignty" which attempted to mask the repeal of the Missouri Compromise—"it being the true intent and meaning of this act not to legislate slavery into any Territory or State, nor to exclude it therefrom, but to leave the people thereof perfectly free to form and regulate their domestic institutions in their own way, subject only to the Constitution of the United States."[390] Douglas had defended his doctrine: "Opponents of the Nebraska Bill do not like the principle which allows the people to settle the slavery question themselves. Is that principle right? Oh yes, exclaim some, but, say they, you should not disturb the Missouri Compromise."[391] In his own speech at Peoria, Douglas had argued that "the people of the north who emigrated to new territories were as capable of managing their domestic affairs as those who remained behind. They allowed legislation upon every question affecting their welfare as a people, but they were not deemed capable of deciding the question of slavery for themselves [because of the Missouri Compromise]. They were permitted to legislate upon every subject affecting the white man, but were to be told that they had not sufficient intelligence to legislate for the black man—or to decide the question of slavery for themselves."[392]

Lincoln examined the logic by which popular sovereignty might apply to slavery: "If this be the rule, you must leave it to each individual to say for himself whether he will have slaves. What better moral right have thirty-one citizens of Nebraska to say, that the thirty-second shall not hold slaves, than the people of the thirty-one States have to say that slavery shall not go into the thirty-second State at all?"[393] According to Lincoln, the logic of popular sovereignty was that every person must be sovereign in deciding whether or not to hold slaves. And thus no territory under such a doctrine, perhaps no state, no democratic majority could decide the slavery question. Ultimately, unrestricted popular sovereignty must mean unrestrained personal choice, even the taking of a human being as a slave.

Lincoln believed popular sovereignty was a treacherous rationale whose logic led progressively to slavery without limit: "But if it is a sacred right for the people of Nebraska to take and hold slaves there, it is equally their sacred right to buy them where they can buy them cheapest; and that undoubtedly will be on the coast of Africa; provided you will consent to not hang them for going there to buy them." Here, Lincoln referred to the death penalty for importing slaves into the United States, a law enacted in 1820. He argued that the logic of popular sovereignty would require reversing the ban on slave importation: "You must remove this restriction too, from the sacred right of self-government. I am aware you say that taking slaves from the States to Nebraska, does not make slaves of freemen; but the African slave-trader can say just as much. He does not catch free negroes and bring them here. He finds them already slaves in the hands of their black captors, and he honestly buys them at the rate of about a red cotton handkerchief a head." With severe irony, Lincoln then remarked: "This is very cheap, and it is a great abridgement of the sacred right of self-government to hang men for engaging in this profitable trade!"[394]

Moreover, under the Kansas-Nebraska Act, this doctrine of popular sovereignty would be used by the original settlers permanently to determine territorial laws concerning slavery; the more numerous residents arriving later were to be denied these same rights. In the new territories "popular sovereignty" would give rights to the few over the many. Lincoln demurred: "Another important objection to this application of the right of self-government, is that it enables the first FEW, to deprive the succeeding MANY, of a free exercise of the right of self-government. The first few may get slavery IN, and the subsequent many cannot easily get it OUT. How common is the remark now in the slave States—'If we were only clear of our slaves, how much better it would be for us.' . . . The same thing was true of the whole nation at the time our constitution was formed."[395]

Lincoln argued that the few should not decide fundamental national issues such as slavery. In a democracy, these issues must be decided by the many. Slavery was a national, not a local, concern: "Whether slavery shall go into Nebraska, or other new territories, is not a matter of exclusive concern to the people who may go there. The whole nation is interested that the best use shall be made of these territories. We want them for the homes of free white people. This they cannot be, to any considerable extent, if slavery shall be planted within them. Slave States are places for poor white people to remove FROM; not to remove TO. New free States are the places for poor people to go to and better their condition. For this use, the nation needs these territories."[396] Thomas Lincoln, his father, had moved from Kentucky to Indiana for this and other reasons. After he sys-

tematically examined the principles and policies by which new states had
been admitted to the Union, Lincoln brought down his hammer directly
upon the repeal of the Missouri Compromise: "I think, and shall try to
show, that it is wrong; wrong in its direct effect, letting slavery into Kansas
and Nebraska—and wrong in its prospective principle, allowing it to
spread to every other part of the wide world, where men can be found
inclined to take it." In a single passage Lincoln summarized an essential
theme of the Peoria speech:

> This *declared* indifference, but as I must think, covert *real* zeal for
> the spread of slavery, I can not but hate. I hate it because of the
> monstrous injustice of slavery itself. I hate it because it deprives
> our republican example of its just influence in the world—
> enables the enemies of free institutions, with plausibility, to taunt
> us as hypocrites—causes the real friends of freedom to doubt our
> sincerity, and especially because it forces so many really good men
> amongst ourselves into an open war with the very fundamental
> principles of civil liberty—criticising the Declaration of Inde-
> pendence, and insisting that there is no right principle of action
> but *self-interest.*[397]

Lincoln opposed the extension of slavery on principle, but he was
mindful of the daunting complexity of America's peculiar institution. Historian Richard Striner has observed that "any working politician who
ignored the force of white supremacy, either within or beyond his own
political base, was too naïve for the work that lay before him."[398] In most
of the North as well as the South, he could never be elected. The scholarship of the past two generations has emphasized the pervasive national
prejudice in the antebellum North against African-Americans, which was
particularly strong in Illinois. Lincoln understood this, having been born
in Kentucky and reared in antiblack southwest Indiana. He had married
the daughter of a Kentucky slaveowner; he had visited slave plantations.
He understood the beliefs and rationalizations of the planters. He had
rafted down the Mississippi River twice, passing by great slave plantations
on both shores. As a congressman, he witnessed slavery and the slave

trade in the nation's capital. So he well understood the prejudice of the North and the practical as well as the legal impediments to ending slavery in the South—especially the difficulty of returning freed slaves to Africa:

> If they [freed slaves] were all landed there [in Africa] in a day, they would all perish in the next ten days; and there are not surplus shipping and surplus money enough in the world to carry them there in many times ten days. What then? Free them all, and keep them among us as underlings? Is it quite certain that this betters their condition? I think I would not hold one in slavery, at any rate; yet the point is not clear enough for me to denounce people upon. What next? Free them, and make them politically and socially, our equals? My own feelings will not admit of this; and if mine would, we well know that those of the great mass of white people will not. Whether this feeling accords with justice and sound judgment, is not the sole question, if indeed, it is any part of it. A universal feeling, whether well or ill-founded, can not be safely disregarded. We can not, then, make them equals. It does seem to me that systems of gradual emancipation might be adopted; but for their tardiness in this, I will not undertake to judge our brethren of the south.[399]

Like his political model Henry Clay, Lincoln supported the abstract idea of colonization, but in the end he retained few illusions about its efficacy. At Peoria Lincoln did not presume to spell out a comprehensive solution to the slavery problem. What he did was to insist that Congress had the constitutional power to restrict the extension of slavery into new territories and it should do so. Thus could the American democratic republic put slavery gradually and peacefully on the road to extinction. Repeatedly in the Peoria speech, Lincoln rejected the claim by Douglas that popular sovereignty, rather than legal restrictions, would limit the spread of slavery: "It is argued that slavery will not go to Kansas and Nebraska, *in any event.* This is a *palliation*—a *lullaby.* I have some hope that it will not; but let us not be too confident. As to climate, a glance at the map shows that there are five slave States—Delaware, Maryland, Virginia,

Kentucky, and Missouri—and also the District of Columbia, all north of the Missouri compromise line. The census returns of 1850 show that, within these, there are 867,276 slaves—being more than one-fourth of all the slaves in the nation."[400]

The example of the Missouri territory before 1820 showed that slavery, once introduced into a territory, was difficult to extinguish: "But it is said, there now is *no* law in Nebraska on the subject of slavery; and that, in such case, taking a slave there, operates his freedom. That *is* good book-law; but is not the rule of actual practice. Wherever slavery is, it has been first introduced without law. The oldest laws we find concerning it, are not laws introducing it; but regulating it, as an already existing thing. A white man takes his slave to Nebraska now; who will inform the negro that he is free? Who will take him before court to test the question of his freedom? In ignorance of his legal emancipation, he is kept chopping, splitting and plowing. Others are brought, and move on in the same track. At last, if ever the time for voting comes, on the question of slavery, the institution already in fact exists in the country, and cannot well be removed. The facts of its presence, and the difficulty of its removal will carry the vote in its favor."[401] Only congressional prohibitions, such as the Northwest Ordinance and the Missouri Compromise, could restrict the slaveowners' disposition to take slaves into the territories.

In the historic controversy over the suitability of climate and soil for slavery, economists and historians of the past half-century have shown that Lincoln's analysis was substantially correct. Neither climate, nor soil, nor even the passage of time would halt the spread of slavery. That the new territories might themselves exclude slavery for economic reasons, Lincoln thought implausible, given the precedents and the evidence. Because slave labor was in fact profitable, and moreover a tradeable asset, it could go anywhere that free labor could go. Slave labor was not merely confined to large-scale plantations. Slaves could be employed in mines, manufacturing, commerce, services, and households. After the value of land, the monetary value of slaves in antebellum America was the largest category of national investment. Lincoln explicitly recognized this fact as an overpowering economic interest in the South and a commercial interest of the north. Cotton plantations of the South needed the bankers, shipowners, and textile producers of the North. Thus, only an unequivocal congressional statute prohibiting the extension of slavery to the territories could put the peculiar institution on the road to ultimate extinction. More than a century later, Robert Fogel and Stanley Engerman demonstrated that slavery could be profitable almost anywhere.[402] Political scientist Harry V. Jaffa had earlier contended: "There is no reason to suppose that should slavery in the mines, foundries, factories, and fields of the free states have proved advantageous to powerful groups therein, new systems of discipline might not have been invented to make the exploitation of slave labor highly profitable there."[403] The wasting away of slavery, under pressures of competition and climate, was a specious economic argument in 1854; it became misleading history when taught to subsequent generations of American students.

Lincoln did not confine his arguments to issues of economic interest and the sanctity of the Missouri Compromise line. Drawing upon the Declaration of Independence, he invoked its equality principle—citing this fundamental American proposition in order to counter growing national acquiescence to the spread of slavery. The Kansas-Nebraska precedent would surely be used to extend slavery into all the territories under the rubric of popular sovereignty: "That future use [of popular sovereignty] is to be the planting of slavery wherever in the wide world, local and unorganized opposition can not prevent it. Now if you wish to give them this endorsement—if you wish to establish this principle—do so. I shall regret it; but it is your right. On the contrary if you are opposed to the principle—intend to give it no such endorsement—let no wheedling, no sophistry, divert you from throwing a direct vote against it."[404] This was an essential purpose of Lincoln's antislavery campaign that fall—to mobilize votes to overturn Kansas-Nebraska and its popular sovereignty principle. In a democratic nation, Lincoln argued, major public issues should be resolved by the voters. He had no illusions about the legislative precedent and force of the Kansas-Nebraska law. To restore the Missouri line by voters was imperative:

The question is asked us, "If slaves will go in, notwithstanding the general principle of [common] law liberates them, why would they not equally go in against positive statute law?—go in, even if the Missouri restriction were maintained?" I answer, because it takes a much bolder man to venture in, with his property, in the latter case, than in the former—because the positive congressional enactment is known to, and respected by all, or nearly all, whereas the negative principle that *no* law is free law, is not much known except among lawyers. We have some experience of this practical difference. In spite of the Ordinance of '87, a few negroes were brought into Illinois, and held in a state of quasi slavery; not enough, however to carry a vote of the people in favor of the institution when they came to form a constitution. But in the adjoining Missouri country, where there was no ordinance of '87—was no restriction—they were carried ten times, nay a hundred times, as fast, and actually made a slave State. This is fact—naked fact.[405]

The spread of slavery could best be stopped by a federal law. The founding principles of equality and liberty implied that it should be restricted. Lincoln rebuked those who would deny the humanity of slaves and their God-given inalienable rights:

Equal justice to the south, it is said, requires us to consent to the extending of slavery to new countries. That is to say, inasmuch as you do not object to my taking my hog to Nebraska, therefore I must not object to you taking your slave. Now, I admit this is perfectly logical, if there is no difference between hogs and negroes. . . . The great majority, south as well as north, have human sympathies, of which they can no more divest themselves than they can of their sensibility to physical gain. These sympathies in the bosoms of the southern people, manifest in many ways, their sense of the wrong of slavery, and their consciousness that, after all, there is humanity in the negro. If they deny this, let me address them a few plain questions. In 1820 you joined the north, almost unanimously, in declaring the African slave trade piracy, and in annexing to it the punishment of death. Why did you do this? If you did not feel that it was wrong, why did you join in providing that men should be hung for it? . . . But you never thought of hanging men for catching and selling wild horses, wild buffaloes, or wild bears."[406]

The popular sovereignty of Douglas could make of a Negro slave the legal equal of a wild bear. Although Lincoln acknowledged the right of self-government, he denied that self-government included the right to take slaves: "I trust I understand, and truly estimate the right of self-government. My faith in the proposition that each man should do precisely as he pleases with all which is exclusively his own, lies at the foundation of the sense of justice there is in me. I extend the principles to communities of men, as well as to individuals. I so extend it, because it is politically wise, as well as naturally just; politically wise, in saving us from broils about matters which do not concern us. Here, or at Washington, I would not trouble myself with the oyster laws of Virginia, or the cranberry laws of Indiana."[407]

President Thomas Jefferson had argued in his First Inaugural Address of 1801 that if in a democracy, it is the right of the majority to rule, such rule may be justified only if the majority rules reasonably: "All, too, will bear in mind this sacred principle, that though the will of the majority is in all cases to prevail, that will to be rightful must be reasonable; that the minority possess their equal rights, which equal law must protect, and to violate would be oppression."[408] In the case of taking slaves, popular sovereignty denied the natural and inalienable rights of other human beings, and thus committed a fundamental injustice. Lincoln applied Jefferson's "sacred principle" to slavery: "The doctrine of self government is right—absolutely and eternally right—but it has no just application, as here attempted. Or perhaps I should rather say that whether it has such just application depends upon whether a negro is *not* or *is* a man. If he is *not* a man, why in that case, he who *is* a man may, as a matter self-government, do just as he pleases with him. But if the negro *is* a man, is it not to that extent, a total destruction of self-government, to say that he too shall not govern *himself?* When the white man governs himself, that is self-government; but when he governs himself and also governs *another* man, that is *more* than self-government—that is despotism. If the negro is a *man*, why then my ancient faith teaches me that 'all men are created equal;' and that there can be no moral right in connection with one man's making a slave of another."[409] With Socratic simplicity, Lincoln provided what Harry V. Jaffa called the "classic refutation" of Douglas's assumption "that the doctrine of popular sovereignty was such that the duty of statesmanship was exhausted when the people's power of decision was secured to them."[410] There could be no "right" in the taking of slaves unless might makes right. Only naked power and self-interest could explain the prevalence of slavery, not only in America but throughout the world.

Popular sovereignty could be reasonable if acts of legislatures ruled out unjust applications. Lincoln emphasized "that the application of the principle of self-government, as contended for [by Douglas], would require the revival of the African slave trade—that no argument could be made in favor of a man's right to take slaves to Nebraska, which could not be equally well made in favor of his right to bring them from the coast of Africa." Lincoln reminded his Peoria audience that Senator Douglas had contended "that the constitution requires the suppression of the foreign slave trade; but does not require the prohibition of slavery in the territories. That is a mistake, in point of fact. The constitution does NOT require the action of Congress in either case; and it does AUTHORIZE it in both. And so, there is still no difference between the cases."[411] At Peoria, Lincoln demonstrated that he was a meticulous analyst of the Constitution. Prudent by nature, Lincoln remained measured in debate. Though shrewd enough to avoid the abolitionist embrace, his emphasis on consent and the equality principle of the Declaration meant serious disputes to come with the slave states. Lincoln did suggest that the ultimate extinction of slavery might take more than a hundred years, but the slavemasters feared for the immediate future of their peculiar institution.

Race and Prejudice

Lincoln's Peoria speech elevated the moral issue and explicitly rejected indifference to slavery. Richard J. Carwardine wrote: "Lincoln founded his tolerant, encompassing nationalism, however, not on moral concessions to slaveholding but on a conviction that most southerners, in continuing to hold firm to the principles of the Declaration of Independence, shared his own view of slavery as a 'monstrous injustice.'"[412] Southern slaveholders themselves found the practice of slave trading morally repugnant. Lincoln astutely emphasized at Peoria that southern society shunned slavetraders: "Again, you have amongst you, a sneaking individual, of the class of native tyrants, known as the 'SLAVE-DEALER.' He watches your necessities, and crawls up to buy your slave, at a speculating price. If you cannot help it, you sell to him; but if you can help it, you drive him from your door. You despise him utterly. You do not recognize him as a friend, or even as an honest man. Your children must not play with his; they may rollick freely with the little negroes, but not with the 'slave-dealers' children. If you are obliged to deal with him, you try to get through the job without so much as touching him. It is common with you to join hands with the men you meet; but with the slave dealer you avoid the ceremony—instinctively shrinking from the snaky contact. If he grows rich and retires from business, you still remember him, and still keep up the ban of non-intercourse upon him and his family. Now why is this? You do not so treat the man who deals in corn, cattle or tobacco."[413]

Lincoln argued that no slave owner could reasonably deny the self-evident humanity of the slave. He noted that in 1850 there were over 400,000 free blacks in the United States, worth over $200 million: "How comes this vast amount of property to be running about without owners? We do not see free horses or free cattle running at large. How is this? All these free blacks are the descendants of slaves, or have been slaves themselves, and they would be slaves now, but for SOMETHING which has operated on their white owners, inducing them, at vast pecuniary sacrifices, to liberate them. What is that SOMETHING? Is there any mistaking it? In all these cases it is your sense of justice, and human sympathy, continually telling you, that the poor negro has some natural right to himself—that those who deny it, and make mere merchandise of him, deserve kickings, contempt and death."[414] For slavery apologists, these last were hard words.

There were still practical limits to what Lincoln might say in Illinois in order to build a political majority to oppose the expansion of slavery.

"As an ambitious politician, he was sensitive to the power of antiblack sentiment in Illinois and frankly conceded that most whites, including himself, would not accept former slaves as political and social equals," wrote William E. Gienapp.[415] This is not exactly so. Lincoln had suggested that even if he were to accept them as equals, it would be of no practical effect. Most residents of Illinois were antiblack even if they were antislavery. Under state law free blacks elsewhere could not migrate to Illinois to become residents. Vocal abolitionists such as Elijah Lovejoy were sparse in number in Illinois and marginalized in elective politics. In Lovejoy's case, he was murdered by a mob in late 1837, a vicious injustice that Lincoln alluded to with regret during an 1838 speech on American law and government.[416]

Thus, antiblack sentiment put some antislavery men on the defensive in Illinois. At Peoria, Lincoln was forced to respond to race-baiting by Douglas who repeatedly declared that Lincoln favored complete equality of the races, including intermarriage. Lincoln answered: "Let it not be said I am contending for the establishment of political and social equality between the whites and blacks. I have already said the contrary. I am not now combating the argument of NECESSITY, arising from the fact that the blacks are already amongst us; but I am combating what is set up as MORAL argument for allowing them to be taken where they have never yet been—arguing against the EXTENSION of a bad thing, which where it already exists, we must of necessity, manage as we best can."[417] This argument was the reasoning of a prudent but ambitious Illinois politician, well aware that his antislavery cause must win public sentiment and a majority at the polls in order to restore the Missouri Compromise and thus to prohibit any further extension of slavery. Lincoln formulated his arguments "to prevent the feeling against social and political equality from undermining the feeling against slavery," argued Harry V. Jaffa. "Among the motives in the free-soil movement for keeping slavery out of Kansas was that of keeping out blacks, whether free or slave."[418]

Lincoln respected the authority of the Constitution; William E. Gienapp noted that Lincoln had no "intention of interfering with slavery in the southern states, acknowledging that there was no power under the Constitution to do so."[419] Lincoln the lawyer-politician was keenly aware that there was a prescribed procedure of constitutional amendment. In January 1865 President Lincoln would himself press that power in order to abolish slavery. Until then he embraced the necessity in a democracy to persuade public opinion. Twenty-three years before, Lincoln had explained the importance of persuasion in public policy. "If you would win a man to your cause, *first* convince him that you are his sincere friend," Lincoln had told a temperance meeting in 1842. "Therein is a drop of honey that catches his heart, which, say what he will, is the great high road to his reason, and which, when once gained, you will find but little trouble in convincing his judgment . . ."[420]

Lincoln never altered his view that to lead, one must persuade. In 1856 at Chicago, Lincoln would declare: "Our government rests in public opinion. Whoever can change public opinion, can change the government, practically just so much. Public opinion . . . [on] any subject, always has a '*central idea*,' from which all its minor thoughts radiate. That 'central idea' in our political public opinion, at the beginning was, and until recently has continued to be, 'the equality of men.' And although it was always submitted patiently to whatever of inequality there seemed to be as matter of actual necessity, its constant working has been a steady progress towards the practical equality of all men."[421]

Nationhood and Union

In the debate at Peoria, Senator Douglas tried to make the case that his was the truly national and unifying policy, but Lincoln's was merely sectional and divisive. As reported by the Peoria *Daily Union*, Douglas argued: "His sentiments could be uttered in any locality. His principles were broad and national, and could be proclaimed with equal freedom in New England or New Orleans—in the east or the west—the north or the south. Not so with his opponents. Their principles were too sectional to extend [south of] the Ohio, and were designed to array the North against the South."[422] To be accused of fomenting national strife was a grave charge. So at the beginning of his Peoria speech, Lincoln contended: "I also wish to be no less than National in all the positions I may take; and whenever I take ground which others have thought, or may think, narrow, sectional and dangerous to the Union, I hope to give a reason, which will appear sufficient, at least to some, why I think differently."[423]

National discord, Lincoln argued, had been provoked by Senator Douglas and his allies who had repealed the Missouri Compromise. It was their Kansas-Nebraska Act which had disturbed the nation's tranquility. "The councils [*sic*] of that genius seem to have prevailed, the Missouri compromise was repealed; and here we are, in the midst of a new slavery agitation, such, I think as we have never seen before. Who is responsible for this? Is it those who resist the measure; or those who, causelessly, brought it forward, and pressed it through, having reason to know, and, in fact, knowing it must and would be so resisted? It could not but be expected by its author, that it would be looked upon as a measure for the extension of slavery, aggravated by a gross breach of faith."[424]

It was also a "gross breach of faith" with the 1776 congressional act of union—the Declaration of Independence. For Lincoln this act was the foundation of American organic law. The Kansas-Nebraska Act was not only a direct challenge to the Declaration, but also to that national comity preserved by the Missouri Compromise. Kansas-Nebraska gratuitously violated the Declaration's inalienable right to liberty. The act was "an aggravation . . . of the only one thing which ever endangers the Union"—slavery. Lincoln invoked Franklin Pierce's 1853 comments wherein the new president had declared that the nation's peace and "repose is to suffer no shock during my official term if I have power to avert it, those who placed me here may be assured."[425] With this presidential hope, Lincoln agreed: "When [the Kansas-Nebraska Act] came upon us, all was peace and quiet. The nation was looking to the forming of new bonds of Union; and a long course of peace and prosperity seemed to lie before us. In the whole range of possibility, there scarcely appears to me to have been any thing, out of which the slavery agitation could have been revived, except the very project of repealing the Missouri compromise."[426]

Under these provocative circumstances, Lincoln analyzed the Union-threatening issue of slavery extension. Harry V. Jaffa emphasized his caution: "The meaning of prudence, in the context of the politics of the ante-bellum United States, may be gathered from this passage in Lincoln's Peoria speech of 1854: 'Much as I hate slavery, I would consent to the extension of it, rather than see the Union dissolved, just as I would consent to any GREAT evil, to avoid a GREATER one.'"[427] Still, Lincoln would not consent to the Missouri repeal, and he passionately contested the extension of slavery because "when I go to Union saving, I must believe, at least, that the means I employ has some adaptation to the end. To my mind, Nebraska has no such adaptation." Quoting Hamlet, he added: "It hath no relish of salvation in it."[428]

The stakes were immense. Douglas, Lincoln believed, had sown chaos. The nation might reap the whirlwind. Lincoln foresaw the coming violence in Kansas. Not only did the repeal of the Missouri Compromise disturb the national peace, Lincoln warned, but: "Through all this, bowie-knives and six-shooters are seen plainly enough; but never a glimpse of the ballot-box. And, really, what is to be the result of this? Each party WITHIN [Kansas], having numerous and determined backers WITH-OUT, is it not probable that the contest will come to blows and blood-shed? Could there be a more apt invention to bring about collision and violence, on the slavery question, than this Nebraska project is? I do not charge, or believe, that such was intended by Congress; but if they had literally formed a ring, and placed champions within it to fight out the controversy, the fight could be no more likely to come off, than it is. And if this fight should begin, is it likely to take a very peaceful, Union-saving turn? Will not the first drop of blood so shed, be the real knell of the Union?"[429] Lincoln would not be intimidated by slaveholder menaces. Neither did he believe that southerners would secede from the Union. Still, he had premonitions of secession and war.

Principle and Policy

Lincoln's essential antislavery policy can be traced from the Peoria court house in 1854 to Ford's Theatre in 1865. To save the Union from the threat of division was paramount. To save the Union on the basis of the

Declaration of Independence made the Union worth saving. To perpetuate the Union was the indispensable condition by which to maintain the promise of the Declaration of Independence throughout America. As a practical matter, only the Union under the Constitution could preserve the possibility of the "ultimate extinction" of slavery in America. If the Union were divided into sovereign slave and free nations, gradual action to end slavery in the whole of the Union would be foreclosed.

At Peoria Lincoln presented a stark moral conflict: "Slavery is founded in the selfishness of man's nature—opposition to it, [in] his love of justice. These principles are an eternal antagonism; and when brought into collision so fiercely, as slavery extension brings them, shocks, and throes, and convulsions must ceaselessly follow. Repeal the Missouri compromise—repeal all compromises—repeal the declaration of independence—repeal all past history, you still can not repeal human nature. It still will be the abundance of man's heart, that slavery extension is wrong; and out of the abundance of his heart, his mouth will continue to speak."[430] Hoping for this abundance, Lincoln dared to lead the antislavery coalition of Illinois to victory.

For Lincoln and much of the North, antislavery was not only a moral issue. Excluding slavery from the territories was also a pragmatic economic program. No slaves in the territories meant virtually no blacks—neither competition from rich plantation owners for farmland, nor competition from free blacks in the labor market. The supposed threat to racial integrity also persisted as a social subtext of economic policy. For a majority of Americans, restrictions on slavery were perceived to be in their economic and social self-interest. Slavery and ideas of racial inferiority were as old as the recorded history of the human species, as historian David Brion Davis has extensively documented. They reflected a social prejudice prevalent the world over in the nineteenth century and much of the twentieth.[431] Lincoln knew these prejudices from firsthand experience. Indeed, while rejecting the invidious racial pejoratives used by Douglas, he deployed certain rhetorical devices to show he understood the ambiguous economic and social arguments of the free-soil movement, even their racist overtones. Lincoln probably took as advanced an antislavery position as any Illinois politician could sustain and hope to be elected to statewide office. "Lincoln," wrote historian James Oliver Horton, "understood that in the volatile world of mid-nineteenth century politics too strong an antislavery stance was dangerous. To hold the support of his party and that of all but a small minority of Republican constituents, he must continually distinguish himself from [William Lloyd] Garrison and the true abolitionists."[432] Even leading antislavery Republicans such as Ohio Senator Benjamin F. Wade unashamedly voiced strong racist sentiments.[433]

Lincoln held fast to the belief that Illinoisans could understand the right to the fruit of one's labor. This human right trumped any property claim to a slave. As Lincoln scholar Gabor Boritt wrote, Lincoln's lifetime of devotion to "the right to rise" in a free economy strengthened the moral imperative.[434] A thorough reading of Lincoln's economic commentaries in the *Collected Works of Abraham Lincoln* suggests that no president has been more the master of the basic principles of economics than Lincoln. He saw that the doctrine of popular sovereignty when combined with free market theory and unrestricted property rights could, unregulated by moral and legal principle, rationalize slavery: "I particularly object to the NEW position which the avowed principle of this Nebraska law gives to slavery in the body politic. I object to it because it assumes that there CAN be a MORAL RIGHT in the enslaving of one man by another. . . . I object to it because the fathers of the republic eschewed, and rejected it. The argument of 'Necessity' was the only argument they ever admitted in favor of slavery . . ."[435]

Citing the arguments Thomas Jefferson made in drafting the Declaration of Independence, Lincoln said the country's Fathers "found the institution [slavery] existing among us, which they could not help; and they cast blame upon the British King for having permitted its introduction. BEFORE the constitution, they prohibited its introduction into the north-western Territory—the only country we owned, then free from it. At the framing and adoption of the constitution, they forbore to so much as mention the word 'slave' or 'slavery' in the whole instrument. In the provision for the recovery of fugitives, the slave is spoken of as a 'PERSON

HELD TO SERVICE OR LABOR.'"[436] Lincoln pressed the point by noting that " the African slave trade" was "spoken of [in the Constitution] as 'the migration or importation of such persons as any of the States NOW EXISTING, shall think proper to admit,' &c. These are the only provisions alluding to slavery. Thus, the thing is hid away, in the constitution, just as an afflicted man hides away a wen or a cancer, which he dares not cut out at once, lest he bleed to death; with the promise, nevertheless, that the cutting may begin at the end of a given time."[437]

Medical metaphors recur in Lincoln's writings. Lincoln's favorite metaphor for slavery was cancer. He would resurrect the comparison in 1860 while on a speaking tour through New England. On March 5 in Hartford, Connecticut, Lincoln talked of a recent train ride: "There was an old gentleman in the car, seated in front of us, whose coat collar was turned far down upon the shoulders. I saw directly that he had a large wen on his neck. I said to . . . [Kentucky Republican Cassius] Clay, [t]hat wen represents slavery, it bears the same relation to that man that slavery does to the country. That wen is a great evil; the man that bears it will say so. But he does not dare to cut it out. He bleeds to death if he does, directly. If he does *not* cut it out, it will shorten his life materially."[438] Lincoln's proposed policy was to cut the cancer carefully so as to save the patient. By sustaining the cancer, slaveholders would shorten the life of the Republic, but the abolitionist, who would promptly cut out slavery, might cause the Republic to bleed to death. As Lincoln would suggest in 1864, it is wrong to lose a life to save a limb, whereas it is prudent to give a limb to save a life.[439] By restricting slavery the nation could be made ready for the ultimate removal of the cancer, thereby assuring the permanence of the Union—and a healthy body politic grounded on the Declaration of Independence.

By almost every test of Lincoln's logic, Douglas failed in his arguments for Kansas-Nebraska—the "love of justice" yielding in Douglas to "the selfishness of man's nature."[440] Lincoln frequently reminded his audience of the senator's declared indifference to slavery. In the peroration of the Peoria speech, he directed his fire upon the speech Douglas had delivered thirteen days before at Springfield: "Senator Douglas

LINCOLN VERSUS DOUGLAS, 1854 AND 1858

☆ Freeport

Chicago ●

☆ Ottawa

☆ Galesburg

● Peoria

● Bloomington

● Urbana

☆ Quincy

● Winchester ● Springfield

☆ Charleston

☆ Alton

☆ Jonesboro

● Lincoln Speeches, 1854
☆ Lincoln-Douglas Debates, 1858

remarked, in substance, that he had always considered this government was made for the white people and not for the negroes. Why, in point of mere fact, I think so too. But in this remark of the Judge, there is a significance, which I think is the key to the great mistake (if there is any such mistake) which he has made in this Nebraska measure. It shows that the Judge has no very vivid impression that the negro is a human; and consequently has no idea that there can be any moral question in legislating about him. In his view, the question of whether a new country shall be slave or free, is a matter of utter indifference, as it is whether his neighbor shall plant his farm with tobacco, or stock it with horned cattle. Now, whether this view is right or wrong, it is very certain that the great mass of mankind take a totally different view. They consider slavery a great moral wrong; and their feelings against it, is not evanescent, but eternal. It lies at the very foundation of their sense of justice; and it cannot be trifled with. It is a great and durable element of popular action, and, I think, no statesman can safely disregard it."[441] Lincoln argued that no statesman could "safely disregard" a widespread public prejudice; nor could he ignore the sentiment that slavery was wrong. Although the history of mankind was punctuated by the persistence of slavery, Lincoln said he knew of no instance where an individual had volunteered to be a slave himself.

In the words of Allan Nevins, Douglas was "tone-deaf" to the moral aspect of slavery. Nevins noted also that Douglas was a tireless man of action who was born to improvise.[442] Further, Douglas was obsessed with American transcontinental development, subordinating other issues to this priority. Historian Eric Foner made a different case: "There is a common critique of Douglas's politics, expressed perhaps most persuasively by Allan Nevins, which argues that, as a man with no moral feelings about slavery, Douglas was incapable of recognizing that this moral issue affected millions of northern voters. This, in my opinion, is a serious misunderstanding of Douglas's politics. What he insisted was not that there was no moral question involved in slavery but that it was not the function of the politician to deal in moral judgments. To Lincoln's prediction that the nation could not exist half slave and half free, Douglas replied that it had so existed for seventy years and could continue to do so if northerners stopped trying to impose their own brand of morality upon the South."[443]

Professor Foner's argument comes from a distinguished American historian of the period. But does this imply that there might be equally legitimate moralities commanding the two regions? If there be two legitimate moralities on slavery, on what principle does one justify congressional legislation, such as ruling out the African slave trade for the whole nation? On what principles does one restrict slaveholders' access to slave imports? Power alone? Does might by itself make right? Lincoln insisted there was only one moral principle with respect to the humanity of the black slave—that "all men are created equal," even if throughout history different races had different civil rights at different times and in different places. At Cooper Union in February of 1860, Lincoln concluded that only "right makes might."[444]

The attitude of Senator Douglas toward the morality of slavery has been a disputed question. Historian Graham A. Peck has noted that "Nevins's forceful judgments have not been widely shared by Douglas scholars, who agree that Douglas personally opposed slavery. Acclaimed biographer Robert W. Johannsen has repeatedly claimed that Douglas was antislavery, and virtually all other Douglas scholars have come to the same conclusion, including Frank E. Stevens, George Fort Milton, Gerald Mortimer Capers, Damon Wells and Jean H. Baker. Moreover, distinguished Civil War historians David Potter and David Herbert Donald have seconded their individual judgments." Peck disagreed with this consensus, arguing that "despite the heavy preponderance of scholarly opinion, the case for Douglas's personal antislavery beliefs is not compelling."[445] After reviewing the four primary sources underlying the arguments that Douglas was antislavery, Peck concluded that "there is little reason for historians to credit Douglas with antislavery views." Peck wrote: "Douglas should in fact be considered moderately proslavery. By my definition, a proslavery figure must have expressed some kind of support for slavery, even if that person did not advocate slavery's expansion. Douglas's record meets this criterion. The available evidence indicates that he considered black slavery to be moral and just. Moreover, and not incidentally, he predicated his popular sovereignty policy on the right of whites to enslave blacks. . . . Douglas also defended slavery against antislavery attacks through his career. Not all northern Democrats made this choice."[446]

American legislators had voted to outlaw the international slave trade, affixing to it the penalty of death. The Declaration of Independence implied that to rob a person of his inalienable right to liberty is an objective wrong. Given the standing of the Declaration, in Lincoln's view, no American legislator should justify moral indifference to slavery. In the end, the fundamental dispute between Lincoln and Douglas at Peoria was more than an American contest. The universal claims of the Declaration of Independence and Lincoln's interpretation of the equality principle made of the Peoria debate a moment of global consequence. As historian David H. Donald wrote, Lincoln insisted "that the American struggle over slavery must be viewed in world perspective. He had always shown sympathy for liberal movements abroad, for instance, expressing sympathy with the efforts of the Hungarian revolutionary Louis Kossuth in his struggles against the Hapsburg monarchy, but only in recent years had he come to see the importance of America as an example to lovers of freedom everywhere."[447]

For Lincoln the legacy of the Founding Fathers had become inextricably linked to America's example in world affairs. At Peoria, Lincoln the private citizen, immersed in the politics of parochial central Illinois, insisted upon raising the sights of his countrymen: He warned that in the eyes of America's friends, slavery was "undermining the principles of progress, and fatally violating the noblest political system the world ever saw." Lincoln acknowledged: "This is not the taunt of enemies, but the warning of friends. Is it quite safe to disregard it—to despise it? Is there no danger to liberty itself, in discarding the earliest practice, and first precept of our ancient faith [that 'all men are created equal']? In our greedy chase to make profit of the negro, let us beware, lest we 'cancel and tear to pieces' even the white man's charter of freedom."[448]

Lincoln had first used that phrase—"white man's charter of freedom"—in his 1852 eulogy of Henry Clay. After acknowledging that Clay had owned slaves, Lincoln spoke of Clay's criticism of radical abolitionists

"who would shiver into fragments the Union of these States, tear to tatters
its now venerated constitution, and even burn the last copy of the Bible,
rather than slavery should continue a single hour. . . . But I would also, if
I could, array his name, opinions, and influence against the opposite
extreme—against a few but an increasing number of men who, for the
sake of perpetuating slavery, are beginning to assail and to ridicule the
white man's charter of freedom, the declaration that 'all men are created
free and equal.'" Lincoln quoted at length from a speech wherein Henry
Clay said:

> If they would repress all tendencies toward liberty, and ultimate
> emancipation, they must do more than put down the benevolent
> efforts of this society. They must go back to the era of our liberty
> and independence, and muzzle the cannon which thunders its
> annual joyous return. They must renew the slave trade with all its
> train of atrocities. They must suppress the workings of British phi-
> lanthropy, seeking to meliorate the condition of the unfortunate
> West Indian slave. They must arrest the career of South American
> deliverance from thraldom. They must blow out the moral lights
> around us, and extinguish that greatest torch of all which America
> presents to a benighted world—pointing the way to their rights,
> their liberties, and their happiness. And when they have achieved
> all those purposes their work will be yet incomplete. They must
> penetrate the human soul, and eradicate the light of reason and
> the love of liberty. Then, and not till then, when universal dark-
> ness and despair prevail, can you perpetuate slavery and repress all
> sympathy, and all humane, and benevolent efforts.[449]

Lincoln feared the Kansas-Nebraska Act might mean the extension
and perpetuation of slavery. So, he did not relent in his attack on the
repeal of the Missouri Compromise. "The Peoria speech spoke of 'the liberal party throughout the world': their representatives in America ('lovers
of liberty' appalled by a great moral wrong) expected their political leaders to address the ethical concerns that shaped public opinion," wrote

Richard J. Carwardine. "Implicit in much of Lincoln's subsequent course was a recognition that the moral constituencies brought into focus by the Nebraska Act needed effective and articulate political leadership. Whether through a continuing Whig party or the subsequent Republican coalition, Lincoln acted from 1854 to 1860 in a way that sought to clarify and publicize the lines dividing what he saw as the two fundamental moral constituencies in the nation, those who saw slavery as wrong, and those who either did not care or praised it as a positive good."[450]

The Peoria speech "was a masterpiece of simplicity, of lucidity. It showed the great jury lawyer at his best," wrote Lincoln biographer Nathaniel Wright Stephenson. "Its temper was as admirable as its logic; not a touch of anger nor of vituperation."[451] Undaunted by the Douglas race-baiting, Lincoln impeached the logic by which the senator denied the proslavery tendency of the Missouri repeal: "If a man will stand up and assert, and repeat, and re-assert, that two and two do not make four, I know nothing in the power of argument that can stop him. I think I can answer the Judge [Douglas] so long as he sticks to the premises; but when he flies from them, I can not work an argument into the consistency of a maternal gag, and actually close his mouth with it."[452]

Lincoln strenuously objected when Douglas argued that the slaveholder had an incontestable property right to take his slave into the territories. In 1857 Lincoln would be stunned when the Supreme Court in *Dred Scott v. Sanford* agreed with Douglas by holding unconstitutional the Missouri Compromise restriction on slavery. But in 1854 at Peoria he responded that "this argument strikes me as not a little remarkable in another particular—in its strong resemblance to the old argument for the 'Divine right of Kings.' By the latter, the King is to do just as he pleases with his white subjects, being responsible to God alone. By the former the white man is to do just as he pleases with his black slaves, being responsible to God alone. The two things are precisely alike; and it is but natural that they should find similar arguments to sustain them."[453] In the 1858 Lincoln-Douglas debates, Lincoln would repeat this argument.

At another point Lincoln warned Douglas that his interpretation of property law, as whatever legislators defined it to be, could justify the enslaving of whites. Lincoln biographer Albert J. Beveridge emphasized that Lincoln's tone at Peoria, unlike that of Douglas, was generally "unstained by abuse."[454] Lincoln ally Joseph Gillespie recalled that Lincoln was characterized by "his extreme fairness. He would rather disoblige a friend than do an act of injustice to a political opponent."[455] Don E. Fehrenbacher contended that Lincoln's case at Peoria was not only an "indictment of the Kansas-Nebraska policy and the consequent opening of federal territories to slavery. . . . When Lincoln eventually joined with men of more advanced beliefs in forming the Republican party, he adopted their name, but they accepted a platform that was closer to his way of thinking."[456]

Lincoln was fair-minded. In and out of the courtroom he could concede the minor points of opponents. On the main issues, however, he did not yield. Not a few contemporaries remarked on the even disposition which regulated his iron will. "He had not a particle of envy in his nature," wrote friend Joseph Gillespie. "He always admitted that Douglass [sic] was a wonderfully gr[e]at political leader and with a good cause to advocate he thought he would be invincible."[457] Lincoln was keenly aware not only of the intense public and private criticism of his own views, but he also observed the fearsome verbal assaults Douglas made on antislavery men. Regarding the slave plantation his sons inherited in Mississippi, Douglas received no quarter from free-soil men. Nor did opponents accommodate his advocacy of popular sovereignty, which they construed to embrace not only slavery, but also polygamy in Utah. If Congress could not prohibit slavery in the territories, then logically it could not prohibit polygamy either. "To these and similar charges [such as Douglas's slaveholding] Lincoln paid no heed. But other speakers did, and the anti-Douglas press was burdened with savage references to Douglas's advocacy of Catholicism, his ownership of slaves, his partiality to Mormonism," wrote Albert J. Beveridge. "All these things and the other influences described went to swell the current running heavily against him and the Democratic Party."[458]

These ferocious critics of the personal life of Douglas did what Lincoln forbore to do. Lincoln began his Peoria speech in a "respectful" tone his friends might have expected: "As I desire to present my own con-nected view of this subject, my remarks will not be, specifically, an answer to Judge Douglas; yet, as I proceed, the main points he has presented will arise, and will receive such respectful attention as I may be able to give them." He added: "I wish further to say, that I do not propose to question the patriotism, or to assail the motives of any man, or class or men; but rather to strictly confine myself to the naked merits of the question."[459]

On the merits, Douglas would disagree with Lincoln for seven more years.

"I particularly object to the NEW position which the avowed principle of this Nebraska law gives to slavery in the body politic. I object to it because it assumes that there CAN be MORAL RIGHT in the enslaving of one man by another. I object to it as a dangerous dalliance for a [free] people—a sad evidence that, feeling prosperity we forget right—that liberty, as a principle, we have ceased to revere. I object to it because the fathers of the republic eschewed, and rejected it."

ABRAHAM LINCOLN,
OCTOBER 16, 1854

V.

The Road from Peoria

Themy Kansas-Nebraska Act turned out to be a pyrrhic victory for Senator Douglas and President Pierce. "The President is and will be more than heretofore embarrassed by the inducements held out during the pendency of Nebraska," wrote Sidney Webster, secretary to President Pierce.[460] Hindsight, the comparative advantage of historians, leads to the same conclusion. David M. Potter wrote: "Few events have swung American history away from its charted course so suddenly or so sharply as the Kansas-Nebraska Act."[461] Many northerners were outraged by the repeal of the Missouri Compromise and punished the Democratic Party at the polls in 1854. But if one considers the contingency of every historical outcome, as well as the limits to what Douglas and sympathetic senators and congressmen knew in May of 1854, it was plausible for Douglas to believe that the Kansas-Nebraska Act could resolve the territorial issue without impeding his White House ambitions. Douglas could only guess at the future. If a weak-willed New England doughface like Franklin Pierce could win the presidency in 1852, then a western powerhouse like Stephen A. Douglas might stampede his way to the White House in 1856.

Old party coalitions did fracture under the stress of the struggles over slavery. New parties did not come together quickly. At the end of his Peoria speech, Lincoln acknowledged that there were differences among anti-Nebraska partisans. He said that Senator Douglas "reminds me that in my firm adherence to the constitutional rights of the slave States, I differ widely from others who are co-operating with me in opposing the Nebraska bill; and he says it is not quite fair to oppose him in this variety of ways. He should remember that he took us by surprise—astounded us—by this measure. . . . But we rose each fighting, grasping whatever he could first reach—a scythe—a pitchfork—a chopping axe, or a butcher's cleaver. We struck in the direction of the sound; and we are rapidly closing in upon him. He must not think to divert us from our purpose, by showing us that our drill, our dress, and our weapons, are not entirely perfect and uniform. When the storm shall be past, he shall find us still Americans; no less devoted to the continued Union and prosperity of the country than heretofore."[462]

The storm did not pass. It intensified. Douglas's dream legislation turned into a nightmare. David Potter wrote: "In an era of many futile measures, the Kansas-Nebraska Act approached the apex of futility. . . . Even at the level of a mere political combination, it did not fulfill anyone's expectations, for though it combined the votes of northerners who hoped to gain a transcontinental railroad and southerners who hoped or were induced to hope for the extension of slavery, the ensuing railroad bill failed to pass, and despite years of turmoil, Kansas never had slavery except in a nominal sense."[463] Historian John S. Wright noted that "Douglas had underestimated three important considerations" about the state of the nation: "(1) The weakness of the political parties . . . (2) The intensity of the undercurrent of sectional animosity beneath the surface of the purely political compromise of 1850; and (3) The swelling moral sentiment that had made its last uneasy compromise with slavery."[464] Rather than pacifying the country, the Kansas-Nebraska law awakened its sleeping passions. Historian Glyndon G. Van Deusen contended: "More than any other measure passed or threatened during the decade, this bill was responsible for the Civil War."[465] But in 1854, amidst the fog of political warfare, few could foresee the approaching conflagration.

Unintended Consequences of Kansas-Nebraska

A Civil War seemed improbable, but sectional divisions prompted by the legislation helped to kill the Whig Party—by further splitting northern and southern Whigs in Congress. They cooperated no longer, even on nonslavery legislation.[466] The effects were equally profound in the Democratic Party—as Whig Senator William H. Seward had suggested a few days before Pierce signed the legislation: "The great support of Slavery in the South has been its alliance with the Democratic party of the North. By means of that alliance it obtained paramount influence in this [Federal] Government about the year 1800 which, from that time to this, with but few and slight interruptions, it has maintained. While Democracy in the North has thus been supporting Slavery in the South, the people of the North have been learning more profoundly the principles of republicanism and of free government."[467] By September 1854, Ohio Democrat Salmon P. Chase was writing Massachusetts Senator Charles Sumner: "I am now without a party."[468] More than two thirds of Democratic congressional seats in northern states switched hands in the elections at the end of 1854.[469] Douglas, a consummate party loyalist, had authored the legislation which unwittingly broke the antebellum Democratic Party.

Senator Seward spoke plainly of the great philosophical divide in Congress. "Slavery and Freedom are antagonistical elements in this country," observed Seward in his speech on the Senate floor just before the bill's final passage. "The founders of the Constitution framed it with a knowledge of that antagonism, and suffered it to continue, that it might work out its own ends. There is a commercial antagonism, an irreconcilable one, between the systems of free labor and slave labor. They have been at war with each other ever since the Government was established, and that war is to continue forever. The contest, when it ripens between these two antagonistic elements, is to be settled somewhere; it is to be settled in the seat of central power, in the Federal Legislature. The Constitution makes it the duty of the central Government to determine questions as often as they shall arise in favor of one or the other party, and refers the decision of them to the majority of the votes in the two Houses of Congress. It will come back here, then, in spite of all the efforts to escape from it."[470] As Seward and Lincoln understood the Constitution and legislative precedents, the issue between slave labor and free labor in the territories could not be separated from the constitutional authority of Congress to resolve it.

A revolution in American politics began in 1854. "The Kansas-Nebraska Act wrought the greatest party realignment in United States history. It shattered party loyalties in the North, fostered a solid South, and rent the nation," wrote historian James A. Rawley.[471] As the transition from the Federalist to the Jeffersonian party became known as the "Revolution of 1800," so the party revolution of 1854 would soon submerge the Whigs in the anti-Nebraska coalition, which became the victorious Republican Party in 1860. The crisis over the extension of slavery proved a disaster for the Democratic Party. "Never before have the democracy of Illinois been so completely vanquished," declared the *Joliet Signal* after the 1854 election.[472] Although the U.S. Senate remained under Democratic control, Democrats became a minority in the U.S. House of Representatives by the end of 1855.[473] Among the victims of the Kansas-Nebraska Act was one of its architects, Missouri Senator David Rice Atchison. Potter wrote that "it quickly became evident that Kansas-Nebraska had destroyed the ascendancy of the Democratic party in the free states and had also upset the bisectional balance within the Democratic party."[474] Lincoln biographer Kenneth J. Winkle summed up the shift: "In 1852, Whigs had won only two northern states. In 1854, the Anti-Nebraska coalition lost only two."[475] The Whig Party had failed to seize the occasion to lead a coalition opposed to slavery extension. Seward himself did not immediately understand the opportunity.[476] Michael F. Holt noted that "Seward was especially adamant in spurning Free-Soilers' advances and insisting that the northern Whig Party was the only antislavery party Northerners needed." Shrewd as Seward was, he miscalculated the rise of the new antislavery coalition.

Douglas disclaimed responsibility for the disaster. He denied that the cause of the Democrats' defeat was Kansas-Nebraska—blaming instead the American Party and the anti-immigration "Know-Nothing" movement.[477] In fact Douglas had sought to exploit Know-Nothingism, at first believing it to be a foil rather than a hindrance to Democratic victory. He saw in its anti-immigration policy a millstone to be hung around the necks of his anti-Nebraska opponents. Opposition to Know-Nothings could rally the base of the Democratic Party, especially among Irish and German Catholic immigrants. A month before the Peoria debate, Douglas wrote to the editor of the *Daily Chicago Times*: "We will gain more votes than we will lose on Nebraska and No Nothingism. You ought to publish the exposition of No Nothingism . . . and charge into them every day boldly and disputedly. That will bring the Germans and all other foreigners and Catholics to our side."[478]

The results of the 1854 elections in Illinois reflected the Douglas tactics. Many German-Americans were reluctant to vote for candidates alleged to have Know-Nothing support. The German-American votes narrowed the victory margin of anti-Nebraska Democrat Lyman Trumbull, and they contributed to a loss by another congressional candidate for whom Lincoln campaigned.[479] But historian Michael F. Holt denied "that the Kansas-Nebraska Act alone caused the Democratic defections and the subsequent realignment of voters between 1854 and 1856. . . . By the middle of that decade, the Democratic party no longer answered the needs of many northern voters; indeed, it seemed to defend the interests of groups those voters could not tolerate."[480] Working men in the North needed a party which would give preference to the economic interests of free labor, not to slave masters and slave labor in the South. For non-Catholic workers, the Know-Nothing movement, both nativist and anti-slavery, was an option because it stood against economic competition from immigrants and slaves. Many northern Protestant workers were no longer willing to defer to the interests of plantation owners in the South and their allies in the North.[481] Indeed, many Know-Nothings were not only antislavery, but also antiblack. In addition, northern Democrats increasingly objected to domination of the national party and the government by a minority of southern advocates and sympathizers of slavery.

The political irony of Kansas-Nebraska is inescapable. Rather than reinforcing two generations of Democratic ascendancy under the doctrine of popular sovereignty, Douglas had unleashed contending forces that would dominate the politics of the country for the next seventy-five years. From this contest issued a new majority party, the Republican Party, which would displace the antebellum party of Jefferson and Jackson, the so-called "democracy." Intended to resolve a territorial issue, passage of Kansas-Nebraska gave the slavery issue a new urgency. The desire for a transcontinental railroad was sidetracked by the threat of slavery extension into the territories.[482] The Kansas-Nebraska Act would lead to unexpected consequences. Senator Chase confided such a sentiment to Senator Sumner after the Senate vote in 1854: "They celebrate a present victory, but the echoes they awake will never rest till slavery itself shall die."[483]

In Illinois some longtime Democratic allies broke from Douglas. The minority Whigs, lacking the populist appeal of Jackson's party, became even weaker. As the Whig and Democratic parties split apart, the established and emerging leaders were compelled to embrace or reject the extension of slavery. Some old line Whigs, affronted by the antislavery rhetoric of Lincoln and his colleagues, left their party to join Douglas and his Democrats. Other Whigs defected to make coalitions with Know-Nothings and temperance advocates. The largest Whig faction ultimately moved into the new Republican Party. In Illinois the Republican Party was slow to come together, but in Michigan and Wisconsin Republicans began organizing in February 1854.[484]

In January 1854, few might have plausibly predicted defeat either for the Democrats or for Douglas. But by 1855, the consequences of Kansas-Nebraska had diminished Douglas and his party. Don E. Fehrenbacher wrote that by 1855 Douglas himself "realized that the midterm election results virtually killed his own presidential ambitions for 1856. Nevertheless, he continued to nurture hopes of one day heading a national ticket with the help of southern votes."[485] The presidential opening for the ambitious Douglas was closing in the South as well as in the North.

Moreover, some of the political and economic objectives sought by Douglas were now unattainable. In their comprehensive work on *The Impending Crisis*, historian David M. Potter, in collaboration with Don E. Fehrenbacher, wrote that "the organization of two new territories on the Northern Plains accomplished nothing that anyone intended and a great deal that no one intended. It did not lead on to the railroad which was Douglas's objective, or to the extension of slavery which was the southerners' objective. . . . And it undermined the structure of the Democratic party, which was the strongest national organization that still sustained the Union."[486] Potter emphasized the devastating impact on Douglas, whose transcontinental railroad bill failed to win approval in the House of Representatives although it passed the Senate: "Thus the Kansas-Nebraska Act did not lead to the Pacific Railroad bill which was its intended sequel, but it did lead to a deeply intensified renewal of the slavery contest, which was not intended."[487]

Election Results and Realignment in Illinois

Unwittingly, Kansas-Nebraska legislation created a major statewide rival to the political ambitions of Stephen A. Douglas in Illinois. The politics of the state were geographically divided, not unlike those of the Union as a whole; and they were as complicated as the politics of any other state. Northern Illinois was substantially antislavery. Southern Illinois was sympathetic to slavery. Central Illinois included representatives of both attitudes. In this context, the Douglas bill led to a split in the Democratic Party, the disintegration of the Whigs, the growth of the Know-Nothings, the persistence of the temperance movement, and the gradual development of a new Republican coalition. At the end of 1854, the anti-Nebraska coalition triumphed at the Illinois polls—virtually sweeping the northern part of the state where the Republican fusion effort was strongest. Senator Douglas had accepted the challenge as a referendum on Kansas-Nebraska. He fought his opponents at every turn. Senator James Shields acknowledged that it was a "test . . . of Douglas to make men acknowledge that the act was all right."[488] Douglas failed this test.

In the 1854 congressional elections, pro-Douglas Democrats won only four of the nine House seats in Illinois. The winners included Douglas ally William A. Richardson (who defeated Archibald Williams for whom Lincoln had campaigned in late October), James Cameron Allen (who narrowly defeated William R. Archer, who had Know-Nothing support), and Samuel Scott Marshall (who was virtually unopposed). Know-Nothings and abolitionists helped to reelect Whig Jesse O. Norton and to elect James Knox from the Peoria district where the People's Party was the anti-Nebraska opposition to the Democrats. Congressman Elihu B. Washburne, an old line Whig friend of Lincoln, won reelection despite an opposing Republican fusion effort in the Rockford-Galena district.

Anti-Nebraska Democrat Assemblyman James H. Woodworth replaced Congressman "Long John" Wentworth, a Chicago Democrat whose anti-Nebraska credentials were deemed insufficiently militant in Chicago. Wentworth did not seek reelection in a four-way race. Other winning congressmen included anti-Nebraska Democrat Lyman Trumbull, who defeated a pro-Douglas Democrat in the Alton area. Trumbull attracted Whig and German support after Whig Joseph Gillespie withdrew. Among the losers in central Illinois was Congressman Richard Yates for whom Lincoln had campaigned. Yates was defeated by Douglas ally Thomas L. Harris in a campaign in which temperance, slavery, and Utah polygamy each played a part. Yates "was doubtless injured," noted Arthur Charles Cole, "by the participation of Ichabod Codding in the canvass and the charge that he [Yates] was the candidate of the abolitionists. Harris showed great confidence in his support of the principle of popular sovereignty; he permitted himself to be placed on record as willing on this principle to admit a state with a constitution recognizing and permitting polygamy."[489] In Lincoln's home district in central Illinois, fear of abolitionism proved stronger than fear of slavery and polygamy. Near the end of Lincoln's sole term in Congress, the Whigs had lost this district to Harris in 1848. Lincoln was gratified when Yates retook the seat in 1850, but its loss in 1854 suggested the hard road ahead for Lincoln and the free-soil coalition in Illinois.

By a slim margin, Democrats allied with Douglas lost control of the Illinois legislature—a body that Douglas had previously used as a pliant tool.[490] Combative as usual, he sustained the pretense that he was neither defeated nor downcast. Speaking at a testimonial dinner in Chicago on November 9 he declared himself committed to the principle of popular sovereignty: "That the people of each State of this Union, and each Territory, with the view to its admission into the Union, have the right and ought to be permitted to enjoy its exercise, to form and regulate their domestic institutions, and internal matters in their own way, subject only to the Constitution."[491] Douglas maintained that the doctrine of popular sovereignty rightfully encompassed both the Constitution and the slavery issue. For Lincoln, however, "[s]ubject only to the constitution" implied recognition of the fundamental basis of the constitution—namely the Declaration of Independence, its equality principle, and thus the humanity of the Negro. "Subject only to the constitution" meant for Lincoln the constitutional authority of Congress to prohibit slavery in the territories.

At the end of 1854, it was a subdued Douglas who returned to Washington for the next session of Congress. "The fierce opposition he had encountered and the rebuke administered to his leadership in the legislative elections had dealt a sobering blow to his confidence," wrote Douglas biographer Robert W. Johannsen. "His conviction that his position was right, however, remained unshaken. The onslaughts against him had aroused an uncompromising defense of his past actions which seemed to leave little room for flexibility and pragmatic adjustment."[492]

The 1854–1855 Senate Campaign

During his 1854 grassroots campaign against Kansas-Nebraska, Lincoln became something of a folk hero as well as a key anti-Nebraska leader in Illinois. He had shed the aristocratic stigma fixed upon him in the 1840s because of his marriage to a well-born Kentuckian and his involvement in the Whig elite of Springfield. Gradually, his bootstrap success—a frontier boy who made good—became the story. "Wherever Lincoln had appeared before or wherever he spoke thereafter," wrote Albert J. Beveridge, "such tales of his humble origin, his early hardships and struggles, and his rise in spite of all drawbacks, were industriously told. In this fashion, as well as by his manner and talk, the feeling steadily grew that Lincoln was indeed a man of the people—a poor boy who had surmounted the hardest and highest obstacles, a typical American whose career showed what any hard working and right living young man of natural talent, could do for himself."[493] After the November 1854 election in Illinois Lincoln saw what he had surely hoped for—a state legislature that favored an anti-Nebraska candidate for the Senate. Lincoln pressed his campaign for the U.S. Senate. But he had two problems. He was still a Whig. Worse, he had just been elected to the state legislature, membership in which barred him under the state constitution in Illinois from election to the U.S. Senate. He solved this problem by resigning the legislative seat. The Whig issue was not so easily resolved.

Like Lincoln, Democrat Lyman Trumbull was a gifted lawyer who had been largely out of politics for several years. Like Lincoln, he had been drawn back into the political arena by the Kansas-Nebraska legislation.[494] But the transition was not easy for the phlegmatic Trumbull, whose wife was a close friend of Mary Todd Lincoln. Trumbull had been seriously ill during the winter and spring of 1854. "You were perhaps surprised to learn that I had gone into politics again," Trumbull wrote his brother. "I am surprised at myself and but for the slavery question . . . I should not have taken any active part in recent elections."[495] Trumbull was nevertheless a potent figure in central Illinois. Compared to Lincoln, Trumbull had two major political advantages in 1854: First, his election to Congress did not bar him from consideration for the Senate seat. Second, he was an articulate and respected Democrat. If combined, Douglas Democrats and anti-Nebraska Democrats would control the state legislature.

Trumbull himself was not optimistic about the prospects for opponents of Douglas: "The Anti-Nebraska men will have a majority in the Legislature, but can they be brought to act together, that is the important question. . . . How this is to be brought about I scarcely know. If all Anti-Nebraska men could be fully persuaded as I am, that we are to receive no quarter from Douglas and his friends, a common sense of danger, would, I think, bring us to act in concert; but some of those who agree with us in principle and ought to act openly with us, are I fear inclined to cooperate with the Nebraska men. . . ." Nor was Trumbull sanguine about his own chances to win the Senate seat held by Shields: "As for the Senate I am for any good Anti-Nebraska Democrat. There are many reasons why I wish to see Shields defeated and I would be for almost any man as against him. My own position, having just been elected to the lower House, is such that I think it would be exceedingly impolitic for me to think of being a candidate. It would not do for me to be a candidate for every office in the land. That very fact, if nothing else would defeat me; but I am willing to do all that in me lies in an honorable way to elect an Anti-Nebraska Democrat in Shields place and I will not be particular about the man. How will Koerner do?"[496] As a German-American, Lieutenant Governor Gustave Koerner would not appeal to Whigs and Know-Nothings with anti-immigrant sympathies. Thus, in Trumbull's suggestion of Koerner can be detected his own subtle ambition for the Senate seat.

Senator Shields had a related problem. His Irish birth was an advantage in the Democratic Party but, given the growing nativist sentiment, a hindrance outside it.[497] Senator Douglas saw the problem and tried to demonize Know-Nothings as the cause of Shields's vulnerability. Douglas wrote editor Charles H. Lanphier: "At all events our friends should stand by Shields and throw the responsibility on the Whigs of beating him *because he was born in Ireland.* The Nebraska fight is over, and Know Nothingism has taken its place as the chief issue in the future."[498] The evidence suggests that there was plausibility in Douglas's assertion that the American Party was rising and that nativism might be an effective target for Douglas allies. Nativism had also been an issue in the fall campaign. Knowing a useful devil when he saw one, Douglas flayed the American Party whenever he could. In his Peoria speech, Douglas had argued that the Know-Nothing movement was "anti-republican and subversive of the principles of the Constitution. He referred briefly to the effect which this spirit of intolerance would have exerted if it had been adopted in the early history of our country."[499] Douglas's attitude toward the Know-Nothings was cynical, according to historians Stephen Hansen and Paul Nygaard. They wrote that Douglas actually saw Know-Nothings as a wedge to split the anti-Nebraska coalition. He even provided the nativists with financial assistance after 1854. In his 1858 Senate campaign against Lincoln, Douglas would court these nativist votes—votes that helped him narrowly win that election.[500]

Senator Shields understood that Kansas-Nebraska, not Know-Nothingism, was the principal issue in the state. There was anti-Irish prejudice in Illinois, but it was not the central factor in the fall election, nor would it determine the state legislative vote for Shields's Senate seat in February 1855. Shields saw anti-Douglas, rather than anti-Irish, sentiment at work. He wrote Charles H. Lanphier that Douglas's enemies "don't care two pence about Nebraska. But Douglass [*sic*] they have sworn to destroy. My election will help him so they have already made an arrangement with" Lincoln.[501] Shields was probably right about the relative unimportance of his place of birth compared to the intense enmity toward Douglas. Lyman Trumbull wrote anti-Nebraska Democrat John M. Palmer that pro-Douglas Democrats were so angry with Douglas's free-soil opponents that "[t]hey would, some of them, sooner vote for a Whig than an Anti-Nebraska Democrat. There is no making terms or getting along in harmony with such men."[502]

Just before the November election, Douglas had visited Palmer and urged him to attend a Democratic caucus at which all participants would pledge themselves to vote for the party's consensus candidate. When Palmer refused, Douglas responded: "You may join the abolitionists if you choose to do so, but, if you do, there are enough patriotic Whigs to take your place and elect Shields." Palmer was enraged: "So help me God, I'll never vote for Shields. You know how warmly I have supported you. . . . From this time forward, I'll fight you and will never speak to you until you are beaten and lose your power to make and unmake men."[503] Palmer himself had doubts about fellow Democrat Trumbull's prospects, writing his wife in late January 1855 "that I think Governor [Joel] Matteson will be elected senator. The chances are that both whigs and the democracy will unite on him. He is anti-slavery in all his antecedents and is a decided anti-Douglas man, which is the real point involved in the controversy. The great end we have in view is the reorganization of the Democratic Party on the basis of personal independence of its members. Shields goes now, which will be a warning that Douglas cannot disregard. He will see the hand-writing on the wall."[504] But, the handwriting was not so clear. There were plenty of ambitious, would-be senators in Illinois.[505] Congressman Jesse O. Norton, who supported Lincoln, wrote him from Washington: "I am satisfied that there are men, *in our own ranks, waiting & longing for you to be set aside,* for the chance it may give *them* of an election."[506] Among those who were interested was outgoing Congressman Yates, who wrote Lincoln: "In answer to such persons as have written to me on the subject of my being a candidate I have replied that in the event you could not succeed I should like to have my name presented—and in such an event I hope I should have your aid—"[507]

Lincoln's candidacy encountered trouble on several fronts—among the old line Douglas Democrats on one hand, and some antislavery

Republicans on the other. For both groups, he was too much a Whig.[508] Undaunted, Lincoln began to campaign for the Senate seat promptly after the November 1854 elections—simultaneously resigning the Illinois legislative post to which he had been elected. Thinking his vacated seat secure for an anti-Nebraska successor, Lincoln concentrated on the U.S. Senate race, neglecting the special election to fill his seat. Democrats pretended to ignore the race. Surprising the Whigs with a strong showing on a rainy election day, the Democrats captured Lincoln's legislative seat for use in the forthcoming U.S. Senate election. (Until a constitutional amendment for the direct election of senators was ratified in 1913, federal senators were chosen by state legislatures.) Politicking for the Senate seat accelerated in late January 1855 after state legislators struggled into Springfield through unrelenting snowstorms. "All are unable to get here," Palmer wrote his wife. "Such a state of things as now exists never was known before in my recollection."[509]

When in February 1855 the state legislature got down to work on the Senate seat, State Representative Stephen T. Logan nominated Lincoln, his former law partner, while John M. Palmer nominated Trumbull. With seventy-five members of the House and twenty-five members of the Senate voting for the office, the votes of fifty-one state legislators would reelect Shields or elect his successor. In the first vote on February 8, Lincoln led Shields, 44–41. Just five votes went for Trumbull and eight more were scattered among minor candidates. Shields biographer Callan wrote that the incumbent senator "was not prepared to succumb without a struggle. Like a tired boxer clinging to the ropes, he fought tooth and nail for his political life, button-holing one delegate after another, seeking their hearts, their heads and their help."[510]

After nine ballots in the legislature Lincoln concluded he could not win. He believed the options were anti-Nebraska Democrat Trumbull or Democratic Governor Joel A. Matteson, whose stand on Kansas-Nebraska was ambiguous and whose maneuvering was duplicitous. Ominously on the ninth ballot, Matteson had received forty-seven votes, Trumbull thirty-five votes and Lincoln only fifteen. Lincoln then decided the contest. He directed his supporters to vote for the antislavery Trumbull, who defeated Matteson, 51–47. Arthur Charles Cole noted that "Matteson, indeed, might well have been elected had it not been that Lieutenant Governor

Koerner, a foreigner and an anti-Nebraskaite, would then have been automatically promoted to the gubernatorial chair."[511]

Only reluctantly did Stephen T. Logan announce Lincoln's withdrawal: "Lincoln's friends were inconsolable," historian Doris Kearns Goodwin wrote, "believing that this was 'perhaps his last chance for that high position.' Logan put his hands over his face and began to cry, while [David] Davis stormily announced that had he been in Lincoln's situation, 'he never would have consented to the 47 men being controlled by the 5.'"[512] But Lincoln proved the better strategist. Of the five Democrats who initially supported Trumbull, several became important in the future Republican Party of Illinois: State Senators Burton C. Cook of Ottawa, John M. Palmer of Carlinville, and Norman B. Judd of Chicago. Another future Republican leader was Lieutenant Governor Koerner. All would be in Chicago at the 1860 Republican presidential convention to support the nomination of Abraham Lincoln.

Lincoln was disappointed by the senatorial vote, but the Democrats were shocked. Pro-Douglas Democrats "were more disappointed by it than they would have been by the election of Lincoln," wrote Horace White. The Douglas majority considered anti-slavery "Trumbull as an arch traitor. That he and his fellow traitors, Palmer, Judd and Cook should have carried off the great prize was an unexpected and most bitter pill, but they did not know how bitter it was until Trumbull took his seat in the Senate and opened fire on the Nebraska iniquity."[513] After the vote a forthright Lincoln wrote Congressman Jesse O. Norton: "It is not true, as might appear by the first ballot, that Trumbull had only five friends who preferred him to me. I know the business of all the men tolerably well, and my opinion is, that if the 51 who elected him, were compelled to a naked expression of preference between him and me, he would . . . at the outside, have 16 and I would have the remainder. And this again would depend substantially upon the fact that his 16 came from the old democratic ranks & the remainder from the whigs."[514]

Lincoln's equanimity in defeat was exemplified in his letter to Congressman Elihu B. Washburne: "I could have headed off every combination and been elected, had it not been for Matteson's double game—and his defeat, now gives me more pleasure than my own gives me pain. On the whole, it is perhaps as well for our general cause that Trumbull is elected. The Neb. men confess that they hate it worse than anything that could have happened. It is a great consolation to see them worse whipped than I am. I tell them it is their own fault—that they had abundant opportunity to choose between him & me, which they declined, and instead forced it on me to decide between him [Trumbull] & Matteson."[515] Lincoln dispassionately anchored his analysis in the facts, the circumstances, and the importance of his antislavery policy. He wrote the father of one Illinois legislator: "My larger number of friends had to surrender to Trumbull's smaller, in order to prevent the election of Matteson, which would have been a Douglas victory. I started with 44 votes & T. with 5. It was rather hard for the 44 to have to surrender to the 5—and a less good humored man than I, perhaps would not have consented to it—and it would not have been done without my consent. I could not, however, let the whole political result go to ruin, on a point merely personal to myself."[516]

For Lincoln the defeat of Kansas-Nebraska was primary. Years later, he wrote: "The election of Judge Trumbull strongly tended to sustain and preserve the position of that portion of the Democrats who condemned the repeal of the Missouri compromise, and left them in a position of joining with us in forming the Republican party."[517] In early 1855 Lincoln himself was not quite ready for the demise of the Whig Party. Still, he had helped to organize a winning coalition in Illinois to oppose Douglas and the extension of slavery. His immediate political goal, the Senate, had been lost, but his leadership of a free-soil coalition in Illinois had been recognized. As historian Robert Pierce Forbes noted, the "most important long-term effect of the Kansas-Nebraska Act . . . may have been to prompt Lincoln's return to politics."[518]

In the process, Lincoln gradually abandoned his Whig partisanship. Anti-Nebraska Democrat Lyman Trumbull was worthy of Lincoln's trust and respect. Trumbull biographer Mark M. Krug wrote that "in February of 1855 many people in Illinois considered Trumbull a greater man and a more effective politician than Abraham Lincoln. There was a widespread feeling that Trumbull, as a Democrat, would be able to fight it out with Douglas in the Senate more effectively than would the Whig Lincoln."[519] As Gustave Koerner observed: "No Democrat, I knew very well from my intimate knowledge of Trumbull's peculiar ability, could cope with Douglas better than he. He was as untiring and indefatigable in argument as Douglas; indeed no one could wear him out. While he could not perhaps present his views as strongly and impressively as Douglas, he was a master in discovering every weak point in the aims of his antagonist and never failed to hit it."[520] Trumbull, hitherto a Democrat without a national following, had been catapulted into the Senate limelight. Four years later, Douglas argued that Trumbull and Lincoln had struck an unholy alliance in 1854 in which Trumbull had pledged his support to Lincoln against Douglas in 1858 in exchange for Lincoln's votes in 1854. Douglas was wrong. There had been no bargain—as the lasting enmity of Mary Lincoln to her longtime friend and bridesmaid, Julia Jayne Trumbull, would suggest. Mary would never forgive or forget the election of Lyman Trumbull in 1855. But she could not foreclose a political alliance between her prudent husband and Trumbull.

Even as he aimed for the Senate seat, Lincoln did not give up his larger goal, the repudiation of Douglas's popular sovereignty and a victory for free-soil principles. Lincoln would ultimately prove that a disciplined, single-issue campaign, focused entirely on the restriction of slavery, could prevail in the multi-issue world of conventional American politics.[521] But neither did Shields give up after defeat; he subsequently represented two other states (Minnesota and briefly Missouri) in the U.S. Senate—demonstrating that political mobility in America was as robust as social and economic mobility. The fate of Senator Douglas was more tortured. The Kansas-Nebraska Act, "intended to smooth a presidentially ambitious Northerner's troubled courting of [the South], was to destroy the suitor's political fortunes," wrote historian David Grimsted.[522] Douglas did not attain his ambition to lead the Democratic Party in 1856, but he would become the presidential nominee of its northern wing in 1860.

Having been described during his one term in Congress as the "lone whig star" of Illinois, Lincoln saw his light fading in 1855.[523] Others in Washington believed his star on the rise. "You would feel flattered at the great interest that is felt for you here by all who know you, either by reputation or personally," Congressman Elihu Washburne had written Lincoln from the nation's capital a few weeks before the Senate election in Febru-

Pro-Nebraska Leaders in Illinois

Charles H. Lanphier

Courtesy of the Abraham Lincoln Presidential Library, reference number I-956

William A. Richardson

The Gilder Lehrman Collection, courtesy of the Gilder Lehrman Institute of American History, on deposit at the New-York Historical Society, New York, reference number GLC 5597.26

Thomas L. Harris

Courtesy of the Abraham Lincoln Presidential Library, reference number I-9424

James Shields

The Gilder Lehrman Collection, courtesy of the Gilder Lehrman Institute of American History, on deposit at the New-York Historical Society, New York, reference number GLC 5111.02.0726

ary 1855. Senator Trumbull wrote Lincoln from Washington, confirming their alliance and soliciting his views: "I shall be happy to hear from you frequently, & particularly to know your views as to the best means of meeting and overwhelming the Slavery expansionists in Illinois-"[524] Trumbull well appreciated Lincoln's energy and leadership of the antislavery cause in Illinois. Early in 1855, Lincoln had drafted a farsighted resolution for the Illinois State General Assembly, condemning the Kansas-Nebraska Act. The resolution was tantamount to a campaign platform for the growing antislavery coalition.

> Resolved by the General Assembly of the State of Illinois, that our Senators in Congress be instructed and, our Representatives requested, to use their best endeavors to procure the repeal of the above recited parts of said Act to organize the Territories of Nebraska and Kansas—
>
> Resolved further, that our said Senators be instructed, and our said Representatives requested; to procure the revival and re-enactment, of the eighth section of the act preparatory to the admission of Missouri into the Union, approved March sixth, eighteen hundred and twenty—
>
> Resolved further, that they use their utmost endeavors to prevent the said Ter[r]itories of Nebraska and Kansas, or either of them, or any part of either of them, ever coming into this Union as a Slave-state or states—
>
> Resolved further, that they use their utmost constitutional endeavors to prevent Slavery ever being established in any county or place, where it does not now legally exist—[525]

This resolution would inspire the Republican platform of 1860 when Abraham Lincoln would be its presidential candidate. Uncompromising opposition to any extension of slavery had become the single issue upon which turned the axis of the Republican Party. From Peoria to the presidency, antislavery policy became the hallmark of Lincoln's strategy for the Republican Party. Historian Reinhard H. Luthin observed that there was a hidden blessing in Lincoln's failure to win the Senate election—"not being a public servant who had to cater to the tastes of a fickle constituency, he could better engage in independent thought on slavery."[526]

Realignment and the Republican Party

The national realignment of political parties was underway. The American people and their parties were drawn toward the opposing poles of the slavery question.[527] The Whig Party in the South expired quickly. Georgia Whig Alexander H. Stephens, given his role in the House passage of the Kansas-Nebraska bill, rang the party's death knell. Many Whigs in the North moved to the nativist Know-Nothing movement, or the Republican Party. Most Whigs in the South gravitated to the Democratic Party. This process had gained momentum after the 1848 election of President Zachary Taylor, a slaveholder whom Southern Whigs found insufficiently sympathetic to their section's interests.[528]

Still, the Whig Party in the North lingered on life support. Kansas-Nebraska was only one cause of a declining Whig Party. Michael F. Holt wrote that "once Whigs focused on developments within the states, rather than those in Washington during the first half of 1854, they collided with a burgeoning Know Nothing movement that abruptly shattered all calculations based on the potential impact of 'this Nebraska business' and that threatened, far more seriously than did the entreaties from Free Soilers for a new antislavery organization, to disembowel the Whig party."[529] In some northern states, slavery seemed less of a threat to citizens than did the tide of European immigrants who appeared around them as neighbors and economic competitors. American politics was and still is local.

The American Party filled part of the vacuum left by Whig decay. Anti-Nebraska forces in 1854 coalesced elsewhere in new Republican organizations, but Illinois moved more slowly than other northern states.[530] Know-Nothingism appealed to many Whigs in Illinois, where Irish-American laborers became a bulwark of the Democratic Party. Being anti-immigrant was more than prejudice. It was also an attempt at economic and political self-preservation.[531] Within two years, however, nativism would peak as leaders of the American Party softened its anti-immigrant identity and thus its sectarian appeal. Gradually, antislavery "Know-Nothings" would be absorbed by the rising Republican Party. The temperance movement had already peaked in 1846—when Maine prohibited the sale of liquor. Eventually, most temperance sympathizers found their way to the Republican Party. The abstemious Lincoln was among them. More importantly, anti-Nebraska Democrats embraced the Republican fusion effort. Lyman Trumbull of Illinois, Salmon P. Chase of Ohio, Gideon Welles of Connecticut, Hannibal Hamlin of Maine, and Montgomery Blair of Maryland would become leaders of the Republican Party and key partners of President Lincoln during the Civil War. Some former Democrats, such as free-soiler Salmon P. Chase, were more antislavery than their Whig counterparts. Still, most new Republicans were not abolitionists, even though many were vigorously antislavery.[532]

The leadership of the antislavery political movement slowly shifted to "practical politicians" like Lincoln.[533] The abolitionist movement had always been divided between those who would not compromise to gain modest ground for the antislavery cause, and those who would. Illinois abolitionists, including Owen Lovejoy, were ready to cooperate with practical antislavery politicians like Abraham Lincoln—as Lovejoy had already demonstrated in organizing the Republican convention at Springfield in early October 1854. Republicans did emerge in Illinois—but mostly in the northern part of the state. Lincoln himself, naturally conservative, was slow to join this new movement—inclined to identify himself as an old line Whig. "I think I am a whig; but others say there are no whigs, and that I am an abolitionist," Lincoln wrote to Joshua F. Speed in August 1855.

"I am not a Know-Nothing," he added. "That is certain. How could I be? How can any one who abhors the oppression of negroes, be in favor of degrading classes of white people? Our progress in degeneracy appears to me to be pretty rapid." Then, he rephrased a line from his Peoria speech: "As a nation, we began by declaring that 'all men are created equal.' When the Know-Nothings get control, it will read 'all men are created equal, except negroes, *and foreigners, and catholics.*' When it comes to this I should prefer emigrating to some country where they make no pretence of loving liberty—to Russia, for instance, where despotism can be taken pure, and without the base alloy of hypocracy [*sic*]."[534] Despite his rejection of nativism, Lincoln recognized the importance of friends like

Joseph Gillespie and Ozias M. Hatch who were involved in the American Party organization. In the fight to repeal Kansas-Nebraska the emerging Republican Party needed them. Massachusetts politician Henry Wilson wrote that organizing the new party was a "work of great delicacy and difficulty."[535] As a Whig who turned Know-Nothing before he became a Republican, Wilson personally experienced the fits and starts by which the Republican Party came together.

Don E. Fehrenbacher wrote that "with just the single bond of anti-Nebraska sentiment uniting its diverse membership, Republicanism could not at first enunciate a comprehensive political program."[536] Too many different strains of antislavery thought were embraced by Republicans. According to Fehrenbacher, "Perhaps the oldest variety was that associated with national pride and the traditions of the Revolution. However bitterly divided on the issue of slavery they may have been at home, Americans presented to the rest of the world the face of a slaveholding nation, and that made a mockery of their asserted belief that the United States had a special mission to lead mankind into a better, freer way of life."[537] Lincoln saw this contradiction clearly. His Peoria speech had emphasized that only the principles of the Declaration could overturn the spirit of Kansas-Nebraska and restore the spirit of 1776. Without Douglas's provocative legislation, the political realignment of Illinois might never have happened. "Prior to the year 1854, Illinois was a strong Democratic state; in fact, never had elected a Whig senator or a Whig state government, and but few Whig congressman," noted Lincoln ally Henry Clay Whitney.[538] Another Lincoln partisan, State Senator John M. Palmer recalled, "No one can doubt that Mr. Douglas in his action upon the Kansas-Nebraska bill, committed the tactical mistake of his life time. He relied upon the strength of merely partisan organization. He did not understand what he afterwards found to be true; that the questions he had raised were of the most dangerous character and would destroy the Democratic party."[539] The answers to these questions would determine whether America would be a free or a slave republic.

Chicago journalist Horace White sympathetically described the disparate leadership of the emerging coalition: "The opponents of the Nebraska bill in Illinois were ranged in three camps, as Whigs, Anti-

Nebraska Democrats, and Free-Soilers or Republicans. Of the first Mr. Lincoln soon became the recognized leader. . . . The second was without a distinctive head, but Lyman Trumbull, by the promptness and energy he had shown in combating the Nebraska bill in the St. Clair district, seemed to be the coming man. The Free-Soilers, were led by Owen Lovejoy and Ichabod Codding, two Congregational clergymen, whose lips had been touched by a live coal from off the altar of eternal justice."[540] Senator Douglas had created the conditions under which the anti-Nebraska coalition emerged, but Lincoln's rhetoric, his field work, and his allies defined its strategy. Subsequent conflict in Kansas led to the expansion of the national Republican Party just as the Douglas legislation had energized and augmented the antislavery coalition in Illinois. "The Kansas-Nebraska Act itself, for all the indignation it aroused, did not constitute a durable issue, especially since there was no hope of repealing the measure," wrote Don E. Fehrenbacher. "Soon, however, the struggle had been transferred to the Western plains. It was the disorder and violence in Kansas that kept the anti-Nebraska coalition alive and helped convert it into a major political party."[541]

Bleeding Kansas

The repeal of the Missouri Compromise disturbed not only the politics of every state in the nation, but also the politics of the territories. The Nebraska territory's northern location placed it largely outside the zone of contiguous contact with slavery. But Kansas itself, west of slaveholding Missouri, made this part of the old Louisiana territory a natural battleground for both slaveholders and their opponents.[542] Senator Seward had prophesied before the bill's passage: "I feel quite sure that Slavery at most can get nothing more than Kansas; while Nebraska, the wider northern region, will, under existing circumstances, escape, for the reason that its soil and climate are uncongenial with the staples of slave culture—rice, sugar, cotton, and tobacco. Moreover, since the public attention has been so well and so effectually directed toward the subject, I cherish a hope that Slavery may be prevented even from gaining a foothold in Kansas. Congress only gives consent, but it does not and cannot introduce Slavery there."[543]

Lincoln believed slavery would go wherever slavemasters themselves were permitted to take their slaves. He predicted that the Kansas-Nebraska Act would incite aggressive Missouri slaveholders to clash with antislavery residents on the plains of Kansas. The conflict among the voters there would decide slavery's fate in the territory before Kansas applied for statehood. But according to Michael F. Holt, the wording of the final legislation "perpetuated the artful ambiguity" of slavery's status in the territories.[544] Delay would thus provide time for slavery to settle in Kansas. Later, upon application for statehood, slavery having been fastened on the territory, it could be recognized under the state constitution submitted to Congress. New York *Tribune* editor Horace Greeley complained: "The pretense of Douglas & Co. that not even Kansas is to be made a slave state by his bill is a gag of the first water. Ask any Missourian what he thinks about it. . . ."[545]

Having lost the congressional vote on the Kansas-Nebraska Act, northerners like Seward were determined not to lose the competition for organizing the territory. Antislavery men were exhorted to go to Kansas. The Emigrant Aid Society, led by Massachusetts legislator Eli Thayer, financed many antislavery settlers. They knew the fate of Kansas could be decided by their votes. Advocates of slavery in neighboring Missouri, whence the transportation of slaves and voters was convenient, took the same initiative. Horace Greeley saw what Seward did not: Missouri slaveholders could rig the election.[546]

In his Peoria speech Lincoln had foreseen the conflict: "Some yankees, in the east, are sending emigrants to Nebraska [including Kansas], to exclude slavery from it; and, so far as I can judge, they expect the question to be decided by voting, in some way or other. But the Missourians are awake too. They are within a stone's throw of the contested ground. They hold meetings, and pass resolutions, in which not the slightest allusion to voting is made. They resolve that slavery already exists in the territory; that more shall go there; that they, remaining in Missouri will protect it; and that abolitionists shall be hung, or driven away."[547]

During 1854, both sides moved men and weapons to the disputed territory. Slaves were few and violence rare in 1854, but by the spring of 1855 armed disputes erupted on the plains of Kansas. A territorial election was scheduled for March 30. Proslavery forces—supported from Missouri—intended to commandeer the electoral process. Missouri's David Rice Atchison, no longer in the Senate, promoted these tactics. Antislavery men boycotted the election. Proslavery election results followed and were duly certified by Kansas Territorial Governor Andrew H. Reeder. A meeting of the new proslavery legislature was called for July 1855 at Lecompton. Predictably, the Lecompton legislature passed laws to support slavery and to inhibit its opponents. A counter-legislature was set up at Lawrence by antislavery forces who believed the first election fraudulent. Predictably, the Lawrence legislature prohibited slavery. The Lecompton government counterattacked in May 1856—serving warrants and violence upon the residents of Lawrence.[548]

Blood-soaked Lawrence gave antislavery forces the issue around which to rally. "Lawrence in Ruins" declared the headline in Greeley's New York *Tribune*. Much about the struggle in Kansas was exaggerated by both sides. But many events were incendiary. Abolitionist John Brown's murder of five Pottawatomie Creek residents in May 1856 inflamed the South, confirming the slaveholders' belief in a provocative, abolitionist North. Revenge became the rallying cry in North and South. South Carolina Congressman Preston S. Brooks asserted: "The admission of Kansas into the Union as a slave state is now a point of honor with the House. . . . It is my deliberate conviction that the fate of the South is to be decided with the Kansas issue."[549] The repeal of the Missouri Compromise did permit slavery in Kansas, but only 200 slaves resided in the territory. To slaveholders such as Brooks this fact was irrelevant. As Lincoln had suggested at Peoria, residents of Missouri and slaveholders of the South would try to turn popular sovereignty into slave law in the new territory. "Bleeding Kansas" provoked a bitter antislavery speech on the U.S. Senate floor by Senator Charles Sumner during which he excoriated South Carolina Senator Andrew P. Butler, one of the F Street Mess from 1854. Sumner charged that Butler overflowed "with rage at the simple suggestion that Kansas has applied for admission as a free state, and with incoherent phrases, discharges the loose expectoration of his speech, now upon her representatives, and then upon her people."[550] On May 22, 1856, Congressman Brooks avenged his cousin's honor by severely caning Senator

Sumner on the floor of the Senate, inflaming passions throughout the nation.

In August 1855, Lincoln reviewed his case against the Kansas-Nebraska Act in a letter to Joshua F. Speed, a Kentuckian who remained his closest friend: "In 1841 you and I had together a tedious low-water trip, on a Steam Boat from Louisville to St. Louis. You may remember, as I well do, that from Louisville to the mouth of the Ohio there were, on board, ten or a dozen slaves, shackled together with irons. That sight was a continual torment to me; and I see something like it every time I touch the Ohio, or any other slave-border. It is hardly fair for you to assume, that I have no interest in a thing which has, and continually exercises, the power of making me miserable. You ought rather to appreciate how much the great body of the Northern people do crucify their feelings, in order to maintain their loyalty to the constitution and the Union." This sentiment reinforced the logic of Lincoln's argument to Speed:

> I do oppose the extension of slavery, because my judgement and feelings so prompt me; and I am under no obligation to the contrary. If for this you and I must differ, differ we must. . . .
>
> That Kansas will form a Slave constitution, and, with it, will ask to be admitted into the Union, I take to be an already settled question; and so settled by the very means you so pointedly condemn. By every principle of law, ever held by any court, North or South, every negro taken to Kansas is free; yet in utter disregard of this— in the spirit of violence merely—that beautiful Legislature gravely passes a law to hang men who shall venture to inform a negro of his legal rights. This is the substance, and real object of the law. If, like Haman, they should hang upon the gallows of their own building, I shall not be among the mourners for their fate.
>
> In my humble sphere, I shall advocate the restoration of the Missouri Compromise, so long as Kansas remains a territory; and when, by all these foul means, it seeks to come into the Union as a Slave-state, I shall oppose it. . . . In my opposition to the admission of Kansas I shall have some company; but we may be beaten. If we are, I shall not, on that account, attempt to dissolve the

Union. On the contrary, if we succeed, there will be enough of us
to take care of the Union. . . .

In this last sentence, Lincoln's hard tone and careful choice of words
suggest his resolve to preserve the Union, a determination clearly shown
at Peoria. So too, as President-elect, Mr. Lincoln would not be moved to
compromise on the extension of slavery to the territories. Even in 1855,
he lectured Joshua Speed about the realities of southern politics, using
some arguments from the Peoria speech: "You say if Kansas fairly votes
herself a free state, as a christian you will rather rejoice at it. All decent
slave-holders *talk* that way; and I do not doubt their candor. But they
never *vote* that way. Although in a private letter, or conversation, you will
express your preference that Kansas shall be free, you would vote for no
man for Congress who would say the same thing publicly. No such man
could be elected from any district in any slave-state. . . . The slave-breeders
and slave-traders, are a small, odious and detested class, among you; and
yet in politics; they dictate the course of all of you, and are as completely
your masters, as you are the masters of your own negroes."[551]

The ongoing struggle over Kansas led to a meeting in Decatur, Illinois, of a dozen antislavery editors on February 22, 1856. More than two
dozen were invited, but a major snowstorm prevented or delayed the
arrival of some. Senator Trumbull had been invited, but Lincoln was the
only noneditor in attendance.[552] He had arranged his legal schedule to be
in town for the meeting. There, he helped the editors draft a Republican
Party manifesto, which according to one editor, "bears the stamp of his
peculiar intellect."[553] Historian Reinhard H. Luthin described Lincoln's
"conciliatory" impact on the editors' work: "The resolutions . . . made no
demand for repeal of the fugitive-slave law, no demand against the admission of new slave states, no demand for the abolition of slavery in the District of Columbia. Upon such a program could Lincoln's Anti-Nebraska
Whigs and Trumbull's Anti-Nebraska Democrats unite—and Lovejoy's
and Codding's Republicans and George Schneider's and Gustave
Koerner's Germans might acquiesce."[554] Upon the narrowly defined issue
of opposition to the extension of slavery, Lincoln believed, the inclusive-
ness and the success of the antislavery coalition would depend.

The prudent and precise language of the Decatur platform came easily to Lincoln, who had used it before. "The platform, while disavowing any intention to interfere in the internal affairs of any State in reference to slavery," reported one Illinois newspaper, "amounted to an emphatic protest against the introduction of slavery into territory already free, or its further extension; demanded the restoration of the Missouri compromise; insisted upon the maintenance of the doctrine of the Declaration of Independence as essential to freedom of speech and of the press, and that, under it, 'freedom' should be regarded 'as the rule and slavery the exception'. . . ."[555] Know-Nothingism was rejected as "we should welcome the exiles and emigrants from the Old World, to homes of enterprise and of freedom in the New. . . ." That night in Decatur, Lincoln was asked to deliver a speech at a public dinner of the assembled editors. He did so reluctantly, but in his "usual masterly manner."[556] Lincoln had become a Republican.

The 1856 Bloomington Convention

While Kansas bled, the Republican Party of Illinois was officially inaugurated in May of 1856. Delegates convened at a meeting in Major's Hall in Bloomington. The planned program did not include Lincoln, but he was called on to give a speech to close the proceedings. No reliable text of his remarks has survived. Journalists later claimed they were too absorbed by Lincoln's eloquence to take notes. Law partner William H. Herndon exulted that Lincoln's "speech was full of fire and energy and force; it was logic; it was pathos; it was enthusiasm; it was justice, equity, truth, and right set ablaze by the divine fires of a soul maddened by the wrong; it was hard, heavy, knotty, gnarly, backed with wrath. I attempted for about fifteen minutes as was usual with me then to take notes, but at the end of that time I threw pen and paper away and lived only in the inspiration of the hour."[557] The emotional and partisan Herndon was not alone in his report.

Some historians have suggested that Lincoln's language was so radical that he neither wanted it transcribed nor reported. One antislavery journalist, Joseph Medill of Chicago, recalled: "My belief is, that after Mr. Lincoln cooled down, he was rather pleased that his speech had not been reported, as it was too radical in expression on the slavery question for the digestion of central and southern Illinois at that time, and that he preferred to let it stand as a remembrance in the minds of his audience.'"[558] Years later, another Illinois editor wrote, "The truth of it is the great mass of the leaders felt that Lincoln made too radical a speech and they did not want it produced for fear it would damage the party. Lincoln himself said he had put his foot into it and asked the reporters to simply report the meeting and not attempt to record his words and they agreed to it."[559] Lincoln scholar Robert S. Harper observed: "The Bloomington convention was guided by a radical spirit; Kansas antislavery agitators had been imported for the occasion. Lincoln gave them the talk they wanted to hear."[560]

Although the "Lost Speech" has been described as passionate, there is evidence that Lincoln used the sober logic of his Peoria speech. "His points were unanswerable, and the force and power of his appeals were irresistible and were received with a storm of applause," reported the Bloomington *Pantagraph.*[561] Judge Reuben M. Benjamin remembered that its thrust "was opposition to extension of slavery into the territories. The speech Mr. Lincoln gave at the Bloomington convention was very like what is known as the Peoria speech, delivered in 1854."[562] Lincoln knew the value of repetition, especially of a well-received speech.

More importantly, Lincoln understood the power of ideas. Peoria themes recur in his speeches, letters, and official documents until the day of his death. Judge Benjamin recalled that the Bloomington Speech "was not rhetorical, but it was logical. Every now and then Mr. Lincoln threw in some statement like a blow from a sledgehammer. Familiar as I felt I was with the subject of extension of slavery in the territories, from having heard the leaders of both parties discuss it exhaustively at that session in the Senate, I was deeply moved by the manner in which Mr. Lincoln handled the subject."[563] Some observers thought the speech not radical at all. James S. Emory, a refugee from the violence in Kansas, recalled that the speech was actually "quite conservative; his chief contention all through it was that Kansas must come in free, not slave, he said he did not want to meddle with slavery where it existed and that he was in favor of a reasonable fugitive slave law. . . . He was at his best and the mad insolence of the slave power as at that time exhibited before the country furnished plenty of material for his unsparing logic to effectively deal with before a popular audience."[564]

Praise for the Bloomington speech was unstinting. The Chicago *Press* reported that Lincoln "held the assembly spellbound."[565] One witness, William Pitt Kellogg, recalled: "Lincoln began very slowly, holding in his left hand a card upon which he had evidently jotted down some of his leading thoughts. From time to time as he reached some climax in his argument, he would advance to the front of the platform as he spoke, and with a peculiar gesture hurl the point, so to speak, at his audience, then as the audience rose to their feet to cheer, he would walk slowly backward, bowing and glancing at the card he held in his hand; again he would resume his speech, making his points in the same manner with like effect."[566]

Lincoln's speech at Bloomington infused the new and diverse Republican Party in Illinois with a winning spirit and an unlikely unity. Chicago *Democratic Press* editor John L. Scripps was "a man of gravity little likely to be carried off his feet by spoken words," according to fellow journalist Horace White. Nonetheless, Scripps recalled: "Never was an audience more completely electrified by human eloquence. Again and again during its delivery they sprang to their feet and upon the benches and testified by long-continued shouts and the waving of hats how deeply the speaker had wrought upon their minds and hearts."[567] John M. Palmer, the former Democrat who chaired the Bloomington convention, observed that "Lincoln made the greatest speech in his life."[568] Fellow attorney Henry C. Whitney wrote years later that he never "heard a speech so thrilling as this one from Lincoln. No one who was present will forget its climax. I have since talked with many who were present, and all substantially concur in enthusiastic remembrances of it." Whitney remembered an ominous moment when Lincoln "with a mien and gesture that no language can describe, exclaimed (referring to threatened secession), 'when it comes to that, we will say to our Southern Brethren: we won't go out of the Union; and you SHAN'T' . . . I have never seen such excitement among a large body of men, and scarcely ever expect to again."[569] Lincoln had invoked the unyielding spirit of his Peoria speech—never to accept the dissolution of the Union nor to accommodate the extension of slavery.

Lincoln continued the campaign several days later in Springfield. According to the Illinois *State Journal,* he "took the stand and pronounced the most logical and finished argument against the evils to be apprehended from the continued aggression of the slave power that it has been our good fortune to listen to. We shall not mar its beauty by an attempt to give a synopsis of it. The speaker's manner was calm and unimpassioned, he preferring rather to appeal to reason than to excite the feelings of his hearers."[570] Lincoln scholar Earl Wiley wrote that this report "suggests strongly that Lincoln's Bloomington speech [too] was not the impassioned exhortation that we have been led to think it was."[571] But impassioned or not, the Bloomington speech had galvanized Republicans into action. The Illinois *State Journal* reported: "Old line Whigs, Jefferson and Jackson Democrats, Republicans, American and foreign born citizens, laying aside all past differences, united together there in one common brotherhood to war against the allied forces of nullification, disunion, slavery propagandism, ruffianism and gag law, which make up the present administration party of the country."[572]

In June 1856, about three weeks after the Bloomington convention, private citizen Lincoln received national recognition in the very first Republican national convention in Philadelphia where he received surprising support for the party's vice-presidential nomination. It went to New Jersey's William L. Dayton. Lincoln then commenced a campaign on behalf of the national Republican ticket. Allen C. Guelzo wrote that Lincoln reviewed "again the antislavery intentions of the Founders (and 'of that Declaration "That all men are born free and equal"'), the folly of Kansas-Nebraska in turning those intentions upside down, and the need for the restoration of the Missouri Compromise."[573] Still, Lincoln entertained few illusions about his political prospects. Senator Douglas remained the dominant figure of Illinois and of the national Democratic Party. Lincoln acknowledged that Douglas's "name fills the nation; and is not unknown, even, in foreign lands. I affect no contempt for the high eminence he has reached. So reached, that the oppressed of my species, might have shared with me in the elevation, I would rather stand on that eminence, than wear the richest crown that ever pressed a monarch's brow." Lincoln was ambitious, but he had joined his ambition to the just cause of "the oppressed of my species."[574]

Lincoln believed that the new Republican Party could prevail as a principled antislavery coalition. "In 1856, while Douglas was using the Kansas-Nebraska issue as a test of party loyalty in Illinois the Republican party appeared in that state with a view to building a constituency of former Whigs and other persons opposed to the extension of slavery in the territories," wrote historian Thomas F. Schwartz of the presidential election of 1856. "For Lincoln the main issue in the election was the extension of slavery into the territories."[575] As he had done in 1848 when he campaigned as a Whig against Free Soil Party presidential candidate Martin Van Buren, Lincoln argued that only a united antislavery force could stop proslavery Democrats. In 1856, Lincoln's Republican antislavery strategy was designed to attract those who were tempted to support former President Millard Fillmore, an erstwhile Whig then running on the American Party ticket.

The Illinois *State Journal* reported on the Republican coalition strategy. Lincoln addressed "himself principally to that portion of the so-called Democratic party who are sincerely opposed to the extension of the institution of slavery into the free territories on our western frontier; and in his own terse, logical, and convincing style of argument proved to them that notwithstanding that they may be theoretically opposed to the Kansas iniquity, they do but sustain it in practice if they cast their suffrages for Mr. Buchanan and the party acting in concert with him, the assertions of defenders to the contrary notwithstanding."[576] On October 9, 1856, Lincoln returned to Peoria to give one of dozens of speeches he delivered during the presidential campaign. There in 1856, as in 1854, Lincoln did not deceive himself about public opinion on race and slavery. Historian Kenneth M. Stampp wrote that Republicans were racial realists: "Given the racial attitudes of the 1850s, no party, not even one appealing primarily to northern voters—could have adopted a platform advocating equal political and legal rights for blacks without suffering total defeat."[577] As a prudent man of affairs, Lincoln's political strategy did recognize the undeniable fact of public prejudice, even as he made arguments to oppose the extension of slavery.

Democrat James Buchanan, an experienced diplomat and Pennsylvania politician, was elected to succeed President Franklin Pierce. The Republican candidate, John C. Frémont, did unexpectedly well in the North, even though former President Millard Fillmore of New York siphoned off some of Frémont's potential support. To some Republicans, the 1856 results seemed promising. In a speech to a Republican dinner at Chicago after the November vote, Lincoln urged his new party to maintain the fight. Not only did they have right on their side, Lincoln argued, but they had the numbers as well: "All of us who did not vote for Mr. Buchanan, taken together, are a majority of four hundred thousand. But, in the late contest we were divided between Fremont and Fillmore. Can we not come together, for the future. . . . Let past differences, as nothing be; and with steady eye on the real issue, let us reinaugurate the good old 'central ideas' of the Republic. We *can* do it. The human heart *is* with us—God is with us. We shall again be able not to declare, that 'all States as States, are equal,' nor yet that 'all citizens are equal,' but to renew the broader, better declaration, including both these and much more, that 'all *men* are created equal.'"[578]

Bleeding Kansas continued to dominate not only Kansas but congressional politics. In 1857, the proslavery Lecompton constitution for Kansas split the national Democratic Party. One faction was led by President Buchanan; another by Senator Douglas. Buchanan, a southern sympathizer like Pierce, held that the Lecompton constitution had been lawfully authorized. Douglas believed, as did antislavery northerners, that Lecompton had been fraudulently ratified. "Unlike Buchanan, Douglas had little real choice in determining his course," wrote Don E. Fehrenbacher. "His senate seat was up for election in 1858. If he followed [Michigan Senator Lewis] Cass in backing Buchanan, he knew that his career as an elected official would be over, such was the popular animus in Illinois against the Lecompton fraud."[579] So the bold and enterprising Douglas began a crusade against the proslavery Lecompton constitution, making a virtue of political necessity, thereby mitigating the negative consequences of his Kansas-Nebraska legislation.[580] Michael F. Holt observed that "Douglas realized that northern Democrats would be crushed by Republicans in subsequent elections if Kansas became a slave state over the objections of the majority of its residents."[581]

Lincoln worried about the Republican Party strategy. Until 1863, he would believe that abolitionism by itself would not doom slavery to extinction, but instead might doom the antislavery coalition. He had learned to handle the issue of slavery extension with great care. Historian Paul Finkelman noted that antebellum Illinois "was in many ways as much a southern state as a northern one . . . most who came north to Illinois brought with them their pro-Southern, proslavery biases."[582] Illinois had become a state divided against itself. The northern part of the state had been settled increasingly by antislavery northerners. Immigrants from slave states dominated "Little Egypt," as southern Illinois was known. Kentuckians like Lincoln were numerous in central Illinois. These geographic divisions within Illinois paralleled the geographic split of the nation.

Historian Benjamin Quarles insisted: "Lincoln was not anti-Negro . . . despite the strong racial prejudices so prevalent where he lived. In the campaign for the Senate in 1858, the jibes of his opponent forced him to declare himself in opposition to Negro [social and political] equality. But Lincoln regarded the issue of racial equality as something of a bug bear, a mysterious specter with uncanny power to affright."[583] Better not to attack a general prejudice head on, but to hit it indirectly. Public sentiment in a democracy could not, after all, "be safely disregarded." Quarles contended that "Lincoln's . . . cardinal belief is well summed up in his own words: 'toleration by necessity where it [slavery] exists, with unyielding hostility to the spread of it.'"[584] Only thereby would America's peculiar institution be put on the road of ultimate extinction.[585]

For the first time since he departed Congress, Lincoln campaigned outside of Illinois in 1856. In Kalamazoo, Michigan he delivered a speech at a Republican rally for the Frémont ticket. Lincoln stuck to his Peoria theme: "The question of slavery, at the present day, should be not only the greatest question, but very nearly the sole question. Our opponents, however, prefer that this should not be the case. To get at this question, I will occupy your attention but a single moment. The question is simply this:— Shall slavery be spread into the new Territories, or not? This is the naked question." He argued that opponents of slavery should not waste their votes on the American Party's Millard Fillmore, who had no chance of election, but should concentrate them on the Republicans. Lincoln returned to favorite themes about the nation's Founding and its legacy of economic opportunity: "We are a great empire. We are eighty years old. We stand at once the wonder and admiration of the whole world, and we must enquire what it is that has given us much prosperity, and we shall understand that to give up that one thing, would be to give up all future prosperity. This cause is that every man can make himself."[586] Lincoln embraced the American "right to rise," as Gabor S. Boritt emphasized. This mobility originated in the inalienable right to liberty proclaimed in the Declaration of Independence.

Lincoln also campaigned energetically in Illinois for Frémont. He delivered a speech in Peoria on October 9. He had said two years earlier in the same place that the nation's "republican robe" was "soiled." Now he asserted that the country's legacy had been "defiled." The local *Weekly Republican* enthused: "On this occasion he went over the whole battle field of the two great contending armies, one *for* and the other *against* slavery and slave labor, and showed, most triumphantly, that our young, gallant and world-renowned commander [Frémont] was the man for the day— the man to right the ship of State, and, like the stripling of Israel, to slay the boasting Goliaths of slaveocracy that have beset the national capitol and defiled the sanctums of liberty, erected and consecrated by the old prophets and fathers of this republic."[587]

The power of elected public officials to change policy in a democracy is conditioned by the reality, as Lincoln believed, that ideas must repeatedly meet the test of the ballot box. But in 1856 no public office of interest was open to him. He had quietly rejected a run for governor.[588] Douglas, meanwhile, still hoped to be nominated by the Democratic Party, then elected president in November. The senator's ambitions were thwarted by southern Democratic support for Pennsylvania's James Buchanan. Though Buchanan prevailed in both Illinois and the nation, Republican William H. Bissell defeated Douglas ally William A. Richardson in the race for governor of Illinois.[589]

In a speech before the U.S. House of Representatives a few months after the 1856 election, Congressman Alexander H. Stephens alleged that the voters had directly endorsed the Kansas-Nebraska Act:

It is because the measure, so directly in issue, has been so triumphantly sustained, that I so much rejoice in the result. No man can say that this issue was dodged. It was presented by its friends in the organization of this House at the beginning of the last session. It was the basis of the organization at [the Democratic national convention in] Cincinnati, and formed one of the most prominent features in the programme of principles there announced. And while it was not named in so many words in the Philadelphia programme, yet all know that the [Republican] party there assembled was organized mainly in opposition to that measure and the principles upon which it was based. In the newspapers, and on the hustings, nothing was railed against so bitterly and unceasingly as the 'iniquity,' 'the cheat,' and 'the infamy,' of the Kansas bill. This measure, therefore, may be considered as one of the things most emphatically indorsed by the people in the late election.[590]

Stephens was not alone in this judgment on the election of 1856, but the conventional wisdom underestimated the plausibility of a stunning change four years later. Lincoln had done the math and saw in Buchanan's unconvincing plurality the opportunity for Republican victory.

"Our republican robe is soiled, and trailed in the dust. Let us repurify it. Let us turn and wash it white, in the spirit, if not the blood, of the Revolution. Let us turn slavery from its claims of "moral right," back upon its existing legal rights, and its arguments of "necessity." Let us return it to the position our fathers gave it; and there let it rest in peace. Let us re-adopt the Declaration of Independence, and with it, the practices, and policy, which harmonize with it. Let north and south—let all Americans—let all lovers of liberty everywhere—join in the great and good work."

ABRAHAM LINCOLN,
OCTOBER 16, 1854

VI.

Challenging Dred Scott, *the Supreme Court, and Douglas*

L ike Franklin Pierce in 1853, President-elect James Buchanan in 1857 was determined to quiet the country. Buchanan tried to do so by accommodating the extension of slavery. "The great object of my administration," he wrote after his 1856 election, "will be to arrest, if possible, the agitation of the Slavery question."[591] Both Pierce and Buchanan abhorred the sectional discord besetting the country. To make peace, they deferred to southern slaveholders.

Every pacification proved temporary. Just as the Kansas-Nebraska Act of 1854 had given way to Bloody Kansas, so too the Lecompton crisis of 1856 gave way to the Supreme Court decision in the *Dred Scott* case. In one of the most controversial cases the Court has ever decided, it ruled in March 1857 that under the Constitution, neither Congress nor territorial legislatures could prohibit slavery in the territories. The Missouri line of 1820 was thus unconstitutional. Moreover, the Supreme Court ruled that slave property was protected by the property clause of the Fifth Amendment. According to Chief Justice Roger B. Taney's *obiter dicta*, blacks could not be American citizens and were not covered by the Declaration of Independence at the time of its adoption by Congress in 1776. The Supreme Court decision effectively destroyed Buchanan's hope for peace because it explicitly ruled out the principal policy of Lincoln and the Republican Party—prohibition by Congress of the extension of slavery. Implicitly, the Supreme Court had also ruled out popular sovereignty which would have left decisions regarding slavery to early residents of a territory.

In his inaugural address just two days before the *Dred Scott* decision, President James Buchanan had endorsed the Kansas-Nebraska Act and laid the groundwork for a ruling by the Supreme Court: "What a happy conception then was it for Congress to apply this simple rule—that the will of the majority shall govern—to the settlement of the question of domestic slavery in the Territories! Congress is neither 'to legislate slavery into any Territory or State, nor to exclude it therefrom, but to leave the people thereof perfectly free to form and regulate their domestic institutions in their own way, subject only to the Constitution of the United States.' As a natural consequence, Congress has also prescribed that, when the Territory of Kansas shall be admitted as a State it 'shall be received into the Union, with or without slavery, as their constitution may prescribe at the time of their admission.' A difference of opinion has arisen in regard to the point of time when the people of a territory shall decide this question for themselves. This is, happily, a matter of but little practical importance." Having virtually repeated the vocabulary of Senator Douglas, President Buchanan then revealed his intuition about the pending Supreme Court ruling. "Besides, it is a judicial question, which legitimately belongs to the Supreme Court of the United States, before whom it is now pending, and will, it is understood, be speedily and finally settled. To their decision, in common with all good citizens, I shall cheerfully submit, whatever this may be."[592] Well aware of the proslavery disposition of the court majority under Chief Justice Taney, Buchanan behind the scene had pressed the court for an early ruling and urged northern justices to side with their southern colleagues.[593] In *Dred Scott*, the president got the ruling he wanted but not the cheerful submission he desired.

Senator Douglas, ever able to rationalize irreconcilable positions, insisted that the Supreme Court had not only decided the permissibility of slavery in the territories, but he also argued, *Dred Scott* notwithstanding, that local jurisdictions could still discourage slaveholders by not enforcing rules to sustain the peculiar institution. That is, even though the Supreme

Court denied Congress and the territories the power to prohibit slavery, merely local ordinances in the territories might indirectly do so. Douglas biographer Damon Wells summarized the contradiction inherent in the Douglas stand: "When Stephen Douglas qualified the powers a territory might exercise over slavery with the phrase 'subject only to the Constitution of the United States,' he left the door open for intervention in territorial affairs from a number of quarters, principally the Supreme Court, whose job it was to interpret the Constitution."[594] Chief Justice Taney did so on March 6, 1857. Not only did the Court rule out popular sovereignty in the territories, but in Taney's opinion declared that Dred Scott, a slave taken into free territory, "had no rights which the white man was bound to respect; and that the negro might justly and lawfully be reduced to slavery for his benefit."[595] Perhaps Douglas was unprepared for the sweeping *obiter dicta* of Chief Justice Taney. Taney did not simply decide that Dred Scott, under common law, had not escaped from servitude by his sojourn in the free states of Illinois and Wisconsin. Taney ruled that neither Congress nor territorial legislatures could prohibit slavery in the territories. Taney wrote that "if Congress itself cannot do this—if it is beyond the powers conferred on the Federal Government—it will be admitted, we presume, that it could not authorize a Territorial Government to exercise them." Historian David M. Potter wrote that this extraordinary ruling "made freedom local—an attribute of those states which abolished slavery, but not of the United States; it made slavery national, in the sense that slavery would be legal in any part of the United States where a state government had not abolished it. Apart from the morality of it, this was a ruinous decision because, in the process of splitting logical hairs, it arrived at a result which converted the charter of freedom into a safeguard of slavery."[596] Taney incorrectly justified this effect by arguing that the intent of the Declaration of Independence did not include Negroes.

The Republican Reaction

Taney's sweeping decision challenged Douglas and popular sovereignty. The senator felt compelled to defend the indefensible—that popular sovereignty was still viable even after the court had ruled that neither the

U.S. Congress nor a territory could restrict slavery. Republicans were astonished that the Supreme Court presumed to take away not only popular sovereignty, but also the constitutional power of Congress to prohibit slavery's extension. Historian George T. McJimsey wrote that Republicans branded *Dred Scott* a conspiracy of the slave owners and their northern allies. But McJimsey argued that while the decision seemed "to undermine the Republicans' major principle [namely, the constitutional authority of Congress to prohibit slavery in the territories, it] actually helped to strengthen its appeal. In the long run, the Dred Scott Case more seriously hurt the Democrats."[597] Lincoln and free-soilers in the North were determined to "overthrow" this notorious ruling of the Supreme Court. Don E. Fehrenbacher emphasized: "Republicans were handed a new weapon—that being the well-grounded speculation that Chief Justice Roger Taney's court intended eventually to nationalize slavery by legalizing it within the northern states themselves."[598] The speculation was well-grounded, not least because a case (*Lemmon vs. the People*) was then in the New York courts which, if the *Dred Scott* precedent prevailed, might sweep away the prohibition against slavery in northern states as well.[599]

Fehrenbacher wrote that for "Republicans like Abraham Lincoln . . . a decision so defective in its logic, so contrary to precedent, and so repugnant to a large part of the population did not immediately become binding on the other branches of the government or upon the American people as settled law of the land."[600] Lincoln explicitly rejected the Supreme Court ruling as valid national policy. As a lawyer, he did accept the ruling, but only as it applied to the specific case of *Dred Scott*. With respect to congressional authority to restrict slavery in the territories, Lincoln and the Republican Party would not defer to the Supreme Court, and its chief justice. Lincoln and his allies had become progressively alarmed by the threat posed by government advocates of slavery. Now, a Supreme Court decision had demonstrated that there were judicial as well as legislative and executive threats to the principles of the Declaration of Independence. Benjamin Quarles wrote that "comforting beliefs about the peaceful passing of slavery received a mortal blow in the Dred Scott decision. . . . To him [Lincoln] the Dred Scott decision meant that slavery was again on the march and would possibly be forced upon the free states themselves."[601]

On June 26, 1857, in a speech as well-crafted as the Peoria address, Lincoln carefully defined the problems the Supreme Court had created. He integrated the themes of his Peoria speech with a review of events in Kansas, and an analysis of the *Dred Scott* case: "Three years and a half ago, Judge Douglas brought forward his famous Nebraska bill. The country was at once in a blaze. He scorned all opposition, and carried it through Congress. Since then he has seen himself superseded in a Presidential nomination, by one indorsing the general doctrine of his measure, but at the same time standing clear of the odium of its untimely agitation, and its gross breach of national faith; and he has seen that successful rival Constitutionally elected, not by the strength of friends, but by the division of adversaries, [Buchanan] being in a popular minority of nearly four hundred thousand votes. He has seen his chief aid[e]s in his own State, Shields and Richardson, politically speaking, successively tried, convicted, and executed, for an offense not their own, but his. And now he sees his own case, standing next on the docket for trial."[602] The trial would come in the U.S. Senate race of 1858. Applying the logic of the Peoria speech to the Supreme Court's ruling, Lincoln stressed the incompatibility of the Declaration of Independence and the *Dred Scott* opinion:

> Chief Justice Taney, in his opinion in the Dred Scott case, admits that the language of the Declaration is broad enough to include the whole human family, but he and Judge Douglas argue that the authors of that instrument did not intend to include negroes, by the fact that they did not at once, actually place them on an equality with the whites. Now this grave argument comes to just nothing at all, by the other fact, that they did not at once, *or ever afterwards*, actually place all white people on an equality with one or another. And this is the staple argument of both the Chief Justice and the Senator, for doing this obvious violence to the plain unmistakable language of the Declaration. I think the authors of that notable instrument intended to include *all* men, but they did not intend to declare all men equal *in all respects*. They did not

mean to say all were equal in color, size, intellect, moral developments, or social capacity. They defined with tolerable distinctness, in what respects they did consider all men created
equal—equal in "certain inalienable rights, among which are life,
liberty, and the pursuit of happiness." This they said, and this
meant. They did not mean to assert the obvious untruth, that all
were then actually enjoying that equality, nor yet, that they were
about to confer it immediately upon them. In fact they had no
power to confer such a boon. They meant simply to declare the
right, so that the *enforcement* of it might follow as fast as circumstances should permit. They meant to set up a standard maxim
for free society, which should be familiar to all, and revered by
all; constantly looked to, constantly labored for, and even though
never perfectly attained, constantly approximated, and thereby
constantly spreading and deepening its influence, and augmenting the happiness and value of life to all people of all colors
everywhere. The assertion that "all men are created equal" was of
no practical use in effecting our separation from Great Britain;
and it was placed in the Declaration, not for that, but for future
use. Its authors meant it to be, thank God, it is now proving itself,
a stumbling block to those who in after times might seek to turn
a free people back into the hateful paths of despotism. They
knew the proneness of prosperity to breed tyrants, and they
meant when such should re-appear in this fair land and com-
mence their vocation they should find left for them at least one
hard nut to crack.[603]

Lincoln then quoted from a recent speech in which Senator Douglas
agreed with Chief Justice Taney and claimed that "when [the Founders]
declared all men to have been created equal—that they were speaking of
British subjects on this continent being equal to British subjects born
and residing in Great Britain—that they were entitled to the same
inalienable rights, and among them were enumerated life, liberty and
the pursuit of happiness. The Declaration was adopted for the purpose
of justifying the colonists in the eyes of the civilized world in withdrawing

their allegiance from the British crown, and dissolving their connection with the mother country."[604] Lincoln disagreed: "My good friends, read that carefully over some leisure hour, and ponder well upon it—see what a mere wreck—mangled ruin—it makes of our once glorious Declaration." His historical critique and homespun metaphors continued: "I had thought the Declaration promised something better than the condition of British subjects; but no, it only meant that we should be *equal* to them in their own oppressed and *unequal* condition. According to that, it gave no promise that having kicked off the King and Lords of Great Britain, we should not at once be saddled with a King and lords of our own."[605]

Lincoln then sought to arouse his fellow citizens to action: "And now I appeal to all—to Democrats as well as others,—are you really willing that the Declaration shall be thus frittered away?—thus left no more at most, than an interesting memorial of the dead past? thus shorn of vitality, and practical value; and left without the *germ* or even the *suggestion* of the individual rights of man in it?"[606] Harry V. Jaffa wrote: "Lincoln's 1857 response to Dred Scott is among his remarkable dialectical tours de force. It is an answer to Douglas's endorsement of Taney's opinion, as well as to Taney himself. . . . In it, we can see the precise ways in which Lincoln later exploited these differences and how he shaped decisively the issues of the election of 1860 and of the crisis that followed upon it."[607] The compelling logic of Peoria had been brought to bear not only upon Douglas, but also upon the Supreme Court of the United States. Lincoln delivered these rigorous speeches to thousands of Americans of different educational backgrounds.

In Lincoln's attack on the Supreme Court's decision, his target was Taney and the slave-power dominance of the federal government. The jury to which he appealed was the American people. Writing together, Robert W. Johannsen and Harry V. Jaffa declared: "Lincoln's argument, vis-à-vis the Court, was simple: we shall never interfere with any disposition of property in accordance with a Court decision; who the Court decides is a slave shall be a slave. But the dicta of the Court shall not determine the policy of the Congress and the President, it shall not nullify the will of the American people, deliberately expressed through free elections."[608] Citing as precedent the opinion of Thomas Jefferson, Lincoln denied that a Supreme Court ruling such as *Dred Scott* could become a final political rule against the will of the sovereign American people or their representatives in Congress. Lincoln's interpretation of the Constitution, building upon the authority of opinions of Presidents Thomas Jefferson and Andrew Jackson, arose from the co-equal powers of each of the three branches of government to decide constitutional questions with respect to the authority of each of their departments. Jefferson had maintained that "to consider judges as the ultimate arbiters of all constitutional questions [is] a very dangerous doctrine indeed, and one which would place us under the despotism of an oligarchy."[609]

Jackson similarly disputed the authority of the Supreme Court to overrule Congress, saying that the judges have no more authority over Congress than Congress has over the Court. Lincoln quoted Jackson's veto message: "The Congress, the executive and the court, must each for itself be guided by its own opinion of the Constitution. Each public officer, who takes an oath to support the Constitution, swears that he will support it as he understands it, and not as it is understood by others."[610] By endorsing the bitterly contested *Dred Scott* opinion, Douglas gave Lincoln political ammunition to challenge the senator in the 1858 election. Journalist Horace White wrote: "The Springfield and Peoria debates of 1854 were the prelude and introduction to the more famous joint debates of 1858. Although four years intervened, the issues were not changed."[611]

The 1858 Senate Campaign

"I shall have my hands full," Douglas told Philadelphia editor John W. Forney about the upcoming 1858 campaign with Lincoln. "He is the strong man of his party—full of wit, facts, dates, and the best stump-speaker, with his droll ways and dry jokes, in the West. He is as honest as he is shrewd; and if I beat him, my victory will be hardly won."[612] The reluctance Douglas expressed was understandable. "We can somewhat appreciate the feeling with which Douglas, aggressive and fearless though he was, welcomed a contest with such a man as Lincoln," wrote William Herndon.[613] Douglas could not easily avoid his Republican opponent as he knew Lincoln would surely follow him. Nor was it Douglas's style to give the appearance of cowardice by refusing to debate. Douglas knew how formidable Lincoln could be. Lincoln partisans knew it as well. "All persons who know these two men," reported the Chicago *Tribune*, "know that Lincoln is more than Douglas's equal, politically or legally—head or heart."[614]

On June 16, 1858, Illinois Republicans gathered in Springfield for their state convention in the same House chamber of the State Capitol where Douglas and Lincoln had contested the repeal of the Missouri Compromise in October 1854. This time, enthusiastic Republicans overflowed the ornate hall. Former Congressman Richard Yates was the temporary chairman of the convention and former Lieutenant Governor Gustave Koerner, the permanent one. In an unusual move, the convention endorsed a resolution naming Lincoln "the first and only choice of the Republicans of Illinois for the United States Senate."[615] So complete was his dominance of the party that convention delegates left no discretion for Republican state legislators who would do the actual voting for U.S. senator.

"The hall of the house of representatives was crowded to its utmost capacity when Lincoln arrived, and he was received with a prolonged shout, waving of handkerchiefs and swinging of hats," recalled Illinois editor Jeriah Bonham. "He bowed his acknowledgments from the speaker's desk, and was introduced by the president of the convention, Hon. Gustavus A. Koerner, and rising to his full height he surveyed the vast audience, and commencing slowly and deliberately at first, his voice increasing in force and power as he advanced."[616] Lincoln began his "House Divided" speech by reformulating many themes from Peoria—refitting some with new arguments, others with new evidence and extended metaphors. He began with an implicit reference to the Kansas-Nebraska Act, to the spread of slavery in Kansas, and to the *Dred Scott* ruling. These events, taken together, had brought America to a great divide:

> If we could first know *where* we are, and *whither* we are tending, we could then better judge *what* to do, and *how* to do it.
>
> We are now far into the *fifth* year, since a policy was initiated, with the *avowed* object, and *confident* promise, of putting an end to slavery agitation.

Under the operation of that policy, that agitation has not only, *not ceased*, but has *constantly augmented.*

In *my* opinion, it *will* not cease, until a *crisis* shall have been reached, and passed.

"A house divided against itself cannot stand."

I believe this government cannot endure, permanently half *slave* and half *free.*

I do not expect the Union to be *dissolved*—I do not expect the house to *fall*—but I *do* expect it will cease to be divided.

It will become *all* one thing, or *all* the other.

Either the opponents of slavery, will arrest the further spread of it, and place it where the public mind shall rest in the belief that it is in course of ultimate extinction; or its *advocates* will push it forward till it shall become alike lawful in *all* the States, *old* as well as *new*—North as well as *South*.[617]

The national stage had been set for the debates. Lincoln, still relatively unknown outside Illinois, had become an authentic Republican alternative to Douglas and his policies. Some of Mr. Lincoln's supporters and opponents thought his convention speech so radical that it would doom his chances to win the Senate seat in Illinois. So did Douglas. One month later, talking in Springfield on July 17, Douglas argued: "In his Chicago speech [Lincoln] says in so many words that [Negroes] were endowed by the Almighty with the right of equality with the white man, and therefore that that right is divine—a right under the higher law; that the law of God makes them equal to the white man, and, and therefore that the law of the white man cannot deprive them of that right. . . . I do not doubt that he in his conscience, believes that the Almighty made the negro equal to the white man. He thinks that the negro is his brother. [Laughter.] I do not think the negro is any kin of mine at all. [Laughter and cheers.] And here is the difference between us."[618] The race-baiting of Senator Douglas appealed to many listeners and readers.

By contrast Lincoln began his 1858 campaign in the same magnanimous spirit which he had exhibited in his "debates" with Douglas in 1854 at Peoria. Now in 1858, he again followed Douglas around Illinois. In late

1856 & Dred Scott

John C. Frémont

The Gilder Lehrman Collection, courtesy of the Gilder Lehrman Institute of American History, on deposit at the New-York Historical Society, New York, reference number GLC 5111.02.0378

James Buchanan

The Gilder Lehrman Collection, courtesy of the Gilder Lehrman Institute of American History, on deposit at the New-York Historical Society, New York, reference number GLC 1453

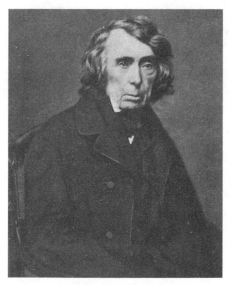

Roger B. Taney

The Gilder Lehrman Collection, courtesy of the Gilder Lehrman Institute of American History, on deposit at the New-York Historical Society, New York, reference number GLC 05111.02.0998

Dred Scott

Courtesy of the Abraham Lincoln Presidential Library, reference number NI-4597

July Lincoln attended a speech by Douglas at Clinton. When the crowd demanded that he too speak, Lincoln replied: "This is Judge Douglas's meeting. I have no right and therefore no disposition to interfere, but if you ladies and gentlemen desire to hear what I have to say on these questions, and will meet me tonight at the Court-house yard, I *will try* and answer the gentleman."[619] Lincoln had already sent Douglas a formal challenge on July 24 which would lead to the legendary Lincoln-Douglas debates, but Douglas bristled at these attempts to piggyback a Lincoln appearance onto his well-attended speeches. "On the road from Monticello to Bement, he passed Lincoln, hastening to Monticello to answer him," wrote George Fort Milton. "Lincoln had better come on to Bement with him, Douglas hailed jocularly, he would give his rival a much bigger crowd than Lincoln could get 'on his own.'"[620] But this was hollow humor for Douglas, who was now under siege and knew it. His fractured party required help. An old ally from the Kansas-Nebraska battles, Georgia Congressman Alexander H. Stephens, came to Illinois to restore his own health. Stephens denied, despite rumors to the contrary, that he attempted to broker peace between pro-Douglas and pro-Buchanan factions in the Illinois Democratic Party.[621]

At Clinton on July 27, 1858, Lincoln renewed the Peoria themes of 1854. As attorney Lawrence Weldon recalled his message that night: "Judge Douglas charges me with being in favor of negro equality. . . . *I am guilty* of hating servitude and loving freedom; and while I would not carry the equality of the races to the extent charged by my adversary, I am happy to confess before you that in some things the black man is the equal of the white man. In the right to eat the bread his own hands have earned he is the equal of Judge Douglas or any other living man." Weldon wrote: "When Lincoln spoke the last sentence he had lifted himself to his full height, and as he reached his hands toward the stars of that still night, then and there fell from his lips one of the most sublime expressions of American statesmanship." When he received the congratulations of friends on the felicity of his phrasing, Lincoln asked: "Do you think that is fine?" When Weldon assured him that it was, Lincoln laughed: "Well, if you think so, I will get that off again."[622] And so he did.

Douglas could not escape a public confrontation; he therefore structured a series of debates that would give him an edge. In 1854, he had been wary of joint appearances; in 1858 he negotiated to obtain the advantage. Because many Illinois constituents believed Lincoln had won the argument in 1854, Douglas sought to go first and last—as he did at Springfield and Peoria in 1854. In four of the seven debates of 1858, Douglas would open and close, including the first and last debates. Lincoln would have that opportunity in three debates.

During August, both candidates continued their separate speaking engagements across Illinois. At Peoria, Lincoln met with supporters and discussed how to hold on to old line Whigs who were drifting to Douglas. Lincoln again spoke at the county court house—this time to an overflow crowd. According to one witness, Lincoln's "arguments were a reiteration of the grand truths enunciated in his Springfield ["House Divided"] speech, with perhaps some change of terms and language, with new illustrations to enforce them. . . . It convinced the doubting, confirmed the wavering, and converted many from the democratic [party] faith that were open to receive the truths so plainly told."[623] In another speech at Beardstown, Lincoln closed with a spirited paean to the intent of the Founders to end slavery by ending the slave trade—thus putting slavery on the road to extinction. The following day, Horace White reconstructed Lincoln's remarks:

Now, if slavery had been a good thing, would the Fathers of the Republic have taken a step calculated to diminish its beneficent influences among themselves, and snatch the boon wholly from their posterity? These communities, by their representatives in old Independence Hall, said to the whole world of men: "We hold these truths to be self evident: that all men are created equal; that they are endowed by their Creator with certain unalienable rights; that among these are life, liberty and the pursuit of happiness." This was their majestic interpretation of the economy of the Universe. . . . In their enlightened belief, nothing stamped with the Divine image and likeness was sent into the world to be trodden on, and degraded, and imbruted by its fellows. They grasped not only the whole race of man then living, but they reached forward and seized upon the farthest posterity.

Lincoln again acknowledged his ambition for the Senate: "While pretending no indifference to earthly honors, I *do claim to* be actuated in this contest by something higher than an anxiety for office. I charge you to drop every paltry and insignificant thought for any man's success. It is nothing; I am nothing; Judge Douglas is nothing. *But do not destroy that immortal emblem of Humanity—the Declaration of American Independence.*"[624]

From the outset of the 1858 debates, Lincoln and Douglas focused on the arguments of 1854, the subsequent events in Kansas, and the *Dred Scott* decision of 1857. At the first debate in Ottawa on August 21, Douglas charged that Lincoln had participated in the Republican organizing committee at Springfield in 1854 that Douglas alleged had approved several radical measures against slavery. The source of the allegation was a speech given by Congressman Thomas L. Harris, the Democrat who had ousted Congressman Richard Yates in 1854. A few days before the Ottawa debate, Douglas had written the editor of the *Springfield Register*: "I find in the State Register of August 28th, 1856, a speech delivered by Major Harris in the House of Reps. on the 9th of August, 1856, in which is copied a resolution described as adopted at the first state convention of the Black Republican party as a part of their platform. I desire to know the time and place at which that convention was held, whether it was a mass meeting or a delegate Convention, whether Lincoln was present and made a speech and such other facts concerning the matter as you may be able to give. This information is very important and I want it immediately. Please consult Major Harris, hunt up the facts and write to me instantly directed to Ottawa. I must have it before next Saturday."[625]

The pre-debate speeches suggest that Douglas had no intention of being put on the defensive. David Zarefsky, a scholar of Lincoln rhetoric, noted: "Douglas's basic strategy was . . . to focus attention away from his own Senate record, which he would have to defend, and to concentrate instead on Lincoln, so that he might attack and shift to his challenger the burden of proof."[626] Lincoln's position was also aggressive. His focus was the inconsistency between the policy of Douglas and the policy of the Founders. He was confident. As one of Robert Todd Lincoln's friends remembered it, Lincoln "carried on the fight of his life; was earnest, fighting a fight he expected to win . . ."[627]

The Lincoln-Douglas Debates

At Ottawa, Lincoln received the opening challenge from Douglas, whose strident allegations against Lincoln turned out to be based on inaccurate information from Douglas friend Charles H. Lanphier. The radical antislavery resolutions that Douglas cited at Ottawa had not in fact been passed at the Springfield meeting in October 1854. Nor had Lincoln been present at that meeting. Horace White recalled:

> Finding Lincoln's name in the list of members of the Republican State committee there appointed, [Douglas] assumed that Lincoln had been present and had taken part in the proceedings. So he wrote to Charles H. Lanphier, editor of the *Register*, the Democratic organ at Springfield, asking for a copy of the resolution passed at the meeting. Lanphier replied by sending him two copies of the *Register* of October 16, 1854, which purported to give a brief report of the meeting, including a copy of the resolutions in full. But for some reason, a different set of resolutions had been substituted for the real ones in the *Register*'s report. The bogus resolutions demanded, among other things, an entire repeal of the fugitive slave law. The real resolutions contained no such demand. There were also other material differences. Lincoln came to the conclusion eventually that Lanphier himself had made the substitution in order to help Thomas L. Harris in his local Congressional campaign against Richard Yates, and that when Douglas, four years later, called for a copy of the resolutions, he [Lanphier] had forgotten the circumstances of the change. At all events, the resolutions were substantially a forgery. They had been passed at some irresponsible gathering in Kane County and had been substituted for the real resolutions of the

Springfield meeting. Douglas was not a party to the forgery, but, as it turned out, was the principal victim of it.[628]

In his response at Ottawa, Lincoln wove together the causes and consequences of the Kansas-Nebraska Act—resurrecting the precise language and logic he had used in 1854. He began by quoting extensively from his own Peoria address, but he prefaced his quotation by saying: "Now gentlemen, I hate to waste my time on such things, but in regard to that general abolition tilt that Judge Douglas makes, when he says I was engaged at the time in selling out and abolitionizing the old Whig party—I hope you will permit me to read a part of a printed speech that I made then at Peoria...in that contest of 1854." He then put on his spectacles and read six paragraphs from the Peoria speech, beginning by noting the effect of the Kansas-Nebraska Act: "This is the *repeal* of the Missouri Compromise. . . ." He ended this self-quotation by emphasizing the logic of repeal: "The law which forbids the bringing of slaves from Africa; and that which has so long forbid the taking of them to Nebraska, can hardly be distinguished on any moral principle, and the repeal of the former could find quite as plausible excuses as that of the latter."[629] Lincoln quoted the exact words of his Peoria speech to distinguish between his own antislavery policy and the more radical program of the abolitionists. He then added: "I have reason to know that Judge Douglas *knows* that I said this." In case the Judge did not get the point, Lincoln drove it home with a variation on another theme from Peoria. "Now gentlemen, I don't want to read at any greater length, but this is the true complexion of all I have ever said in regard to the institution of slavery and the black race. This is the whole of it, and anything that argues me into his idea of perfect social and political equality with the negro, is but a specious and fantastic arrangement of words, by which a man can prove a horse chestnut to be a chestnut horse. [Laughter.] I will say here, while upon this subject, that I have no purpose directly or indirectly to interfere with the institution of slavery in the States where it exists. I believe I have no lawful right to do so, and I have no inclination to do so"[630] Once again, Lincoln proved as much a master of metaphor as he was a master of logic. He continued to make a careful distinction between what was lawful and what was not.

Lincoln later said Ottawa was his favorite presentation: "I was better pleased with myself at Ottawa than at any other place."[631] Shortly after Ottawa, Lincoln remarked that he and Douglas "crossed swords here yesterday; the fire [fur] flew some, and I am glad to know I am yet alive. There was a vast concourse of people—more than could get near enough to hear."[632] In his speech at Carlinville on August 31, Lincoln again quoted from Peoria.[633] He did so again at Clinton on September 2, and again at Bloomington on September 4.[634] In many ways, Peoria of 1854 had been a rehearsal for the debates of 1858. By the summer of 1858, Lincoln had compiled a scrapbook of speech materials—starting with the printed Declaration of Independence and including speeches by Douglas and himself.[635] Lincoln knew from careful research what he had said, when he had said it, and where it was in print. One Republican candidate, Capt. James N. Brown, wrote Lincoln for advice on how to handle criticism in 1858 of Lincoln's positions. Lincoln put together a notebook of clippings for Brown with the preface: "The following extracts are taken from various speeches of mine delivered at various times and places, and I believe they contain all I have ever said about 'Negro equality.'" He began with three crucial excerpts from the Peoria speech of 1854.[636]

Douglas had tried to verify Lincoln's role in the organization of the Republican Party, but Douglas ally Lanphier had not done his research carefully. So, at the Ottawa debate, Douglas repeated the resolutions published in Lanphier's *State Register*, a Democrat paper. Douglas asserted they came from the October 1854 Republican convention in Springfield. Subsequently, the Chicago *Press and Tribune*, a Republican paper, reported that the resolutions Douglas used were the ones adopted at Aurora, not Springfield. Lincoln was present at neither meeting. The tables had been turned and by the Freeport debate, it was Douglas who was under attack for deceptive campaign statements.[637]

The 1858 debates dealt with the salient slavery issues, the competing policies to resolve them, and the intent of the Founders. Both candidates tried to define principles and practical measures to distinguish their positions. Douglas pressed the case that Lincoln was a radical abolitionist. And in the words of historian Theodore Clarke Smith, Lincoln "showed also that the fundamental difference between himself and Douglas lay in the fact that he regarded slavery as wrong, while Douglas reiterated his entire indifference."[638] Don E. Fehrenbacher emphasized that Lincoln stuck to his theme: "The basic strategy of convincing the public that slavery should be placed on the course of extinction through its elimination in the federal territories remained constant."[639] David Zarefsky went further when he wrote that Lincoln: "wanted to portray Douglas as actually favoring the spread of slavery and to place on Douglas the responsibility for denying the charge."[640] In 1858, as at Peoria in 1854, the moral issue of slavery preoccupied Lincoln. At the final debate in Alton, Lincoln employed an argument from Peoria:

> That is the real issue. That is the issue that will continue in this country when these poor tongues of Judge Douglas and myself shall be silent. It is the eternal struggle between these two principles—right and wrong—throughout the world. They are the two principles that have stood face to face from the beginning of time; and will ever continue to struggle. The one is the common right of humanity and the other the divine right of kings. It is the same principle in whatever shape it develops itself. It is the same spirit that says, "You work and toil and earn bread, and I'll eat it." [Loud applause.] No matter in what shape it comes, whether from the mouth of a king who seeks to bestride the people of his own nation and live by the fruit of their labor, or from one race of men as an apology for enslaving another race, it is the same tyrannical principle. I was glad to express my gratitude at Quincy, and I re-express it here to Judge Douglas—*that he looks to no end of the institution of slavery.* That will help the people to see where the struggle really is. It will hereafter place with us all men who really do wish the wrong may have an end. And whenever we can get rid of the fog which obscures the real question—when we can get Judge Douglas and his friends to avow a policy looking to its perpetuation—we can get out from among them that class of men and bring them to the side of those who treat it as a wrong. Then there will soon be an end of it, and that end will be its ultimate extinction.[641]

Slavery was wrong. That was the nub of Lincoln's argument. The Constitution of 1787 had protected slavery in the states where it already existed, but there was no constitutional protection for its extension. Furthermore, Congress was authorized by Article IV, Section III of the Constitution to prohibit slavery in the territories.[642] Indeed, there was a presumption at the birth of the republic on behalf of free-soil, beginning with the Declaration of Independence and the Northwest Ordinance.[643] Lincoln reminded his audiences that extinction of slavery, even shame at its existence in the early republic, was implied by the Constitution's omission of the word "slavery." Gabor S. Boritt wrote that Lincoln "could declare that slavery was not 'distinctly' and 'expressly' affirmed in the Constitution. In contrast, like countless nationalists before him, he noted that the Constitution 'expressly charged' the federal government 'with the duty of providing for the general welfare.'"[644] Lincoln said at Dayton, Ohio, in 1859: "We believe that the spreading out and perpetuity of the institution of slavery impairs the general welfare. We believe—nay, we know, that that is the only thing that has ever threatened the perpetuity of the Union itself."[645]

Lincoln argued that freedom in America was national, but slavery was local. He held that the moral issue of the black man's right to the fruit of his labors derived not only from the Declaration's inalienable right to liberty, but also from economic justice. At Alton, Lincoln centered the debate: "The real issue in this controversy—the one pressing upon every mind—is the sentiment on the part of one class that looks upon the institution of slavery *as a wrong*, and of another class that *does not* look upon it as a wrong."[646] To repeat this proposition was a fundamental strategy of Lincoln's rhetoric, made necessary because Douglas contrived to avoid the fundamental moral dimension of the slavery issue. As Douglas biographer William Garrott Brown wrote: "Douglas did not, and perhaps he could not, follow Lincoln when he passed from the Declaration and the Constitution to the 'higher law,' from the question of rights to the question of right and wrong; for there Lincoln rose not merely above Douglas, but above all that sort of politics which both he and Douglas came out of. There, indeed, was the true difference between these men and their causes. Douglas seems to shrink backward into the past, and Lincoln to come nearer and grow larger as he proclaims: 'That is the issue which will continue in this country when these poor tongues of Judge Douglas and myself shall be silent. It is the eternal struggle between these two principles, right and wrong, throughout the world.'"[647] For Lincoln the objective moral order did exist. Thus, he insisted that if "you admit that [slavery] is wrong," Douglas "cannot logically say that anybody has a right to do wrong "[648]

In January 1859 the Illinois state legislature would again elect a U.S. senator. The defection to Douglas of some old Whig allies like T. Lyle Dickey hurt Lincoln. Although in November 1858 Republicans had won many more individual votes for their state legislative candidates, they trailed the Democrats in elected members of the legislature. The difference was due to malapportionment and incumbent Democrat state senators who were not up for reelection in 1858. Democrats thus had enough votes to reelect Senator Douglas by a 54–46 margin.

Lincoln had few regrets about his defeat in the 1858 campaign, writing: "In the last canvass I strove to do my whole duty both to our cause, and to the kind friends who had assigned me the post of honor; and now if those friends find no cause to regret that they did not assign that post to other hands, I have none for having made the effort, even though it has ended in personal defeat. I hope and believe seed has been sown that will yet produce fruit. The fight must go on. Douglas managed to be supported both as the best means to *break down*, and to *uphold* the slave power. No ingenuity can long keep those opposing elements in harmony. Another explosion will come before a great while."[649] As events would unfold over the next three years, Lincoln's Peoria platform would ultimately prevail. Lincoln took care that the seven debates, carefully edited, were printed as a large pamphlet. Chicago Republican Isaac N. Arnold contended that "the speeches of Lincoln published, circulated, and read throughout the Free States, did more than any other agency in creating the public opinion, which prepared the way for the overthrow of slavery."[650]

At Peoria in 1854, and elsewhere in 1857 and 1858, Lincoln remarked that in a democracy public policy could not be effectively influenced without a prudent respect for public opinion. "Public sentiment is everything," he said.[651] By debating the nation's most prominent Democrat, Lincoln aimed to change public sentiment—inside and outside of Illinois. Hugh McCulloch, who in 1865 would become President Lincoln's third secretary of the treasury, recalled that he saw Lincoln speak in Indianapolis, Indiana, after the 1858 campaign—probably in September 1859: "The subject was slavery—its character, its incompatibility with Republican institutions, its demoralizing influences upon society, its aggressiveness, its rights as limited by the Constitution; all of which were discussed with such clearness, simplicity, earnestness, and force as to carry me with him to the conclusion that the country could not long continue part slave and part free—that freedom must prevail throughout the length and breadth of the land, or that the great Republic, instead of being the home of the free and the hope of the oppressed, would become a by-word and a reproach among the nations."[652] In the Lincoln-Douglas debates of 1858 the most fundamental issue of the early American republic had been joined: Would America ultimately become a slaveholding republic or a free-soil republic?

The Presidential Campaign

In 1858, Democratic Congressman Thomas L. Harris died. In the fall of 1859, an election was held to replace him. Five years after his unsuccessful campaign to support Whig Richard Yates, Lincoln campaigned for John M. Palmer, the erstwhile Democrat whom he had urged to stay quiet in the Yates-Harris congressional race of 1854. It was an uphill race for Republican Palmer; Douglas Democrat John A. McClernand won the Harris seat. Still, Lincoln and his allies served notice that the Republican campaign and its growing coalition would persist until victorious.

In almost every place Lincoln spoke, he pressed the distinction between the right of freedom and the wrong of slavery. In Chicago, in March 1859, Lincoln implored his listeners: "Never forget that we have before us this whole matter of the right or wrong of slavery in this Union, though the immediate question is as to its spreading out into new Territories and States."[653] In a speech at Columbus, Ohio, in September 1859, Lincoln said that Senator Douglas "is so put up by nature that a lash upon his back would hurt him, but a lash upon anybody else's back does not hurt him." Lincoln suggested that "Judge Douglas ought to remember when he is endeavoring to force this policy upon the American people that while he is put up in that way a good many are not. He ought to remember that there was once in this country a man by the name of Thomas Jefferson, supposed to be a Democrat" who wrote of slavery: "I tremble for my country when I remember that God is just!"[654] Lincoln's sense of justice was expressed in the memorable aphorism, committed privately to paper: "As I would not be a *slave*, so I would not be a *master.*"[655]

Senator Douglas had been scheduled to campaign in Ohio in early September 1859. Ohio Republican leaders recruited Lincoln to answer him. Although the Illinois Republican spoke to smaller crowds, he may have had the bigger impact with his biting critique of an important *Harper's* magazine article written by Douglas. Douglas campaigned again in Ohio after Lincoln left, but Republicans won the state's gubernatorial election in early October. Though they did not debate face to face, each engaged the arguments of the other. Lincoln tried to mitigate Republican admiration for the way that the indomitable Douglas had fought the Buchanan administration over the Lecompton constitution. "Lincoln's great strategic aim," wrote Harry V. Jaffa and Robert W. Johannsen, "both in the Illinois campaign of 1858 and the Ohio campaign of 1859, was to destroy Douglas' credentials as a free-soil champion, credentials which he had gained in large measure because of his leadership of the fight against Lecompton, in which the Republican Congressional delegation had been his followers."[656] Some eastern Republicans such as Horace Greeley, the powerful and impulsive Republican editor of the New York *Tribune*, had fallen into this trap.

In defending popular sovereignty, Douglas argued that Taney's *Dred Scott* ruling notwithstanding, the people of a territory could still restrict slavery if they did not legally protect it. Lincoln at Colombus was devastating in his critique of Douglas and his response to the *Dred Scott* decision: "When all the trash, the words, the collateral matter was cleared away from it; all the chaff was fanned out of it, it was a bare absurdity—*no less than a thing may be lawfully driven away from where it has a lawful right to be.* [Cheers and laughter.] Clear it of all the verbiage, and that is the naked truth of his proposition—that a thing may be lawfully driven from the place where it has a lawful right to stay."[657]

It was timely, therefore, that in late 1859 Lincoln visited Kansas— Atchison on December 2 and Leavenworth on December 4–5. (Atchison had been founded in 1854 and named for Missouri Senator David Rice Atchison.) At his first Kansas stop in Elwood on November 30, Lincoln returned to the historical narrative of his Peoria speech: "The general feeling in regard to Slavery has changed entirely since the early days of the republic. You may examine the debates under the Confederation, in the Convention that framed the Constitution and in the first session of Congress and you will not find a single man saying that Slavery is a good thing. They all believed it was an evil. They made the Northwest Territory, the only Territory then belonging to the government, forever *free*. They prohibited the African Slave trade. Having thus prevented its extension and cut off the supply, the Fathers of the Republic believed Slavery must soon disappear."[658]

Lincoln's speech and manner in Atchison in 1859 were as distinctive as they had been at Peoria in 1854. Typically, one listener in Atchison described Lincoln's address as "most logical and vigorous."[659] At Leavenworth, "Mr. Lincoln argued that those who thought Slavery right ought to unite on a policy which should deal with it as being right; that they should go for a revival of the Slave Trade; for carrying the institution everywhere, into Free States as well as Territories; and for a surrender of fugitive slaves in Canada, or war with Great Britain." But Lincoln insisted that "all those who believe slavery is wrong should unite on a policy, dealing with it as a wrong. They should be deluded into no deceitful contrivances, pretending indifference, but really working for that to which they are opposed."[660] For Lincoln indifference was a deceit, the subtle siren of popular sovereignty and slavery.

During 1859 Lincoln the private citizen began to think of his dark horse availability for the 1860 Republican presidential nomination. Noah Brooks had earlier asked Lincoln, "Do you think we shall elect a Free-Soil President in 1860?" The future President replied: "Well, I don't know. Everything depends on the course of the Democracy. . . . There's a big antislavery element in the Democratic party, and if we could get hold of that, we might possibly elect our man in 1860. But it's doubtful—*very* doubtful. Perhaps we shall be able to fetch it by 1864; perhaps not. As I said before, the Free-Soil party is bound to win in the long run."[661] One of the first boosters of Abraham Lincoln's presidential nomination was Peoria *Republican* editor Thomas J. Pickett—the same journalist who had witnessed Lincoln's Peoria campaign speech of 1844. When asked by Pickett in April 1859 if he might promote such a candidacy, Lincoln replied: "I must in candor, say I do not think myself fit for the Presidency."[662] Pickett and other Illinois editors did not agree.

Lincoln's answer to Pickett was modest, but he did not disclaim an interest. His Peoria speech of 1854 had led to his first Senate candidacy in January 1855. His "House Divided" speech and the Lincoln-Douglas debates of 1858 had gained Lincoln national attention during his second bid for a Senate seat. These efforts triggered a series of political actions and reactions, which led to more speeches, which led to more political invitations, which led to more speeches. In late 1859 came an invitation to speak in New York City early in 1860. At Cooper Union in Manhattan on February 27, 1860, Lincoln mobilized the techniques and themes of his Peoria speech. As Lincoln scholar Harold Holzer detailed, Lincoln spelled out the history of slavery with particular emphasis on the Founders' intentions and their actions. Many days in the library of the Illinois Supreme Court enabled him to unearth more facts and circumstances to reinforce the case he had made at Peoria. Statements of historical fact preoccupied Lincoln the litigator and he worked assiduously to assure their accuracy. When James O. Putnam made a mistake in a speech he delivered, Lincoln generously wrote Putnam: "You must not lay much stress on the blunder about Mr. Adams; for I made a more mischievous one, in the first printed speech of mine, on the Slavery question—Oct. 1854—I stated that the prohibition of slavery in the North West Territory was made a condition in the Virginia deed of cession—while, in fact, it was not. Like yourself, I have since done what I could to correct the error."[663]

Lincoln habitually corrected not only his opponents, but also his own statements. In June 1860, he wrote Chicago journalist John L. Scripps to make sure that "in any reprint of the [1854] speech, the text should be preserved, but there should be a note stating the error" heretofore described.[664] Lincoln took great care that his major speeches were printed accurately. When possible, he edited them personally. But as this letter to Scripps suggests, he was scrupulous in urging that his original error continue to be reprinted as part of the original text, only correcting it in a footnote. Lincoln was well aware of his widening readership. He understood the increasing importance of his speeches to the national antislavery cause. Their originality and persuasiveness had become his trademark. Moreover in 1854, Lincoln had largely abandoned his old habit of ridicule. His rhetoric had become more temperate, even magnanimous at times. But on the extension of slavery, he remained uncompromising. In the concluding appeal of his Cooper Union speech, Lincoln invoked the tone of Peoria:

> Wrong as we think slavery is, we can yet afford to let it alone where it is, because that much is due to the necessity arising from its actual presence in the nation; but can we, while our votes will prevent it, allow it to spread into the National Territories, and to overrun us here in these Free States? If our sense of duty forbids this, then let us stand by our duty, fearlessly and effectively. Let us be diverted by none of those sophistical contrivances wherewith we are so industriously plied and belabored—contrivances such as groping for some middle ground between right and the wrong, vain as the search for a man who should be neither a living man nor a dead man—such as a policy of "don't care" on a question about which all true men do care—such as Union appeals beseeching true Union men to yield to Disunionists, reversing the divine rule, and calling, not the sinners, but the righteous to repentance—such as invocations to Washington, imploring men to unsay what Washington said, and undo what Washington did.
>
> Neither let us be slandered from our duty by false accusations against us, nor frightened from it by menaces of destruction to the Government nor of dungeons to ourselves. LET US HAVE FAITH THAT RIGHT MAKES MIGHT, AND IN THAT FAITH, LET US, TO THE END, DARE TO DO OUR DUTY AS WE UNDERSTAND IT.[665]

With this memorable exhortation, Lincoln concluded. Lincoln scholar Harold Holzer noted that "the Cooper Union address was a magnificent anomaly, both lawyerly and impassioned; empirical and scholarly; a
moderation of Lincoln's style and tone, accompanied by a stiffening reiteration of moral purpose; no 'house divided' jeremiad, but instead a
clear vision of national justice, animated by the confident expectation
that it would prevail."[666] When Lincoln delivered his Cooper Union
speech, the South had for some time been threatening disunion. Southerners had been accustomed to dominating the Washington government
and they feared the Republican Party's free-soil program. The shifting
national balance of power had often before led to discussion of the
South's withdrawal from the union. "Over the decades, the federal government had effectively become a proslavery instrument by means of
multiple little decisions and unconscious drift," wrote Don E. Fehrenbacher. "But with a northern majoritarian impulse threatening to over-
whelm past practices, the South demanded that the federal government
enforce what it had come to regard as binding constitutional guarantees
[of slavery]. . . . If the federal government failed to fulfill its constitutional
duty, as southerners perceived it, the dismemberment of the Union itself
would necessarily follow."[667]

Lincoln generally dismissed the intimidating threats of the slave
power. Further, he insisted that Congress had not only the constitutional
power but also the duty to prohibit slavery in the territories. Aware of
slaveholder threats of disunion which he believed to be exaggerated, Lincoln at Cooper Union provided a comprehensive rationale for the Republican presidential campaign of 1860. Thereafter, he was recognized as a
national Republican leader and a dark horse presidential contender.
Nearly three months later, Lincoln acknowledged the upcoming presidential contest in a letter to Senator Lyman Trumbull: "As you request, I
will be entirely frank. The taste *is* in my mouth a little; and this, no doubt,
disqualifies me, to some extent, to form correct opinions. You may confidently rely, however, that by no advice or consent of mine, shall my pre-
tentions [*sic*] be pressed to the point of endangering our common
cause."[668] Friends of Lincoln pressed the case for him. The taste was
much more than a little in their mouths.

In mid-May 1860 the Republican National Convention met at Chicago. Lincoln's allies produced what many thought a political miracle by engineering his presidential nomination on the third ballot. The leaders of this effort included three anti-Nebraska Democrats who had voted against Lincoln in the Senate contest of February 1855. Republican State Chairman Norman B. Judd had shrewdly negotiated the selection of Chicago as the site for the national convention. In May 1860 at Decatur, John M. Palmer had nominated Lincoln for President at the Illinois Republican State Convention. A third pro-Trumbull vote from 1855, Burton C. Cook, helped orchestrate the Lincoln campaign demonstration on the floor of the Chicago convention. These three were joined by a remarkable coalition of old Whigs and Democrats, many of them longtime legal and political friends and associates of Lincoln. They worked tirelessly in Chicago to derail the candidacy of New York Senator William H. Seward, the favorite, and to nominate Lincoln in his place. Anticipating victory in the general election, Republicans united behind the one-term congressman, now "the railsplitter" or "Honest Abe" from Illinois. In the four-way presidential election of November 1860, Lincoln defeated three well-known opponents: Senator Stephen A. Douglas, Vice President John C. Breckinridge, and former Tennessee Senator John Bell.

President-elect Lincoln would go to Washington, but he would take with him the antislavery principles first defined at Peoria.

"Let north and south—let all Americans—let all lovers of liberty everywhere—join in the great and good work. If we do this, we shall not only have saved the Union; but we shall have so saved it, as to make, and to keep it, forever worthy of the saving. We shall have so saved it, that the succeeding millions of free happy people, the world over, shall rise up, and call us blessed, to the latest generations."

ABRAHAM LINCOLN,
OCTOBER 16, 1854

VII.

Peoria Characterizes the Lincoln Presidency

Mary A. Livermore was a Bostonian transplanted to Chicago a few years before the Civil War. Her husband edited a religious periodical to which she contributed. Together, they attended the Republican National Convention in May 1860. Seated in the journalists' section on the platform near the podium, Mrs. Livermore gained a closer, clearer picture of the nomination of Abraham Lincoln than other women, who were confined to the balcony of the cavernous Wigwam. Over 9,000 delegates and observers had gathered there to choose the Republican presidential candidate.

Pandemonium broke out the moment Abraham Lincoln of Illinois triumphed over Senator Seward of New York. Mrs. Livermore, however, remained unmoved and skeptical. In her memoirs she recalled: "It seemed to me these demonstrations were made rather because the antislavery principles had triumphed than because Lincoln himself was a special favorite." So she inquired of a Massachusetts reporter near her: "Is it *certain* that Mr. Lincoln is an uncompromising anti-slavery man? . . . Mr. Lincoln is not anti-slavery just now for the sake of getting votes, is he?" The reporter then took "from his pocketbook a little fragment of newspaper, which contained this extract from his 'Peoria, Ill., speech,' made Oct. 16,

1854, and passed it to me with the simple query, 'Do you think he can back track after saying that?'" Mrs. Livermore then read the clipping:

> "Slavery is founded in the selfishness of man's nature—opposition to it, in the love of justice. These principles are an eternal antagonism; and when brought into collision as fiercely as slavery extension brings them, shocks and throes and convulsions must follow ceaselessly. Repeal the Missouri Compromise; repeal all compromises; repeal the Declaration of Independence; repeal all past history; you cannot repeal human nature. It will still be in the abundance of man's heart that slavery extension is wrong, and out of the abundance of the heart his mouth will continue to speak."[669]

Not only did Lincoln's Peoria speech lay the intellectual groundwork for his presidential nomination, but it also spelled out the principles and some of the polices which guided the Lincoln presidency. In a footnote to their *Complete Works of Abraham Lincoln*, erstwhile White House aides John G. Nicolay and John Hay wrote that "the Peoria speech, together with one delivered twelve days before at Springfield, made Lincoln a power in national politics. He had had little to do with politics since the expiration of his term in Congress, but the repeal of the Missouri Compromise aroused him to instant action. . . . When closely studied the Peoria speech reveals germs of many of the powerful arguments elaborated by Lincoln later in his career."[670]

Many who later studied the Peoria speech discovered these "germs" of presidential policies. Biographer Albert J. Beveridge observed "that, in the winter of 1854–55, no human being, so far as is known, had an inkling of Lincoln's greatness; nor, at that time, did a ray of that fame which was to blaze about his name a decade later penetrate backward from the future through those hidden years."[671] To borrow the usage of historian Don Fehrenbacher, Lincoln's years from Peoria to the presidency were a "prelude to greatness." Lincoln biographer Ida Tarbell, using the Nicolay-Hay metaphor that Lincoln himself had used, noted that the Peoria speech contained "the germ of many of the arguments which he elaborated in the next six years and used with tremendous effect."[672] His stream of arguments for freedom, equality, and the perpetuity of the union ran fast through the decade from the Peoria speech to the abolition of slavery in 1865. "Lincoln's speeches usually drew upon previous speeches, notes, or earlier spontaneous remarks," noted Lincoln scholar Ronald C. White Jr. "Lincoln never started out to write a speech from scratch."[673] Peoria did have a few echoes from the past, but the *Collected Works of Abraham Lincoln* prior to 1854 show that the Peoria speech is substantially a new work without precedent in the Lincoln canon. Thus did it become a political turning point for Lincoln. The controversies of Bleeding Kansas and *Dred Scott* further intensified his determination to attain leadership in the fight against the extension of slavery.[674]

Though as a boy and a young man Lincoln lacked the advantage of academic training, it is a mistake to underestimate the sophistication of his intellect. The philosophical, economic, and legal reasoning evident in his speeches, letters, and papers mark Lincoln among America's most intellectually gifted presidents. His judgment was comprehensive and his learning deep. His program to restrict the spread of slavery, while preserving the Union, even at the risk of war, was presented in a temperate, disciplined tone. Political philosopher Joseph R. Fornieri wrote: "The design of Lincoln's argument at Peoria drew upon and integrated various constitutional, biblical, legal and republican sources against slavery extension."[675] Essential to Lincoln's antislavery nationalism was his belief that if the American Union were divided between slave states and free states, the extinction of slavery in the South would become implausible. So too, would an American schism diminish the hope of freedom around the world.

Lincoln's demeanor and his vocabulary after 1854 became nearly as important as his message. His rhetoric became serious and self-confident; he used fewer stories and less sarcasm. William O. Stoddard observed that "Mr. Lincoln, in his political speeches, resorted to none of the tricks common among what are called stump speakers. He was thoroughly in earnest and always closely argumentative. If he told stories, it was not to amuse a crowd, but to illustrate a point. The real questions at issue engaged his entire attention, and he never undertook to raise a false issue or to dodge a real one. Indeed, he seemed incapable of the tricks so often resorted to for the discomfiture of an opponent."[676] At Peoria, Lincoln had diverged not only from rival Stephen A. Douglas in style and substance, but he had also abandoned the personal attacks of his stump speeches of the 1830s and 1840s.

As president, Lincoln held fast to his program—even after three years of unavailing war when armistice with the Confederacy beckoned. In July 1864, Lincoln prepared a note for use in peace negotiations being promoted by the editor of the New York *Tribune*, Horace Greeley: "Any proposition which embraces the restoration of peace, the integrity of the whole Union, and the abandonment of slavery, and which comes by and with an authority that can control the armies now at war against the United States will be received and considered by the Executive government of the United States, and will be met by liberal terms on other substantial and collateral points; and the bearer, or bearers thereof shall have safe-conduct both ways."[677] Lincoln used precise language. Peace without union was unthinkable. Peace with slavery was unacceptable. Peace must come with emancipation and union.

When "the tug came"—between Lincoln and secessionists in the winter of 1860–1861—he did not compromise his opposition to the extension of slavery despite great pressure from Congress. In December 1860, President-elect Lincoln wrote Illinois Senator Trumbull in Washington: "Let there be no compromise on the question of *extending* slavery."[678] A day later, determined to lead the Republicans in Washington, Lincoln wrote Congressman William Kellogg: "Entertain no proposition for a compromise in regard to the *extension* of slavery. The instant you do, they have us under again; all our labor is lost and sooner or later must be done over. Douglas is sure to be again trying to bring in his 'Pop. Sov.' Have none of it. The tug has to come & better now than later."[679] Lincoln's leadership and tenacity as president contrasted sharply with the passivity and irresolution of James Buchanan, who believed that secession might be unconstitutional, but he had no power to resist it. Even Senator

Seward, who aspired to be President Lincoln's chief minister, desperately sought compromise with the South.

In the secession winter of 1860–61, Illinois Democrats sought to appease the South. One Lincoln friend, Dr. Franklin Blades, then a member of the Illinois House of Representatives, witnessed a Democratic Party convention in the State Capitol. "I was a lobby onlooker of that convention, and the incendiary speeches which were made and applauded to the echo, and the misapprehensions of Mr. Lincoln, were so vividly impressed on my memory that now, nearly fifty years after, they are recalled with almost startling distinctness." Blades noted that most Democratic speeches opposed the use of force against the South. He quoted one Chicago representative: "The tone and feeling of this convention responds to my own; and I am satisfied that, if such a conflict ever comes, it will be war *in the North, and not in the South.* (Applause.) It will be war in Chicago—war in Springfield—war on the broad prairies of Illinois. (Loud applause.) Before the patriotic people of this State will allow an invading force to pass beyond its border to subjugate the South, they will make one vast mausoleum of your State. (Continued applause.)"[680] Illinois, like the Union, was a house divided. But only twelve days after the surrender of Fort Sumter on April 13, 1861, a company of "National Blues" entrained at Peoria for Springfield, where they became Company E, 18th Regiment Illinois Volunteers for the Union.

Declaration of Independence and the Constitution

Perhaps no president, nor even any Founder, embraced the Declaration so often, so publicly, and so unequivocally as did Lincoln after Peoria. When he stopped at Independence Hall in Philadelphia on the way to Washington in February 1861, he admitted: "that all the political sentiments I entertain have been drawn, so far as I have been able to draw them, from the sentiments which originated, and were given to the world, from this hall in which we stand. I have never had a feeling politically that did not spring from the sentiments embodied in the Declaration of Independence."[681]

Two years and almost nine months later, President Lincoln spoke at Gettysburg. At the outset of his brief address on November 19, 1863, the president invoked the Founding act of Union: "Four score and seven years ago our fathers brought forth, on this continent, a new nation, conceived in Liberty, and dedicated to the proposition that all men are created equal."[682] That is, America had been founded by a congressional act of Union on July 4, 1776, not in 1788 by ratification of the new Constitution. Thus the Declaration and its principles had the standing of national law. John Patrick Diggins noted that the Gettysburg "speech never mentions the Constitution and it has little to do with legal compromises about slavery. Rather than giving the American people 'a new past,' Lincoln gave them an old past, the eighteenth-century America that 'offered a new nation, conceived in Liberty, and dedicated to the proposition that all men are created equal.'"[683] Restoration, not revolution, was Lincoln's purpose.

A self-described conservative, Lincoln was determined to conserve the Founding principles of liberty and equality upon which the Constitution had been constructed. Lincoln's commitment to the Constitution was as steadfast as his embrace of the Declaration. His mastery and understanding of both documents informed his leadership. Shortly before leaving Springfield in February 1861, Lincoln reportedly told William H. Herndon: "I am decided; my course is fixed; my path is blazed. The Union and the Constitution shall be preserved and the laws enforced at every and at all hazards. I expect the people to sustain me. They have never yet forsaken any true man."[684] He repeated similar sentiments along his extended trip to Washington. Still, he would not be tested until he had sworn upon the Bible the unique oath, prescribed by the Constitution for the president, to "preserve, protect and defend the Constitution of the United States."

Faced with secession upon taking the presidential oath of office, Lincoln declared in his First Inaugural of March 4, 1861: "I therefore consider that, in view of the Constitution and the laws, the Union is unbroken."[685] Four months later, in a special message to Congress he further spelled out his interpretation of the Constitution: "The Constitution provides, and all the states have accepted the provision, that 'The United

States shall guarantee to every state in this Union a republican form of government.' But if a state may lawfully go out of the Union, having done so it may also discard the republican form of government; so that to prevent its going out is an indispensable *means* to the *end* of maintaining the [republican] guaranty mentioned; and when an end is lawful and obligatory, the indispensable means to it are also lawful and obligatory."[686]

President Lincoln brought to bear his every skill to sustain the Constitution, to uphold the Union, and to prohibit the extension of slavery. He knew his constitutional powers, even in war, were limited in practice by public opinion. At Peoria and thereafter, he had duly acknowledged the protections afforded slavery by the Constitution. He had opposed a premature campaign to abolish slavery because he believed, wrote Lincoln scholars Kenneth L. Deutsch and Joseph R. Fornieri, that "the forcible abolition of slavery in the Southern states would constitute an egregious violation of the Constitution, which could precipitate the dissolution of the Union, the death knell of the American experiment, and the triumph of slavery over freedom."[687] Nonetheless secession came, and in the end the permanence of the Union was resolved by war and the end of slavery was settled by a constitutional amendment.

The American Founding, its history, and its organic law provided Lincoln with not only the principles, but also the yardsticks by which to measure the duties of all American citizens. When General Winfield Scott resigned his Army command, President Lincoln praised "the important public services rendered by him to his country during his long and brilliant career, among which will ever be gratefully distinguished his faithful devotion to the Constitution, the Union, and the Flag, when assailed by parricidal rebellion."[688] Mr. Lincoln held fast to his belief that the Declaration and the Constitution, if upheld by American citizens, might influence not only the future of slavery in America but also the "vast" future of all peoples the world over. In his special message to Congress on July 4, 1861, President Lincoln emphasized that "this issue [of rebellion and secession] embraces more than the fate of these United States. It presents to the whole family of man, the question, whether a constitutional republic, or a democracy—a government of the people, by the same people—

can, or cannot, maintain its territorial integrity, against its own domestic foes. It presents the question, whether discontented individuals, too few in numbers to control administration, according to organic law, in any case, can always, upon the pretences made in this case, or on any other pretences, or arbitrarily, without any pretence, break up their Government, and thus practically put an end to free government upon the earth. It forces us to ask: 'Is there, in all republics, this inherent, and fatal weakness?' 'Must a government, of necessity, be too *strong* for the liberties of its own people, or too *weak* to maintain its own existence?'"[689] There may be no more succinct summary of the perennial dilemmas of a free people.

With victory close at hand, President Lincoln prudently moved loyal unionists toward what was impractical in 1854—amending the Constitution so as to abolish slavery. When a committee from the Union Republican National Convention of 1864 came to the White House to inform him officially of his nomination, President Lincoln endorsed the proposed Thirteenth Amendment: "I approve the declaration in favor of so amending the Constitution as to prohibit slavery throughout the nation. . . . [S]uch [an] amendment of the Constitution as [is] now proposed, became a fitting, and necessary conclusion to the final success of the Union cause. Such alone can meet and cover all cavils. Now, the unconditional Union men, North and South, perceive its importance, and embrace it. In the joint names of Liberty and Union, let us labor to give it legal form, and practical effect."[690] The amendment languished during the presidential campaign, but President Lincoln pushed for its approval after his reelection in November. He did so forcefully—uncharacteristically lobbying congressmen to assure approval of the amendment by the House of Representatives on January 31, 1865.

Preserving the Union

To preserve the Union required not only forceful persuasion and coalition politics, but above all, relentless prosecution of the war effort. In his July 4, 1861, special Message to Congress, Mr. Lincoln said: "The seceders insist that our Constitution admits of secession. They have assumed to make a National Constitution of their own, in which, of necessity, they have either *discarded*, or *retained*, the right of secession, as they insist, it exists in ours. If they have discarded it, they thereby admit that, on principle, it ought not to be in ours. If they have retained it, by their own construction of ours they show that to be consistent they must secede from one another, whenever they shall find it the easier way of settling their debts, or effecting any other selfish, or unjust object. The principle itself is one of disintegration, and upon which no government can possibly endure." Having stated the principle, the president continued:

> If all the States, save one, should assert the power to *drive* that one out of the Union, it is presumed the whole class of seceder politicians would at once deny the power, and denounce the act as the greatest outrage upon State rights. But suppose that precisely the same act, instead of being called "driving the one out," should be called "the seceding of the others from that one," it would be exactly what the seceders claim to do; unless, indeed, they make the point, that the one, because it is a minority, may rightfully do, what the others, because they are a majority, may not rightfully do. These politicians are subtle, and profound, on the rights of minorities. They are not partial to that power which made the Constitution, and speaks from the preamble, calling itself "We, the People."[691]

President Lincoln, cautious at first, proved himself a match for the "fire-eaters" in the South who had drawn a line of secession through the Union and attacked Fort Sumter. Echoing Whig Senator Daniel Webster in a previous national crisis, President Lincoln believed there could be no liberty without union and no union without liberty—at least none worthy of the Declaration. "For Lincoln, saving the Union was not separate from the eventual elimination of slavery from American life," wrote Don E. Fehrenbacher. "For him, any Union worth preserving had as a prerequisite that slavery should first be restricted and ultimately be eliminated."[692] Fehrenbacher's interpretation is an inescapable inference from Lincoln's speeches and papers from Peoria in 1854 until his death in 1865. Historian Doris Kearns Goodwin wrote: "His conviction that we are one nation, indivisible, 'conceived in Liberty, and dedicated to the proposition that all men are created equal,' led to the birth of a union free of slavery. And he expressed this conviction in a language of enduring clarity and beauty, exhibiting a literary genius to match his political genius."[693]

To retain the allegiance of divergent Union factions—from slaveowners in the loyal border states to abolitionists in New England—Lincoln marshaled his every power of persuasion. In August 1862, the mercurial Horace Greeley demanded in his "Prayer of Twenty Millions" that President Lincoln take immediate action to emancipate the nation's slaves. Amidst the setbacks of war and the limitations they imposed, President Lincoln replied with characteristic logic and prudence:

> I would save the Union. I would save it the shortest way under the Constitution. The sooner the national authority can be restored; the nearer the Union will be "the Union as it was." If there be those who would not save the Union, unless they could at the same time *save* slavery, I do not agree with them. If there be those who would not save the Union unless they could at the same time *destroy* slavery, I do not agree with them. My paramount object in this struggle *is* to save the Union, and is *not* either to save or to destroy slavery. If I could save the Union without freeing *any* slave I would do it, and if I could save it by freeing *all* the slaves I would do it; and if I could save it by freeing some and leaving others alone I would also do that. What I do about slavery, and the colored race, I do because I believe it helps to save the Union; and what I forbear, I forbear because I do *not* believe it would help to save the Union. I shall do *less* whenever I shall believe what I am doing hurts the cause, and I shall do *more* whenever I shall believe doing more will help the cause. I shall try to correct errors when shown to be errors; and I shall adopt new views so fast as they shall appear to be true views.[694]

In these last two sentences, the deft hand of the practical statesman was at work, managing and moving public opinion toward the adoption of emancipation. Mr. Lincoln had been drafting a proclamation of emancipation for more than a month when he replied to Greeley. He had already informed his cabinet. Before he told the American people, he needed to cultivate those Unionists opposed to emancipation.

If maintaining the Union was the key to national emancipation, so too did the logic of a desperate war lead to the wartime limitation of civil liberties. President Lincoln justified these military priorities in a public letter to New York State Democrats who complained that civil liberties had been violated. He reviewed the rebel planning by which the Constitution and the Union had been imperilled by insurrection and invasion:

Prior to my instalation [*sic*] here it had been inculcated that any State had a lawful right to secede from the national Union; and that it would be expedient to exercise the right, whenever the devotees of the doctrine should fail to elect a President to their own liking. I was elected contrary to their liking; and accordingly, so far as it was legally possible, they had taken seven states out of the Union, had seized many of the United States Forts, and had fired upon the United States Flag, all before I was inaugerated [*sic*]; and, of course, before I had done any official act whatever. The rebellion, thus began soon ran into the present civil war; and, in certain respects, it began on very unequal terms between certain parties. The insurgents had been preparing for it more than thirty years, while the government had taken no steps to resist them. The former had carefully considered all the means which could be turned to their account. It undoubtedly was a well pondered reliance with them that in their own unrestricted effort to destroy Union, constitution, and law, all together, the government would, in great degree, be restrained by the same constitution and law, from arresting their progress. Their sympathizers pervaded all departments of the government, and nearly all communities of the people.[695]

In this 1863 letter to Erastus Corning and other New York Democrats who objected to war measures affecting civil liberties, President
Lincoln reflected upon the history, the logic and the constitutional basis
for his policy:

> I was slow to adopt the strong measures, which by degrees I have
> been forced to regard as being within the exceptions of the Con-
> stitution, and as indispensable to the public safety. Nothing is bet-
> ter known to history than that courts of justice are utterly
> incompetent to such cases. Civil courts are organized chiefly for
> trials of individuals, or, at most, a few individuals acting in con-
> cert; and this in quiet times, and on charges of crimes well
> defined in the law. Even in times of peace, bands of horse-thieves
> and robbers frequently grow too numerous and powerful for the
> ordinary courts of justice. But what comparison, in numbers, have
> such bands ever borne to the insurgent sympathizers even in
> many of the loyal states? Again, a jury too frequently have at least
> one member, more ready to hang the panel than to hang the trai-
> tor. And yet again, he who dissuades one man from volunteering,
> or induces one soldier to desert, weakens the Union cause as
> much as he who kills a union soldier in battle. Yet this dissuasion,
> or inducement, may be so conducted as to be no defined crime of
> which any civil court would take cognizance.[696]

By the logic of the Constitution applied to insurrection, and by reason of the laws of war, President Lincoln considered secessionists to be
traitors—especially West Point–trained officers who had sworn an oath of
allegiance to the United States of America. Rebellion and treason put the
secessionist leaders beyond the customary civil and criminal law, to be
dealt with as outlaws by the hard hand of a constitutional government
determined to preserve the Union.[697]

Ten weeks later in August, President Lincoln decided to use a Union
rally in Springfield, Illinois, to answer complaints about his Emancipation
Proclamation and to reinforce the principles of his war strategy. He sent a
letter to attorney James C. Conkling to be read at a Union rally in Spring-

field on September 3, 1863. Lincoln intended it then to be printed for the whole nation to see: "But the [emancipation] proclamation, as law, either is valid, or is not valid. If it is not valid, it needs no retraction. If it is valid, it can not be retracted, any more than the dead can be brought to life. Some of you profess to think its retraction would operate favorably for the Union. Why better *after* the retraction, than *before* the issue? There was more than a year and a half of trial to suppress the rebellion before the proclamation issued, the last one hundred days of which passed under an explicit notice that it was coming, unless averted by those in revolt, returning to their allegiance."[698] There would be no retraction.

Increasingly confident in his public purposes, the president well understood the constitutional basis for his authority as commander-in-chief. But he did not rely upon legal authority alone. He relied as well upon the ultimate sovereign authority—the American people. He appealed to them with his pen, using what Lincoln scholar Douglas L. Wilson has aptly called "Lincoln's Sword."[699] After reelection in November 1864, President Lincoln in his final message to Congress of December gave his interpretation of American democratic politics: "The most reliable indication of public purpose in this country is derived through our popular elections. Judging by the recent canvass and its result [a general victory for the President and his party], the purpose of the people, within the loyal States, to maintain the integrity of the Union, was never more firm, nor more nearly unanimous, than now. . . . There have been much impugning of motives, and much heated controversy as to the proper means and best mode of advancing the Union cause; but on the distinct issue of Union or no Union, the politicians have shown their instinctive knowledge that there is no diversity among the people [i.e.,the loyal citizens voting]. In affording the people the fair opportunity of showing, one to another and to the world, this firmness and unanimity of purpose, the election has been of vast value to the national cause."[700] Even at war, President Lincoln suggested that American democracy showed that the ballot need not be surrendered entirely to the bullet. Still, three months later, President Lincoln reminded the American people in his Second Inaugural that it was "the progress of our arms, upon which all else chiefly depends."[701]

Slavery and Equality

The equality principle of the Declaration, the immorality of slavery, the preservation of the Union, and the destruction of the rebel army were the refrains to which President Lincoln often returned during his presidency. In his Second Inaugural he reminded Americans that "all knew" that slavery "was somehow the cause of the war."[702] Devoted as he was to the inalienable rights of the Declaration, those "endowed by the Creator," he believed public policy was constrained not only by the Constitution but also by public opinion. "In the Peoria speech, as in all his speeches thereafter, until his inauguration as president, Lincoln tried to make his fellow citizens understand that by right, as opposed to power, the same principles applied to the slaves as to themselves," wrote Harry V. Jaffa. "But here [in the Peoria speech] he is notably ambiguous as to his own feelings about political and social equality."[703] Ambiguity was a tactic used by Lincoln to deal not only with racist public opinion, but also with war strategy and war aims—even as he was explicit that in principle all men are created equal. Lincoln argued that this abstract principle was objectively true even though throughout history and around the globe, slavery persisted and equality before the law had never been fully achieved.

President Lincoln had to battle not only the Confederate insurrection but also a rebel worldview radically different from the one announced in the Declaration of Independence. There may be no starker contrast to Lincoln's Peoria argument on the immorality of slavery than the racial attitudes expressed by his erstwhile friend—Alexander H. Stephens. Historian Michael Davis wrote: "Of all Southern men with 'living positions' perhaps Alexander Hamilton Stephens knew best that Lincoln was neither a rabid abolitionist nor the tool of a wicked party."[704] Stephens wrote a friend in July 1860: "In point of merit as a man I have no doubt that Lincoln is just as good, safe and sound a man as Mr. Buchanan, and would administer the Government so far as he is individually concerned just as safely for the South and as honestly and faithfully *in every particular*. I know the man well. He is not a bad man. He will make as good a President as [Millard] Fillmore did and better too in my opinion. He has a great deal more practical common sense. Still his party may do mischief."[705] In 1865 while he was imprisoned in Boston by the Union government, the former Confederate vice president recalled: "I knew Mr. Lincoln, thought well of him personally, believed him to be a kind-hearted man."[706]

At the onset of the secession crisis in late 1860, Stephens had been an opponent of secession. After Lincoln's election, Stephens addressed the Georgia state legislature: "I do not anticipate that Mr. Lincoln will do anything to jeopardize our safety and security, whatever may be his spirit to do it; for he is bound by the constitutional checks which are thrown around him; which at this time render him powerless to do any great mischief. . . . " Stephens told the Georgia legislature: "Shall the people of the South secede from the Union in consequence of the election of Mr. Lincoln to the Presidency of the United States? My countrymen, I tell you frankly, candidly, and earnestly, that I do not think that they ought. In my judgment, the election of no man, constitutionally chosen to that high office, is sufficient cause for any State to separate from the Union."[707] Only a month later, President-elect Lincoln wrote to Stephens, succinctly noting their differences about the nation's future: "Do the people of the South really entertain fears that a Republican administration would, *directly*, or *indirectly*, interfere with their slaves, or with them, about their slaves? If they do, I wish to assure you, as once a friend, and still, I hope, not an enemy, that there is no cause for such fears. . . . You think slavery is *right* and ought to be extended; while we think it is *wrong* and ought to be restricted. That I suppose is the rub. It certainly is the only substantial difference between us."[708]

By March 21, 1861, Stephens had embraced secession. He had also been elected vice president of the Confederacy. Called upon to speak in Savannah, Georgia, Stephens spelled out the principles which he believed grounded the new Confederacy. Unselfconsciously and unapologetically, he explained that the new civil structure of the Confederacy had been literally founded on justifiable slavery. In this "Cornerstone" speech, Stephens said of the new Confederate constitution that it set "the proper status of the negro in our form of civilization."[709] Not only is the equality principle of the Declaration false, but: "Our new [Confederate] government is founded upon exactly the opposite idea; its foundations are laid, its corner-stone rests upon the great truth, that the negro is not equal to the white man; that slavery—subordination to the superior race—is his natural and normal condition. [Applause.] This, our new government, is the first, in the history of the world, based upon this great physical, philosophical, and moral truth."[710]

After the Civil War, Stephens maintained: "The war was inaugurated and waged by those at the head of the Federal Government, against these States, or the people of these States, to prevent their withdrawal from the Union. On the part of these States, which had allied themselves in a common cause, it was maintained and carried on purely in defence of this great Right, claimed by them, of State Sovereignty and Self-government, which they with their associates had achieved in their common struggle with Great Britain, under the Declaration of 1776, and which, in their judgment, lay at the foundation of the whole structure of American free Institutions."[711] Stephens had grown to political maturity under the ascendancy of the Democratic party and its doctrine of states' rights. Through state legislation in the South, this doctrine assured the property right to a black slave. In 1857 the Supreme Court upheld this property right. As Lincoln suggested, this policy ruling meant that if a man could bring his hog from a slave state to a free territory, then a slaveowner could transport his slave there too. And no third party could intervene.

Then came secession, Fort Sumter, and Civil War. In his Second Inaugural, President Lincoln clearly defined the cause of the war: "One eighth of the whole population were colored slaves, not distributed generally over the Union, but localized in the Southern part of it. These slaves constituted a peculiar and powerful interest. All knew that this interest was, somehow, the cause of the war. To strengthen, perpetuate, and extend this interest was the object for which the insurgents would rend the Union, even by war, while the government claimed no right to do more than to restrict the territorial enlargement of it."[712] After the Civil War, Alexander H. Stephens and Jefferson Davis continued to disagree with Lincoln's analysis. They claimed that states' rights rather than slavery was the cause of the war.

In April 1864, several weeks before the Republican National Convention in Baltimore renominated him, President Lincoln traveled to that city to speak at a fund-raising fair for the U.S. Sanitary Commission. He said: "The world has never had a good definition of the word liberty, and the American people, just now, are much in want of one. We all declare for liberty; but in using the same *word* we do not all mean the same *thing*. With some the word liberty may mean for each man to do as he pleases with himself, and the product of his labor; while with others the same word may mean for some men to do as they please with other men, and the product of other men's labor. Here are two, not only different, but incompatable [*sic*] things, called by the same name—liberty. And it follows that each of the things is, by the respective parties, called by two different and incompatable names—liberty and tyranny."[713] Lincoln believed that slavery was tyranny—the theft by force of another man's labor.

Invoking the biblical metaphor of the good shepherd, Lincoln continued: "The shepherd drives the wolf from the sheep's throat, for which the sheep thanks the shepherd as a *liberator*, while the wolf denounces him for the same act as the destroyer of liberty, especially as the sheep was a black one. Plainly the sheep and the wolf are not agreed upon a definition of the word liberty; and precisely the same difference prevails to-day among us human creatures, even in the North, and all professing to love liberty. Hence we behold the processes by which thousands are daily passing from under the yoke of bondage, hailed by some as the advance of liberty, and bewailed by others as the destruction of all liberty."[714] The biblical metaphor made clear that the Declaration of Independence should protect not the wolf but the sheep. The wolf was ever well-armed for tyranny.

In his final message to Congress in December 1864, President Lincoln summed up his case for the Union: "The public purpose to re-establish and maintain the national authority is unchanged, and, as we believe, unchangeable. The manner of continuing the effort remains to choose. On careful consideration of all the evidence accessible it seems to me that no attempt at negotiation with the insurgent leader could result in any good. He would accept nothing short of severance of the Union—precisely what we will not and cannot give. His declarations to this effect are explicit and oft-repeated. He does not attempt to deceive us. He affords us no excuse to deceive ourselves. He cannot voluntarily reaccept the Union; we cannot voluntarily yield it. Between him and us the issue is distinct, simple, and inflexible. It is an issue which can only be tried by war, and decided by victory. If we yield, we are beaten; if the Southern people fail him, he is beaten."[715]

At Peoria, Lincoln had set forth his purpose to prohibit the extension of slavery, to maintain the permanence of the union, and finally to place slavery in the course of ultimate extinction. From Peoria, Lincoln steered prudently and relentlessly toward these goals. Faced with intractable constitutional and practical issues at the onset of the Civil War, President Lincoln had forborne to act from moral principles alone, lacking as he believed both the constitutional warrant to deal directly with slavery and also sufficient public support to do so. At war, having concluded that the Constitution gave the commander-in-chief the power to act on slavery as an indispensable means to end the insurrection and preserve the union, Lincoln invoked military necessity—and the moral principle implicit in the slavery controversy. On September 22, 1862, he gave the South 100 days to renounce secession before he might issue the Emancipation Proclamation. He did so on January 1, 1863. Lincoln declared the Emancipation Proclamation an "act of justice" based "on military necessity."[716] Lincoln's proclamation generally applied to slaves in those areas of the Confederacy not yet under Union control, but it did not apply to slaves in the Border States or sections of the South where the Union army had regained power. Lincoln explained the distinction between his constitutional power and his moral convictions in an open letter to Horace Greeley in August 1862: "I have here stated my purpose according to my view of *official* duty; and I intend no modification of my oft expressed *personal* wish that all men every where could be free."[717]

After January 1, 1863, there was no retreat on emancipation. In late July 1863, President Lincoln wrote to General Stephen A. Hurlbut, the commander of Union forces in Arkansas: "The emancipation proclamation applies to Arkansas. I think it is valid in law, and will be so held by the

Lincoln Presidency

Mary Livermore

*Courtesy of the Kentucky Historical Society,
reference number 1987PH29.alb1.p16n47*

Erastus Corning

*Courtesy of the Library of Congress Prints &
Photographs Div., reference number:
LC-BH82-5232*

James C. Conking

*Courtesy of the Abraham Lincoln Presidential
Library, reference number I-239*

Archibald Dixon

Courtesy of the U.S. Senate Historical Office

courts. I think I shall not retract or repudiate it. Those who shall have tasted actual freedom I believe can never be slaves, or quasi slaves again."[718] The president not only informed his generals but responded to northern adversaries of emancipation with great confidence: "You say you will not fight to free negroes. Some of them seem willing to fight for you; but, no matter. Fight you, then, exclusively to save the Union. I issued the proclamation on purpose to aid you in saving the Union. Whenever you shall have conquered all resistance to the Union, if I shall urge you to continue fighting, it will be an apt time, then, for you to declare you will not fight to free negroes."[719] He hammered his critics: "I thought that in your struggle for the Union, to whatever extent the negroes should cease helping the enemy, to that extent it weakened the enemy in his resistance to you. . . . But negroes, like other people, act upon motives. Why should they do any thing for us, if we will do nothing for them? If they stake their lives for us, they must be prompted by the strongest motive—even the promise of freedom. And the promise being made, must be kept."[720]

Eight months later Lincoln returned to this same theme. On April 4, 1864, a delegation of Kentuckians visited the White House. It included newspaper editor Albert G. Hodges, Governor Thomas E. Bramlette, and former Senator Archibald Dixon, the same Whig whose amendment to the Kansas-Nebraska bill in January 1854 had prompted the repeal of the Missouri Compromise. Then in a letter directed to Hodges and intended for publication, President Lincoln returned to the arguments of Peoria:

I am naturally anti-slavery. If slavery is not wrong, nothing is wrong. I can not remember when I did not so think, and feel. And yet I have never understood that the Presidency conferred upon me an unrestricted right to act officially upon this judgment and feeling. It was in the oath I took that I would, to the best of my ability, preserve, protect, and defend the Constitution of the United States. I could not take the office without taking the oath. Nor was it my view that I might take an oath to get power, and break the oath in using the power. I understood, too, that in ordinary civil administration this oath even forbade me to practically indulge my primary abstract judgement on the moral question of slavery. I had publicly declared this many times, and in many ways. And I aver that, to this day, I have done no official act in mere deference to my abstract judgment and feeling on slavery. I did understand, however, that my oath to preserve the constitution to the best of my ability, imposed upon me the duty of preserving, by every indispensable means, that government—that nation—of which that constitution was the organic law. Was it possible to lose the nation, and yet preserve the constitution? By general law life *and* limb must be protected; yet often a limb must be amputated to save a life; but a life is never wisely given to save a limb. I felt that measures, otherwise unconstitutional [in the civil administration of peacetime], might become lawful [by military necessity], by becoming indispensable to the preservation of the constitution, through the preservation of the nation. Right or wrong, I assumed this ground, and now avow it. I could not feel that, to the best of my ability, I had even tried to preserve the constitution, if, to save slavery, or any minor matter, I should permit the wreck of government, country, and Constitution all together.[721]

His was a bold and active strategy to save the Union. Lincoln did claim "not to have controlled events, but confess plainly that events have controlled me." But this subtle conceit hid Lincoln's active hand at work. His deft maneuvers helped create political space for his emancipation politics in the North and more opportunity for blacks in the South to emancipate themselves. As historians James O. Horton and Lois Horton wrote, "Lincoln had not always enjoyed great popularity among black Americans, but after the Emancipation Proclamation . . . most considered him their friend and ally."[722] Although northern skeptics may not have taken the proclamation literally, many southern blacks did. The president recognized not only the humanity of the slaves, but also their strategic importance to a Union victory. Southern blacks recognized that his policies created the opportunity to flee their slave owners—particularly when Union troops were in the vicinity.

In his final Message to Congress on December 6, 1864, Lincoln pronounced the death sentence on America's peculiar institution: "I retract nothing heretofore said as to slavery. I repeat the declaration made a year ago, that 'while I remain in my present position I shall not attempt to retract or modify the emancipation proclamation, nor shall I return to slavery any person who is free by the terms of that proclamation, or by any of the Acts of Congress.' If the people should, by whatever mode or means, make it an Executive duty to re-enslave such persons, another, and not I, must be their instrument to perform it."[723] The president had come a long way from Illinois, but echoes of Peoria could still be heard.

Union, Morality, and Reality

At Peoria, Lincoln had emphasized the linkage of the American Union and the Declaration of Independence. On the way to Washington in 1861, President-elect Lincoln had expanded his Peoria theme: "I recollect thinking then, boy even though I was, that there must been something more than common that those men struggled for . . . that something even more than National Independence; that something that held out a great promise to all the people of the world to all time to come; I am exceedingly anxious that this Union, the Constitution, and the liberties of the people shall be perpetuated in accordance with the original idea for which that struggle was made, and I shall be most happy indeed if I shall be an humble instrument in the hands of the Almighty, and of this, his almost chosen people, for perpetuating the object of that great struggle."[724] The original idea, the object of the American Revolution, was to vindicate the inalienable right to liberty, grounded in the proposition that "all men are created equal."

Lincoln rarely missed an opportunity to anchor his abstract principles in the express and implied provisions of the Constitution. In his Amnesty Proclamation of December 1863, he quoted the Constitution: "The United States shall guaranty to every State in this union a republican form of government, and shall protect each of them against invasion; and, on application of the legislature, or the executive, (when the legislature cannot be convened), against domestic violence."[725] To guarantee a republican government to each state, each state must remain in the Union, its sole constitutional guarantor.

"Abraham Lincoln is the greatest of all interpreters of America's moral meaning. He surpasses even Thomas Jefferson," wrote University of Virginia scholar William Lee Miller.[726] Lincoln's achievement was not only to understand America's peculiar institution in historical, legal, and philosophic terms, but also as chief executive to know how to persuade, organize, and manage Americans for victory in war. Abolitionists were absorbed in the moral problems, but they underestimated the governing realities by which slavery might actually be limited, then terminated. Accommodationists were so focused on maintaining the semblance of national unity that antislavery leaders such as William H. Seward were prepared to yield when "the tug" of secession came. Harry V. Jaffa wrote that "Lincoln understood [that] the task of statesmanship" is "to know what is good or right, to know how much of that good is attainable, and to act to secure that much good but not to abandon the attainable good by grasping for more."[727]

Lincoln acted upon the ancient aphorism that the perfect should not be made the enemy of the good. "As a politician, Lincoln was a pragmatist willing to adjust to events and to adapt different policies to different circumstances, ever ready to revise positions based on new developments," wrote John Patrick Diggins. "As a philosopher, however, Lincoln was a moralist and even an absolutist, unswerving in his belief that natural rights are inalienable and hence inviolable, that the Republic's founding principles have the capacity, if properly understood, to remain immune to change, and that the meaning of right and wrong is not relative and dependent upon time and place."[728] President Lincoln, in his last public address three nights before his assassination, made the point: "Important principles may, and must, be inflexible."[729] Always open to practical means to attain constitutional and moral ends, he was no relativist. In Lincoln's judgment, the objective moral order of the Declaration of Independence was timeless, universal, and immutable.

In Hartford in March 1860, before he was a well-known presidential contender, Lincoln explained his unwavering moral standard: "We understand that the 'equality of man' principle which actuated our forefathers in the establishment of the government is right; and that slavery, being directly opposed to this, is morally wrong. I think that if anything can be proved by natural theology, it is that slavery is morally wrong."[730] Lincoln also made it clear that the objective moral order, with which the Founders had underpinned constitutional democracy, was at stake in the secessionist dispute: "We suppose slavery is wrong, and that it endangers the perpetuity of the Union. Nothing else menaces it. Its effect on free labor makes it what Seward has been so roundly abused for calling, an irrepressible conflict. Almost every man has a sense of certain things being wrong, and at the same time, a sense of its pecuniary value. These conflict in the mind, and make a riddle of man. If slavery is considered upon a property basis, public opinion must be forced to its support. The alternative is its settlement upon the basis of its being wrong."[731] Lincoln insisted that right principle trumped the widespread, ancient claim to hold slaves as property. At New Haven later the same day, Lincoln addressed the question of Union: "Again . . . does anything in any way endanger the perpetuity of this Union but that single thing, Slavery? Many of our adversaries are anxious to claim that they are specially devoted to the Union, and take pains to charge upon us hostility to the Union. Now we claim that we are the only true Union men, and we put to them this one proposition: What ever endangered this Union, save and except Slavery? . . . Can any man believe that the way to save the Union is to extend and increase the only thing that threatens the Union, and to suffer it to grow bigger and bigger?"[732]

Upon taking the oath of office in March 1861, President Lincoln did not flinch in the manner of his predecessors, Franklin Pierce and James Buchanan. In his First Inaugural Address, he observed that: "One section of our country believes slavery is *right,* and ought to be extended, while the other believes it is *wrong,* and ought not to be extended. This is the only substantial dispute."[733] Having issued the Emancipation Proclamation on January 1, 1863, President Lincoln did not retreat. As Richard Yates, by then governor of Illinois, recalled, Lincoln would not be rushed into issuing the proclamation. Neither would he be forced to withdraw it once issued. Speaking in New York City shortly before the dedication of the Gettysburg cemetery in November 1863, Governor Yates recalled being told by President Lincoln: "Dick, hold fast and see the salvation of God."[734] There would be no reconsideration of emancipation. In August 1863, the president wrote the military commander of Louisiana: "For my own part I think I shall not, in any event, retract the emancipation proclamation; nor, as executive, ever return to slavery any person who is free by the terms of that proclamation, or by any of the acts of Congress."[735] A year later, as he considered his options during the agonizing political and military uncertainty of August 1864, Lincoln did appear to waver for a moment while he considered peace negotiations with the secessionists. Many Republicans, including Lincoln himself, doubted his prospects for reelection. Nevertheless, he resolutely returned to the aims of his presidential policy—victory in war, emancipation of the slaves, and preservation of the Union.

The South

At Peoria, Lincoln remarked that though he hated slavery, he would not condemn the slaveholders of the South. He held both North and South to be complicit in America's peculiar institution and therefore did not speak of the South with the contempt that characterized many abolitionists and other antislavery politicians. Lincoln rarely affected a patronizing, moral superiority. In his first major, recorded speech of the 1854 campaign—the Bloomington *Pantagraph* reported that Lincoln "declared that the Southern slaveholders were neither better nor worse than we of the North, and that we of the North were no better than they. If we were situated as they are, we should act no better than they. If we were situated as they are, we should act and feel as they do; and if they were situated as we are, they should act and feel as we do; and we never ought to lose sight of this fact in discussing the subject."[736]

Speaking in Hartford, Connecticut, in March 1860, Lincoln had rejected any self-righteous, northern claim to moral superiority: "In this we do not assume that we are better than the people of the South—neither do we admit that they are better than we. We are not better, barring circumstances, than they. Public opinion is formed relative to a property basis. Therefore, the slaveholders battle any policy which depreciates their slaves as property. What increases the value of this property, they favor. When you tell them that slavery is immoral, they rebel, because they do not like to be told they are interested in an institution which is not a moral one. When you enter into a defence of slavery, they seize upon it, for they like justification. The result is, that public opinion is formed among them which insists upon the encouragement or protection, the enlargement or perpetuation of slavery—and secures them property in the slave."[737] As Gabor Boritt made clear, the economic analysis Lincoln developed in the 1830s and 1840s was well integrated into his slavery policy.[738] If there were no fixed rules in a free market to prohibit slavery, Lincoln believed, amoral and profit-seeking men would be at liberty to take slaves.

In his special Message to Congress on July 4, 1861, Lincoln recapitulated the policies he had patiently put before the people of the South in his First Inaugural Address: "The policy chosen looked to the exhaustion of all peaceful measures, before a resort to any stronger ones. It sought only to hold the public places and property, not already wrested from the Government, and to collect the revenue; relying for the rest, on time, discussion, and the ballot-box. It promised a continuance of the mails, at government expense, to the very people who were resisting the government; and it gave repeated pledges against any disturbance to any of the people, or any of their rights. Of all that which a president might constitutionally, and justifiably, do in such a case, everything was foreborne, without which, it was believed possible to keep the government on foot."[739]

More than deference to the constitutional limitations on his presidential office caused the president to avoid using force in March 1861. He temporized, hoping to avoid civil war. The secessionists would decide. The Confederate attack on Fort Sumter on April 12 made the war necessary. In the 1850s, Lincoln had often dismissed the threat of secession, but he was still a hard-headed realist. At Cooper Union in 1860, Lincoln spoke directly to the dominant southern leadership: "Your purpose, then plainly stated, is that you will destroy the Government, unless you be allowed to construe and enforce the Constitution as you please, on all points in dispute between you and us. You will rule or ruin in all events."[740] In 1862 as President Lincoln began to prepare the Emancipation Proclamation, he showed how deeply he understood the intractability of slavery. "Gentlemen, this American slavery is no small affair, and it cannot be done away with at once. It is a part of our national life. It is not of yesterday. It began in colonial times. In one way or another it has shaped nearly everything that enters into what we call government. It is as much northern as it is southern. It is not merely a local or geographical institution. It belongs to our politics, to our industries, to our commerce, and to our religion," Lincoln told visitors to the Soldiers' Home. "Every portion of our territory in some form or another has contributed to the growth and the increase of slavery. It has been nearly two hundred years coming up to its present proportions. It is wrong, a great evil indeed, but the South is no more responsible for the wrong done to the African race than is the North."[741] In this even-handed judgment, Lincoln anticipated much recent historiography on the pervasiveness of American slavery.[742]

Lincoln understood the historical disputes over American slaveholding, but he was impatient with any rationalization of secession. It was treason. He disdained tortured justifications for secession and servitude. In his special Message to Congress of July 4, 1861, he argued: "It might seem, at first thought, to be of little difference whether the present movement at the South be called 'secession' or 'rebellion.' The movers [of the Confederacy], however, well understand the difference. At the beginning, they knew they could never raise their treason to any respectable magnitude, by any name which implies *violation* of law. . . . They knew they could make no advancement directly in the teeth of these strong and noble sentiments. . . . They invented an ingenious sophism, which, if conceded, was followed by perfectly logical steps, through all the incidents, to the complete destruction of the Union. The sophism itself is, that any state of the Union may, *consistently* with the national Constitution, and therefore *lawfully*, and *peacefully*, withdraw from the Union, without the consent of the Union, or of any other state. The little disguise that the supposed right is to be exercised only for just cause, themselves to be the sole judge of its justice, is too thin to merit any notice."[743]

The Civil War came, President Lincoln believed, because the leaders of the Confederacy, mostly slavemasters, would not accept the lawful election of a President who considered slavery a wrong to be put "in the course of ultimate extinction." Only after the Confederate attack on Fort Sumter and general southern insurrection did Lincoln brand secession as traitorous. Thereafter, he did not cavil at condemning Confederate leaders while holding out hope for the people of the South. By his Fourth Annual Message to Congress in December 1864, Lincoln wrote that he and Jefferson Davis could never agree: "Between him and us the issue is distinct, simple, and inflexible."[744] The war for the Union and emancipation must end in unconditional victory. But this had not been Lincoln's strategy in 1861. At the close of his First Inaugural, President Lincoln had extended a magnanimous hand to the South:

> In *your* hands, my dissatisfied fellow countrymen, and not in *mine*, is the momentous issue of civil war. The government will not assail *you*. You can have no conflict, without being yourselves the aggressors. *You* have no oath registered in Heaven to destroy the government, while *I* shall have the most solemn one to "preserve, protect, and defend" it.
>
> I am loth to close. We are not enemies, but friends. We must not be enemies. Though passion may have strained, it must not break our bonds of affection. The mystic chords of memory, stretching from every battle-field, and patriot grave, to every living heart and hearthstone, all over this broad land, will yet swell the chorus of the Union, when again touched, as surely they will be, by the better angels of our nature.[745]

The pathos of the First Inaugural was followed by the absence of triumphalism in the Second Inaugural, even as victory drew near: "On the occasion corresponding to this four years ago [the First Inaugural], all thoughts were anxiously directed to an impending civil-war. All dreaded it—all sought to avert it. While the inaugeral [*sic*] address was being delivered from this place, devoted altogether to *saving* the Union without war, insurgent agents were in the city seeking to *destroy* it without war—seeking to dissol[v]e the Union, and divide effects, by negotiation. Both parties deprecated war; but one of them would *make* war rather than let the nation survive; and the other would *accept* war rather than let it perish. And the war came." President Lincoln admonished his countrymen in the North, as well as the slaveholders of the South, that all were complicit in the "great evil" of slavery. "Fondly do we hope—fervently do we pray— that this mighty scourge of war may speedily pass away. Yet, if God wills that it continue, until all the wealth piled by the bond-man's two hundred and fifty years of unrequited toil shall be sunk, and until every drop of blood drawn with the lash, shall be paid by another drawn with the sword, as was said three thousand years ago, so still it must be said 'the judg-ments of the Lord, are true and righteous altogether.'"[746]

The president implied that the remorseless war he tried to avert in 1861 might have been sustained by providential intervention. Perhaps through Civil War, both North and South together suffered for the sin of slavery. And so in victory, magnanimity characterized the president's atti-tude: "With malice toward none; with charity for all; with firmness in the right, as God gives us to see the right, let us strive on to finish the work we are in; to bind up the nation's wounds; to care for him who shall have borne the battle, and for his widow, and his orphan—to do all which may achieve and cherish a just, and a lasting peace, among ourselves, and with all nations."[747] Only weeks later, Lincoln concluded his last public address: "In the present '*situation*' as the phrase goes, it may be my duty to make some new announcement about reconstruction to the people of the South. I am considering, and shall not fail to act, when satisfied that action will be proper."[748] With reconstruction, as with war, Lincoln was deliberate, ready to act upon new facts and circumstances.

Douglas and Lincoln

Temperateness had characterized Mr. Lincoln's debates with Stephen A. Douglas, his chief adversary of the 1850s. Douglas, often good-natured, could be mean-spirited and mean-tongued. As a young man in the 1830s,

Lincoln occasionally showed the same tendencies and he was often pained by the results. But by the 1850s, he had abandoned these tactics, having matured into the disciplined politician the nation would observe in his presidency. During his contests with Senator Douglas, "Lincoln's estimate of the 'Little Giant' was generous. He conceded him great hardihood, pertinacity and magnetic power," wrote Lincoln scholar Robert Gerald McMurtry.[749] "Lincoln truly embodied," wrote Joseph Fornieri, "biblical magnanimity."[750] Lincoln also respected the truth—and so he disdained the cavalier way Douglas sometimes abused it. McMurtry noted: "Of all the men he had ever seen, Mr. Lincoln thought Douglas had the most audacity in maintaining an untenable position. . . ."[751] Douglas's ability in public to stonewall the facts of history confounded Lincoln. "In the summer of 1858, Douglas made a speech at Pontiac during the course of which he ventured to quote from [William M.] Holland's Life of van Buren,'" recalled a contemporary, Clifton H. Moore. "A day or so later Lincoln passed through here and among other things told me that Douglas in his speech at Pontiac had seriously misquoted Holland, a fact he could easily establish if he only had Holland's book; but unfortunately not a copy was to be found in Clinton. The next morning he pushed on to Bloomington. He was still so wrought up over Douglas's misrepresentation that [Judge] David Davis was finally induced to send a man on horseback to Springfield with a note from Lincoln asking for the book. In due time the messenger returned with the desired volume which he turned over to Lincoln, who took it with him, threatening to confront Douglas with it at the earliest opportunity." Lincoln later told Moore: "Douglas will tell a lie to ten thousand people one day, even though he knows he may have to deny it to five thousand the next."[752]

In the final months of his life, Senator Douglas distinguished himself, giving unstinting support to Lincoln's policy to preserve the Union. Shortly after the election of 1860, Douglas wrote a group of New Orleans citizens: "No man in America regrets the election of Mr. Lincoln more than I do; none made more strenuous exertions to defeat him; none differ with him more radically and irreconcileably upon all the great issues involved in the contest. No man living is [more] prepared to resist, by all the legitimate means, sanctioned by the Constitution and laws of our country, the aggressive policy which he and his party are understood to represent. But, while I say this, I am bound, as a good citizen and law-abiding man, to declare my conscientious conviction that mere election of any man to the Presidency by the American people, in accordance with the Constitution and laws, does not of itself furnish any just cause or reasonable ground for dissolving the Federal Union."[753]

Despite their profound disagreements, both Illinois antagonists revered the Union. The first Confederate blow, the attack on Fort Sumter, converted Douglas into an ally of President Lincoln in defense of the Union. They met at the White House shortly after the rebel occupation of Fort Sumter. After the meeting, Douglas wrote out a statement to share with the press: "Mr[.] Douglas called on the President and had an interesting conversation on the present condition of the country. The substance of the conversation was that while Mr D was unalterably opposed to the administration on all its political issues, he was prepared to sustain the president in the exercise of all his constitutional functions to preserve the Union, and maintain the government, and defend the Federal Capital. A firm policy and prompt action was necessary. The Capital of our Country was in danger, and must be defended at all hazards, and at any expense of men & money. He spoke of the present & future, without reference to the past."[754]

To preserve the Union, old adversaries had become new allies. Douglas traveled to Illinois to rally the state behind the president. Douglas biographer William Garrott Brown noted: "On his way homeward he was everywhere besought to speak. Once he was aroused from sleep to address an Ohio regiment marching to the front, and his great voice rolled down upon them, aligned beneath him in the darkness, a word of loyalty and courage."[755] Douglas declared: "There can be no neutrals in this war, only patriots and traitors."[756] He saw that the house dividing against itself could not stand. From Chicago, Douglas wrote President Lincoln: "I found the state of feeling here and in some parts of our State much less satisfactory than I could have desired or expected when I arrived. There will be no outbrake [*sic*] however and in a few days I hope for entire unanimity in the support of the government and the Union."[757] Exhausted and sick, Douglas died a few weeks later.

The Bible and the World

At Peoria in 1854, Lincoln had impatiently corrected Senator Douglas: "In the course of my main argument, Judge Douglas interrupted me to say, that the principle [of] the Nebraska bill was very old; that it originated when God made man and placed good and evil before him, allowing him to choose for himself, being responsible for the choice he should make. At the time I thought this was merely playful; and I answered it accordingly. But in his reply to me he renewed it, as a serious argument. In seriousness then, the facts of this proposition are not true as stated. God did not place good and evil before man, telling him to make his choice. On the contrary, he did tell him there was one tree, of the fruit of which, he should not eat, upon pain of certain death. I should scarcely wish so strong a prohibition against slavery in Nebraska."[758] In this artful argument, a master of the English language was at work. William Blackstone's *Commentaries on the Laws of England*, the King James Bible, and the histories and tragedies of Shakespeare had been studied, even internalized, by Lincoln, so as to give him command of their teachings and the subtleties of the English language. Perhaps they inspired the elegant simplicity and power of his mature prose.

The divine prohibition in Genesis against eating the fruit of only one tree was the parable Lincoln used to show that no one complicit in the sin of slavery might escape the penalty. The right and wrong of slavery had always been clear to him. He could not understand Springfield ministers who supported Douglas over him in the 1860 presidential election: "These men well know that I am for freedom in the territories, freedom everywhere as far as the Constitution and laws will permit, and that my opponents are for slavery. They know this; and yet, with this book [the Bible] in their hands, in the light of which human bondage cannot live a moment, they are going to vote against me. I do not understand it at all."[759] Religious historian Mark A. Noll wrote, "It is one of the great ironies of the history of Christianity in America that the most profoundly religious analysis of the nation's deepest trauma came not from a clergyman or a theologian but from a politician who was self-taught in the ways of both God and humanity."[760]

From Peoria on, Lincoln's rhetoric increasingly integrated biblical metaphors with rigorous argument. Garry Wills observed that "Lincoln was a master of the Bible's extraordinary hold on the Protestant imagination of nineteenth-century America. . . . In his 1854 Peoria address, he had already used the Magnificat ['We shall have so saved it, that the succeeding millions of free happy people, the world over, shall rise up and call us blessed to the latest generation'] to describe America's special status among nations. . . ."[761] Joseph R. Fornieri noted that the Peoria speech is replete with biblical references. The speech was "a clear expression of Mr. Lincoln's moral vision." Eight times in the speech he makes reference to "faith." Fornieri summed up: "Lincoln's civil theological intention to articulate and clarify the nation's political creed is evident through the speech. He uses the expressions 'ancient faith' and 'old faith' synonymously on five different occasions, in contradistinction to the 'New Faith' of slavery's extension preached by the Kansas-Nebraska Act."[762] During the period between his Lyceum Speech in 1838 and the Second Inaugural in 1865, Lincoln developed an American civil religion which today permeates the rhetoric of both political parties. The "almost chosen" people needed a civil religion.

If, as Don Fehrenbacher wrote, Lincoln's leadership in the 1850s was *A Prelude to Greatness*, the Peoria speech was the first major movement of the symphony. But no great work is completed without sustained preparation. The Peoria speech could have been written only by a man who had mastered the history and the issues of his era. Only intense study could enable such a man to link ancient truths in a compelling way to modern realities in order "that the succeeding millions of free happy people, the world over, shall rise up, and call us blessed, to the latest generations."[763] Allen C. Guelzo wrote of the frequent scriptural allusions of the 1850s: "Kansas-Nebraska was 'a woful coming down from the early faith of the republic' and had no 'relish of salvation'. . . . Above all the notion of purifying the republican robe of liberty in a sacrificial washing sounded eerily like the millennial imagery of the martyrs in St. John's Revelation whose white robes had been washed and made white 'in the blood of the Lamb.'"[764]

With the same scriptural brush used at Peoria, Lincoln painted a tight canvas during the Second Inaugural: "The Almighty has His own purposes. 'Woe unto the world because of offences! for it must needs be that offences come; but woe to that man by whom the offence cometh!'"[765] Religious historian Ronald C. White Jr. wrote that the "biblical and theological language" of the Second Inaugural was unique. "Within 701 words Lincoln mentions God fourteen times, quotes the bible four times, and invokes prayer three times."[766] Lincoln was not an orthodox Christian, nor even officially a member of a Christian church. Still, he embraced the Judeo-Christian moral order at work in America's common culture at the birth of the republic. At Peoria Lincoln declared that America must cleanse its "republican robe" from the stain of slavery. Slavery "deprives our republican example of its just influence in the world."[767] The degradation of the Declaration of Independence in the despotism of slavery corrupted the American republic. Such a decline would not be without dire consequences—including the extinction of America's example to the world. For, as Lincoln observed in 1857, the Declaration of 1776 had the implicit power for "augmenting the happiness and value of life to all people of all colors everywhere. . . ."[768]

Lincoln at Peoria had emphasized that America's experiment had consequences far beyond its borders. "The President was deeply imbued with the belief that the American Dream had a worldwide significance, and it must have been heartening for him to receive the congratulatory message of the workingmen of Manchester, England, in 1863," wrote Gabor Boritt. "This spoke of America as 'a singular, happy abode for the working millions' and of Lincoln as the leader who decisively upheld the great belief that all men are created free and equal. Here was evidence for Lincoln that the laboring folk not only of his nation but also of the entire world understood the meaning of the Civil War."[769] Indeed, Lord Godfrey Charnwood noted in his classic biography of 1916: "Beyond his own country some of us recall his name as the greatest among those associated with the cause of popular government."[770] President Lincoln had popular government in mind when he responded to the Manchester workers: "I have understood well that the duty of self-preservation rests solely with the American people. But I have at the same time been aware that favor or disfavor of foreign nations might have a material influence in enlarging and prolonging the struggle with disloyal men in which the country is engaged. A fair examination of history has seemed to authorize a belief that the past action and influences of the United States were generally regarded as having been beneficent towards mankind."[771]

Lincoln, the antislavery nationalist, maintained the striking American narrative set forth at Peoria in 1854. "[A] fair examination of history" persisted as a constant theme in his writing and speaking. In December 1862, President Lincoln spoke of America as the "last best hope" of the world. Lincoln regularly invoked providential and global themes. At Trenton in February 1861, he called his countrymen God's "almost chosen people." In his special Message to Congress in July 1861, Lincoln wrote that the Civil War "embraces more than the fate of these United States. It presents to the whole family of man, the question, whether a constitutional republic, or a democracy—a government of the people, by the same people— can, or cannot, maintain its territorial integrity, against its own domestic foes."[772] Lincoln argued that the war was "a struggle for maintaining in the world, that form, and substance of government, whose leading object is, to elevate the condition of men—to lift artificial weights from all shoulders—to clear the paths of laudable pursuit for all—to afford all, an unfettered start, and a fair chance, in the race of life."[773] No one shackled in iron could make the "race of life."

In July 1862, Lincoln implored several congressmen from the Border States to accept compensated emancipation for their slaves: "As you would perpetuate popular government for the best people in the world, I beseech you that you do in no wise omit this [proposal of compensated emancipation]. Our common country is in great peril, demanding the loftiest views, and boldest action to bring it speedy relief. Once relieved, it's form of government is saved to the world; it's beloved history, and cherished memories, are vindicated; and it's happy future fully assured, and rendered inconceivably grand. To you, more than to any others, the privilege is given, to assure that happiness, and swell that grandeur, and to link your own names therewith forever."[774]

In the 1600s, Lincoln's humble ancestors had gone to America from the modest precincts of Puritan East Anglia. He had described to others his lineage. He was interested in the opinions of ordinary Englishmen— especially since the English aristocracy tended to be pro-Confederacy. The great contest of the Royalists and Roundheads in seventeenth-century England had not been forgotten in nineteenth-century America. Two centuries after the English Civil War, Great Britain had become the dominant imperial power in the world. English opinion and parliamentary policy were crucial to Union foreign policy during the American Civil War. The Lincoln Administration was determined to prevent any European intervention on behalf of the Confederacy. The president tried, therefore, to mold foreign opinion, as he did the domestic electorate, by rational and principled argument. In April 1863, he devised a way for English citizens to support the war effort. As Massachusetts Senator Charles Sumner wrote to British statesman John Bright: "Two days ago the President sent for me to come at once. When I arrived he said that he had been thinking of a matter on which we had often spoken, the way in which English opinion should be directed, & that he had drawn up a resolution embodying the ideas which he should hope to see adopted by public meetings in England. I inclose the resolution, in his autograph, as he gave it to me. He thought it might serve to suggest the point which he regarded as important."[775] In the resolution, the president had invoked the specter of a slave civilization:

Whereas, while, *heretofore*, States, and Nations, have tolerated slavery, *recently*, for the first in the world, an attempt has been made to construct a new Nation, upon the basis of, and with the primary, and fundamental object to maintain, enlarge, and perpetuate human slavery, therefore,

Resolved, That no such embryo State should ever be recognized by, or admitted into, the family of christian and civilized nations; and that all ch[r]istian and civilized men everywhere should, by all lawful means, resist to the utmost, such recognition or admission.[776]

Lincoln foresaw the profound effect on Victorian England—heir to the English abolitionist, William Wilberforce—of an appeal to the family of civilized nations and to its values, just as he believed at Peoria such a case would persuade his countrymen. Still, persuading English working men was not as important as persuading American fighting men. In the middle of the 1864 election campaign, President Lincoln told an Ohio regiment passing through Washington on its way home: "In no administration can there be perfect equality of action and uniform satisfaction rendered by all. But this government must be preserved in spite of the acts of any man or set of men. It is worthy [of] your every effort. Nowhere in the world is presented a government of so much liberty and equality."[777]

Lincoln historian Richard N. Current wrote that, in Lincoln's view, "to be an American . . . was a matter of commitment to certain principles, not a matter of racial or cultural inheritance."[778] Current wrote: "Lincoln did not pretend that American democracy was perfect, or anywhere near perfect. He looked upon it as an experiment, and he invited people of all countries, cultures, and creeds to share in the great political experiment as well as the economic opportunities of the United States."[779] On election night in November 1864, President Lincoln told serenaders outside the White House that defeating slavery would preserve the Union and the hope of freedom the Union represented: "I cannot at this hour say what has been the result of the election; but, whatever it may be, I have no desire to modify this opinion—that all who have labored to-day in behalf of the Union organization, have wrought for the best interests of their country and the world, not only for the present, but for all future ages."[780] Two days later, he told another group of serenaders:

But the election, along with its incidental, and undesirable strife, has done good too. It has demonstrated that a people's government can sustain a national election, in the midst of a great civil war. Until now it has not been known to the world that this was a possibility. It shows also how *sound*, and how *strong* we still are. It shows that, even among candidates of the same party, he who is most devoted to the Union, and most opposed to treason, can receive most of the people's votes. It shows also, to the extent yet known, that we have more men now, than we had when the war began. Gold is good in its place; but living, brave, patriotic men, are better than gold.[781]

For Lincoln, patriotism was an indispensable virtue. In his eulogy of Henry Clay in 1852, Lincoln remarked that the Kentucky senator "loved his country partly because it was his own country, but mostly because it was a free country."[782] So too, Lincoln believed, should all Americans. In his last Annual Message to Congress, President Lincoln reemphasized the historical importance of the wartime election: "In affording the people the fair opportunity of showing, one to another and to the world, this firmness and unanimity of purpose, the election has been of vast value to the national cause."[783]

When the Thirteenth Amendment abolishing slavery passed the House on January 31, 1865, Lincoln told serenaders that this American constitutional event had more than national significance: "The occasion was one of congratulation to the country and to the whole world."[784] The amendment was "a king's cure for all the evils. It winds the whole thing up."[785] It confirmed that no American court of law would be able to undo the bloody work of Civil War and Emancipation. The "republican robe," described at Peoria as "soiled, and trailed in the dust," might be repurified.[786]

The Thirteenth Amendment was a crucial outcome brought about by the will of loyal Americans who had gone to war, first to preserve the Union, and later with emancipation, to vindicate their own charter of freedom. As Lincoln had argued at Peoria, Americans could not ignore the Declaration of Independence except at their great peril. In his Second Annual Message to Congress, only weeks before he issued the final Emancipation Proclamation, Lincoln prophesied: "Fellow-citizens, *we* cannot escape history. We of this Congress and this administration, will be remembered in spite of ourselves. No personal significance, or insignificance, can spare one or another of us. The fiery trial through which we pass, will light us down, in honor or dishonor, to the latest generation. We *say* we are for the Union. The world will not forget that we say this. We know how to save the Union. The world knows we do know how to save it. We—even *we here*—hold the power, and bear the responsibility."

More than victory in war was at stake, President Lincoln wrote to Congress on December 1, 1862: "In *giving* freedom to the *slave*, we *assure* freedom to the *free*—honorable alike in what we give, and what we preserve. We shall nobly save, or meanly lose, the last best, hope of earth. Other means may succeed; this could not fail. The way is plain, peaceful, generous, just—a way which, if followed, the world will forever applaud, and God must forever bless."[787]

"God did not place good and evil before man, telling him to make his choice. On the contrary, he did tell him there was one tree, of the fruit of which, he should not eat, upon pain of certain death. I should scarcely wish so strong a prohibition against slavery in Nebraska."

ABRAHAM LINCOLN,
OCTOBER 16, 1854

VIII.

Coda

"The repeal of the Missouri Compromise," recalled Horace White, "found Abraham Lincoln a country lawyer with a not very lucrative practice, but a very popular story-teller." The Chicago journalist underestimated Lincoln's law practice, but he was surely right that the Kansas-Nebraska Act had stirred the North and Abraham Lincoln to political action. "Without that awakening, which came like an electric shock to all the Northern States, he would doubtless have remained in comparative obscurity."[788] White notwithstanding, Lincoln in 1854 was one of the better-recognized attorneys of Illinois. Financially successful, he was a formidable jury lawyer and an accomplished litigator before the Supreme Court of Illinois.[789] As an ambitious lawyer-politician, Lincoln rode the Eighth Judicial Circuit in the spring of 1854, pondering the impact of Senator Stephen Douglas's incendiary legislation. Upon his return to Springfield, he studied the documentary history of the American Founding in the State Library. When in late summer he set out again on the Eighth Circuit, Lincoln had formulated his arguments against the extension of slavery. White noted that in the Peoria speech of October 1854, Lincoln gathered those arguments into a program that would carry him through the political debates of the next decade.

John Todd Stuart recalled that after Lincoln left Congress in 1849, he and Stuart were walking in Springfield when Stuart said: "Lincoln the time is Coming when you & I will have to be Democrats or Abolitionists." Stuart reported that the future President replied: "When that time Comes My mind is fixed—I cant Compromise the Slavery question."[790] In 1854, the time came. Intense study in the State Capitol and vigorous debate in the state courts had made him ready. He had learned that straightforward propositions, appealing to both the intellect and the heart, could drive his arguments home in jury summations. So might they move political debate. There developed in the 1850s a hard, compelling edge to Lincoln's antislavery theme. In a single, unadorned sentence, Lincoln summarized his basic message: "I think that if anything can be proved by natural theology, it is that slavery is morally wrong."[791]

Unlike many Illinois friends, Lincoln could not be indifferent to slavery. After Kansas-Nebraska, he argued, no one could. He reasoned that the spread of slavery meant the abandonment of the principles of the Declaration of Independence. His purpose became increasingly clear. Lincoln's intention "was to emancipate the American republic from the curse of slavery, a curse which lay upon both races, and which in different ways enslaved them both," wrote Harry V. Jaffa.[792] With respect to slavery in the American territories, only action at the national level could limit slavery's growth, because in 1854 the doctrine of popular sovereignty and the repeal of the Missouri Compromise line had opened the door to the national expansion of slavery. As Lincoln said in the final Lincoln-Douglas debate in 1858: "Is it not a false statesmanship that undertakes to build up a system of policy upon the basis of caring nothing about *the very thing that every body does care the most about*?"[793] Thus did Lincoln impeach the proclaimed indifference toward slavery of Senator Douglas.

After Peoria, Lincoln invoked in almost every major speech the authority of the Declaration. It is the bedrock of American constitutional democracy, he insisted, saying in 1856 that the "'central idea' in our political public opinion . . . was, and until recently continued to be, 'the equality of men.'"[794] At Peoria, he had argued that consent and the proposition that all men are created equal were the sheet anchors of the Republic— just as they had become the sheet anchors of his antislavery campaign. He had written notes for a speech on slavery and the American political tradition: "Most *governments* have been based, practically, on the denial of equal rights of men...*ours* began, by *affirming* those rights. *They* said, some men are too *ignorant*, and *vicious*, to share in government. Possibly so, said we; and, by your system, you would always keep them ignorant, and vicious. We proposed to give *all* a chance; and we expected the weak to grow stronger, the ignorant, wiser; and all better, and happier together."[795] This doctrine of the Declaration he would refer to as America's "ancient faith." The elegant simplicity of his prose appeared everywhere in the 1850s— even in a private note to himself, where he wrote "as I would not be a *slave*, so I would not be a *master*."[796]

In a revealing speech on July 10, 1858, Lincoln had said of slavery: "I have always hated it, but I have always been quiet about it until this new era of the introduction of the Nebraska Bill began." He added: "I should like to know if taking this old Declaration of Independence, which declares that all men are equal upon principle and making exceptions to it where will it stop. If one man says it does not mean a negro, why not another say it does not mean some other man? If that declaration is not the truth, let us get the Statute book, in which we find it and tear it out! Who is so bold as to do it! [Voices—'me' 'no one,' &c.] If it is not true let us tear it out!"[797] There could be no compromise on the basic principles of the Declaration of Independence. That document was the first section in the *Statutes of Indiana* that Lincoln probably studied as a youth.[798] During the secession crisis of early February 1861, President-elect Lincoln warned Senator William H. Seward, who was leaning toward appeasement of the South, not to compromise on the expansion of slavery into territories:

I say now, however, as I have all the while said, that on the territorial question—that is, the question of extending slavery under the national auspices,—I am inflexible. I am for no compromise which *assists* or *permits* the extension of the institution on soil owned by the nation. And any trick by which the nation is to acquire territory, and then allow some local authority to spread slavery over it, is as obnoxious as any other.

I take it that to effect some such result as this, and to put us again on the high-road to a slave empire is the object of all these proposed compromises. I am against it.[799]

Lincoln maintained that if a principle were true, objectively true, it must be upheld, even if not promptly applied by policy: "If it is not true let us tear it out."[800] The moral issue of slavery was inescapable—no matter how adroitly Stephen A. Douglas tried to evade it in the debates of 1854 and 1858. Opposed to immediate abolition on constitutional grounds, Lincoln would still contest the evasions of the equality principle. Popular sovereignty, as argued by Douglas, was a convenient rationalization of self-interest: Whatever the people vote for, even slavery, was right. In trying to accommodate the slaveholders of the South, Senator Douglas alienated much more of the populous North. In 1854 Abraham Lincoln began the process by which Illinois would build a majority on the basis of a measured policy to restrict the spread of slavery. At Peoria, his constituents heard that economic and social policy must gradually follow from principles anchored in reason, morality, and public welfare. But philosophic wisdom required practical wisdom to be effective. Erstwhile secretary John Hay recalled his first encounter with Lincoln in 1859: "He came into the law office where I was reading, which adjoined his own, with a copy of Harper's Magazine in his hand, containing Senator Douglas's famous article on Popularity Sovereignty. Lincoln seemed greatly roused by what he read. Entering the office without a salutation, he said: 'This will never do! He puts the moral element out of this question. It won't stay out.'"[801] In Lincoln's last Annual Message to Congress, he reminded his countrymen: "Important principles may, and must be inflexible."[802]

Lincoln recoiled at the prospect that the future of American freedom might be threatened by the advance of slavery. Historian Kenneth M. Stampp wrote: "A year after the passage of the Kansas-Nebraska Act, a pessimistic Lincoln feared that there was no prospect for a peaceful end to slavery in the United States. 'On the question of liberty, as a principle,' he wrote, 'we are not what we have been.'"[803] He regretted the change: "When we were the political slaves of King George, and wanted to be free, we called the maxim that 'all men are created equal' a self evident truth;

but now when we have grown fat, and have lost all dread of being slaves ourselves, we have become so greedy to be *masters* that we call the same maxim 'a self-evident lie'[.] The fourth of July has not quite dwindled away; it is still a great day—*for burning fire-crackers*!!!"[804]

In the same 1855 letter, Lincoln reflected on the animating principles of 1776: "That spirit which desired the peaceful extinction of slavery, has itself become extinct, with the *occasion*, and the *men* of the Revolution. Under the impulse of that occasion, nearly half the states adopted systems of emancipation at once; and it is a significant fact, that not a single state has done the like since. So far as peaceful, voluntary emancipation is concerned, the condition of the negro slave in America, scarcely less terrible to the contemplation of a free mind, is now as fixed, and hopeless of change for the better, as that of the lost souls of the finally impenitent. The Autocrat of all the Russians will resign his crown, and proclaim his subjects free republicans sooner than will our American masters voluntarily give up their slaves." Lincoln, in 1855, anticipated the themes of his "House Divided" speech of 1858: "Our political problem now is 'Can we, as a nation, continue together *permanently—forever*—half slave, and half free?' The problem is too mighty for me. May God, in his mercy, superintend the solution."[805]

Historian James McPherson made the case that "[f]rom 1854, when he returned to politics, until nominated for president in 1860, the dominant, unifying theme of Lincoln's career was opposition to the expansion of slavery as the vital first step toward placing it on the course of ultimate extinction." McPherson isolated a principal cause of disunion: "It was not merely Lincoln's election, but his election as a *principled opponent of slavery on moral grounds* that precipitated secession."[806] Although Senator Douglas tried to cloak the Kansas-Nebraska Act in high principle, he fooled few. Popular sovereignty was a political creed of convenience with respect to slavery, artfully adapted to win favor in the South and the North alike, and to hold the sections together. A bold Senator Douglas and a pliant President Pierce presided over passage of the Kansas-Nebraska Act. Both valued Democratic Party dominance of the Union and thus the accommodation of the slaveholders essential to Democratic majorities and patronage. Lincoln too valued the Union, but especially the opportunities it gave to free labor—not least because free labor followed from the moral imperatives of the Declaration of Independence. "Slavery," Lincoln declared at Peoria, "is founded in the selfishness of man's nature—opposition to it [in] his love of justice. These principles are an eternal antagonism."[807]

Lincoln friend Joseph Gillespie maintained that after 1854 slavery was the sole subject "on which he would become excited." Some biographers have suggested that Lincoln's resistance to unjust subordination may have originated in his resentment of an overbearing father, who was legally entitled to the value of his son's labor, which he appropriated until Lincoln reached twenty-one years of age. Moreover, there were antislavery religious moorings in Lincoln's Baptist boyhood in slaveholding Kentucky. Perhaps principle and provenance were joined in Lincoln's early commitment to just compensation for free labor. Gillespie recalled "meeting with him once at Shelbyville when he remarked that something must be done or slavery would overrun the whole country[.] He said there were about 600,000 non slave holding whites in Kentucky to about 33,000 slave holders[.] That in the convention then recently held it was expected that the delegates would represent these classes about in proportion to their respective numbers but when the convention assembled there was not a single representative of the non slaveholding class[.] Every one was in the interest of the slaveholders and said he this thing is spreading like wild fire over the Country[.] In a few years we will be ready to accept the institution in Illinois and the whole country will adopt it[.]"[808] Lincoln's opposition to slavery had theoretical roots in the works of the classical economists David Ricardo and Adam Smith. Lincoln's reading of American economic writer Francis Wayland, and probably Henry Carey, were sources for his free-labor ideas. In his First Annual Message to Congress in December 1861, he wrote: "Labor is the superior of capital, and deserves much the higher consideration. Capital has its rights, which are as worthy of protection as any other rights."[809]

Consistent with his economic principles, Lincoln in 1854 opposed the spread of slavery's unrequited toil to free territory. Although slavery could not be eliminated by congressional action in the states where it already existed, Congress did have the constitutional authority to prohibit slavery in the territories. Lincoln's respect for the authorized procedures of the

Constitution cannot be underestimated when trying to understand his deference to slavery in the original states. There, slavery was protected by the Constitution—a concession necessitated at the Convention of 1787 in order to create the Union of thirteen states. Given his judicial temperament, Lincoln could not be indifferent to the law. As a politically ambitious man in a constitutional democracy, his only open field was to reform bad law by persuasion and election. In 1859, a midwestern journalist heard Lincoln give a campaign speech in Indianapolis. He would later recall: "The part of the speech . . . which most strongly impressed me, at the time, and has remained the longest in my memory is what he said about reverence for the law. I noticed that he never used the term obedience to the law, but always reverence, seeming to regard that term higher and more comprehensive than the other."[810] Reverence for the law was an imperative of the American civil religion, spelled out by Lincoln at age twenty-eight in his 1838 Lyceum speech: "Let reverence for the laws, be breathed by every American mother, to the lisping babe, that prattles on her lap—let it be taught in schools, in seminaries, and in colleges;—let it be written in Primmers, spelling books, and in Almanacs;—let it be preached from the pulpit, proclaimed in legislative halls, and enforced in courts of justice. And, in short, let it become the *political religion* of the nation; and let the old and the young, the rich and the poor, the grave and the gay, of all sexes and tongues, and colors and conditions, sacrifice unceasingly upon its altars."[811]

Sixteen years after the Lyceum speech, Lincoln, now an accomplished lawyer, rose to speak in Peoria. Ward Hill Lamon's ghost-written biography of Lincoln has long been criticized, but his ghostwriter got it right when he wrote: "The speech was really a great one, almost perfectly adapted to produce conviction upon a doubting mind. It ought to be carefully read by every one who desires to know Lincoln's power as a debater, after his intellect was matured and ripened by years of hard experience." Addressing those who believed in the redeeming powers of climate and economics to halt slavery's expansion, Lincoln dismissed this "lullaby" that slavery might waste away and gradually disappear in the inhospitable environment of the new territory. Many advocates of the Kansas-Nebraska Act, and later many historians, would argue that the decline of slavery was inevitable by reason of climate and economics. But, as James McPherson observed: "On the eve of the Civil War, plantation agriculture was more profitable, slavery more entrenched, slave owners more prosperous, and the 'slave power' more dominant within the South if not in the nation at large than it had ever been."[812]

Climate was a critical issue, but the force of the *Dred Scott* decision of the U.S. Supreme Court loomed larger. In ruling the Missouri Compromise line unconstitutional, and declaring no black man could ever be an American citizen, the court legitimated the unrestricted spread of slavery to the territories, heightening Lincoln's fear for the future of freedom in the Republic. In light of the Supreme Court's ruling, a slave republic might be the result. By 1858, slavery had become the preeminent national issue. But contrary to the opinion of Chief Justice Taney, Lincoln believed that Congress did have the constitutional authority, even the duty, to prohibit slavery's extension. "I am impliedly, if not expressedly pledged to a belief in the *right* and *duty* of Congress to prohibit slavery in all the United States Territories," he said in 1858 at the Freeport debate with Douglas.[813] Moreover, Congress could under certain circumstances, Lincoln argued, "overthrow" an opinion of the Supreme Court.

With care and foresight, Lincoln in 1854 had begun to edit and print his major speeches, a hallmark technique of his future campaigns. This deliberate strategy made his edited texts, especially those printed at his initiative, the accepted rendition of his thinking, not only for his contemporaries, but for all posterity. By nature, Lincoln was meticulous, and in his maturity, he was generally temperate, deliberate, patient. He did harbor a streak of melancholy which has been much debated and sometimes exaggerated. Perhaps the melancholy moments made him more reflective and creative. His melancholy notwithstanding, bold, but well-timed decisions characterized his politics and policies after 1854. According to his law partner, Lincoln's "ambition was a little engine that knew no rest," but in the climate of contemporary public opinion Lincoln did not employ radical tactics toward his ambitious goals.[814] Although he knew what simple justice required of his countrymen, he sensed when the American people were ready for decisive measures. He was also relentless in moving public sentiment toward his position. "Mr. Lincoln's confidence in the justness of the antislavery battle never faltered through the years I knew him," recalled attorney Charles S. Zane.[815] "In January, 1859, while the Democrats were celebrating the election of Stephen A. Douglas to the United States Senate, Archibald Williams . . . came into Lincoln's office and finding him writing said: 'Well, the Democrats are making a great noise over their victory.' Looking up Lincoln replied: 'Yes, Archie, Douglas has taken this trick, but the game is not played out.'"[816]

Indeed, the polls had barely closed on the November 1858 election when Jeriah Bonham wrote an editorial for the *Illinois Gazette* wherein he predicted the candidates for the 1860 presidential election: "Douglas will lead the cohorts of slavery. Lincoln should lead the hosts of freedom in this 'irrepressible conflict.' Who has earned the proud position as well as he? as he is in himself the embodiment and exponent of our free institutions. These two men have fought the battles over the plains of Illinois. What is so proper as their being the champions of the two principles on the national field?"[817]

The national campaign of 1860 resolved itself into a dispute over a single moral and social issue. The conventional wisdom of American politics suggests that elections should not turn on moral issues and that single-issue candidates cannot prevail in presidential contests. Lincoln thought otherwise. He had declared at Columbus, Ohio, in September 1859: "Looking at these things, the Republican party, as I understand its principles and policy, believe that there is great danger of the institution of slavery being spread out and extended, until it is ultimately made alike lawful in all the States of this union; so believing, to prevent that incidental and ultimate consummation, is the original and chief purpose of the Republican organization. . . . This chief and real purpose of the Republican party is eminently conservative. It proposes nothing save and except to restore this government to its original tone in regard to this element of slavery, and there to maintain it, looking for no further change . . . than that which the original framers of the government themselves expected and looked forward to."[818] This "chief and real purpose"—to restrict "this element of slavery"—became the primary issue to be resolved in the presidential elections of 1860 and 1864. As Lincoln had stated in his "House Divided" speech of 1858, "Our cause, then, must be intrusted to, and conducted by its own undoubted friends—those whose hands are free, whose hearts are in the work—who do care for the result."[819]

The radical aim of some in the South was to make America a vast slaveholding Republic. If they succeeded, and "if this principle is established, that there is no wrong in slavery . . . when this is done, where this doctrine prevails, the miners and sappers will have formed public opinion for the slave trade," said Lincoln at Columbus in 1859. "They will be ready for Jeff. Davis and [Alexander] Stephens and other leaders of that company, to sound the bugle for the revival of the slave trade, for the second Dred Scott decision, for the flood of slavery to be poured over the free States, while we shall be here tied down and helpless and run over like sheep."[820] Only two years later, Lincoln and the Union would be embattled by a slaveholder insurrection led by Jefferson Davis and Alexander H. Stephens as president and vice president of the Confederacy. In that contest, Lincoln, a self-described conservative bent on using persuasion and the ballot to restore the founding principles of the republic, would in the end wage a remorseless war for the union, and ultimately, for abolition of slavery in America. Ohio journalist David R. Locke recalled visiting with Lincoln after he gave the Columbus speech. He reported that Lincoln told him: "Slavery is doomed, and that within a few years. . . . In discussing it we have taught a great many thousands of people to hate it who had never given it a thought before. What kills the skunk is the publicity it gives itself. What a skunk wants to do is to keep snug under the barn—in the day-time, when men are around with shot-guns."[821]

In his speeches after Peoria, Lincoln appealed primarily to the intelligence, rationality, and fairness of his listeners. One reporter, who heard him speak in Indianapolis in 1859, remembered: "He seemed to be addressing himself to the intelligence and thinking powers of his auditors rather than to their imagination. His words were simple, but every one was weighted with meaning, and when delivered they formed an argument that was irresistible or a statement of fact that was conclusive."[822] When Lincoln spoke in Kansas at the end of 1859, a local slaveholder was called on to reply. He began: "I have heard, during my life, all the best public speakers, all the eminent statesmen of the past and the present generation, and while I dissent utterly from the doctrines of this address and shall endeavor to refute some of them, candor compels me to say that it is the most able—the most logical—speech I ever listened to."[823]

Lincoln brought the concentrated powers of research and reason to bear on his adversaries. In the Cooper Union address of February 1860, he rejected the slaveholders' argument that the North was the provocative power: "Again, you [the slaveholders] say we [Republicans] have made the slavery question more prominent than it formerly was. We deny it. We admit that it is more prominent, but we deny that we made it so. It was not we, but you, who discarded the old policy of the fathers [the restriction of slavery]. We resisted, and still resist, your innovation; and thence comes the greater prominence of the question. Would you have that question reduced to its former proportions? Go back to that old policy. What has been will be again, under the same conditions. If you would have the peace of the old times, readopt the precepts and policy of the old times."

The future of slavery remained in doubt throughout most of the Civil War, but Lincoln's reelection in November 1864 heralded its ultimate extinction in the Union. At Appomattox in April 1865 the South surrendered, and with its surrender, its slave-based economy collapsed. Then, the Thirteenth Amendment to the Constitution, abolishing slavery, rang the death knell of America's peculiar institution. The promise of emancipation, having been made, was kept. Even the failures of Reconstruction and segregation could not extinguish the promise of constitutional equality in the Thirteenth, Fourteenth, and Fifteenth amendments. The moral and legal framework of American fundamental law had been so reconstructed that, at some future time, it might house the civil rights reforms which would come a century after President Lincoln's death. Then, with the Civil War constitutional amendments teaching Americans by example, racism too could be put in the course of ultimate extinction.

The promise of the Peoria speech and of the Declaration of Independence might still be fulfilled.

"I wish further to say, that I do not propose to question the patriotism, or to assail the motives of any man, or class of men; but rather to strictly confine myself to the naked merits of the question."

ABRAHAM LINCOLN,
OCTOBER 16, 1854

IX.

The Peoria Speech and the Historians' Record

That the Springfield-Peoria speech was the turning point in Lincoln's political life was grasped by many of Lincoln's contemporaries. Fellow attorney Samuel C. Parks said: "The occasion of his becoming a great antislavery leader was the agitation of the Repeal of the Missouri Compromise[.] His first great speech in opposition to that measure & in reply to Mr[.] Douglas in Spring field [*sic*] was one of the ablest & most effective of his life."[824] Illinois newspaper editor Paul Selby thought the speech was "one of the noblest efforts of Mr. Lincoln's life, and advocated the truest and boldest anti-slavery doctrine."[825] Chicago journalist Horace White, then just twenty, recalled a half century later: "The speech of 1854 made so profound an impression on me that I feel under its spell to this day."[826] White believed that Lincoln had set forth most of the arguments at Peoria which would carry him through every contest before and after his elevation to the presidency.

Early Lincoln biographers also recognized the importance of the Peoria speech. Journalist John L. Scripps, who composed a partisan campaign biography in 1860, wrote that "the triumph" of Lincoln's Peoria speech "was even more marked than Springfield. . . . It was a thorough and unanswerable exposition of all the sophisms and plausible pretences with which Douglas up to that time had invested the Kansas-Nebraska Bill . . ."[827]

Lincoln's younger law partner, William H. Herndon, became the preeminent collector of anecdotal evidence about his life. In his Lincoln biography, Herndon and collaborator Jesse W. Weik quoted from a newspaper editorial Herndon had written after the Springfield speech in early October—one which "may seem rather strongly imbued with youthful enthusiasm, yet on reading it in maturer years I am still inclined to believe it reasonably faithful to the facts and the situation." Herndon had written in the Illinois *State Journal* at the time of the Peoria speech: "The anti-Nebraska speech of Mr. Lincoln was the profoundest in our opinion that he had made in his whole life."[828]

Another contemporary biographer, Illinois Congressman Isaac N. Arnold, wrote: "As printed it lacks the fire and vehemence of the extemporaneous speech, but as an argument against the extension of slavery it has no equal in the anti-slavery literature of the country."[829] Arnold shared Herndon's view that Senator Stephen A. Douglas, already America's most powerful senator and a leading contender for the presidency, was knocked off balance by the Lincoln speeches at Springfield and Peoria. Arnold contended "on these two occasions, more perhaps than any other in his life . . . Douglas [was] disconcerted by the vigor and power of the reply to him. A consciousness of being in the wrong may have contributed to this result. It was perfectly clear that Mr. Lincoln spoke from the most deep and earnest conviction of right, and his manner indicated this."[830]

New York Times editor Henry J. Raymond, a biographer and close Lincoln political ally during the Civil War, wrote that Senator Douglas "always claimed to have voted for the repeal of the Missouri Compromise because he sustained the 'great principle' of popular sovereignty, and desired that the inhabitants of Kansas and Nebraska should govern themselves, as they were well able to do. The fallacy of drawing from these premises the conclusion that they therefore should have the right to establish slavery there, was most clearly and conclusively exposed by Mr. Lincoln, so that no one could thereafter be misled by it, unless he was a willing dupe of pro-slavery sophistry."[831]

Noah Brooks was an Illinois journalist who moved to California before coming to Washington to cover the Lincoln administration. He subsequently wrote his own Lincoln biography. Compared to the earlier Springfield address, Brooks wrote that the Peoria "speech was materially different, but it was, as subsequently written out by him, more skilful and elaborate in its treatment of the great question. Those who heard both of these memorable addresses have said that the Peoria speech, while perfect in its construction, a marvel of logical force, was not so stirring as that delivered at Springfield. It was, however, distinguished above all others for it's manifestation of a full and exhaustive knowledge of the slavery question and of all that had at that time grown out of it. Probably no other man then living could have produced so complete and comprehensive a view of the subject presented, both as to itself and its collateral branches."[832] One cannot escape the inference that Lincoln intended the Springfield speech to be heard—but that he intended the Peoria speech to be heard and to be read widely.

John G. Nicolay and John Hay—President Lincoln's youthful secretaries who a generation later published their sympathetic biography—wrote that prior to the Springfield speech, "Lincoln had hitherto been the foremost man in his [congressional] district. That single effort made him the leader on the new question in his State." Composing their ten-volume biography of Mr. Lincoln in the late nineteenth century, Nicolay and Hay insisted: "After the lapse of more than a quarter of a century the critical reader still finds [the Peoria speech] a model of brevity, directness, terse diction, exact and lucid historical statement, and full of logical propositions so short and so strong as to resemble mathematical axioms. Above all it is pervaded by an elevation of thought and aim that lifts it out of the commonplace of mere party controversy. Comparing it with his later speeches, we find it to contain not only the argument of the hour, but the premonition of the broader issues into which the new struggle was destined soon to expand."[833]

Massachusetts editor Josiah G. Holland never knew Lincoln personally, but he published his biography well before Nicolay and Hay. In 1866, Holland recorded the impact that the Peoria speech evoked twelve years earlier: "Owing very materially to Mr. Lincoln's efforts, a political revolution swept the state."[834] Another Lincoln presidential secretary, William O. Stoddard, was also a young Illinois journalist in the 1850s. He observed that "Lincoln's Peoria speech was printed and widely read. By it his followers were supplied with forcible verbal formulas for the expression of their thoughts and feelings, and all the local speakers of the fall campaign were given a magazine of fresh material to draw upon."[835] Charles A. Church, who wrote an early history of the Republican Party in Illinois, concluded that after the Springfield address, Lincoln's "audience felt that a man of power had arisen, a Moses to lead the people."[836]

Several decades later, Lincoln biographer Ida Tarbell wrote of the 1854 addresses: "These speeches . . . form really the first of the series of Lincoln-Douglas Debates. They proved conclusively to the anti-Nebraska politicians in Illinois that Lincoln was to be their leader in the fight they had begun against the extension of slavery." Tarbell noted: "Lincoln's friends expected him to do well in his reply [to Douglas], but his speech was a surprise even to those who knew him best. It was profound, finished, vigorous, eloquent."[837] In the 1920s, Lincoln biographer Nathaniel Wright Stephenson wrote that the Peoria speech was "a landmark in his career. It sums up all his long, slow development in political science, lays the abiding foundation of everything he thought thereafter.'"[838] That Peoria formed the substance and style of future prepared statements was recognized even by biographers who were unsympathetic to the Lincoln legacy. Written about the same time as Stephenson's, former Indiana Senator Albert J. Beveridge's two-volume biography often criticized the pre–Civil War Lincoln. But Beveridge acknowledged the merit of Lincoln's 1854 rhetoric when he entitled the chapter on Kansas-Nebraska: "Political Merger: The First Great Speech."[839]

"It was Lincoln's first great speech," agreed Lincoln scholar Paul M. Angle. "Floridity had given way to short, plain words, each finding its proper place in a logical development as strict and uncompromising as the Euclidian demonstrations its author had mastered. With these characteristics were others which future generations were to recognize as distinguishing marks—the fair-mindedness which impelled him to remind his hearers that for the sting of slavery the North bore equal responsibility with the South; the humility which caused him to confess that even though all earthly power were his, he should not know what to do with slavery as an existing institution."[840]

In the 1920s, poet Carl Sandburg wrote that the Peoria speech led "many politicians and people in Illinois" to see that "there was one man in the state who could grapple and hold his own with Stephen A. Douglas. Among Whig and anti-Nebraska politicians it was recognized that a mind was among them [that] could strip a political issue to what he called its 'naked merits.' And among thousands of plain people was an instinct, perhaps a hope, that this voice was their voice."[841] In the mid-twentieth century, Lincoln biographer Benjamin Thomas suggested that the Peoria speech transformed an "essentially self-centered small-town politician of self-developed but largely unsuspected talents into democracy's foremost spokesman."[842] The Peoria speech brought Lincoln to the center of Illinois politics, even put him on the nation's political map. Historian T. Harry Williams wrote: "More than any Republican, Lincoln stressed that slavery was on the march, that it was aggressively reaching out into new areas: the territories and possibly the free states themselves. He did not say positively that this thrust was the result of a deliberate plan, of an organized movement, but he hinted strongly at the possibility."[843]

Some Lincoln biographers have provided other perspectives. In the early 1930s Lincoln critic Edgar Lee Masters spent more time on events surrounding Lincoln's handling of the nascent Republican Party organization after his Springfield speech than on the speech itself. Masters saw Lincoln as more a creature of ambition than principle.[844] Stephen A. Douglas biographer George Fort Milton minimized the relative importance of Lincoln's efforts: "While the Springfield and Peoria speeches constituted a high point in Abraham Lincoln's career, to Douglas they probably represented little more than two arduous days in a State-wide campaign."[845] Lincoln biographer Benjamin Thomas later noted: "While the Springfield and Peoria addresses were high points in Lincoln's career, to Douglas they were merely part of the daily grind of speechmaking. . . ."[846]

In the 1940s, James G. Randall, the dominant Lincoln biographer of the period, virtually skipped over the Peoria address. He preferred to spend time on Lincoln's famous "lost speech" of 1856 for which there is no reliable text.[847] In his multi-volume study of Lincoln's presidency, Randall wrote two sentences about the 1854 speech: "Lincoln was in his best campaigning form as he urged his countrymen to purify the republican robe, to wash it white, to readopt the Declaration of Independence, to turn slavery 'back upon its existing legal rights,' to save the Union, and in doing so to 'make and to keep it forever worthy of the saving.' This he urged in terms of 'Fellow-countrymen, Americans, South as well as North,' joining in 'the great and good work.'"[848]

Doctoral student David Herbert Donald helped Professor Randall do his research. A half century later, Harvard professor Donald gave the speech much more attention than Randall. "Though Lincoln's argument was terse and powerful, his audience found little in its substance that was new," wrote the Harvard University historian. "What listeners did find different and significant in Lincoln's speech was his tone of moral outrage when he discussed 'the monstrous injustice of slavery.'" Indeed, the Peoria arguments were not entirely new if his listeners had heard either his speech at Springfield or those given at Bloomington and Winchester. But for many of Lincoln's listeners, the reasoning was fresh, cogent, and moving. Donald argued, "With this [speech] Lincoln reached the bedrock of his political faith, with his assurance that all men are created equal." Donald thought the Springfield speech "a remarkable address, more elevated in sentiment and rhetoric than any speech Lincoln had previously made, and when he finished, the women in the audience waved their white handkerchiefs in support and men gave loud and continuous hurrahs."[849]

Also writing in the second half of the twentieth century, Historian Allan Nevins wrote that Lincoln struck "with deadly aim at the central point: the assumption in the Nebraska Act that no moral issue was involved in the spread of slavery."[850] According to Nevins: "Here was a voice, fresh as the prairie world itself, such as no man had raised in the East. It lifted the argument at once to a new plane; to the level of high moral considerations. It tested the Kansas-Nebraska Act not by old laws, compacts and precedents, or by new expediencies, but by those fundamental principles of freedom, right and humanity on which the republic had been founded."[851]

Some recent historians have expressed reservations about the Peoria speech. Historian Mark E. Neely Jr. acknowledged: "The Peoria speech was his first great speech, better than any he would give in the famous

Lincoln-Douglas debates four years later." Nevertheless, Neely wrote: "Lincoln's argument, which may seem unanswerable today, was in his own day politically vulnerable on at least two scores. First, it was sectional and threatened the continuing existence of the Union. Second, the time and manner in which slavery was to end were not specified, and many whites felt threatened by the lack of a program to deal with slaves after they became free black men and women." Lincoln did know that antislavery principles could not be argued without suggesting a "sectional" appearance. Emphasizing that his view was truly national, Lincoln denied that universal ethical principles could be sectional in nature. According to Neely, "Lincoln's vagueness about the eventual 'extinction' of slavery, which betrayed the second political vulnerability of his doctrine, was perhaps the most intellectually dishonest part of his platform. Neither he nor any other anti-Nebraska politician much wanted to deal with the question of race. They did so only to the degree that Douglas and the Democrats, through mean-spirited, demagogic race-baiting, forced them."[852] On Lincoln's part, vagueness about the future of slavery was a circumspect humility in the face of a distant, contingent outcome, which Lincoln suggested could come generations in the future.

Much more critical was Richard Hofstadter, the Columbia history professor who questioned the moral basis of Lincoln's thought, instead emphasizing Lincoln's maneuvering. "Lincoln's ambition and interests were aroused, and he proceeded to rehabilitate his political fortunes," wrote Hofstadter. "His strategy was simple and forceful. He carefully avoided issues like the tariff, internal improvements, the Know-Nothing mania, or prohibition, each of which would alienate important groups of voters. He took pains in all his speeches to stress that he was not an abolitionist and at the same time to stand on the sole program of opposing the extension of slavery. On October 4, 1854, at the age of forty-five, Lincoln *for the first time in his life* denounced slavery in public."[853] Stanford historian Don E. Fehrenbacher made a different judgment, arguing that "the depth and sincerity of Lincoln's conviction can be affirmed without the slightest discounting of his intense, unsleeping ambition. He simply had the good fortune to find that a cause which moved him deeply also offered glittering rewards."[854]

Fehrenbacher noted that "those 'revisionist' scholars who sympathize more with Douglas than with his anti-Nebraska critics are likely to lay emphasis upon Lincoln's self-interest and opportunism. Donald W. Riddle, for example, sees only hunger for office in his famous Peoria speech of 1854, with its 'specious arguments' against popular Sovereignty." Riddle wrote that Lincoln "was not fighting for a cause. He was using the slavery issue, conveniently presented by the Kansas-Nebraska Act, to advance his own political standing."[855] Opposition to the Kansas-Nebraska Act in 1854 might have been a useful vehicle to an ambitious politician, but it was not a very likely victory strategy in Illinois, much of whose population had emigrated from the South and shared many southern attitudes toward race and slavery. Indeed much of antislavery Illinois was antiblack. Illinois was also home base of the author of the Kansas-Nebraska Act. "That Douglas was from Illinois enabled Lincoln to make him the primary target of his attacks with an eye toward building an anti-Democratic [Party] coalition in the state," wrote historian Brooks D. Simpson.[856] Circumstances had again provided Lincoln with a personal target in the popular Douglas. Lincoln and Douglas had long been on opposing partisan sides. Nevertheless, the hindsight of the historian should not diminish Mr. Lincoln's achievement in forging an improbable antislavery coalition in Illinois. Contingency in the event characterizes almost every historical episode. Knowing only what Americans knew in 1854, victory of the antislavery coalition in Illinois appeared unlikely. Senator Douglas surely believed this.

Donald W. Riddle emphasized Lincoln's ambition. "Obviously his own interests . . . had been served in his campaigning in the Congressional election of 1854. For in the discussions with Douglas in Springfield and in Peoria he was bent upon enhancing his own political standing by opposing Douglas," wrote Riddle. "The famous Peoria speech was clearly so pointed. Shrewdly omitting a fair estimate of the purpose of the Kansas-Nebraska Act, Lincoln centered attention upon the repeal of the compromise, and painted in the darkest colors the evils which he claimed would result from it."[857] Riddle's view is a curiosity. In fact, a comprehensive estimate of the purpose and effect of the Kansas-Nebraska Act runs throughout the Peoria speech. Lincoln did foresee grave consequences because of Kansas-Nebraska, "Bleeding Kansas," and the ensuing *Dred Scott* Supreme

Court decision of 1857. These events might have led, Lincoln believed, to the nationalization of slavery. "Plainly the Peoria speech marks a great advance in Lincoln's literary and forensic power; it is easy to see that when he made use of this power he had passed across the dividing line, from the ordinary to the superior in the composition and delivery of his speeches," admitted Riddle. "But not much can be said for the logic of the speech, nor for Lincoln's fairness" in his treatment of Douglas.[858] It is hard to reconcile Riddle's last pithy sentence with a careful reading of the full Peoria text itself. Others noted that Lincoln's transparent logic and fairness were hallmarks of his speech.

Douglas scholar Robert W. Johannsen also emphasized Lincoln's ambition in the formulation of the Peoria speech. He criticized Lincoln scholars who have minimized Lincoln's ambition. He did acknowledge the centrality of the speech in Lincoln's political life. But, Johannsen questioned the importance of its idealism: "Writers and scholars over the years have elevated the Peoria Speech to the level of infallible truth, viewing it as a statement of moral indignation and urgency against slavery, as a lofty and eloquent appeal to restore the ideals of the Founding Fathers, and as one of the imperishable speeches of all time. With proper allowance for the excessive adulation and hyperbole identified with all things Lincoln, one may find suggestions of these in his words. What is usually overlooked, however, is the speech's unmistakable political character and purpose. It provided Lincoln with a foundation upon which he built an antislavery career that eventually carried him to political heights he did not even dream of in 1854."[859]

Johannsen argued that Lincoln had been unfair "by singling out Douglas as the sole target for his assaults as if the Illinois senator had accomplished the repeal of the Missouri Compromise by himself. For the slaveholding South, in whose interest Douglas had allegedly acted, Lincoln had only benign words."[860] Johannsen maintained that Lincoln was too accommodating to southern slaveholders: "By focusing on the threat of slavery expansion implied in the repeal of the Missouri Compromise while virtually excusing Southerners for holding slaves in their states, Lincoln was able to place his argument on the broad spectrum of whig thought and to be, as he said, truly national in his position. . . . [W]hile

Lincoln credited Southerners with knowing that slavery was wrong, he had no such concession to Douglas. His enemy was Douglas, not the South. To achieve his ends, it was necessary to portray the Little Giant in extreme terms, as representing the proslavery argument in its most insidious form."[861] The "pretended indifference" of Douglas to slavery was, however, insidious compared to the open advocacy of slavery by southern planters, which was transparent. And Lincoln was determined to unmask the former and defeat the latter.

That Lincoln was an ambitious man is true—as Lincoln himself acknowledged. As a twenty-three-year-old entering politics in 1832, Lincoln had publicly stated, "Every man is said to have his peculiar ambition. Whether it be true or not, I can say for one that I have no other so great as that of being truly esteemed of my fellow men, by rendering myself worthy of their esteem. How far I shall succeed in gratifying this ambition, is yet to be developed."[862] Three decades later as President, he would write General Joseph Hooker, "You are ambitious, which, within reasonable bounds, does good rather than harm."[863] Recognizing ambition in himself, he did not unctuously reject it in others. The Kansas-Nebraska Act, permitting slavery to spread to the formerly restricted territories, ignited Lincoln's moral indignation, which fired his ambition. To a public man the goal of political office was a necessary means to carry out a public policy. If the Kansas-Nebraska Act were to be repealed and slavery's expansion contained, political leadership would be indispensable. Lincoln's principled response to Kansas-Nebraska was not unique. Thousands of leaders of all parties joined Lincoln in 1854 to oppose the Douglas legislation and eventually create the Republican Party.

The 1860 platform of the Republican Party would rest on Lincoln's emphasis at Peoria on the Declaration of Independence. Joseph R. Fornieri wrote that Lincoln's "principled orientation should be kept in mind to balance recent scholarship that has made much of his personal ambition. Lincoln maintained that the Kansas-Nebraska Act profoundly jeopardized the founding ideals of the republic by placing slavery on a new basis. It extended the institution into the virgin territories and promoted the idea that it was a matter of moral indifference to the Union. In sum, the Kansas-Nebraska Act polarized sectional conflict, precipitated an incipient civil war in Kansas, caused a realignment resulting in the formation of the Republican Party, and led to the emergence of Lincoln in national politics."[864]

Oxford University historian Richard J. Carwardine maintained that after the introduction of the Kansas-Nebraska legislation Lincoln "saw early on the political opportunities that Douglas's dangerous measure had opened up. If he could harness the popular revolt against Douglas into the service of an enlarged Whig party, conservative and antislavery, he would both serve the cause of freedom and construct the means by which he might return to Washington, this time as a United States senator."[865] In his political efforts, as Carwardine noted, Lincoln, a Whig conservative himself, adhered to the settled arrangements of the Missouri Compromise of 1820 and to the economic policies of the conservative Whig party. However, Lincoln did add the edge of an aggressive antislavery patriotism, going beyond the Founders he revered.

William Lee Miller of the University of Virginia wrote: "After his enlargement of his purpose in 1854, even though the stakes were higher and the conflict fiercer, Lincoln would become not less but more disciplined in his generosity and would begin to tie his ambition to a larger end."[866] Not unmindful of the negative consequences of narrow personal ambition, Lincoln could give up a short-term political goal for antislavery principle—as his actions attested in the Illinois legislative election for U.S. senator of February 1855. Lincoln was the initial frontrunner in the votes of the State Legislature, but he threw his votes to an antislavery Democrat in order to insure the election of an Illinois senator who was anti-Nebraska. Lincoln's faith in the victor, Lyman Trumbull, would prove justified, particularly in 1864 when Senator Trumbull guided through the Senate the Thirteenth Amendment to abolish slavery.

Lincoln's political rise was temporarily arrested by the 1855 defeat for the U.S. Senate seat. Historian John Niven noted: "Lincoln failed in his campaign for the United States Senate. His speeches and impromptu replies to Douglas, however, marked him as a powerful and persuasive free-soil Whig and as the most articulate orator of the anti-Nebraska politicians in Illinois."[867] Illinois had taken note of private citizen Lincoln, and so had the national antislavery movement. National recognition came not merely because of Lincoln's moral logic, but also in response to the sense of urgency his speeches conveyed. Biographer Stephen B. Oates emphasized the change at Peoria, writing that Lincoln's "best oratory had always been charged with a certain moral eloquence, [and] his colleagues had never heard him give such an inspired address as this, never heard him declaim his antislavery convictions so fiercely and openly, never heard him defend the ideals of the Republic with such moral urgency as he had this day."[868] At Peoria Lincoln "spoke with an urgent sense of mission that gave his speeches a searching eloquence—a mission to save the American experiment, turn back the tide of slavery expansion, restrict the peculiar institution once again to the South, and place it back on the road to extinction, as Lincoln believed the Founding Fathers had so placed it."[869]

At Peoria, Lincoln harnessed personal ambition to high principle in opposing the spread of slavery in divided America. Here, concluded Don E. Fehrenbacher, Lincoln had sown the seeds of the 1858 "House Divided" speech. Fehrenbacher contended that "the expectation that the 'house' would some day 'cease to be divided' was virtually native to his thinking. The Kansas-Nebraska Act, from his point of view, amounted to a revolution. It impaired the hope for ultimate extinction, opened the way of slavery's ultimate expansion, and made this corrosive issue paramount in American politics. From the beginning, too, Lincoln objected to popular sovereignty as a doctrine of moral evasion. The germ [of the House Divided speech] . . . can be detected in a sentence from his famous Peoria speech of October 16, 1854: 'this *declared* indifference, but as I must think, covert *real* zeal for the spread of slavery, I can not but hate.'"[870]

Lincoln sustained his moral zeal. "The year 1854 was both a watershed in antebellum politics and the defining passage of Lincoln's pre-presidential public life," wrote Professor Richard Carwardine. The Peoria speech's "intellectual quality, moral force and rhetorical power made it the greatest speech of his political career to date, and its qualities provide their own argument that his campaign utterances were prompted by something more than political opportunism or convenience. The 'Peoria speech' contained most of the essential elements of his public addresses over the next six years."[871]

The clarity and originality of the prose, the organization and the substance of the speech—rather more than its delivery—contributed to Peoria's intellectual and emotional power. "It was well prepared and beautifully organized. Indeed, it may have been the best of Lincoln's campaign speeches," wrote historian John S. Wright. "It was a good speech, in the main, because it represented a fusion of the political and the personal viewpoints to a degree that gave the speech a ring of integrity rarely present in campaign addresses."[872] The Peoria speech took on the same intense qualities that Lincoln cited in his eulogy for Senator Henry Clay in 1852. Lincoln said that the Great Pacificator's "eloquence has not been surpassed. In the effective power to move the heart of man, Clay was without an equal. . . ."[873] Lincoln had noted that "Clay's eloquence did not consist, as many fine specimens of eloquence does [do], of types and figures—of antithesis, and elegant arrangement of words and sentences; but rather of that deeply earnest and impassioned tone, and manner, which can proceed only from great sincerity and a thorough conviction, in the speaker of the justice and importance of his cause. This it is, that truly touches the chords of sympathy; and those who heard Mr. Clay never failed to be moved by it, or ever afterwards, forgot the impression. All his efforts were made for practical effect. He never spoke merely to be heard."[874]

This moral earnestness became the standard for Lincoln's oratory. The Peoria speech contained little of the bitter ridicule of his previous two decades in Whig-Democrat combat. Historian Doris Kearns Goodwin wrote: "For the first time in his public life, his remarkable array of gifts as historian, storyteller, and teacher combined with a lucid, relentless, yet always accessible logic."[875]

His straightforward style—preferring the simpler Anglo-Saxon forms to polysyllabic Latinates—distinguished Lincoln from many national and Illinois politicians. His manner of speech earned the respect of his listeners at Peoria and thereafter. Historian Matthew Pinsker wrote: "Lincoln had always received praise for his oratorical abilities, but the response to his standard stump speech in 1854 was overwhelming. Unlike many other public speakers of the day, Lincoln carefully refrained from hyperbole, pretentious allusions, or personal vindictiveness. Instead, in speeches that routinely lasted for hours, he patiently built arguments rooted in American history and based on the plainest, most homespun logic."[876] Literary scholar John Channing Briggs wrote that Lincoln's "lengthy, calculated, sometimes passionate arguments brought years of thought to fruition in a public forum. What to Herndon seemed a sudden transformation in the face of crisis was a galvanizing moment, a manifestation of the secret processes Herndon had always thought were at work within his partner's silences."[877] Lincoln had seized the moment provided by Kansas-Nebraska. To the challenge, he applied intellectual honesty and moral gravity, moved by tenacious ambition and organizational skill. These virtues and talents came together in his presidency to prove him a great chief executive.

The Springfield-Peoria speeches marked Lincoln's decisive shift from the issue of economic growth—free markets, property rights, and nationalist economics—to the principles of the Declaration of Independence and the struggle for a republican Constitution. In *Lincoln and the Economics of the American Dream*, Gabor Boritt wrote: "For the first period of his political life economics provided the central motif. Antislavery was also there but was pushed far in the background with its triumph placed at a very distant day. After 1854 antislavery became Lincoln's immediate goal, and the economic policies that he continued to esteem highly and work for when possible were relegated to the background and to a future triumph."[878] According to the Gettysburg College historian, "after 1854 slavery became the most direct antithesis of the American Dream in his thought, the diametrical opposite of the central idea of the Republic."[879] As Professor Boritt noted, one irony of Lincoln's presidency was that in the midst of saving the Union, abolishing slavery, and winning the war, Lincoln completed his Whig economic program of the 1840s.

Along with Boritt, recent Lincoln scholars such as Michael Burlingame, Joseph R. Fornieri, Allen C. Guelzo, James A. Rawley, Richard Striner, and Douglas L. Wilson have insisted upon the singularity of the Peoria speech in determining Lincoln's future course. In his forthcoming multi-volume biography of Lincoln, Michael Burlingame has written that Lincoln "prepared a long, masterful speech arraigning Douglas, the Kansas-Nebraska Act, and slavery with a passionate eloquence that heralded the emergence of a new Lincoln. Like a butterfly emerging from a caterpillar's chrysalis, the partisan warrior of the 1830s and 1840s was transformed into a statesman. Abandoning his earlier 'slasher-gaff' style, he began to speak with authority as a principled, high-minded champion of the antislavery cause. He dissected Douglas's popular sovereignty doctrine with surgical precision, forceful logic, and deep moral conviction."[880] Allen C. Guelzo wrote that "Lincoln was determined that there must be no further extension of slavery, no more fearful backtracking to Southern demands, and no more clever manipulations of the law to purchase a few more years of life for the Slave Power. He took his election to the presidency as a vindication of this policy, and a sign that enough national rage and resistance had accumulated against slavery that the hour to begin the dismantling of the Slave Power had arrived."[881] Having made the turn toward Zion, Lincoln never turned back.

Douglas L. Wilson called the Peoria address Lincoln's "breakthrough speech." and "the keystone of Lincoln's political career."[882] Richard Striner called the speech "the most vivid demonstration of the change in the political outlook of Lincoln that began in 1854. It heralded the fiery orations that would blaze his path to the White House. And it established the moral fundamentals of his whole political creed."[883]

So, from 1854 onward, Lincoln built his campaign platform upon a coherent understanding of the promise of the American Founding. Historian James A. Rawley wrote: "Lincoln's Peoria speech was notable for its high moral tone, its intellectual rigor, its insight into the American dilemma, and its essential conservatism. He wished to maintain the ideals of the Declaration of Independence as well as the Constitution and the Union, restore the old [Missouri] compromise, and reject what he termed the new morality that slavery is right."[884] Rawley concluded: "The year 1854 was a turning point in Lincoln's life, during which he returned to politics and took the path that would lead him to the White House with deepened antislavery convictions about the danger of slavery to national unity, republican principles, majority rule, and American morality. It transformed the Western lawyer and small-time politician into the nascent statesman."[885] Historian William E. Gienapp wrote that the speeches of 1854 "possessed a new moral earnestness at the same time that his language became more crisp and lean. The earlier rhetorical flourishes and hyperbole were conspicuously absent as he appealed for the restoration of what he considered the policy of the Founding Fathers on slavery."[886]

The future president could not know what awaited him and his countrymen, but Lincoln knew where he was headed. The underlying historical judgment of this volume is how little of the future can be foreseen by men and women of affairs, how unpredictable are all outcomes, how many motives drive each human decision; how leadership can influence what might be otherwise, in the event, improbable outcomes. It was perhaps his sense of historical contingency that caused Lincoln to emphasize the Declaration's principle of consent; and thus to rely not upon the limited foresight of one ambitious statesman, but, as he suggested, upon the ballots of a democratic people. As Lincoln queried, is there any better hope? In dismissing the doctrine of popular sovereignty which Senator Douglas had tried to apply to the Kansas-Nebraska territories, Lincoln said: "Well I doubt not that the people of Nebraska are, and will continue to be as good as the average of people elsewhere. I do not say the contrary. What I do say is, that no man is good enough to govern another man, *without that other's consent.* I say this is the leading principle—the sheet anchor of American republicanism. Our Declaration of Independence says:

> We hold these truths to be self evident: that all men are created equal; that they are endowed by their Creator with certain inalienable rights; that among these are life, liberty and the pursuit of happiness. That to secure these rights, governments are instituted among men, DERIVING THEIR JUST POWERS FROM THE CONSENT OF THE GOVERNED.[887]

Getting right with the Declaration of Independence was a driving passion of Mr. Lincoln as he fought his way back into state and national politics in 1854. Armed with the "sheet anchor of American republicanism," he was determined to set right the historical record, and America's future, as he was given to see it.[888]

What do we now know of Lincoln's statecraft, the effect of which Lincoln could not foresee in 1854? Did he help to set right America's future? With the benefit of hindsight, what can the prudent historian conclude about the consequences for American history of Mr. Lincoln's economic, political, and antislavery constitutional principles? We do know from his economic philosophy that he rejected the idea of any necessary conflict between labor and capital, believing them to be cooperative in nature. Cooperation as well as competition could, he believed, lead to economic growth and increasing opportunity for all. In fact, Lincoln argued that capital was, itself, the result of the savings of free labor. Wrought by the mind and muscle of people, the exchange of the products of labor gave rise to savings which were then deployed as capital. Free people are thus the most important resource, not wealth. This humane proposition Lincoln set forth in his first Annual Message of 1861 to Congress—that "labor is prior to, and independent of capital. Capital is only the fruit of labor, and could never have existed if labor had not first existed."[889]

Lincoln's speeches roll down like thunder in the twentieth-century voice of Martin Luther King Jr. Mr. Lincoln defined the essence of the American dream. "There is not, of necessity any such thing as the free hired laborer being fixed to that condition for life. . . . The prudent, penniless beginner in the world labors for wages awhile, saves a surplus with which to buy tools or land for himself; then labors on his own account for awhile, and at length hires another new beginner to help him. This is the just, and generous, and prosperous system, which opens the way to all— gives hope to all, and, energy, and progress, and improvement of conditions to all."[890] More than 100 years later, Dr. King reminded all Americans that the black man's "unpaid labor made cotton king and established America as a significant nation in international commerce. Even after his release from chattel slavery, the nation grew over him, submerging him. . . . And so we still have a long, long way to go before we reach the promised land of freedom."[891]

Born poor, Abraham Lincoln was truly a self-made man, believing as he said that "work, work, work is the main thing."[892] His economic policy was designed not only "to clear the path for all," but to spell out incentives to encourage entrepreneurs to create new jobs, new products, new wealth. He believed in what historian Gabor Boritt has called "the right to rise."[893] Lincoln's America was, in principle, a color-blind America. "I want every man to have the chance," Lincoln announced in New Haven in March

1860, "and I believe a black man is entitled to it . . . when he may look forward and hope to be a hired laborer this year and the next, work for himself afterward, and finally to hire men to work for him! That is the true system."[894] In Lincoln's American system, government fosters growth. Equal opportunity leads to social mobility. Intelligence, hard work, and free labor lead to savings and innovation. Such a color-blind economic system was the counterpart of the Declaration's color-blind equality principle. The great black abolitionist, Frederick Douglass, saw this clearly, pronouncing the fitting tribute when he said of President Lincoln that he was "the first great man that I talked with in the United States freely, who in no single instance reminded me of the difference of color." He attributed Lincoln's attitude to the fact that he and Lincoln were self-made men—"we both starting at the lowest rung of the ladder."[895]

President Lincoln's political, constitutional, and wartime legacy has transformed American history. He had accepted war to preserve the Union, and with war, to free the slaves . . . "It is an issue which can only be tried by war, and decided by victory." His determination to fight on to victory was not imprudent, he argued. "The national resources . . . are unexhausted, and, as we believe, inexhaustible."[896] Without his leadership and resolve, separate slave and free countries might have competed as neighbors on the same continent. Thus there might have been no integrated, continental, American economy based on free labor. But without continental American industrial power, which Lincoln self-consciously advocated, the industrial means would not have been available to contain Imperial Germany as it reached for European hegemony in 1914. Neither would there have been a national power strong enough to destroy its successor, Hitler's Nazi Reich, nor to crush the aggressions of Imperial Japan. And, in the end, there would have been no unified, continental American power to oppose and overcome the Communist empire of the second half of the twentieth century. Nations based upon the invidious distinctions of race and class, the defining characteristics of the malignant world powers of our era, were preempted by the force and leadership of the United States of America. In Lincoln's words, "We made the experiment; and the fruit is before us. Look at it—think of it. Look at it, in its aggregate grandeur, of extent of country, and numbers of population—of ship, and steamboat, and rail-[road]. . . ."[897]

Hovering over the whole history of Mr. Lincoln's pilgrimage, there lingers the enigma of a very private man—the impenetrable shadow of his profile. We scrutinize Lincoln's character; but we see him through a glass darkly. So we mine his papers, sap the memoirs left by those who knew him, plumb his personal relationships. Still, he escapes us. Like a luminous comet, he had for a twinkling thrust himself before our eyes, the eyes of the world, there to vanish into the deep whence he came.

On October 27, eleven days after Lincoln's speech at Peoria, Johan Carl Frederic Polycarpus Von Schneidau made a daguerrotype when Lincoln spoke in Chicago against the Kansas-Nebraska Act. That image was doctored in 1858 for use in the Lincoln-Douglas Senate campaign. This later image is courtesy of the Chicago Historical Society.

FULL TEXT OF SPEECH
AT PEORIA, ILLINOIS
OCTOBER 16, 1854[898]

O n Monday, October 16, Senator DOUGLAS, by appointment, addressed a large audience at Peoria. When he closed, he was greeted with six hearty cheers; and the band in attendance played a stirring air. The crowd then began to call for LINCOLN, who, as Judge Douglas had announced was, by agreement, to answer him. Mr. Lincoln then took the stand, and said—

"I do not arise to speak now, if I can stipulate with the audience to meet me here at half past 6 or at 7 o'clock. It is now several minutes past five, and Judge Douglas has spoken over three hours. If you hear me at all, I wish you to hear me thro'. It will take me as long as it has taken him. That will carry us beyond eight o'clock at night. Now every one of you who can remain that long, can just as well get his supper, meet me at seven, and remain one hour or two later. The Judge has already informed you that he is to have an hour to reply to me. I doubt not but you have been a little surprised to learn that I have consented to give one of his high reputation and known ability, this advantage of me. Indeed, my consenting to it, though reluctant, was not wholly unselfish; for I suspected if it were understood, that the Judge was entirely done, you democrats would leave, and not hear me; but by giving him the close, I felt confident you would stay for the fun of hearing him skin me."

The audience signified their assent to the arrangement, and adjourned to 7 o'clock P.M., at which time they re-assembled, and Mr. LINCOLN spoke substantially as follows:

The repeal of the Missouri Compromise, and the propriety of its restoration, constitute the subject of what I am about to say.

As I desire to present my own connected view of this subject, my remarks will not be, specifically, an answer to Judge Douglas; yet, as I proceed, the main points he has presented will arise, and will receive such respectful attention as I may be able to give them.

I further wish to say, that I do not propose to question the patriotism, or to assail the motives of any man, or class or men; but rather to strictly confine myself to the naked merits of the question.

I also wish to be no less than National in all the positions I may take; and whenever I take ground which others have thought, or may think, narrow, sectional and dangerous to the Union, I hope to give a reason, which will appear sufficient, at least to some, why I think differently.

And, as this subject is no other, than part and parcel of the larger general question of domestic-slavery, I wish to MAKE and to keep the distinction between the EXISTING institution, and the EXTENSION of it, so broad, and so clear, that no honest man can misunderstand me, and no dishonest one, successfully misrepresent me.

In order to [get?] a clear understanding of what the Missouri Compromise is, a short history of the preceding kindred subjects will perhaps be proper. When we established our independence, we did not own, or claim, the country to which this compromise applies. Indeed, strictly speaking, the confederacy then owned no country at all; the States respectively owned the country within their limits; and some of them owned territory beyond their strict State limits. Virginia thus owned the North-Western territory—the country out of which the principal part of Ohio, all Indiana, all Illinois, all Michigan and all Wisconsin, have since been formed. She also owned (perhaps within her then limits) what has since been formed into the State of Kentucky. North Carolina thus owned what is now the State of Tennessee; and South Carolina and Georgia, in separate parts, owned what are now Mississippi and Alabama. Connecticut, I think owned the little remaining part of Ohio—being the same where they now send Giddings to Congress, and beat all creation at making cheese. These territories, together with the States themselves, constituted all the country over which the confederacy then claimed any sort of jurisdiction. We were then living under the Articles of Confederation, which were superceded by the Constitution several years afterwards. The question of ceding these territories to the general government was set on foot. Mr. Jefferson, the author of the Declaration of Independence, and otherwise a chief actor in the revolution; then a delegate in Congress; afterwards twice President; who was, is, and perhaps will continue to be, the most distinguished politician of our history; a Virginian by birth and continued residence, and withal, a slave-holder; conceived the idea of taking that occasion, to prevent slavery ever going into the north-western territory. He prevailed on the Virginia Legislature to adopt his views, and to cede the territory, making the prohibition of slavery therein, a condition of the deed. Congress accepted the cession, with the condition; and in the first Ordinance (which the acts of Congress were then called) for the government of the territory, provided that slavery should never be permitted therein. This is the famed ordinance of '87 so often spoken of. Thenceforward, for sixty-one years, and until in 1848, the last scrap of this territory came into the Union as the State of Wisconsin, all parties acted in quiet obedience to this ordinance. It is now what Jefferson foresaw and intended—the happy home of teeming millions of free, white, prosperous people, and no slave amongst them.

Thus, with the author of the declaration of Independence, the policy of prohibiting slavery in new territory originated. Thus, away back of the constitution, in the pure fresh, free breath of the revolution, the State of Virginia, and the National congress put that policy in practice. Thus through sixty odd of the best years of the republic did that policy steadily work to its great and beneficent end. And thus, in those five states, and five millions of free, enterprising people, we have before us the rich fruits of this policy. But *now* new light breaks upon us. Now congress declares this ought never to have been; and the like of it, must never be again. The sacred right of self government is grossly violated by it! We even find some men, who drew their first breath, and every other breath of their lives, under this very restriction, now live in dread of absolute suffocation, if they should be restricted in the "sacred right" of taking slaves to Nebraska. That *perfect* liberty they sigh for—the liberty of making slaves of other people—Jefferson never thought of; their own father never thought of; they never thought of themselves, a year ago. How fortunate for them, they did not sooner become sensible of their great misery! Oh, how difficult it is to treat with respect, such assaults upon all we have ever really held sacred.

But to return to history. In 1803 we purchased what was then called Louisiana, of France. It included the now states of Louisiana, Arkansas, Missouri, and Iowa; also the territory of Minnesota, and the present bone of contention, Kansas and Nebraska. Slavery already existed among the French at New Orleans; and, to some extent, at St. Louis. In 1812 Louisiana came into the Union as a slave state, without controversy. In 1818 or '19, Missouri showed signs of a wish to come in with slavery. This was resisted by northern members of Congress; and thus began the first great slavery agitation in the nation. This controversy lasted several months, and became very angry and exciting; the House of Representatives voting steadily for the prohibition of slavery in Missouri, and the Senate voting as steadily against it. Threats of breaking up the Union were freely made; and the ablest public men of the day became seriously alarmed. At length a compromise was made, in which, like all compromises, both sides yielded something. It was a law passed on the 6th day of March, 1820, providing that Missouri might come into the Union *with* slavery, but that in all the remaining part of the territory purchased of France, which lies north of 36 degrees and 30 minutes north latitude, slavery should never be permitted. This provision of law, *is the Missouri Compromise.* In excluding slavery North of the line, the same language is employed as in the Ordinance of '87. It directly applied to Iowa, Minnesota, and to the present bone of contention, Kansas and Nebraska. Whether there should or should not, be slavery south of that line, nothing was said in the law; but Arkansas constituted the principal remaining part, south of the line; and it has since been admitted as a slave state without serious controversy. More recently, Iowa, north of the line, came in as a free state without controversy. Still later, Minnesota, north of the line, had a territorial organization without controversy. Texas principally south of the line, and West of Arkansas; though originally within the purchase from France, had, in 1819, been traded off to Spain, in our treaty for the acquisition of Florida. It had thus become a part of Mexico. Mexico revolutionized and became independent of Spain. American citizens began settling rapidly, with their slaves in the southern part of Texas. Soon they

revolutionized against Mexico, and established an independent government of their own, adopting a constitution, with slavery, strongly resem-
bling the constitutions of our slave states. By still another rapid move,
Texas, claiming a boundary much further West, than when we parted with
her in 1819, was brought back to the United States, and admitted into the
Union as a slave state. There then was little or no settlement in the northern part of Texas, a considerable portion of which lay north of the Missouri line; and in the resolutions admitting her into the Union, the
Missouri restriction was expressly extended westward across her territory.
This was in 1845, only nine years ago.

Thus originated the Missouri Compromise; and thus has it been
respected down to 1845. And even four years later, in 1849, our distinguished Senator, in a public address, held the following language in relation to it:

"The Missouri Compromise had been in practical operation for about
a quarter of a century, and had received the sanction and approbation of
men of all parties in every section of the Union. It had allayed all sectional jealousies and irritations growing out of this vexed question, and
harmonized and tranquilized the whole country. It had given to Henry
Clay, as its prominent champion, the proud sobriquet of the "*Great Pacificator*" and by that title and for that service, his political friends had repeatedly appealed to the people to rally under his standard, as a presidential
candidate, as the man who had exhibited the patriotism and the power to
suppress, an unholy and treasonable agitation, and preserve the Union.
He was not aware that any man or any party from any section of the
Union, had ever urged as an objection to Mr. Clay, that he was the great
champion of the Missouri Compromise. On the contrary, the effort was
made by the opponents of Mr. Clay, to prove that he was not entitled to
the exclusive merit of that great patriotic measure, and that the honor
was equally due to others as well as to him, for securing its adoption—that
it had its origin in the hearts of all patriotic men, who desired to preserve
the blessings of our glorious Union—an origin akin that of the constitution of the United States, conceived in the same spirit of fraternal affection, and calculated to remove forever, the only danger, which seemed to
threaten, at some distant day, to sever the social bond of union. All the

evidences of public opinion at that day, seemed to indicate that this Compromise had been canonized in the hearts of the American people, as a sacred thing which no ruthless hand would ever be reckless enough to disturb."

I do not read this extract to involve Judge Douglas in an inconsistency. If he afterwards thought he had been wrong, it was right for him to change. I bring this forward merely to show the high estimate placed on the Missouri Compromise by all parties up to so late as the year 1849.

But, going back a little, in point of time, our war with Mexico broke out in 1846. When Congress was about adjourning that session, President Polk asked them to place two millions of dollars under his control, to be used by him in the recess, if found practicable and expedient, in negociating a treaty of peace with Mexico, and acquiring some part of her territory. A bill was duly got up, for the purpose, and was progressing swimmingly, in the House of Representatives, when a member by the name of David Wilmot, a democrat of Pennsylvania, moved as an amendment "Provided that in any territory thus acquired, there shall never be slavery."

This is the origin of the far-famed "Wilmot Proviso." It created a great flutter; but it stuck like wax, was voted into the bill, and the bill passed with it through the House. The Senate, however, adjourned without final action on it and so both appropriation and proviso were lost, for the time. The war continued, and at the next session, the president renewed his request for the appropriation, enlarging the amount, I think, to three million. Again came the proviso; and defeated the measure. Congress adjourned again, and the war went on. In Dec., 1847, the new congress assembled. I was in the lower House that term. The "Wilmot Proviso" or the principle of it, was constantly coming up in some shape or other, and I think I may venture to say I voted for it at least forty times; during the short term I was there. The Senate, however, held it in check, and it never became law. In the spring of 1848 a treaty of peace was made with Mexico; by which we obtained that portion of her country which now constitutes the territories of New Mexico and Utah, and the now state of California. By this treaty the Wilmot Proviso was defeated, as so far as it was intended to be, a condition of the acquisition of territory. Its friends however, were still determined to find some way to restrain slavery from getting into the new country. This new acquisition lay directly West of our old purchase from France, and extended west to the Pacific ocean—and was so situated that if the Missouri line should be extended straight West, the new country would be divided by such extended line, leaving some North and some South of it. On Judge Douglas' motion a bill, or provision of a bill, passed the Senate to so extend the Missouri line. The Proviso men in the House, including myself, voted it down, because by implication, it gave up the Southern part to slavery, while we were bent on having it *all* free.

In the fall of 1848 the gold mines were discovered in California. This attracted people to it with unprecedented rapidity, so that on, or soon after, the meeting of the new congress in Dec., 1849, she already had a population of nearly a hundred thousand, had called a convention, formed a state constitution, excluding slavery, and was knocking for admission into the Union. The Proviso men, of course were for letting her in, but the Senate, always true to the other side would not consent to her admission. And there California stood, kept *out* of the Union, because she would not let slavery *into* her borders. Under all the circumstances perhaps this was not wrong. There were other points of dispute, connected with the general question of slavery, which equally needed adjustment. The South clamored for a more efficient fugitive slave law. The North clamored for the abolition of a peculiar species of slave trade in the District of Columbia, in connection with which, in view from the windows of the capitol, a sort of negro-livery stable, where droves of negroes were collected, temporarily kept, and finally taken to Southern markets, precisely like droves of horses, had been openly maintained for fifty years. Utah and New Mexico needed territorial governments; and whether slavery should or should not be prohibited within them, was another question. The indefinite Western boundary of Texas was to be settled. She was received a slave state; and consequently the farther West the slavery men could push her boundary, the more slave country they secured. And the farther East the slavery opponents could thrust the boundary back, the less slave ground was secured. Thus this was just as clearly a slavery question as any of the others.

These points all needed adjustment; and they were all held up, perhaps wisely to make them help to adjust one another. The Union, now, as in 1820, was thought to be in danger; and devotion to the Union rightfully inclined men to yield somewhat, in points where nothing else could have so inclined them. A compromise was finally effected. The south got their new fugitive-slave law; and the North got California, (the far best part of our acquisition from Mexico,) as a free State. The south got a provision that New Mexico and Utah, *when admitted as States* may come in *with* or *without* slavery as they may then choose; and the north got the slave-trade abolished in the District of Columbia. The north got the western boundary of Texas, thence further back eastward than the south desired; but, in turn, they gave Texas ten millions of dollars, with which to pay her old debts. This is the Compromise of 1850.

Preceding the Presidential election of 1852, each of the great political parties, democrats and whigs, met in convention, and adopted resolutions endorsing the compromise of '50; as a "finality," a final settlement, so far as these parties could make it so, of all slavery agitation. Previous to this, in 1851, the Illinois Legislature had indorsed it.

During this long period of time Nebraska had remained, substantially an uninhabited country, but now emigration to, and settlement within it began to take place. It is about one third as large as the present United States, and its importance so long overlooked, begins to come into view. The restriction of slavery by the Missouri Compromise directly applies to it; in fact, was first made, and has since been maintained, expressly for it. In 1853, a bill to give it a territorial government passed the House of Representatives, and in the hands of Judge Douglas, failed of passing the Senate only for want of time. This bill contained no repeal of the Missouri Compromise. Indeed, when it was assailed because it did not contain such repeal, Judge Douglas defended it in its existing form. On January 4th, 1854, Judge Douglas introduces a new bill to give Nebraska territorial government. He accompanies this bill with a report, in which last, he expressly recommends that the Missouri Compromise shall neither be affirmed nor repealed.

Before long the bill is so modified as to make two territories instead of one; calling the Southern one Kansas.

Also, about a month after the introduction of the bill, on the judge's own motion, it is so amended as to declare the Missouri Compromise inoperative and void; and, substantially, that the People who go and settle there may establish slavery, or exclude it, as they may see fit. In this shape the bill passed both branches of congress, and became a law.

This is the *repeal* of the Missouri Compromise. The foregoing history may not be precisely accurate in every particular; but I am sure it is sufficiently so, for all the uses I shall attempt to make of it, and in it, we have before us, the chief material enabling us to correctly judge whether the repeal of the Missouri Compromise is right or wrong.

I think, and shall try to show, that is wrong; wrong in its direct effect, letting slavery into Kansas and Nebraska—and wrong in its prospective principle, allowing it to spread to every other part of the wide world, where men can be found inclined to take it.

This *declared* indifference, but as I must think, covert *real* zeal for the spread of slavery, I can not but hate. I hate it because of the monstrous injustice of slavery itself. I hate it because it deprives our republican example of its just influence in the world—enables the enemies of free institutions, with plausibility, to taunt us as hypocrites—causes the real friends of freedom to doubt our sincerity, and especially because it forces so many really good men amongst ourselves into an open war with the very fundamental principles of civil liberty—criticising the Declaration of Independence, and insisting that there is no right principle of action but *self-interest.*

Before proceeding, let me say I think I have no prejudice against the Southern people. They are just what we would be in their situation. If slavery did not now exist amongst them, they would not introduce it. If it did now exist amongst us, we should not instantly give it up. This I believe of the masses north and south. Doubtless there are individuals, on both sides, who would not hold slaves under any circumstances; and others who would gladly introduce slavery anew, if it were out of existence. We know that some southern men do free their slaves, go north, and become tip-top abolitionists; while some northern ones go south, and become most cruel slave-masters.

When southern people tell us they are no more responsible for the origin of slavery, then we; I acknowledge the fact. When it is said that the institution exists; and that it is very difficult to get rid of it, in any satisfactory way, I can understand and appreciate the saying. I surely will not blame them for not doing what I should not know how to do myself. If all earthly power were given me, I should not know what to do, as to the existing institution. My first impulse would be to free all the slaves, and send them to Liberia,—to their own native land. But a moment's reflection would convince me, that whatever of high hope, (as I think there is) there may be in this, in the long run, its sudden execution is impossible. If they were all landed there in a day, they would all perish in the next ten days; and there are not surplus shipping and surplus money enough in the world to carry them there in many times ten days. What then? Free them all, and keep them among us as underlings? Is it quite certain that this betters their condition? I think I would not hold one in slavery, at any rate; yet the point is not clear enough for me to denounce people upon. What next? Free them, and make them politically and socially, our equals? My own feelings will not admit of this; and if mine would, we well know that those of the great mass of white people will not. Whether this feeling accords with justice and sound judgment, is not the sole question, if indeed, it is any part of it. A universal feeling, whether well or ill-founded, can not be safely disregarded. We can not, then, make them equals. It does seem to me that systems of gradual emancipation might be adopted; but for their tardiness in this, I will not undertake to judge our brethren of the south.

When they remind us of their constitutional rights, I acknowledge them, not grudgingly, but fully, and fairly; and I would give them any legislation for the reclaiming of their fugitives, which should not, in its stringency, be more likely to carry a free man into slavery, than our ordinary criminal laws are to hang an innocent one.

But all this; to my judgment, furnishes no more excuse for permitting slavery to go into our own free territory, than it would for reviving the African slave trade by law. The law which forbids the bringing of slaves *from* Africa; and that which has so long forbid the taking them *to* Nebraska, can hardly be distinguished on any moral principle; and the repeal of the former could find quite as plausible excuses as that of the latter.

The arguments by which the repeal of the Missouri Compromise is sought to be justified, are these:

First, that the Nebraska country needed a territorial government.

Second, that in various ways, the public had repudiated it, and demanded the repeal; and therefore should not now complain of it.

And lastly, that the repeal establishes a principle, which is intrinsically right.

I will attempt an answer to each of them in its turn.

First, then, if that country was in need of a territorial organization, could it not have had it as well without as with the repeal? Iowa and Minnesota, to both of which the Missouri restriction applied had, without its repeal, each in succession, territorial organizations. And even, the year before, a bill for Nebraska itself, was within an ace of passing, without the repealing clause; and this in the hands of the same men who are now the champions of repeal. Why no necessity then for the repeal? But still later, when this very bill was first brought in, it contained no repeal. But, say they, because the public had demanded, or rather commanded the repeal, the repeal was to accompany the organization, whenever that should occur.

Now I deny that the public ever demanded any such thing—ever repudiated the Missouri Compromise—ever commanded its repeal. I deny it, and call for the proof. It is not contended, I believe, that any such command has ever been given in express terms. It is only said that it was done *in principle*. The support of the Wilmot Proviso, is the first fact mentioned, to prove that the Missouri restriction was repudiated in *principle*, and the second is, the refusal to extend the Missouri line over the country acquired from Mexico. These are near enough alike to be treated together. The one was to exclude the chances of slavery from the *whole* new acquisition by the lump; and the other was to reject a division of it, by which one *half* was to be given up to those chances. Now whether this was a repudiation of the Missouri line, in *principle*, depends upon whether the Missouri law contained any *principle* requiring the line to be extended over the country acquired from Mexico. I contend it did not. I insist that it contained no general principle, but that it was, in every sense, specific. That its terms limit it to the country purchased from France, is undenied and undeniable. It could have no principle beyond the intention of those who made it. They did not intend to extend the line to country which they did not own. If they intended to extend it, in the event of acquiring additional territory, why did they not say so? It was just as easy to say, that "in all the country west of the Mississippi, which we now own, or *may here-after acquire* there shall never be slavery," as to say, what they did say; and they would have said it if they had meant it. An intention to extend the law is not only not mentioned in the law, but is not mentioned in any con-temporaneous history. Both the law itself, and the history of the times are a blank as to any *principle* of extension; and by neither the known rules for construing statutes and contracts, nor by common sense, can any such principle be inferred.

Another fact showing the *specific* character of the Missouri law—show-ing that it intended no more than it expressed—showing that the line was not intended as a universal dividing line between free and slave territory, present and prospective—north of which slavery could never go—is the fact that by that very law, Missouri came in as a slave state, *north* of the line. If that law contained any prospective *principle*, the whole law must be looked to in order to ascertain what the *principle* was. And by this rule, the south could fairly contend that inasmuch as they got one slave state north of the line at the inception of the law, they have the right to have another given them *north* of it occasionally—now and then in the indefinite west-ward extension of the line. This demonstrates the absurdity of attempting to deduce a prospective *principle* from the Missouri Compromise line.

When we voted for the Wilmot Proviso, we were voting to keep slavery *out* of the whole . . . [Mexican?] acquisition; and little did we think we were thereby voting, to let it *into* Nebraska, laying several hundred miles distant. When we voted against extending the Missouri line, little did we think we were voting to destroy the only line, then of near thirty years standing. To argue that we thus repudiated the Missouri Compromise is no less absurd than it would be to argue that because we have, so far, for-borne to acquire Cuba, we have thereby, in principle, repudiated our for-mer acquisitions, and determined to throw them out of the Union! No less absurd than it would be to say that because I may have refused to build an addition to my house, I thereby have decided to destroy the existing house! And if I catch you setting fire to my house, you will turn upon me and say I INSTRUCTED you to do it! The most conclusive argu-ment, however, that, while voting for the Wilmot Proviso, and while voting against the EXTENSION of the Missouri line, we never thought of disturbing the original Missouri Compromise, is found in the facts, that there was then, and still is, an unorganized tract of fine country, nearly as large as the state of Missouri, lying immediately west of Arkansas, and south of the Missouri compromise line, by its northern boundary; and consequently is part of the country, in which, by implication, slavery was permitted to go, by that compromise. There it has lain open ever since, and there it still lies. And yet no effort has been made at any time to wrest it from the south. In all our struggles to prohibit slavery within our Mexican acquisitions, we never so much as lifted a finger to prohibit it, as to this tract. Is not this entirely conclusive that at all times, we have held the Missouri Compromise a sacred thing; even when against ourselves, as well as when for us?

Senator Douglas sometimes says the Missouri line itself was, *in principle,* only an extension of the line of the ordinance of '87—that is to say, an extension of the Ohio river. I think this is weak enough on its face. I will remark, however that, as a glance at the map will show, the Missouri line is a long way farther South than the Ohio; and that if our Senator, in proposing his extension, had stuck to the *principle* of jogging southward, perhaps it might not have been voted down so readily.

But next it is said that the compromises of '50 and the ratification of them by both political parties, in '52, established a *new principle,* which required the repeal of the Missouri Compromise. This again I deny. I deny it, and demand the proof. I have already stated fully what the compromises of '50 are. The particular part of those measures, for which the virtual repeal of the Missouri compromise is sought to be inferred (for it is admitted they contain nothing about it, in express terms) is the provision in the Utah and New Mexico laws, which permits them when they seek admission into the Union as States, to come in with or without slavery as they shall then see fit. Now I insist this provision was made for Utah and New Mexico, and for no other place whatever. It had no more direct reference to Nebraska than it had to the territories of the moon. But, say they, it had reference to Nebraska, *in principle.* Let us see. The North consented to this provision, not because they considered it right in itself; but because they were compensated—paid for it. They, at the same time, got

California into the Union as a free State. This was far the best part of all they had struggled for by the Wilmot Proviso. They also got the area of slavery somewhat narrowed in the settlement of the boundary of Texas. Also, they got the slave trade abolished in the District of Colombia. For all these desirable objects the North could afford to yield something; and they did yield to the South the Utah and New Mexico provision. I do not mean that the whole North, or even a majority, yielded, when the law passed; but enough yielded, when added to the vote of the South, to carry the measure. Now can it be pretended that the *principle of the* arrangement requires us to permit the same provision to be applied to Nebraska, *without any equivalent at all?* Give us another free State; press the boundary of Texas still further back, give us another step toward the destruction of slavery in the District, and you present us a similar case. But ask us not to repeat, for nothing, what you paid for in the first instance. If you wish the thing again, pay again. That is the *principle* of the compromises of '50, if indeed they had any principles beyond their specific terms—it was the system of equivalents.

Again, if Congress, at that time, intended that all future territories should, when admitted as States, come in with or without slavery, at their own option, why did it not say so? With such an universal provision, all know the bills could not have passed. Did they, then—could they—establish a *principle* contrary to their own intention? Still further, if they intended to establish the principle that wherever Congress had control, it should be left to the people to do as they thought fit with slavery why did they not authorize the people of the District of Columbia at their adoption to abolish slavery within these limits? I personally know that this has not been left undone, because it was unthought of. It was frequently spoken of by members of Congress and by citizens of Washington six years ago; and I heard no one express a doubt that a system of gradual emancipation, with compensation to owners, would meet the approbation of a large majority of the white people of the District. But without the action of Congress they could say nothing; and Congress said "no." In the measures of 1850 Congress had the subject of slavery in the District expressly in hand. If they were then establishing the principle of allowing the people to do as they please with slavery, why did they not apply the *principle* to that people?

Again, it is claimed that by the Resolutions of the Illinois Legislature, passed in 1851, the repeal of the Missouri compromise was demanded. This I deny also. Whatever may be worked out by a criticism of the language of those resolutions, the people have never understood them as being any more than an endorsement of the compromises of 1850; and a release of our Senators from voting for the Wilmot Proviso. The whole people are living witnesses, that this only was their view. Finally, it is asked "If we did not mean to apply the Utah and New Mexico provision, to all future territories, what did we mean, when we, in 1852, endorsed the compromises of '50?"

For myself, I can answer this question most easily. I meant not to ask a repeal, or modification of the fugitive slave law. I meant not to ask for the abolition of slavery in the District of Colombia. I meant not to resist the admission of Utah and New Mexico, even should they ask to come in as slave States. I meant nothing about additional territories, because, as I understood, we then had no territory whose character as to slavery was not already settled. As to Nebraska, I regarded its character as being fixed, by the Missouri compromise, for thirty years—as unalterably fixed as that of my own home in Illinois. As to new acquisitions I said "sufficient unto the day is the evil thereof." When we make new acquaintances, [acquisitions?] we will, as heretofore, try to manage them some how. That is my answer. That is what I meant and said; and I appeal to the people to say, each for himself, whether that was not also the universal meaning of the free States.

And now, in turn, let me ask a few questions. If by any, or all these matters, the repeal of the Missouri Compromise was commanded, why was not the command sooner obeyed? Why was the repeal omitted in the Nebraska bill of 1853? Why was it omitted in the original bill of 1854? Why, in the accompanying report, was such a repeal characterized as a *departure* from the course pursued in 1850? and its continued omission recommended?

I am aware Judge Douglas now argues that the subsequent express repeal is no substantial alteration of the bill. This argument seems wonderful to me. It is as if one should argue that white and black are not different. He admits, however, that there is a literal change in the bill; and that he made the change in deference to other Senators, who would not support the bill without. This proves that those Senators thought the change a substantial one; and that the Judge thought their opinions worth deferring to. His own opinions, therefore, seem not to rest on a very firm basis even in his own mind—and I suppose the world believes, and will continue to believe, that precisely on the substance of that change this whole agitation has arisen.

I conclude then, that the public never demanded the repeal of the Missouri compromise.

I now come to consider whether the repeal, with its avowed principle, is intrinsically right. I insist that it is not. Take the particular case. A controversy had arisen between the advocates and opponents of slavery, in relation to its establishment within the country we had purchased of France. The southern, and then best of the purchase, was already in as a slave State. The controversy was settled by also letting Missouri in as a slave State; but with the agreement that within all the remaining part south of the line, nothing was said; but perhaps the fair implication was, that it should come in with slavery if it should so choose. The southern part, except a portion heretofore mentioned, afterwards did come in with slavery, as the State of Arkansas. All these many years since 1820, the Northern part had remained a wilderness. At length settlements began in it also. In due course, Iowa, came in as a free State, and Minnesota was given a territorial government, without removing the slavery restriction. Finally the sole remaining part, North of the line, Kansas and Nebraska, was to be organized; and it is proposed, and carried, to blot out the old dividing line of thirty-four years standing, and to open the whole of that country to the introduction of slavery. Now, this, to my mind, is manifestly unjust. After an angry and dangerous controversy, the parties made friends by dividing the bone of contention. The one party first appropriates her own share, beyond all power to be disturbed in the possession of it; and then seizes the share of the other party. It is as if two starving men had divided their only loaf; the one had hastily swallowed his half, and then grabbed the other half just as he was putting it to his mouth!

Let me here drop the main argument, to notice what I consider rather an inferior matter. It is argued that slavery will not go to Kansas and Nebraska, *in any event*. This is a *palliation*—a *lullaby*. I have some hope that it will not; but let us not be too confident. As to climate, a glance at the map shows that there are five slave States—Delaware, Maryland, Virginia, Kentucky, and Missouri—and also the District of Columbia, all north of the Missouri compromise line. The census returns of 1850 show that, within these, there are 867,276 slaves—being more than one-fourth of all the slaves in the nation.

It is not climate, then, that will keep slavery out of these territories. Is there any thing in the peculiar nature of the country? Missouri adjoins these territories, by her entire western boundary, and slavery is already within every one of her western counties. I have even heard it said that there are more slaves, in proportion to whites, in the north western county of Missouri, than within any county of the State. Slavery pressed entirely up to the old western boundary of the State, and when, rather recently, a part of that boundary, at the north-west was moved out a little farther west, slavery followed on quite up to the new line. Now, when the restriction is removed, what is to prevent it from going still further? Climate will not. No peculiarity of the country will—nothing in *nature* will. Will the disposition of the people prevent it? Those nearest the scene, are all in favor of the extension. The yankees, who are opposed to it may be more numerous; but in military phrase, the battle-field is too far from *their* base of operations.

But it is said, there now is *no* law in Nebraska on the subject of slavery; and that, in such case, taking a slave there, operates his freedom. That *is* good book-law; but is not the rule of actual practice. Wherever slavery is, it has been first introduced without law. The oldest laws we find concerning it, are not laws introducing it; but *regulating* it, as an already existing thing. A white man takes his slave to Nebraska now; who will inform the negro that he is free? Who will take him before court to test the question of his freedom? In ignorance of his legal emancipation, he is kept chopping, splitting and plowing. Others are brought, and move on in the same track. At last, if ever the time for voting comes, on the question of slavery, the institution already in fact exists in the country, and cannot well be removed. The facts of its presence, and the difficulty of its removal will carry the vote in its favor. Keep it out until a vote is taken, and a vote in favor of it, can not be got in any population of forty thousand, on earth, who have been drawn together by the ordinary motives of emigration and settlement. To get slaves into the country simultaneously with the whites, in the incipient stages of settlement, is the precise stake played for, and won in this Nebraska measure.

The question is asked us, "If slaves will go in, notwithstanding the general principle of law liberates them, why would they not equally go in against positive statute law?—go in, even if the Missouri restriction were maintained?" I answer, because it takes a much bolder man to venture in, with his property, in the latter case, than in the former—because the positive congressional enactment is known to, and respected by all, or nearly all, whereas the negative principle that *no* law is free law, is not much known except among lawyers. We have some experience of this practical difference. In spite of the Ordinance of '87, a few negroes were brought into Illinois, and held in a state of quasi slavery; not enough, however to carry a vote of the people in favor of the institution when they came to form a constitution. But in the adjoining Missouri country, where there was no ordinance of '87—was no restriction—they were carried ten times, nay a hundred times, as fast, and actually made a slave State. This is fact— naked fact.

Another LULLABY argument is, that taking slaves to new countries does not increase their number—does not make any one slave who otherwise would be free. There is some truth in this, and I am glad of it, but it [is] not WHOLLY true. The African slave trade is not yet effectually suppressed; and if we make a reasonable deduction for the white people amongst us, who are foreigners, and the descendants of foreigners, arriving here since 1808, we shall find the increase of the black population out-running that of the white, to an extent unaccountable, except by supposing that some of them too, have been coming from Africa. If this be so, the opening of new countries to the institution, increases the demand for, and augments the price of slaves, and so does, in fact, make slaves of freemen by causing them to be brought from Africa, and sold into bondage.

But, however this may be, we know the opening of new countries to slavery, tends to the perpetuation of the institution, and so does KEEP men in slavery who otherwise would be free. This result we do not FEEL like favoring, and we are under no legal obligation to suppress our feelings in this respect.

Equal justice to the south, it is said, requires us to consent to the extending of slavery to new countries. That is to say, inasmuch as you do not object to my taking my hog to Nebraska, therefore I must not object to you taking your slave. Now, I admit this is perfectly logical, if there is no difference between hogs and negroes. But while you thus require me to deny the humanity of the negro, I wish to ask whether you of the south yourselves, have ever been willing to do as much? It is kindly provided that of all those who come into the world, only a small percentage are natural tyrants. That percentage is no larger in the slave States than in the free. The great majority, south as well as north, have human sympathies, of which they can no more divest themselves than they can of their sensibility to physical gain. These sympathies in the bosoms of the southern people, manifest in many ways, their sense of the wrong of slavery, and their consciousness that, after all, there is humanity in the negro. If they deny this, let me address them a few plain questions. In 1820 you joined the north, almost unanimously, in declaring the African slave trade piracy, and in annexing to it the punishment of death. Why did you do this? If you did not feel that it was wrong, why did you join in providing that men should be hung for it? The practice was no more than bringing wild negroes from Africa, to sell to such as would buy them. But you never thought of hanging men for catching and selling wild horses, wild buffaloes, or wild bears.

Again, you have amongst you, a sneaking individual, of the class of native tyrants, know as the "SLAVE-DEALER." He watches your necessities, and crawls up to buy your slave, at a speculating price. If you cannot help it, you sell to him; but if you can help it, you drive him from your door. You despise him utterly. You do not recognize him as a friend, or even as an honest man. Your children must not play with his; they may rollick freely with the little negroes, but not with the "slave-dealers" children. If you are obliged to deal with him, you try to get through the job without so much as touching him. It is common with you to join hands with the men you meet; but with the slave dealer you avoid the ceremony—instinctively shrinking from the snaky contact. If he grows rich and retires from business, you still remember him, and still keep up the ban of non-intercourse upon him and his family. Now why is this? You do not so treat the man who deals in corn, cattle or tobacco.

And yet again; there are in the United States and territories, including the District of Columbia, 433,643 free blacks. At $500 per head they are worth over two hundred millions of dollars. How comes this vast amount of property to be running about without owners? We do not see free horses or free cattle running at large. How is this? All these free blacks are the descendants of slaves, or have been slaves themselves, and they would be slaves now, but for SOMETHING which has operated on their white owners, inducing them, at vast pecuniary sacrifices, to liberate them. What is that SOMETHING? Is there any mistaking it? In all these cases it is your sense of justice, and human sympathy, continually telling you, that the poor negro has some natural right to himself—that those who deny it, and make mere merchandise of him, deserve kickings, contempt and death.

And now, why will you ask us to deny the humanity of the slave? and estimate him only as the equal of the hog? Why ask us to do what you will not do yourselves? Why ask us to do for *nothing*, what two hundred million of dollars could not induce you to do?

But one great argument in the support of the repeal of the Missouri Compromise, is still to come. That argument is "the sacred right of government." It seems our distinguished Senator has found great difficulty in getting his antagonists, even in the Senate to meet him fairly on this argument—some poet has said

"Fools rush in where angels fear to tread."

At the hazzard of being thought one of the fools of this quotation, I meet that argument—I rush in, I take that bull by the horns.

I trust I understand, and truly estimate the right of self-government. My faith in the proposition that each man should do precisely as he pleases with all which is exclusively his own, lies at the foundation of the sense of justice there is in me. I extend the principles to communities of men, as well as to individuals. I so extend it, because it is politically wise, as well as naturally just; politically wise, in saving us from broils about matters which do not concern us. Here, or at Washington, I would not trouble myself with the oyster laws of Virginia, or the cranberry laws of Indiana.

The doctrine of self government is right—absolutely and eternally right—but it has no just application, as here attempted. Or perhaps I should rather say that whether it has just such application depends upon whether a negro is *not* or is a man. If he is *not* a man, why in that case, he who *is* a man may, as a matter of self-government, do just as he pleases with him. But if the negro *is* a man, is it not to that extent, a total destruction of self-government, to say that he too shall not govern *himself?* When the white man governs himself, and also governs *another* man, that is *more* than self-government—that is despotism. If the negro is a *man*, why then my ancient faith teaches me that "all men are created equal;" and that there can be no moral right in connection with one man's making a slave of another.

Judge Douglas frequently, with bitter irony and sarcasm, paraphrases our argument by saying "The white people of Nebraska are good enough to govern themselves, *but they are not good enough to govern a few miserable negroes*!!"

Well I doubt not that the people of Nebraska are, and will continue to be as good as the average of people elsewhere. I do not say the contrary. What I do say is, that no man is good enough to govern another man, *without that other's consent.* I say this is the leading principle—the sheet anchor of American republicanism. Our Declaration of Independence says:

"We hold these truths to be self evident: that all men are created equal; that they are endowed by their Creator with certain inalienable rights; that among these are life, liberty and the pursuit of happiness. That to secure these rights, governments are instituted among men, DERIVING THEIR JUST POWERS FROM THE CONSENT OF THE GOVERNED."

I have quoted so much at this time merely to show that according to our ancient faith, the just powers of governments are derived from the consent of the governed. Now the relation of masters and slaves is, PRO TANTO, a total violation of this principle. The master not only governs the slave without his consent; but he governs him by a set of rules altogether different from those which he prescribes for himself. Allow ALL the governed an equal voice in the government, and that, and that only is self government.

Let it not be said I am contending for the establishment of political and social equality between the whites and blacks. I have already said the contrary. I am not now combating the argument of NECESSITY, arising from the fact that the blacks are already amongst us; but I am combating what is set up as MORAL argument for allowing them to be taken where they have never yet been—arguing against the EXTENSION of a bad thing, which where it already exists, we must of necessity, manage as we best can.

In support of his application of the doctrine of self-government, Senator Douglas has sought to bring to his aid the opinions and examples of our revolutionary fathers. I am glad he has done this. I love the sentiments of those old-time men; and shall be most happy to abide by their opinions. He shows us that when it was in contemplation for the colonies to break off from Great Britain, and set up a new government for themselves, several of the states instructed their delegates to go for the measure PROVIDED EACH STATE SHOULD BE ALLOWED TO REGULATE ITS DOMESTIC CONCERNS IN ITS OWN WAY. I do not quote; but this is in substance. This was right. I see nothing objectionable in it. I also think it probable that it had some reference to the existence of slavery amongst them. I will not deny that it had. But had it, in any reference to the carrying of slavery into NEW COUNTRIES? That is the question; and we will let the fathers themselves answer it.

This same generation of men, and mostly the same individuals of the generation, who declared this principle—who declared independence—who fought the war of the revolution through—who afterwards made the constitution under which we still live—these same men passed the ordinance of '87, declaring that slavery should never go to the north-west territory. I have no doubt Judge Douglas thinks they were very inconsistent in this. It is a question of discrimination between them and him. But there is not an inch of ground left for his claiming that their opinions—their example—their authority—are on his side in this controversy.

Again, is not Nebraska, while a territory, a part of us? Do we not own the country? And if we surrender the control of it, do we not surrender the right of self-government? It is part of ourselves. If you say we shall not control it because it is ONLY part, the same is true of every other part; and when all the parts are gone, what has become of the whole? What is then left of us? What use for the general government, when there is nothing left for it [to] govern?

But you say this question should be left to the people of Nebraska, because they are more particularly interested. If this be the rule, you must leave it to each individual to say for himself whether he will have slaves. What better moral right have thirty-one citizens of Nebraska to say, that the thirty-second shall not hold slaves, than the people of the thirty-one States have to say that slavery shall not go into the thirty-second State at all?

But if it is a sacred right for the people of Nebraska to take and hold slaves there, it is equally their sacred right to buy them where they can buy them cheapest; and that undoubtedly will be on the coast of Africa; provided you will consent to not hang them for going there to buy them. You must remove this restriction too, from the sacred right of self-government. I am aware you say that taking slaves from the States to Nebraska, does not make slaves of freemen; but the African slave-trader can say just as much. He does not catch free negroes and bring them here. He finds them already slaves in the hands of their black captors, and he honestly buys them at the rate of about a red cotton handkerchief a head. This is very cheap, and it is a great abridgement of the sacred right of self-government to hang men for engaging in this profitable trade!

Another important objection to this application of the right of self-government, is that it enables the first FEW, to deprive the succeeding MANY, of a free exercise of the right of self-government. The first few may get slavery IN, and the subsequent many cannot easily get it OUT. How common is the remark now in the slave States—"If we were only clear of our slaves, how much better it would be for us." They are actually deprived of the privilege of governing themselves as they would, by the action of a very few, in the beginning. The same thing was true of the whole nation at the time our constitution was formed.

Whether slavery shall go into Nebraska, or other new territories, is not a matter of exclusive concern to the people who may go there. The whole nation is interested that the best use shall be made of these territories. We want them for the homes of free white people. This they cannot be, to any considerable extent, if slavery shall be planted within them. Slave States are places for poor white people to remove FROM; not to remove TO. New free States are the places for poor people to go to and better their condition. For this use, the nation needs these territories.

Still further; there are constitutional relations between the slave and free States, which are degrading to the latter. We are under legal obligations to catch and return their runaway slaves to them—a sort of dirty, disagreeable job, which I believe, as a general rule the slave-holders will not perform for one another. Then again, in the control of the government—the management of the partnership affairs—they have greatly the advantage of us. By the constitution, each State has two Senators—each has a number of Representatives; in proportion to the number of its people—and each has a number of presidential electors, equal to the whole number of its Senators and Representatives together. But in ascertaining the number of the people, for this purpose, five slaves are counted as being equal to three whites. The slaves do not vote; they are only counted and so used, as to swell the influence of the white people's votes. The practical effect of this is more aptly shown by a comparison of the States of South Carolina and Maine. South Carolina has six representatives, and so has Maine; South Carolina has eight presidential electors, and so has Maine. This is precise equality so far; and, of course they are equal in Senators, each having two. Thus in the control of the government, the two States are equals precisely. But how are they in the number of their white people? Maine has 581,812—while South Carolina has 274,567. Maine has twice as many as South Carolina, and 32,679 over. Thus each white man in South Carolina is more than the double of any man in Maine. This is all because South Carolina, besides her free people, has 384,984 slaves. The South Carolinian has precisely the same advantage over the white man in every other free State, as well as in Maine. He is more than the double of any one of us in this crowd. The same advantage, but not to the same extent, is held by all the citizens of the slave States, over those of the free; and it is an absolute truth, without an exception, that there is no voter in any slave State, but who has more legal power in the government, than any voter in any free State. There is no instance of exact equality; and the disadvantage is against us the whole chapter through. This principle, in the aggregate, gives the slave States, in the present Congress, twenty additional representatives—being seven more than the whole majority by which they passed the Nebraska bill.

Now all this is manifestly unfair; yet I do not mention it to complain of it, in so far as it is already settled. It is in the constitution; and I do not, for that cause, or any other cause, propose to destroy, or alter, or disregard the constitution. I stand to it, fairly, fully, and firmly.

But when I am told I must leave it altogether to OTHER PEOPLE to say whether new partners are to be bred up and brought into the firm, on the same degrading terms against me, I respectfully demur. I insist, that whether I shall be a whole man, or only, the half of one, in comparison with others, is a question in which I am somewhat concerned; and one which no other man can have a sacred right of deciding for me. If I am wrong in this—if it really be a sacred right of self-government, in the man who shall go to Nebraska, to decide whether he will be the EQUAL of me, or the DOUBLE of me, then after he shall have exercised that right, and thereby shall have reduced me to a still smaller fraction of a man than I already am, I should like for some gentleman deeply skilled in the mysteries of sacred rights, to provide himself with a microscope, and peep about, and find out, if he can, what has become of my sacred rights! They will surely be too small for detection with the naked eye.

Finally, I insist, that if there is ANY THING which it is the duty of the WHOLE PEOPLE to never entrust to any hands but their own, that thing is the preservation and perpetuity, of their own liberties, and institutions. And if they shall think, as I do, that the extension of slavery endangers them, more than any, or all other causes, how recreant to themselves, if they submit the question, and with it, the fate of their country, to a mere hand-full of men, bent only on temporary self-interest. If this question of slavery extension were an insignificant one—one having no power to do harm—it might be shuffled aside in this way. But being, as it is, the great Behemoth of danger, shall the strong grip of the nation be loosened upon him, to entrust him to the hands of such feeble keepers?

I have done with this mighty argument, of self-government. Go, sacred thing! Go in peace.

But Nebraska is urged as a great Union-saving measure. Well I too, go for saving the Union. Much as I hate slavery, I would consent to the extension of it rather than see the Union dissolved, just as I would consent to any GREAT evil, to avoid a GREATER one. But when I go to Union saving, I must believe, at least, that the means I employ has some adaptation to the end. To my mind, Nebraska has no such adaptation.

<blockquote>"It hath no relish of salvation in it."</blockquote>

It is an aggravation, rather, of the only one thing which ever endangers the Union. When it came upon us, all was peace and quiet. The nation was looking to the forming of new bonds of Union; and a long course of peace and prosperity seemed to lie before us. In the whole range of possibility, there scarcely appears to me to have been any thing, out of which the slavery agitation could have been revived, except the very project of repealing the Missouri compromise. Every inch of territory we owned, already had a definite settlement of the slavery question, and by which, all parties were pledged to abide. Indeed, there was uninhabited country on the continent, which we could acquire; if we except some extreme northern regions, which are wholly out of the question. In this state of case, the genius of Discord himself, could scarcely have invented a way of again getting [setting?] us by the ears, but by turning back and destroying the peace measures of the past. The councils of that genius seem to have prevailed, the Missouri compromise was repealed; and here we are, in the midst of a new slavery agitation, such, I think as we have never seen before. Who is responsible for this? Is it those who resist the measure; or those who, causelessly, brought it forward, and pressed it through, having reason to know, and, in fact, knowing it must and would be so resisted? It could not but be expected by its author, that it would be looked upon as a measure for the extension of slavery, aggravated by a gross breach of faith. Argue as you will, and long as you will, this is the naked FRONT and ASPECT, of the measure. And in this aspect, it could not but produce agitation. Slavery is founded in the selfishness of man's nature—opposition to it, is [in?] his love of justice. These principles are an eternal antagonism; and when brought into collision so fiercely, as slavery extension brings them, shocks, and throes, and convulsions must ceaselessly follow. Repeal the Missouri compromise—repeal all compromises—repeal the declaration of independence—repeal all past history, you still can not repeal human nature. It still will be the abundance of man's heart, that slavery extension is wrong; and out of the abundance of his heart, his mouth will continue to speak.

The structure, too, of the Nebraska bill is very peculiar. The people are to decide the question of slavery for themselves; but WHEN they are to decide; or HOW they are to decide; or whether, when the question is once decided, it is to remain so, or is to be subject to an indefinite succession of new trials, the law does not say, Is it to be decided by the first dozen settlers who arrive there? or is it to await the arrival of a hundred? Is it to be decided by a vote of the people? or a vote of the legislature? or, indeed by a vote of any sort? To these questions, the law gives no answer. There is a mystery about this; for when a member proposed to give the legislature express authority to exclude slavery, it was hooted down by the friends of the bill. This fact is worth remembering. Some yankees, in the east, are sending emigrants to Nebraska, to exclude slavery from it; and, so far as I can judge, they expect the question to be decided by voting, in some way or other. But the Missourians are awake too. They are within a stone's throw of the contested ground. They hold meetings, and pass resolutions, in which not the slightest allusion to voting is made. They resolve that slavery already exists in the territory; that more shall go there; that they, remaining in Missouri will protect it; and that abolitionists shall be hung, or driven away. Through all this, bowie-knives and six-shooters are seen plainly enough; but never a glimpse of the ballot-box. And, really, what is to be the result of this? Each party WITHIN, having numerous and determined backers WITHOUT, is it not probable that the contest will come to blows, and bloodshed? Could there be a more apt invention to bring about collision and violence, on the slavery question, that this Nebraska project is? I do not charge, or believe, that such was intended by Congress; but if they had literally formed a ring, and placed champions within it to fight out the controversy, the fight could be no more likely to come off, than it is. And if this fight should begin, is it likely to take a very peaceful, Union-saving turn? Will not the first drop of blood so shed, be the real knell of the Union?

The Missouri Compromise ought to be restored. For the sake of the Union, it ought to be restored. We ought to elect a House of Representatives which will vote its restoration. If by any means, we omit to do this, what follows? Slavery may or may not be established in Nebraska. But whether it be or not, we shall have repudiated—discarded from the councils of the Nation—the SPIRIT of COMPROMISE; for who after this will ever trust in a national compromise? The spirit of mutual concession–that spirit which first gave us the constitution, and which has thrice saved the Union—we shall have strangled and cast from us forever. And what shall we have in lieu of it? The South flushed with triumph and tempted to excesses; the North, betrayed, as they believe, brooding on wrong and burning for revenge. One side will provoke; the other resent. The one will taunt, the other defy; one agrees [aggresses?], the other retaliates. Already a few in the North, defy all constitutional restraints, resist the execution of the fugitive slave law, and even menace the institution of slavery in the states where it exists.

Already a few in the South, claim the constitutional right to take to and hold slaves in the free states—demand the revival of the slave trade; and demand a treaty with Great Britain by which fugitive slaves may be reclaimed from Canada. As yet they are but few on either side. It is a grave question for the lovers of the Union, whether the final destruction of the Missouri Compromise, and with it the spirit of all compromise will or will not embolden and embitter each of these, and fatally increase the numbers of both.

But restore the compromise, and what then? We thereby restore the national faith, the national confidence, the national feeling of brotherhood. We thereby reinstate the spirit of concession and compromise—that spirit which has never failed us in past perils, and which may be safely trusted for all the future. The south ought to join in doing this. The peace of the nation is as dear to them as to us. In memories of the past and hopes of the future, they share as largely as we. It would be on their part, a great act—great in its spirit, and great in its effect. It would be worth to the nation a hundred years' purchase of peace and prosperity. And what of sacrifice would they make? They only surrender to us, what they gave us for a consideration long, long ago; what they have not now, asked for, struggled or care for; what has been thrust upon them, not less to their own astonishment than to ours.

But it is said we cannot restore it; that though we elect every member of the lower house, the Senate is still against us. It is quite true, that of the Senators who passed the Nebraska bill, a majority of the whole Senate will retain their seats in spite of the elections of this and the next year. But if at these elections, their several constituencies shall clearly express their will against Nebraska, will these senators disregard their will? Will they neither obey, nor make room for those who will?

But even if we fail to technically restore the compromise, it is still a great point to carry a popular vote in favor of the restoration. The moral weight of such a vote can not be estimated too highly. The authors of Nebraska are not at all satisfied with the destruction of the compromise—an endorsement of this PRINCIPLE, they proclaim to be the great object. With them, Nebraska alone is a small matter—to establish a principle, for FUTURE USE, is what they particularly desire.

That future use is to be the planting of slavery wherever in the wide world, local and unorganized opposition can not prevent it. Now if you wish to give them this endorsement—if you wish to establish this principle—do so. I shall regret it; but it is your right. On the contrary if you are opposed to the principle—intend to give it no such endorsement—let no wheedling, no sophistry, divert you from throwing a direct vote against it.

Some men, mostly whigs, who condemn the repeal of the Missouri Compromise, nevertheless hesitate to go for its restoration, lest they be thrown in company with the abolitionist. Will they allow me as an old whig to tell them good humoredly, that I think this is very silly? Stand with anybody that stands RIGHT. Stand with him while he is right and PART with him when he goes wrong. Stand WITH the abolitionist in restoring the Missouri Compromise; and stand AGAINST him when he attempts to repeal the fugitive law. In the latter case you stand with the southern disunionist. What of that? you are still right. In both cases you are right. In both cases you oppose [expose?] the dangerous extremes. In both you stand on middle ground and hold the ship level and steady. In both you are national and nothing less than national. This is good old whig ground. To desert such ground, because of any company, is to be less than a whig— less than a man—less than an American.

I particularly object to the NEW position which the avowed principle of this Nebraska law gives to slavery in the body politic. I object to it because it assumes that there CAN be a MORAL RIGHT in the enslaving of one man by another. I object to it as a dangerous dalliance for a few [free?] people—a sad evidence that, feeling prosperity we forget right— that liberty, as a principle, we have ceased to revere. I object to it because the fathers of the republic eschewed, and rejected it. The argument of "Necessity" was the only argument they ever admitted in favor of slavery; and so far, and so far only as it carried them, did they ever go. They found the institution existing among us, which they could not help; and they cast blame upon the British King for having permitted its introduction. BEFORE the constitution, they prohibited its introduction into the north-western Territory—the only country we owned, then free from it. At the framing and adoption of the constitution, they forbore to so much as mention the word "slave" or "slavery" in the whole instrument. In the pro-vision for the recovery of fugitives, the slave is spoken of as a "PERSON HELD TO SERVICE OR LABOR." In that prohibiting the abolition of the African slave trade for twenty years, that trade is spoken of as "the migra-tion or importation of such persons as any of the States NOW EXISTING, shall think proper to admit," &c. These are the only provisions alluding to slavery. Thus, the thing is hid away, in the constitution, just as an afflicted man hides away a wen or a cancer, which he dares not cut out at once, lest he bleed to death; with the promise, nevertheless, that the cutting may begin at the end of a given time. Less than this our fathers COULD not do; and NOW [MORE?] they WOULD not do. Necessity drove them so far, and farther, they would not go. But this is not all. The earliest Con-gress, under the constitution, took the same view of slavery. They hedged and hemmed it in to the narrowest limits of necessity.

In 1794, they prohibited an out-going slave-trade—that is, the taking of slaves FROM the United States to sell.

In 1798, they prohibited the bringing of slaves from Africa, INTO the Mississippi Territory—this territory then comprising what are now the States of Mississippi and Alabama. This was TEN YEARS before they had the authority to do the same thing as to the States existing at the adoption of the constitution.

In 1800 they prohibited AMERICAN CITIZENS from trading in slaves between foreign countries—as, for instance, from Africa to Brazil.

In 1803 they passed a law in aid of one or two State laws, in restraint of the internal slave trade.

In 1807, in apparent hot haste, they passed the law, nearly a year in advance, to take effect the first day of 1808—the very first day the constitution would permit—prohibiting the African slave trade by heavy pecuniary and corporal penalties.

In 1820, finding these provisions ineffectual, they declared the trade piracy, and annexed to it, the extreme penalty of death. While all this was passing in the general government, five or six of the original slave States had adopted systems of gradual emancipation; and by which the institution was rapidly becoming extinct within these limits.

Thus we see, the plain unmistakable spirit of that age, towards slavery, was hostility to the PRINCIPLE, and toleration, ONLY BY NECESSITY.

But NOW it is to be transformed into a "sacred right." Nebraska brings it forth, places it on the high road to extension and perpetuity; and, with a pat on its back, says to it, "Go, and God speed you." Henceforth it is to be the chief jewel of the nation—the very figure-head of the ship of State. Little by little, but steadily as man's march to the grave, we have been giving up the OLD for the NEW faith. Near eighty years ago we began by declaring that all men are created equal; but now from that beginning we have run down to the other declaration, that for SOME men to enslave OTHERS is a "sacred right of self-government." These principles can not stand together. They are as opposite as God and mammon; and whoever holds to the one, must despise the other. When Petit, in connection with his support of the Nebraska bill, called the Declaration of Independence "a self-evident lie" he only did what consistency and candor require all other Nebraska men to do. Of the forty odd Nebraska Senators who sat present and heard him, no one rebuked him. Nor am I apprized that any Nebraska newspaper, or any Nebraska orator, in the whole nation, has ever yet rebuked him. If this had been said among Marion's men, Southerners though they were, what would have become of the man who said it? If this had been said to the men who captured André, the man who said it, would probably have been hung sooner than André was. If it had been said in old Independence Hall, seventy-eight years ago, the very door-keeper would have throttled the man, and thrust him into the street.

Let no one be deceived. The spirit of seventy-six and the spirit of Nebraska, are utter antagonisms; and the former is being rapidly displaced by the latter.

Fellow countrymen—Americans south, as well as north, shall we make no effort to arrest this? Already the liberal party throughout the world, express the apprehension "that the one retrograde institution in America, is undermining the principles of progress, and fatally violating the noblest political system the world ever saw." This is not the taunt of enemies, but the warning of friends. Is it quite safe to disregard it—to despise it? Is there no danger to liberty itself, in discarding the earliest practice, and first precept of our ancient faith? In our greedy chase to make profit of the negro, let us beware, lest we "cancel and tear to pieces" even the white man's charter of freedom.

Our republican robe is soiled, and trailed in the dust. Let us repurify it. Let us turn and wash it white, in the spirit, if not the blood, of the Revolution. Let us turn slavery from its claims of "moral right," back upon its existing legal rights, and its arguments of "necessity." Let us return it to the position our fathers gave it; and there let it rest in peace. Let us re-adopt the Declaration of Independence, and with it, the practices, and policy, which harmonize with it. Let north and south—let all Americans—let all lovers of liberty everywhere—join in the great and good work. If we do this, we shall not only have saved the Union; but we shall have so saved it, as to make, and to keep it, forever worthy of the saving. We shall have so saved it, that the succeeding millions of free happy people, the world over, shall rise up, and call us blessed, to the latest generations.

At Springfield, twelve days ago, where I had spoken substantially as I have here, Judge Douglas replied to me—and as he is to reply to me here, I shall attempt to anticipate him, by noticing some of the points he made there.

He commenced by stating I had assumed all the way through, that the principle of the Nebraska bill, would have the effect of extending slavery. He denied that this was INTENDED, or that this EFFECT would follow.

I will not re-open the argument upon this point. That such was the intention, the world believed at the start, and will continue to believe. This was the COUNTENANCE of the thing; and, both friends and enemies, instantly recognized it as such. That countenance can not now be changed by argument. You can as easily argue the color out of the negroes' skin. Like the "bloody hand" you may wash it, the red witness of guilt still sticks, and stares horribly at you.

Next he says, congressional intervention never prevented slavery, any where—that it did not prevent it in the north west territory, now [nor?] in Illinois—that in fact, Illinois came into the Union as a slave State—that the principle of the Nebraska bill expelled it from Illinois, from several old States, from every where.

Now this is mere quibbling all the way through. If the ordinance of '87 did not keep slavery out of the north west territory, how happens it that the north west shore of the Ohio river is entirely free from it; while the south east shore, less than a mile distant, along nearly the whole length of the river, is entirely covered with it?

If that ordinance did not keep it out of Illinois, what was it that made the difference between Illinois and Missouri? They lie side by side, the Mississippi river only dividing them; while their early settlements were within the same latitude. Between 1810 and 1820 the number of slaves in Missouri INCREASED 7,211; while in Illinois, in the same ten years, they DECREASED 51. This appears by the census returns. During nearly all of that ten years, both were territories—not States. During this time, the ordinance forbid slavery to go into Illinois; and NOTHING forbid it to go into Missouri. It DID go into Missouri, and did NOT go into Illinois. That is the fact. Can any one doubt as to the reason of it?

But, he says, Illinois came into the Union as a slave State. Silence, perhaps, would be the best answer to this flat contradiction of the known history of the country. What are the facts upon which this bold assertion is based? When we first acquired the country, as far back as 1787, there were some slaves within it, held by the French inhabitants at Kaskaskia. The territorial legislation, admitted a few negroes, from the slave States, as indentured servants. One year after the adoption of the first State constitution the whole number of them was—what do you think? just 117—while the aggregate free population was 55,094—about 470 to one. Upon this state of facts, the people framed their constitution prohibiting the further introduction of slavery, with a sort of guaranty to the owners of the few indentured servants, giving freedom to their children to be born thereafter, and making no mention whatever, of any supposed slave for life. Out of this small matter, the Judge manufactures his argument that Illinois came into the Union as a slave State. Let the facts be the answer to the argument.

The principles of the Nebraska bill, he says, expelled slavery from Illinois? The principle of that bill first planted it here—that is, it first came, because there was no law to prevent it—first came before we owned the country; and finding it here, and having the ordinance of '87 to prevent its increasing, our people struggled along, and finally got rid of it as best they could.

But the principle of the Nebraska bill abolished slavery in several of the old States. Well, it is true that several of the old States, in the last quarter of the last century, did adopt systems of gradual emancipation, by which the institution has finally become extinct within their limits; but it MAY or MAY NOT be true that the principle of the Nebraska bill was the cause that led to the adoption of these measures. It is now more than fifty years, since the last of these States adopted its system of emancipation. If Nebraska bill is the real author of these benevolent works, it is rather deplorable, that he has, for so long a time, ceased working all together. Is there not some reason to suspect that it was the principle of the REVO-LUTION, and not the principle of Nebraska bill, that led to emancipation in these old States? Leave it to the people of those old emancipating States, and I am quite sure they will decide, that neither that, nor any other good thing, ever did, or ever will come of Nebraska bill.

In the course of my main argument, Judge Douglas interrupted me to say, that the principle [of] the Nebraska bill was very old; that it originated when God made man and placed good and evil before him, allowing him to choose for himself, being responsible for the choice he should make. At the time I thought this was merely playful; and I answered it accordingly. But in his reply to me he renewed it, as a serious argument. In seriousness then, the facts of this proposition are not true as stated. God did not place good and evil before man, telling him to make his choice. On the contrary, he did tell him there was one tree, of the fruit of which, he should not eat, upon pain of certain death. I should scarcely wish so strong a prohibition against slavery in Nebraska.

But this argument strikes me as not a little remarkable in another particular—in its strong resemblance to the old argument for the "Divine right of Kings." By the latter, the King is to do just as he pleases with his white subjects, being responsible to God alone. By the former the white man is to do just as he pleases with his black slaves, being responsible to God alone. The two things are precisely alike; and it is but natural that they should find similar arguments to sustain them.

I had argued, that the application of the principle of self-government, as contended for, would require the revival of the African slave trade— that no argument could be made in favor of a man's right to take slaves to Nebraska, which could not be equally well made in favor of his right to bring them from the coast of Africa. The Judge replied, that the constitution requires the suppression of the foreign slave trade; but does not require the prohibition of slavery in the territories. That is a mistake, in point of fact. The constitution does NOT require the action of Congress in either case; and it does AUTHORIZE it in both. And so, there is still no difference between the cases.

In regard to what I had said, the advantage the slave States have over the free, in the matter of representation, the Judge replied that we, in the free States, count five free negroes as five white people, while in the slave States, they count slaves as three whites only; and that the advantage, at last, was on the side of the free States.

Now, in the slave States, they count free negroes just as we do; and it so happens that besides their slaves, they have as many free negroes as we have, and thirty-three thousand over. Thus their free negroes more than balance ours; and their advantage over us, in consequence of their slaves, still remains as I stated it.

In reply to my argument, that the compromise measures of 1850, were a system of equivalents; and that the provisions of no one of them could fairly be carried to other subjects, without its corresponding equivalent being carried with it, the Judge denied out-right, that these measures had any connection with, or dependence upon, each other. This is mere desperation. If they have no connection, why are they always spoken of in connection? Why has he so spoken of them, a thousand times? Why has he constantly called them a SERIES of measures? Why does everybody call them a compromise? Why was California kept out of the Union, six or seven months, if it was not because of its connection with the other measures? Webster's leading definition of the verb "to compromise" is "to adjust and settle a difference, by mutual agreement with concessions of claims by the parties." This conveys precisely the popular understanding of the word compromise. We knew, before the Judge told us, that these measures passed separately, and in distinct bills; and that no two of them were passed by the votes of precisely the same members. But we also know, and so does he know, that no one of them could have passed both branches of Congress but for the understanding that the others were to pass also. Upon this understanding each got votes, which it could have got in no other way. It is this fact, that gives to the measures their true character; and it is the universal knowledge of this fact, that has given them the name of compromise so expressive of that true character.

I had asked "If in carrying the provisions of the Utah and New Mexico laws to Nebraska, you could clear away other objection, how can you leave Nebraska 'perfectly free' to introduce slavery BEFORE she forms a constitution—during her territorial government?—while the Utah and New Mexico laws only authorize it WHEN they form constitutions, and are admitted into the Union?" To this Judge Douglas answered that the Utah and New Mexico laws, also authorized it BEFORE; and to prove this, he read from one of their laws, as follows: "That the legislative power of said territory shall extend to all rightful subjects of legislation consistent with the constitution of the United States and the provisions of this act."

Now it is perceived from the reading of this, that there is nothing express upon the subject; but that the authority is sought to be implied merely, for the general provision of "all rightful subjects of legislation." In reply to this, I insist, as a legal rule of construction, as well as the plain popular view of the matter, that the EXPRESS provision for Utah and New Mexico coming in with slavery if they choose, when they shall form constitutions, is an EXCLUSION of all implied authority on the same subject— that Congress, having the subject distinctly in their minds, when they made the express provision, they therein expressed their WHOLE meaning on that subject.

The Judge rather insinuated that I had found it convenient to forget the Washington territorial law passed in 1853. This was a division of Oregon, organizing the northern part, as the territory of Washington. He asserted that, by this act, the ordinance of '87 theretofore existing in Oregon, was repealed; that nearly all the members of Congress voted for it, beginning in the H.R., with Charles Allen of Massachusetts, and ending with Richard Yates, of Illinois; and that he could not understand how those who now oppose the Nebraska bill, so voted then, unless it was because it was then too soon after both the great political parties had ratified the compromises of 1850, and the ratification therefore too fresh, to be then repudiated.

Now I had seen the Washington act before; and I have carefully examined it since; and I aver that there is no repeal of the ordinance of '87, or of any prohibition of slavery, in it. In express terms, there is absolutely nothing in the whole law upon the subject—in fact, nothing to lead a reader to THINK of the subject. To my judgment, it is equally free from every thing from which such repeal can be legally implied; but however this may be, are men now to be entrapped by a legal implication, extracted from covert language, introduced perhaps, for the very purpose of entrapping them? I sincerely wish every man could read this law quite through, carefully watching every sentence, and every line, for a repeal of the ordinance of '87 or any thing equivalent to it.

Another point on the Washington act. If it was intended to be modelled after the Utah and New Mexico acts, as Judge Douglas, insists, why was it not inserted in it, as in them, that Washington was to come in with or without slavery as she may choose at the adoption of her constitution?

It has no such provision in it; and I defy the ingenuity of man to give a reason for the omission, other than that it was not intended to follow the Utah and New Mexico laws in regard to the question of slavery.

The Washington act not only differs vitally from the Utah and New Mexico acts; but the Nebraska act differs vitally from both. By the latter act the people are left "perfectly free" to regulate their own domestic concerns &c; but in all the former, all their laws are to be submitted to Congress, and if disapproved are to be null. The Washington act goes even further; it absolutely prohibits the territorial legislation [legislature?], by very strong and guarded language, from establishing banks, or borrowing money on the faith of the territory. Is this the sacred right of self-government we hear vaunted so much? No sir, the Nebraska bill finds no model in the acts of '50 or the Washington act. It finds no model in any law from Adam till today. As [Charles] Phillips says of Napoleon, the Nebraska act is grand, gloomy, and peculiar; wrapped in the solitude of its own originality; without a model, and without a shadow upon the earth.

In the course of his reply, Senator Douglas remarked, in substance, that he had always considered this government was made for the white people and not for the negroes. Why, in point of mere fact, I think so too. But in this remark of the Judge, there is a significance, which I think is the key to the great mistake (if there is any such mistake) which he has made in this Nebraska measure. It shows that the Judge has no very vivid impression that the negro is a human; and consequently has no idea that there can be any moral question in legislating about him. In his view, the question of whether a new country shall be slave or free, is a matter of as utter indifference, as it is whether his neighbor shall plant his farm with tobacco, or stock it with horned cattle. Now, whether this view is right or wrong, it is very certain that the great mass of mankind take a totally different view. They consider slavery a great moral wrong; and their feelings against it, is not evanescent, but eternal. It lies at the very foundation of their sense of justice; and it cannot be trifled with. It is a great and durable element of popular action, and, I think, no statesman can safely disregard it.

Our Senator also objects that those who oppose him in this measure do not entirely agree with one another. He reminds me that in my firm adherence to the constitutional rights of the slave States, I differ widely from others who are co-operating with me in opposing the Nebraska bill; and he says it is not quite fair to oppose him in this variety of ways. He should remember that he took us by surprise—astounded us—by this measure. We were thunderstruck and stunned; and we reeled and fell in utter confusion. But we rose each fighting, grasping whatever he could first reach—a scythe—a pitchfork—chopping axe, or a butcher's cleaver. We struck in the direction of the sound; and we are rapidly closing in upon him. He must not think to divert us from our purpose, by showing us that our drill, our dress, and our weapons, are not entirely perfect and uniform. When the storm shall be past, he shall find us still Americans; no less devoted to the continued Union and prosperity of the country than heretofore.

Finally, the Judge invokes against me, the memory of Clay and of Webster. They were great men; and men of great deeds. But where have I assailed them? For what is it, that their life-long enemy, shall now make profit, by assuming to defend them against me, their life-long friend? I go against the repeal of the Missouri compromise; did they ever go for it? They went for the compromise of 1850; did I ever go against them? They were greatly devoted to the Union; to the small measure of my ability, was I ever less so? Clay and Webster were dead before this question arose; by what authority shall our Senator say they would espouse his side of it, if alive? Mr Clay was the leading spirit in making the Missouri compromise; is it very credible that if now alive, he would take the lead in the breaking of it? The truth is that some support from whigs is now a necessity with the Judge, and for thus it is, that the names of Clay and Webster are now invoked. His old friends have deserted him in such numbers as to leave too few to live by. He came to his own, and his own received him not, and Lo! he turns unto the Gentiles.

A word now as to the Judge's desperate assumption that the compromises of '50 had no connection with one another; that Illinois came into the Union as a slave state, and some other similar ones. This is no other than a bold denial of the history of the country. If we do not know that the Compromises of '50 were dependent on each other; if we do not know that Illinois came into the Union as a free state—we do not know any thing. If we do not know these things, we do not know that we ever had a revolutionary war, or such a chief as Washington. To deny these things is to deny our national axioms, or dogmas, at least; and it puts an end to all argument. If a man will stand up and assert, and repeat, and re-assert, that two and two do not make four, I know nothing in the power of argument that can stop him. I think I can answer the Judge so long as he sticks to the premises; but when he flies from them, I can not work an argument into the consistency of a maternal gag, and actually close his mouth with it. In such a case I can only commend him to the seventy thousand answers [anti-Nebraska votes] just in from Pennsylvania, Ohio and Indiana.

ACKNOWLEDGMENTS:
PEOPLE AND IDEAS

I have much to acknowledge. More than two decades in the making, my book is a work of many hands. It is my first on Abraham Lincoln's place in American history. Happily, the spirit of historians claimed me as a young man. Here I must take the time to thank some of the historians and teachers who have held my attention from school days. Inevitably, I shall not be able to name all, nor can I say how much I owe to each. Space does not allow comprehensive inclusion of all the intellectual debts of a lifetime.

As a student of history, I know there is neither a beginning, nor is there an end to my indebtedness to good teachers. My grandfather Louis, whom I revered, and my devoted parents, were my first dedicated teachers. Having raised me in the shadows of the Depression and World War II, in central Pennsylvania, they made me aware of American hardships and victories, at home and abroad. Elsie B. Diven, my gifted teacher in the fifth and sixth grades, quickened my interest in the beauty of the English language, and in everything patriotic, especially West Point, where she had decided I should go. Hers was a strict pedagogy, and I minded her; but I did not make it to West Point, only to Army boot camp at Fort Knox, Kentucky.

Duncan Campbell, "a great Scot" and military historian—my secondary school coach and history teacher—drove me the twenty miles from home to the Gettysburg battlefield. There, he regaled our class with stories of bold warriors, blue and gray. There, I learned of slavery and emancipation, of Union and Confederate heroes and heroines.

In high school Garrett Greene, peering at me through Edwardian horn-rimmed glasses, exacted a mighty toll of my memory, always insisting upon mastery of American milestones—dates, names, places, and ideas.

Facts and circumstances, I learned from this Hill School master, are the stuff of ideas and decisions. "No big theories, Lehrman." The narrative of past things, he taught in his own idiom, is not only the outcome of impersonal forces and the history of ideas, but it is also the contingent record of individual decisions—of men and women, leaders and partisans, with many motives, caught up in the event.

Neither my mother nor my father had gone to college. Thus, I relied on my headmaster—who sent me to Yale. In my senior year, Professor Charles Garside nominated me to be a Carnegie Teaching Fellow in history. Professor George Wilson Pierson, a formidable de Tocqueville scholar, persuaded my practical and reluctant father that I should accept the Carnegie Teaching Fellowship appointment. As an assistant instructor of history on the Yale faculty, I was paid $3,500 for the year. Professors Howard Lamar, Charles Garside, Martin Duberman, Ralph Turner, William Goetzman, Robin Winks, among many others, pressed me deeper into the field. My teaching experience at Yale made an impact on my intellectual development which I can trace to this very day. Professor Lamar encouraged me to apply for a Woodrow Wilson Fellowship to Harvard, where I was subsidized with the princely sum of $2,500 for the year. There, I was awarded my M.A. in history.

I had entered the university in 1956. At that time it was not only my teachers, but also certain books which left permanent marks on my mind's eye. Undergraduate and graduate studies found me focused on European and American history. At the same time, Professor Ralph Turner turned me toward the history of neolithic and early urban cultures. Professor Robert Sabatino Lopez, the historian of medieval and renaissance Europe, at Yale and at Harvard, never let me forget "the economic basement of history." Professor Myron Gilmore of Harvard caused me to study Jacob Burckhardt's *Civilization of the Renaissance in Italy* (1860). With Professor Ernest May I studied *The World War and American Isolation, 1914–1917* (1959). These scholars influenced my way of thinking about America as a distinct civilization and its differences from Europe. They turned my thoughts to the role of culture, institutions, and war in the making of America. They caused me to reflect upon what was unique in the American common culture. Professor Robin L. Winks at Yale made American historiography a part of my intellectual life requiring me to read Carl N. Degler's outstanding 1959 volume on American historical interpretation, *Out of Our Past.* Kenneth M. Stampp in 1956 published his *Peculiar Institution* which swept away the *Gone With the Wind* view of American slavery. Roy P. Basler had edited the *Collected Works of Abraham Lincoln* (1953) in eight volumes. Later came two supplements. They can be read through, from beginning to end, themselves a fascinating "autobiography" in Lincoln's own hand. I cannot describe the profound effect the Basler volumes had on me. Lincoln's 17,000-word Peoria speech of 1854 suffused my consciousness upon the first reading, its lasting imprint finally transferred to the pages of this book. When on the road to Peoria to do research for this book, I did not escape the memory of this first reading. Harry V. Jaffa published his *Crisis of the House Divided* in 1959. In my opinion, this work is the most profound philosophical analysis of the political issues at stake between Abraham Lincoln and Stephen Douglas. Soon, thereafter, came Don E. Fehrenbacher's *Prelude to Greatness*, which reminded American historians that Mr. Lincoln was made ready for the presidency during the 1850s. In *Prelude* one is taught that Lincoln's emergence was not an accident that befell a melancholy railsplitter who somehow became a great president.

These are but a few of the remarkable books I carried with me, even as I ventured into the business world during the 1960s. Wherever my work travels took me, there, too, went new American history books, legacies of the influence of Stampp, Jaffa, Fehrenbacher, and others. Four powerful influences of the 1970s and 1980s were David M. Potter's *Impending Crisis* (1976), Don E. Fehrenbacher's *Dred Scott Case* (1978), Gabor S. Boritt's *Lincoln and the Economics of the American Dream* (1978), and James M. McPherson's *Battle Cry of Freedom: the Civil War Era* (1989). In *Lincoln and the Economics of the American Dream* (1978), Gabor Boritt emphasized the origin of Lincoln's economic ideas. Lincoln campaigned for government-encouraged free markets internally; but he was opposed to unrestrained free trade externally. In this, like Hamilton and Clay, Lincoln was a nationalist interested in building up a diversified national economy open to the talents, and also in protecting American labor and essential American industries. Lincoln supported a revenue-raising tariff and a central bank to supply a stable, uniform currency. His purpose was to bind together a vast, diffuse, national economy. Thus, he also endorsed a forward looking program of public works—roads, canals, railroads—to integrate the new U.S. territories and the states into one inclusive, continental market. I remain sympathetic to his purpose and policy. I summarize here Lincoln's program because I am convinced, by my study of nineteenth-century American economic disputes, that these issues are perennial. For integrated studies of the Civil War era, Potter's *Impending Crisis* seemed to me a masterpiece on the lead up to the war. McPherson's *Battle Cry of Freedom*, more focused on the Civil War, wound the whole thing up. The era of American Reconstruction cannot be separated from the Civil War nor from the Civil Rights reforms of the 1960s. On American Reconstruction after the Civil War, Eric Foner's *Reconstruction: America's Unfinished Revolution* (1988) is indispensable. So too is Herman Belz's *Reconstructing the Union: Theory and Policy during the Civil War* (1969).

There are many outstanding Lincoln books, major biographies, and histories— acknowledged in the Historians' Record, Notes, and Bibliography—to which I direct the reader's attention. As more has been written of Mr. Lincoln than any American, my mentions are a mere fraction of the library of scholarship on the subject. Legal historians and civil rights leaders have contributed to my work. I would be remiss in not citing my time long ago on the board of the NAACP Legal Defense Fund, where I observed the legal scholar Jack Greenberg, so influential in *Brown vs. Board of Education*, still hard at work on research, writing, and civil rights reforms. My intellectual intimacy with the whirlwind of slavery and its consequences was deepened during this period.

Much of my writing, after I left the university, concentrated on the analysis of monetary and economic issues, all viewed from an historical perspective. I summed up my arguments in a book with three university professors in 1976, *Money and the Coming World Order*. The decade of the 1970s witnessed the collapse of the post–World War II Bretton Woods international monetary system. The major economic debates of the 1960s and 1970s reminded me of the national banking, currency, and economic debates of the Lincoln era. I did not fail to make that connection, writing on the contemporary controversies for the *Wall Street Journal, Harper's* magazine, *New Times,* and other publications. Those were avocational efforts, as my commitment to a demanding business schedule kept me constantly on the road, at home and abroad.

I dwell on this period because I owe so much of my intellectual development in the 1970s to a man forty-two years my senior—the French scholar and statesman, an *eminence grise* of President Charles De Gaulle's Fifth Republic, Jacques Rueff. Rueff played a major part in the 1959 DeGaulle economic reforms of the Fifth Republic, which raised France from the depths of the Algerian crisis and near civil war to one of the fastest growing developed economies in the decade of the 1960s. As an economist, Rueff was a younger contemporary, a friend, and a peer of John Maynard Keynes, with whom Rueff debated. Rueff was older, but a friend and peer of Milton Friedman. At the epicenter of monetary theory and diplomacy in France throughout the period between World War I and World War II, Rueff remained a key figure in the intellectual, economic, and diplomatic debates of the post–World War II era until his death in 1978.

I write of him because, without his interest in my intellectual development, my economic and historical understanding would have been less integrated. He also encouraged my writing style. President De Gaulle had publicly described Rueff as the "Poète de finance" and I took notice. He was recognized by his intellectual peers as the first economist ever elected to the "Academie Francaise." With him I studied the monetary history of the Western world so intimately that I decided, with the French publisher, Plon, to assemble and publish Rueff's collected works in seven French volumes (including his scientific essays, plays and autobiography), subsequently overseeing their translation into English by Roger Glemét, the chief economic translator of the United Nations in Geneva. A polymath who was fluent in English, Professor Rueff caused me to rethink causes and consequences in American history, to try to link international diplomacy, economic and monetary institutions with the national politics, ideas, and institutions of our unique American history. In the Anglo-Saxon–dominated world, Jacques Rueff is now a neglected French scholar. No acknowledgment here could repay him sufficient tribute, nor give his gentle genius adequate praise. The coherent and comprehensive analysis of his magnum opus, *L'Ordre Social* (1945), helped me to plumb the intellectual coherence and integrity of Mr. Lincoln's integrated worldview.

I continued to write on monetary and economic policy throughout the 1980s. During this period, Morgan Stanley, the investment bank, published four of my manuscripts on monetary history and policy. To my friend and long-time intellectual collaborator, Barton Biggs, the global investment strategist at Morgan Stanley, I am deeply indebted for the interest he and Morgan Stanley took in my writings. During this period, Robert L. Bartley, editor of the *Wall Street Journal* began publishing my writings, which appeared there, on and off, for two decades. William F. Buckley Jr. published my writings in the *National Review*. During the 1970s, I came to know Robert Silvers, editor of the *New York Review of Books*, which along with *The Times Literary Supplement* (of England), and later the *Claremont Review of Books*, edited by Charles R. Kesler, enabled me to stay abreast of scholarship. John P. Britton, from my undergraduate days to this very moment, has been an intellectual collaborator—even enriching my historical imagination with early Mesopotamian studies.

My work in American history took on an intensified life when my long-time friendship with Richard Gilder led to the building of the Gilder Lehrman Collection of American historical manuscripts, now on deposit at the New-York Historical Society. I had become a modest collector of American documents, even in graduate school, but my partnership with Dick Gilder led to the rapid expansion of the Collection into a major archive of about 60,000 items, chronicling American history in its original documents and manuscripts—from the "discovery" of America until recent times. The strongest parts of the Collection focus on the Colonial, Revolutionary, Founding, Antebellum, and Civil War eras. The collection is described by Yale Sterling Professor of History David Brion Davis and professor Stephen Mintz in *The Boisterous Sea of Liberty* and briefly in Professor James G. Basker's introduction to *The Soldier's Pen*, by Gilder Lehrman Fellow Robert Bonner. Dick and I went on to establish the Gilder Lehrman Institute of American History in 1994, the purpose of which was to refocus the study and teaching of American history, in high schools and colleges, based on the original documents of American history. To this task Professor Basker of Barnard College and Lesley Herrmann brought intellectual entrepreneurship and hard work. President Basker and Executive Director Herrmann continue to lead the Gilder Lehrman Institute into ever more encompassing American history and teaching projects. Dick and I have been fortunate to have their farsighted leadership. Jim Basker, a professor of English literature, proved a leader worthy of every challenge we could put before him. Mary Ross has been tireless in her work with foundations that sponsor our work. Seth Kaller, by study and diligence, became an expert and the agent for the Gilder Lehrman Collection.

There is not space enough here to describe the larger-than-life talent of my friend and partner, Dick Gilder. For almost twenty years, we have labored together in the cause of American history. Without him the landscape of American historical studies would be much the poorer. Professor Gabor Boritt, Lincoln scholar of Gettysburg College, became our partner in 1990 for the purpose of establishing the Lincoln Prize. Later came the Frederick Douglass Prize, inaugurated with Professor David Brion Davis of Yale (1999), and then the Washington Book Prize sponsored with Mount Vernon and Washington College (2005). Professor Davis, a pioneer of global slavery studies, became in 1994 the first Director of the Gilder Lehrman Center for the Study of Slavery, Resistance and Abolition—at Yale University. His research and writing have been an indispensable foundation of this book. To President Gordon A. Haaland, Professor Boritt and also to Professor Michael Birkner of Gettysburg College, I owe the invitation to teach the Lincoln seminar at Gettysburg College. To them I also owe my acquaintance with Sandra Trenholm, the outstanding student of my Lincoln Seminar. She later revealed—to another student of my Lincoln seminar—that I was a pretty good teacher, but a pushover for wily students. Sandy became the assistant curator of the Gilder Lehrman Collection, and then succeeded Paul Romaine as chief curator of the Collection. She also read the manuscript. Her expert eye made a difference. So did the eyes of the accomplished staff of the Gilder Lehrman Collection, including Maribel Diaz, Cindy Muthuveren, Karla Rubio, and Davindra Basdeo.

How do I begin to thank the innumerable teachers—in universities, high schools, think tanks and foundations—who have given their time to the Gilder Lehrman projects, not to mention in certain cases, the research efforts which made this book possible? Among others, there are Professor David Blight, the present director of the Gilder Lehrman Center at Yale; Professor Richard Carwardine of Oxford, so helpful in our efforts in

England; Jean H. Baker, David Herbert Donald, John Hope Franklin, Allen Guelzo, William C. Harris, James and Lois Horton, Stephen Mintz, Kenneth Stampp, and Douglas Wilson. They have discussed with me their books, rehearsed their arguments, then patiently endured my questions. Discussions with Professor Basker, an accomplished historian as well as literature scholar, have made me a more careful student. From my studies, I know that the Lincoln field benefits from a new generation of scholars—among them Brian R. Dirck, Joseph R. Fornieri, Lucas E. Morel, Graham Peck, Matthew Pinsker, Michael Vorenberg, Jennifer Weber, Stewart Winger, and David Work.

In the past two decades, several Lincoln scholars have performed an invaluable archival service for all Americans with their editing of the recollections of Lincoln's contemporaries. Professor Michael Burlingame has relentlessly mined the works of key Lincoln intimates, such as Noah Brooks, John Hay, John G. Nicolay, and William Stoddard. Like countless students and scholars of Lincoln I have been spared the labor of deciphering Horace Greeley's handwriting by the pathbreaking efforts of Rodney Davis and Douglas L. Wilson. Not only did they edit and publish the testimony of William Herndon, Lincoln's law partner, and the memories of *Herndon's Informants*, but they have also supervised the invaluable transcriptions of the Robert Todd Lincoln Collection at the Library of Congress. Doug Wilson read my manuscript and shared his intimate knowledge of the original sources.

Dr. John R. Sellers at the Library of Congress and Dr. Thomas F. Schwartz of the Abraham Lincoln Association and the Abraham Lincoln Presidential Library and Museum have put Abraham Lincoln online—a place where the technologically-oriented sixteenth president would doubtless want to be. That work continues in Springfield, Illinois, with a new compilation of "The Papers of Abraham Lincoln," directed by Daniel W. Stowell and sponsored by the Illinois Historic Preservation Agency and the Abraham Lincoln Presidential Library and Museum. Under the leadership of Richard Norton Smith, Tom Schwartz, and now Rick Beard, the library is an inviting resource for any Lincoln scholar. My own quest at the library was aided by Debbie Hamm, Cheryl Schnirring, Mary Michals, and Roberta Fairburn.

Lincoln for his own reasons, his wife for hers, did not keep a full record of his private and public documents, but he and others were very careful to preserve many important ones. Mr. Lincoln would be amazed at the scale and devotion of the many teams of scholars who have searched, preserved, and published his work. And he would also enjoy, as I did, browsing in Dan Weinberg's peerless Abraham Lincoln Bookstore—a Chicago institution devoted to the study of American history and America's sixteenth president. Lincoln would have appreciated the archives of the Cullom-Davis Library of Bradley University in Peoria. There, Lincoln's notebook, in his own hand, can be found, tabulating the legislative line-up for the 1855 Senate election. It was a gift to Dr. Robert Boal, a Lincoln friend who made his home in Peoria at the end of his life. Charles Frey and Sherri Schneider helped guide me through the Lincoln resources there.

Discussion of Lincoln topics, such as the Peoria speech, has been kept alive by the Abraham Lincoln Association in Springfield, Illinois, the Abraham Lincoln Institute in Washington, D.C., the Civil War Institute in Gettysburg, and the Lincoln Forum, among many other Lincoln and Civil War organizations. For example, each November, hundreds of Lincoln students gather in Gettysburg, to celebrate the words Lincoln said there, and to discuss the sixteenth president—under the auspices of the Lincoln Forum, headed by Frank Williams and Harold Holzer, both distinguished Lincoln authors. Harold is also cochairman of the Abraham Lincoln Bicentennial Commission.

In addition to these colleagues in the study of Lincoln, I have been fortunate over the years to have had many associates in other intellectual enterprises. Though their specialized fields did not include Lincoln, many helped to form my worldview.

I have yet to thank Charles Pierce and Parker Gilbert, Director and President respectively of New York's Pierpont Morgan Library, both of whom responded to my calls for help and advice on the Gilder Lehrman Collection, giving it a distinguished home at the Pierpont Morgan Library in New York for a decade. Gordon Haaland and Katherine Will, successive presidents of Gettysburg College, and Tina Grim and Diane Brennan, Gettysburg overseers of the Lincoln Prize, are friends and colleagues to whom I am annually indebted. To President Richard Levin of Yale and

Sterling Professor of Law Guido Calabresi, now a Federal judge, I am last-ingly grateful—the former indispensable for the Gilder Lehrman Center at Yale, the latter a mentor and friend from early Yale days who encour-aged my scholarship. James Rees, the director of Mount Vernon, keeper of the seals and scholarship at General Washington's home, now a distin-guished history teaching center, and Gay Hart Gaines, the former regent of Mount Vernon, have been crucial allies-in-arms for American history. Working with them has been an inspiration.

Today, the Gilder Lehrman Collection lives at the New-York Historical Society. To Nancy Newcomb, Roger Hertog, Louise Mirrer, and Kenneth Jackson, among many leaders of the New-York Historical Society, I owe so much to their good offices and scholarship. To Josiah Bunting III, scholar and novelist, I am indebted for countless hours rehearsing the events, leaders, and meaning of American history. Ed Feulner, Ken Cribb, and Chris DeMuth have encouraged my work in public policy and American history for decades.

Scholars who have written many books know well the meaning of a production team. Without the indispensable Frank Trotta, Esq., and Susan Tang, both associates of almost thirty years, and Ericka Wright, Deja Lowden, Steve Szymanski, and Patricia Blake, my investment business— during early morning hours at work on this book—would have been on autopilot. "Autopilot" does not bring business results; and I am ever grate-ful for their loyalty and attention to my intellectual enterprises. They have enabled me, at work and while writing, to navigate, simultaneously, the worlds of history research and investment markets. Kathleen Packard did research for the photos and maps, and in so many ways has helped on my Lincoln projects. Among her staff at Kathode Ray Media, Erin Simmons designed the maps and Ashley Rio helped format the images.

Richard Behn has been my colleague in one project or another for about three decades. Among his many learned interests, he came late to American history—he perhaps thinking, a while back, that my zeal for Mr. Lincoln's unique literary and political achievement was a bit peculiar. During the past ten years, Dick has become not only a recognized Lincoln website manager, but also my research associate at The Lincoln Institute and my research assistant for this book. To his tireless efforts and to his editorial oversight, I owe enough to say that this book would have been much longer in coming without him. Not least because of publication timetables and my business schedule, he and I worked weekends and evenings to complete this work. He always understood that my full-time vocation, my large family, especially my wife Louise, had to come first. But goad that he is—he never let up. His tenacity with the footnotes and his patient help with my other historical projects do not exhaust the description of our partnership.

David Detweiler, president, and Judith Schnell, publisher, of Stackpole Books, a select publisher of American history works, believed I could make a "drop dead" deadline. They were almost right. I missed by a few weeks, and capital punishment was commuted. I am grateful that they had confidence in the manuscript from the start. Stackpole's Amy Lerner has contributed her invaluable wisdom and discipline to the publication schedule. Ryan Masteller provided similar scrutiny and discipline to copy editing the manuscript itself. Tracy Patterson and Wendy Reynolds created the book design. Paul Shaw, Susan Drexler, and Peter Rossi assured that the book got into readers' hands.

Michael Burlingame's detailed knowledge of all things Lincoln has been invaluable to me. As he has done for many contemporary scholars, he has been generous with his own extraordinary research and editing skills, reading my manuscript even as he was completing his monumental multivolume biography of Lincoln. To the reading of the manuscript, others also brought eyes to see and ears to hear. I regret that the tight publication schedule did not permit the reading of the manuscript by other scholars and friends who have discussed the themes of the book with me and who have indirectly inspired it. I am indebted to James Basker, Josiah Bunting, Michael Burlingame, David Brion Davis, David Detweiler, Samuel Freedman, Mark Gerson, Doris Kearns Goodwin, James O. Horton, James M. McPherson, Judith Schnell, and Douglas L. Wilson, who did read it. No one cross-examines me with questions like Louise, John, Thomas, Eliza, and Peter Lehrman—all of whom read parts of the manuscript and encouraged the author. To Lee, John, Thomas, Eliza, and Peter, it is sufficient to say that I wrote the book for them. My gratitude to them abides with our dedication to the Lincoln legacy.

Doris Kearns Goodwin, despite her demanding schedule of travel and scholarship, commented on the substance, the style, and the structure of the entire book. No one who has not worked with Doris can appreciate the effect of her infectious enthusiasm and literary judgment. Professor Douglas Wilson, a scholar of Lincoln and Jefferson, brought to bear his deep learning on essential aspects of the manuscript, even over dinner in Peoria. Columbia University Professor Samuel Freedman, a columnist for the *New York Times*, influenced many sections which needed clarification for the general reader. Professors James Oliver Horton and Lois Horton have been pioneers in the history of American slavery. Jim's scholarship on the links among Lincoln, slavery, and American history is essential for the period. Professor James M. McPherson, the dean of Civil War historians, has been an inspiration on my Lincoln pilgrimage. His incisive comments enabled me to have confidence in the title and arguments of the book. My intellectual debts to James Basker and Josiah Bunting go well beyond this book. Save for the remaining errors, mine alone, these dedicated readers remedied many defects of the early manuscripts.

To the great man himself, Abraham Lincoln, and to my grandfather, Louis, who reminded me each February 12 of the president's birthday, I owe more than I can unselfconsciously say here. So I shall merely implore my children, every American, to study Lincoln, then to gird their loins and to strive toward realizing the principles of the Declaration of Independence.

For Louise, the dedication page tells too short a tale of her inspiration for my work. Like Lincoln, born of East Anglian roots—devoted, tenacious, and principled—Louise exemplifies the conscience and power of the culture which gave rise to early America in New England. Thus I knew that marriage entailed standards to which I would ever try to measure up. Nothing, I think, excels marriage and children.

MILESTONES IN THE LIVES OF ABRAHAM LINCOLN AND STEPHEN A. DOUGLAS

1776 Declaration of Independence approved (July 4).

1781 Articles of Confederation.

1787 Constitutional Convention in Philadelphia (May–September). Northwest Ordinance with slavery prohibition passed by Congress (July 13).

1788 U.S. Constitution ratified.

1807 Importation of slaves prohibited by England to all its territories.

1808 Importation of slaves to United States prohibited by Congress.

1809 Abraham Lincoln born in Hardin County, Kentucky (February 12).

1813 Stephen A. Douglas born in Vermont (April 13).

1816 Lincoln family moved to Indiana.

1818 Lincoln's mother Nancy dies (October 5).

1819 Lincoln's father, Thomas, remarries—to widow Sarah Bush Johnston (December 2).

1820 Congress passes Compromise of 1820 (Missouri Compromise) which admits Maine as a free state and Missouri as a slave state. Slavery is prohibited in the Louisiana Purchase above a line at 36° 30'.

1828 Lincoln's sister Sarah dies during childbirth (January 20).

1830 Lincoln family moves from Indiana to Illinois. Illinois endures "Winter of the Deep Snow" (1830–1831).

1831 Abraham Lincoln, legally independent, settles in New Salem, Illinois.

1832   Lincoln serves in the Black Hawk War, elected captain by his
            militia unit.

            Lincoln is defeated in race for Illinois House of Representatives
            (August 6).

1833   Stephen A. Douglas moves to Illinois, settling in Jacksonville
            (November).

1834   Lincoln wins first of four races for Illinois House of
            Representatives (August 4).

            Lincoln commences preparation to become a lawyer.

            Lincoln meets Stephen A. Douglas at session of state legislature,
            which opens in Vandalia (December 1).

1835   Lincoln's friend Ann Rutledge dies (August 25).

1836   After self-study, Lincoln admitted to the practice of law
            (September 9).

1837   Lincoln moves from New Salem to Springfield; rooms with
            Joshua F. Speed above Speed's general store. He begins legal
            partnership with Kentucky-native John Todd Stuart.

            Lincoln and State Representative Dan Stone introduce
            resolution to protest the antiabolitionist resolution passed by
            the Illinois state legislature. The protest includes the phrase
            "that the institution of slavery is founded on both injustice
            and bad policy" (March 27).

            Lincoln and Sangamon County allies engineer the legislation to
            move the state capital from Vandalia to Springfield (April 15).

            Abolitionist Elijah Lovejoy murdered by mob in Alton, Illinois
            (November 7).

1838   Lincoln delivers Lyceum Speech on "Perpetuation of Our
            Political Institutions" (January 27).

            Lincoln campaigns for Whig John Todd Stuart, who defeats
            Democrat Stephen A. Douglas for Congress.

1839   First railroad line in Illinois completed.

            Illinois state capital shifted from Vandalia to Springfield (July 4).

            Douglas and Lincoln are among sixteen men who send
            invitations to a "cotillion" at American House in Springfield

(December 16). It may be at this event that Lincoln meets Mary Todd of Kentucky, visiting her sisters in Springfield.

Several Whigs, including Lincoln, begin a series of debates on political issues in Springfield with a group of Democrats, including Stephen A. Douglas (December).

1840 Lincoln campaigns for Whig presidential candidate William Henry Harrison, who wins election. Douglas campaigns for Democrat Martin Van Buren.

Douglas is named Illinois Secretary of State.

1841 Lincoln ends engagement with Mary Todd (January 1) and suffers a bout of melancholy.

Lincoln switches legal partners from John Todd Stuart to Stephen T. Logan.

Douglas is named to Illinois Supreme Court—an appointment that leads Lincoln to refer to him as "Judge Douglas" in later speeches.

1842 Lincoln is challenged to duel by future Democratic senator James Shields; conflict is mediated by friends (September 22).

Lincoln reconciles with and marries Mary Todd (November 4).

Douglas is elected to Congress for first of two terms.

1843 First Lincoln son, Robert Todd Lincoln, born (August 1).

1844 Lincoln campaigns in Indiana and Illinois for Whig presidential candidate Henry Clay, who loses election to James K. Polk.

Lincoln begins legal partnership with William H. Herndon, which continues until Lincoln's assassination.

1846 Second Lincoln son, Edward Baker Lincoln, born (March 10).

Lincoln is nominated for Congress (May 1) and elected to Congress over Democrat Peter Cartwright (August 3, 1846).

1846–1848

Mexican-American War, which Lincoln opposes on principle. He supports military expenditures.

1847 Stephen A. Douglas is elected to the U.S. Senate by Illinois Legislature. He marries first wife, Martha Martin.

Work started on first railroad line with a Chicago connection.

1847–1849
> Lincoln serves in Congress. Votes repeatedly for Wilmot Proviso, prohibiting slavery in new territories acquired from Mexico. Meets fellow Whig Alexander H. Stephens, future vice president of the Confederacy.

1848
> Lincoln campaigns for Whig presidential candidate Zachary Taylor, who wins election (November 7). On speaking tour of Massachusetts, Lincoln meets William H. Seward for the first time.
>
> Martha Martin Douglas inherits a 2,500-acre Mississippi plantation—along with 100 slaves—when her father dies. Douglas had rejected the plantation when Martin had offered it as a wedding present.

1849
> Congressman Lincoln announces intention to introduce legislation to end slavery in the District of Columbia (January 10).
>
> First Douglas son Robert is born (January).
>
> Lincoln returns to Springfield and the practice of law.

1850
> Congress passes Compromise of 1850 which admits California as a free state and strengthens the provisions of the Fugitive Slave Act. Slave trade in Washington, D.C., is abolished. Territorial organization of New Mexico and Utah is authorized without any prohibition of slavery. Passage of the Compromise is organized by Senator Stephen A. Douglas.
>
> Illinois Central Railroad gets a land grant from the federal government. Second Lincoln son Eddie dies (February 1).
>
> President Zachary Taylor dies (July 9); he is succeeded by Millard Fillmore, who signs all the parts of the Compromise of 1850 (September).
>
> Second Douglas son Stephen is born (November).
>
> Third Lincoln son William is born (December 21).

1851
> Lincoln's father Thomas dies (January 17).
>
> Illinois Central Railroad chartered by Illinois Legislature. Construction, which lasts almost five years, begins.

1852 *Uncle Tom's Cabin* by Harriet Beecher Stowe is published.

Lincoln delivers eulogy for Henry Clay (July 6).

Lincoln campaigns for Whig presidential candidate Winfield Scott, who loses to Democrat Franklin Pierce (November 2) to whom Stephen Douglas had lost his party's nomination (June 12).

1853 Douglas reelected to the U.S. Senate by Illinois state legislature.

Fourth Lincoln son, Thomas ("Tad"), is born (April 4).

Martha Martin Douglas dies (January 19).

Franklin Pierce inaugurated president (March 4).

A grieving Senator Douglas leaves for a tour of Europe; he returns in October.

First Illinois State Fair held in Springfield (October 1–4).

Congress again begins discussion of territorial legislation for Kansas-Nebraska. (December). Chairman Douglas opens hearings of his Senate Committee on Territories (December 5).

Kansas-Nebraska legislation reintroduced in Senate (December 14).

1854 Senator Douglas reports first version of his own Kansas-Nebraska legislation (January 4).

Senator Archibald Dixon offers amendment to Kansas-Nebraska Act which repeals Missouri Compromise line (January 16).

Senator Douglas and the "F Street Mess" go with Secretary of War Jefferson Davis to visit President Franklin Pierce; they convince him to support effective repeal of the Missouri Compromise slavery restriction (January 22).

Senator Salmon P. Chase and others release "Appeal of Independent Democrats" denouncing Douglas legislation (January 24).

Senator Douglas engineers passage of Kansas-Nebraska Act in the Senate, 37-14 (March 4).

Congressman Alexander H. Stephens engineers passage of Kansas-Nebraska Act in the House of Representatives (May 22).

President Franklin Pierce signs Kansas-Nebraska Act (May 30).

Know-Nothing movement opposed to immigration, which had been growing in the North for a decade, strengthens in Illinois and elsewhere. Calling itself the "Native American Party" prior to 1856 and the "American Party" thereafter, it focused its opposition to Catholic immigrants from Ireland and Germany while also opposing slavery.

Congressman Richard Yates, an antislavery Whig, returns to Springfield, intending to retire (August 9). He is met by Lincoln, who urges him to run again.

In first reported address against Kansas-Nebraska, Lincoln speaks at Winchester (August 26).

Kansas-Nebraska opponents shout down speech by Senator Douglas in Chicago (September 1).

Lincoln debates Kansas-Nebraska Act at Springfield court house with John Calhoun (September 9).

Editorial against Kansas-Nebraska Act, written by Lincoln, appears in *Illinois Journal* (September 11).

Lincoln delivers speech against Kansas-Nebraska at Bloomington (September 12).

Lincoln and Douglas deliver competing speeches in Bloomington (September 26).

Second Illinois State Fair opens in Springfield (early October); it is beset by rain.

Douglas delivers three-hour speech in Springfield at State Capitol (October 3); Lincoln replies the next day in the same chamber of the House of Representatives (October 4) at the same length.

Douglas in the afternoon and Lincoln at night deliver speeches on the courthouse square in Peoria (October 16).

Meeting in Lacon, Lincoln agrees to a request by Douglas not to continue joint appearances on Kansas-Nebraska Act (October 17).

Lincoln elected to state House of Representatives (November 7) along with a majority of anti-Nebraska legislators. After declining election to the legislature, Lincoln begins campaign for U.S. Senate seat held by Democrat James Shields.

Democrat wins special election for state legislative seat to which Lincoln had been elected in November (December 23).

Republican Party begins to form as the Whig Party declines in Illinois and elsewhere.

1854–1858

Agitation and conflict in Kansas over slavery.

1855 Lincoln loses state legislative vote for U.S. Senate; he throws his support to an anti-Nebraska Democrat, Lyman Trumbull, who narrowly wins election.

1856 South Carolina Congressman Preston Brooks severely beats Massachusetts Senator Charles Sumner on the floor of the U.S. Senate (May 22).

At organizing convention in Bloomington for Illinois Republican Party, Lincoln delivers a stirring speech, using themes from 1854. Only brief summary of speech is reported (May 29).

Lincoln loses Republican nomination for Vice President (June 19). John C. Frémont receives Republican presidential nomination.

Douglas supports James Buchanan for Democratic nomination after he realizes he can not win it (June 2–6). Lincoln campaigns for Frémont, who loses to Buchanan (November 4). Know-Nothing movement supports former President Millard Fillmore under the "American Party" label.

Senator Douglas marries second wife, Adele Cutts, grand-niece of Dolley Madison (November 19).

1857 James Buchanan inaugurated President (March 4).

Dred Scott decision delivered by Supreme Court Chief Justice Roger B. Taney (March 6).

Lincoln gives speech against *Dred Scott* decision (June 26).

Lecompton Constitutional Convention in Kansas supports slavery for territory (September). Antislavery residents boycott.

Senator Douglas sells the Mississippi River plantation his sons have inherited and buys another one in Mississippi.

Senator Douglas breaks with Buchanan Administration and
announces he will oppose ratification of the Lecompton
Constitution for Kansas.

First ratification vote on Lecompton Constitution, boycotted by
antislavery Kansans (December 21).

1858 Lecompton Constitution rejected in Kansas referendum in
which antislavery forces participate (January 4).

Buchanan administration terminates hundreds of patronage
appointees loyal to Senator Douglas. Split of the Democratic
Party intensifies.

Adele Cutts Douglas suffers a miscarriage; both she and her
husband fall ill.

Lincoln nominated by Illinois Republicans for U.S. Senate seat
occupied by Senator Stephen A. Douglas; Lincoln delivers
"House Divided" speech (June 16).

Douglas responds to House Divided speech with a speech in
Chicago (July 9).

Lincoln and Douglas deliver campaign speeches in the same
towns; Lincoln challenges Douglas to a series of debates
(July 24).

LeCompton Constitution again rejected in Kansas referendum
(August 2).

First Lincoln-Douglas debate held at Ottawa (August 21).

Second debate held at Freeport (August 27).

Third debate held at Jonesboro (September 15).

Fourth debate held at Charleston (September 18).

Fifth debate held at Galesburg (October 7).

Sixth debate held at Quincy (October 13).

Seventh and final debate held at Alton (October 15).

Republican legislative candidates get more popular votes than
Douglas Democrats (November 2). Douglas is nonetheless
reelected to the Senate, 54-46, by Illinois state legislature.

Fellow Democrats loyal to Buchanan strip Douglas of the
chairmanship of the Senate Committee on Territories.

1859 Lincoln campaigns in Iowa, Ohio, Indiana, Wisconsin, and Kansas—delivering antislavery speeches.

Adele Cutts Douglas gives birth to a daughter, who dies a few weeks later. Both Adele and Stephen Douglas become sick again.

1860 Lincoln delivers Cooper Union address (February 27) and other speeches in New Hampshire, Rhode Island, and Connecticut (February 28–March 10).

Lincoln is nominated for president by Republican National Convention in Chicago (May 18).

Douglas receives the presidential nomination (June 23) of northern Democrats after Democratic Party splits in two. Douglas campaigns vigorously around North and South while Lincoln quietly remains at home in Springfield.

Lincoln is elected president over Democrats Stephen A. Douglas and John Breckinridge and Constitutional Union Party candidate John Bell (November 6).

South Carolina secedes from Union (December 20).

1861 Lincoln leaves Springfield, Illinois, (February 11) for Washington by train. He delivers numerous speeches along the way in Indiana, Ohio, Pennsylvania, New York, and New Jersey. He arrives in Washington (February 23).

Confederate President Jefferson Davis and Vice President Alexander H. Stephens inaugurated (February 18).

Lincoln delivers First Inaugural Address (March 4).

Confederates attack Fort Sumter (April 12). Congress not in session, President Lincoln responds to Fort Sumter with a call for 75,000 volunteers to put down rebellion.

President Lincoln meets with Senator Douglas about attack on Fort Sumter; Douglas publicly supports Lincoln response. Douglas dies (June 3).

Lincoln delivers special message to Congress (July 4) outlining causes of conflict.

Kansas admitted to the Union as a free state.

Union loses first major battle of the Civil War at Bull Run (July 21).

1862   After battling typhoid-like illness, Willie Lincoln dies in White
           House (February 20); brother Tad recovers.

           President Lincoln signs legislation for compensated
           emancipation in District of Columbia (April 16).

           President Lincoln signs legislation overturning the *Dred Scott*
           decision and prohibiting slavery in territories (June 19).

           Preliminary Emancipation Proclamation issued (September 22).

1863   Final Emancipation Proclamation signed by President Lincoln
           (January 1).

           Black Americans recruited for Union army.

           President Lincoln writes public letter to Democratic
           Congressman Erastus Corning explaining his policies
           (June 12).

           Union victories at Gettysburg (July 1–3) and Vicksburg (July 4).

           President Lincoln writes another public letter to Illinois
           Republican James Conkling to be read at Union meeting in
           Springfield (August 27).

           President Lincoln delivers Gettysburg Address (November 19).

           President Lincoln proposes program of reconstruction
           (December 8).

1864   Ulysses S. Grant appointed to command all Union armies
           (March 12).

           President Lincoln is renominated by Union-Republican Party
           (June 8).

           General George B. McClellan receives Democratic nomination
           for president at Chicago (August 27).

           Atlanta is captured by Union General William T. Sherman
           (September 2).

           President Lincoln is reelected over General McClellan
           (November 8).

1865   Congress passes Thirteenth Amendment abolishing slavery
           (January 31) after lobbying of House members by President
           Lincoln.

           Peace conference held with three Confederate commissioners at
           Hampton Roads (February 3).

Lincoln delivers Second Inaugural address (March 4).

Confederate general Robert E. Lee surrenders to Union commander Ulysses S. Grant (April 9).

Lincoln delivers final public address on reconstruction (April 11).

Lincoln is assassinated in Ford's Theatre (April 14) and dies the next day.

Thirteenth Amendment is ratified (December 6).

NOTES

The original orthography of documents is used. Grammatical and spelling mistakes are noted by [sic] only when necessary for the reader. CWAL refers to the *Collected Works of Abraham Lincoln*, Roy P. Basler, editor (New Brunswick, NJ: Rutgers University Press, 1953). *Herndon's Lincoln* is published in many editions. The most recent is edited and thoroughly annotated by Douglas L. Wilson and Rodney O. Davis (Urbana, IL: Knox College Lincoln Studies Center and the University of Illinois Press, 2006).

INTRODUCTION
1. William H. Herndon and Jesse W. Weik, *Herndon's Life of Lincoln*, 264–65.
2. Speech at Peoria, October 16, 1854, in CWAL, Volume II, 276.

CHAPTER I
3. Letter from Robert Todd to Ninian Edwards, March 13, 1844, in James T. Hickey, "Lincolniana: Robert S. Todd Seeks a Job for His Son-in-Law, Abraham Lincoln," *Journal of the Illinois Historical Society*, 1979, 275.
4. It is generally assumed that Lincoln's speech took place in May when Lincoln was in Peoria on legal business, which included a scandalous divorce case that required repeated visits to Peoria during 1844.
5. In November 1837, a Democratic convention met at Peoria. It denounced Congressman May who, it was charged had "disregarded and forfeited the pledges given to his constituents before his election to the office which he now occupied, and that he be respectfully requested to resign his seat in Congress, in consideration of his opposition to the party and principles which elevated him to his present station." Earnest E. East Collection, Abraham Lincoln Presidential Library, Springfield, IL, first published in the Washington *Globe*, December 12, 1837.
6. The debate was supposed to take place in the Peoria County Court House, but the sheriff went home with the keys to the building—forcing the debate to another location.
7. Thoms J. Pickett, *Daily State Journal* of Lincoln, Nebraska, April 12, 1881, in Rufus Rockwell Wilson, ed., *Intimate Memories of Lincoln*, 191. Lincoln's reference to crawling out of the pole had metaphorical political significance because the Whig symbol in this election was the racoon. Democrats pejoratively referred to Whigs as "coons."
8. Ibid., 190–91. There are different recollections of the format. One Peoria resident recalled that May had agreed to the debate only if Lincoln refrained from

making any personal references about May's controversial past and that May got to make concluding remarks.

9. Michael Burlingame, ed., *A Reporter's Lincoln*, 164–65. According to Michael Burlingame, Lincoln repeatedly expressed his contempt during the 1840s and early 1850s toward Whigs who switched to the Democratic Party. See Michael Burlingame, *The Inner World of Abraham Lincoln*, 153–54.

10. Pickett, *Daily State Journal*, in Wilson, *Intimate Memories of Lincoln*, 190–91. Historian Don E. Fehrenbacher had some doubts about the accuracy of Lincoln's quote by Pickett, writing: "It is not clear that Pickett was himself an auditor of this exchange" (Don E. Fehrenbacher and Virginia Fehrenbacher, *Recollected Words of Abraham Lincoln*, 358). However, Pickett was then the editor of the pro-Whig Peoria *Register* and it was not unlikely that he would have been present.

11. Ernest E. East, *Abraham Lincoln Sees Peoria*, 13.

12. James M. McPherson, *This Mighty Scourge: Perspectives on the Civil War*, 202.

13. Herndon and Weik, *Herndon's Life of Lincoln*, 130.

14. Ibid., 84. Milton Hay wrote that "John Calhoun was something of a factor in his political education. Calhoun in his late years from habits of dissipation became a moral and political wreck, a tool merely to aid the iniquities of Douglas and Buchanan in Kansas, but at the period to which I refer he was justly regarded as the strongest man intellectually in the Democratic ranks. He had not the declamatory power of Douglas, but in the clear statement of political issues and logical argument thereon he was greatly his superior, and this was Mr. Lincoln's estimate of the two men. Calhoun was specially strong in those colloquial street corner discussions you have referred to. It was in these colloquial discussions that Calhoun and Lincoln not infrequently engaged. Like Lincoln he could fairly state his opponent's side of the question, and argue with fairness and preserve his temper. His educational qualifications had been better than Mr. Lincoln's, and politics seemed to be his only study. I have never heard the argument so effectively put against a protective tariff as Calhoun could put it. Frequent contact and conflict with such an opponent must have had its educational influence on Mr. Lincoln." Letter from Milton Hay to John Hay, February 8, 1887, in Harry E. Pratt, "Recollections of Lincoln," *Bulletin of the Abraham Lincoln Association*, December 1931, 8.

15. Peoria *Democratic Press*, April 17, 1844, in East, *Abraham Lincoln Sees Peoria*, 7, 8.

16. Jeriah Bonham, *Fifty Years' Recollections with Observations and Reflections on Historical Events Giving Sketches of Eminent Citizens—Their Lives and Public Services*, 158–60.

17. Gerald M. Capers, *Stephen A. Douglas Defender of the Union*, 14.

18. Fragment on Stephen A. Douglas, c. December, 1856, in CWAL, Volume II, 382–83.

19. John G. Nicolay and John Hay, *Abraham Lincoln: A History*, Volume I, 209.

20. Thomas J. McCormack, ed., *Memoirs of Gustave Koerner, 1809–1896: Life-Sketches Written at the Suggestion of His Children*, 591.

21. Isaac N. Arnold, *The History of Abraham Lincoln, and the Overthrow of Slavery*, 51.

22. Woodrow Wilson, *A History of the American People*, Volume IV, 165–66.

23. Benjamin Thomas, *Abraham Lincoln*, 138. See Robert Johannsen, *Lincoln, Slavery and the South*, 27–35.

24. William O. Stoddard: *Abraham Lincoln: The True Story of a Great Life*, 136.

25. Allan Nevins and Irving Stone, eds., *Lincoln: A Contemporary Portrait*, 13.

26. Letter from Carl Schurz to Henry Meyer, November 20, 1856, in Carl Schurz, *Intimate Letters of Carl Schurz, 1841 to 1869*, 174.

27. Letter from Abraham Lincoln to John M. Brockman, September 25, 1860, in CWAL, Volume IV, 121.

28. Allan Nevins, *The Emergence of Lincoln*, Volume I, 360.

29. Benjamin Thomas, *"Lincoln's Humor" and Other Essays*, Michael Burlingame, ed., 146.

30. E. L. Kimball, "Richard Yates: His Record as Civil War Governor of Illinois," *Journal of the Illinois State Historical Society*, April 1930, 3.

31. Henry Wilson, *History of the Rise and Fall of the Slave Power*, Volume II, 396.

32. James Miner, in Wilson, *Intimate Memories of Lincoln*, 166, 165.

33. Speech at Winchester, August 26, 1854, in CWAL, Volume II, 227.

34. James Miner in Wilson, *Intimate Memories of Lincoln*, 166.

35. Herndon and Weik, *Herndon's Life of Lincoln*, 226.

36. Frederick Trevor Hill, *Lincoln as Lawyer*, 264.

37. T. Lyle Dickey, quoted in the Bloomington *Pantagraph*, February 12, 1927, in Carl Sandburg, *Abraham Lincoln: The Prairie Years*, 24.

38. "Autobiography" sent to Jesse W. Fell, December 20, 1859, in CWAL, Volume. III, 512.

39. Sunderine Temple and Wayne Temple, *Abraham Lincoln and Illinois' Fifth Capitol*, 56–58.

40. Paul M. Angle and Earl Schenck Miers, *The Living Lincoln*, 158.

41. Nicolay and Hay, *Abraham Lincoln: A History*, Volume I, 203.

42. Herndon and Weik, *Herndon's Life of Lincoln*, 226.

43. Fragment on Slavery, circa July 1854 (exact date uncertain), in CWAL, Volume II, 222–23.

44. Letter to Richard J. Oglesby, September 8, 1854, in CWAL, First Supplement, 24.

45. Burlingame, *The Inner World of Abraham Lincoln*, 30.

46. Richard Yates, "Speech of Richard Yates," delivered in the Wigwam at the Springfield Jubilee, November 20, 1860, quoted in the *Illinois State Journal*, November 22, 1860, 3.

47. Michael F. Holt, *The Rise and Fall of the American Whig Party: Jacksonian Politics and the Onset of the Civil War*, 830.

48. Letter from Stephen Douglas to Charles H. Lanphier, December 18, 1854, in Robert W. Johannsen, ed., *The Letters of Stephen A. Douglas*, 331.

49. Albert J Beveridge wrote: "The *Illinois Journal* [September 14, 1854] charged that Major Thomas L. Harris, the Democratic candidate for Congress in Springfield district, had said that he would vote to admit Utah with polygamy, because every State and Territory must decide domestic questions for itself." Albert J. Beveridge, *Abraham Lincoln, 1809–1858*, Volume II, 236.

50. Letter from Abraham Lincoln to Richard Yates, August 18, 1854, in CWAL, Volume II, 226.

51. William H. Herndon interview with William Jayne, August 15, 1866, in Douglas L. Wilson and Rodney O. Davis, eds., *Herndon's Informants*, 266. Although its name changed several times during the 1840s and 1850s, the *Sangamon Journal* was always known as "the *Journal*."

52. David Herbert Donald, *Lincoln*, 172.

53. Richard J. Carwardine, *Lincoln*, 58.

54. George Thomas Palmer, *A Conscientious Turncoat: The Story of John M. Palmer, 1817–1900*, 29, 28.

55. John M. Palmer, *Personal Recollections of John M. Palmer: The Story of an Earnest Life*, 63.

56. Letter from Abraham Lincoln to John M. Palmer, September 7, 1854, in CWAL, Volume II, 228–29.

57. McCormack, *Memoirs of Gustave Koerner*, 625.

58. Allen C. Guelzo, *Abraham Lincoln, Redeemer President*, 185.

59. Gerald M. Capers, *Stephen A. Douglas: Defender of the Union*, 121.

60. John Senning, "The Know-Nothing Movement in Illinois," Illinois *State Register*, August 16, 1854, quoted in *The Journal of the Illinois State Historical Society*, April 1914.

61. Letter from Stephen A. Douglas to Twenty-five Chicago Clergymen, April 6, 1854, in Johannsen, *The Letters of Stephen A. Douglas*, 310.

62. Letter from Stephen A. Douglas to Charles H. Lanphier, August 25, 1854, in Ibid., 329.

63. Capers, *Stephen A. Douglas*, 120; Thomas, *Abraham Lincoln*, 147.

64. Nicolay and Hay, *Abraham Lincoln: A History*, Volume I, 205.

65. Sandburg, *Abraham Lincoln: The Prairie Years*, Volume II, 9.

66. Nicolay and Hay, *Abraham Lincoln: A History*, Volume I, 205–6.

67. Sandburg, *Abraham Lincoln: The Prairie Years*, Volume II, 9.

68. *Free West*, September 7, 1854, quoted in Arthur Charles Cole, *The Era of the Civil War*, 132.

69. Horace White, "Abraham Lincoln in 1854," *Illinois State Historical Society*, January 1908, 8–9.

70. Nicolay and Hay, *Abraham Lincoln: A History*, Volume I, 205–6.

71. Capers, *Stephen A. Douglas*, 120. Historian Granville D. Davis disputed this account of Douglas's actions prepared by his father-in-law, James Madison Cutts: "Ample evidence exists to indicate that this is merely another fabrication of the unreliable Brief Treatise [upon Constitutional and Party Questions written by Cutts]." He notes that according to press accounts, Douglas stopped talking by 10:30 P.M. and that Cutts had the day of the week wrong; the meeting was on Friday, not Saturday. See Granville D. Davis, "Douglas and the Chicago Mob," *The American Historical Review*, April 1949, 553–56.

72. Nicolay and Hay, *Abraham Lincoln: A History*, Volume I, 205–6.

73. Letter from Stephen Douglas to John C. Breckinridge, September 14, 1854, in Johannsen, *The Letters of Stephen A. Douglas*, 329.

74. Ibid., 457.

75. Allen Johnson, *Stephen A. Douglas*, 265.

76. Cole, *The Era of the Civil War, 1848–1870*, 132.

77. Beveridge, *Abraham Lincoln, 1809–1858*, Volume II, 235. Beveridge wrote: "Douglas's campaign speech, as finally perfected, was made in Chicago, Nov. 9, 1854, and appears in full in the Weekly *National Intelligencer*, Dec. 2, 1854. In this speech he also attacked the Republican Party, then forming, as purely sectional."

78. Letter from Stephen Douglas to James Washington Sheahan, September 14, 1854, in Johannsen, *The Letters of Stephen A. Douglas*, 330.

79. George Fort Milton, *The Eve of Conflict: Stephen A. Douglas and the Needless War*, 185.

80. Nicolay and Hay, *Abraham Lincoln: A History*, Volume I, 373.
81. Calhoun would be appointed surveyor-general of the Kansas-Nebraska territory by President Buchanan in 1854. Calhoun played a prominent role in Kansas government and politics over the next four years, earning him the nickname "Candlestick."
82. Herndon and Weik, *Herndon's Life of Lincoln*, 84.
83. Robert H. Browne, *Abraham Lincoln and Men of his Time*, Volume I, 520.
84. Nicolay and Hay, *Abraham Lincoln: A History*, Volume I, 207.
85. Douglas L. Wilson, "The Unfinished Text of the Lincoln-Douglas Debates," *Journal of the Abraham Lincoln Association*, Winter 1994, Volume 15, No. 1, 73.
86. David C. Mearns, ed., *The Lincoln Papers*, 187.
87. Sherman D. Wakefield, *How Lincoln Became President*, 42–49, 165–73.
88. Editorial on the Kansas-Nebraska Act, *Illinois Journal*, September 11, 1854, in CWAL, Volume II, 230.
89. The Compromise of 1850 was more pro-slavery than it may have appeared. James M. McPherson noted that "the territories of Utah and New Mexico (which also included the future states of Nevada and Arizona) legalized slavery in 1852 and 1859 respectively, that slaveholding setters in California made strenuous and partly successful efforts to infiltrate bondage into that state, and that California's representatives and senators voted mainly with the proslavery South in the 1850s." James M. McPherson, "The Fight for Slavery in California," *New York Review of Books*, October 11, 2007, 13.
90. Speech at Bloomington, Illinois, September 12, 1854, in CWAL, Volume II, 232–33.
91. Bloomington *Weekly Pantagraph*, September 20, 1854, quoted in Sherman D. Wakefield, *How Lincoln Became President*, 41. See Paul M. Angle, ed., *New Letters and Papers of Lincoln*, 133–37.
92. James S. Ewing, speech to the Illinois Schoolmasters' Club, Bloomington, February 12, 1909, quoted in Paul M. Angle, ed., *Abraham Lincoln by Some Men Who Knew Him*, 40–41.
93. Lawrence Weldon, quoted in Allen Thorndike Rice, ed., *Reminiscences of Abraham Lincoln*, 199.
94. Jesse W. Fell, quoted in O. H. Oldroyd, ed. *The Lincoln Memorial: Album Immortelles*, 470–71.
95. Statement of James T. Ewing, quoted in Beveridge, *Abraham Lincoln, 1809–1858*, Volume I, 242.
96. Lawrence Weldon, quoted in Allen Thorndike Rice, ed., *Reminiscences of Abraham Lincoln*, 198–99.
97. Speech at Bloomington, Illinois, September 26, 1854, in the Peoria *Weekly Republican*, October 6, 1854, quoted in CWAL, Volume II, 239–40.
98. Harry E. Pratt, "Abraham Lincoln in Bloomington, Illinois," *Journal of the Illinois State Historical Association*, Volume XXIX, No. 1, April 1936, 53.
99. Walter B. Stevens, (edited by Michael Burlingame), *A Reporter's Lincoln*, 63. (James S. Ewing).
100. Bloomington *Weekly Pantagraph*, September 29, 1854, in Pratt, "Abraham Lincoln in Bloomington, Illinois," 53.
101. Autobiography written for John L. Scripps, ca. June, 1860, in CWAL, Volume IV, 67.
102. Nicolay and Hay, *Abraham Lincoln: A History*, Volume I, 204.

103. Letter from Stephen A. Douglas to Charles Lanphier, February 13, 1854, in Cole, *The Era of the Civil War*, 121.
104. Protest in Illinois Legislature on Slavery, March 3, 1837, in CWAL, Volume I, 75.
105. Beveridge, *Abraham Lincoln, 1809–1858*, Volume II, 238.
106. Letter from Joseph Gillespie to William H. Herndon, December 8, 1866, in Wilson and Davis, *Herndon's Informants*, 507.
107. Although the fragment has been dated as ca. July 1, 1854, its actual date is subject to dispute and may have been written later, perhaps in 1858 or 1859. CWAL, Volume II, 222.
108. Letter from Samuel C. Parks to William H. Herndon, March 25, 1866, in Wilson and Davis, *Herndon's Informants*, 239.

CHAPTER II

109. Clark Ezra Carr, *The Illini: A Story of the Prairies*, 192.
110. Sandburg, *Abraham Lincoln: The Prairie Years*, Volume II, 11. Sandburg used many contemporary sources, but often embellished them with his own imagination.
111. James G. Randall, *Lincoln the President: Springfield to Gettysburg*, Volume I, 104.
112. Sandburg, *Abraham Lincoln: The Prairie Years*, Volume II, 6.
113. John Locke Scripps, *Life of Abraham Lincoln*, 49.
114. Nicolay and Hay, *Abraham Lincoln: A History*, Volume I, 208.
115. Sunderine Temple and Wayne C. Temple speculated: "While Lincoln definitely talked in the Hall of the House on October 4, it is probable that Douglas had stood on the landing of the double-flighted stairs the previous day. Otherwise, nearly 20,000 people could not have heard him." *Abraham Lincoln and Illinois' Fifth Capitol*, 200.
116. Johannsen, *Stephen A. Douglas*, 457.
117. Noah Brooks, *Abraham Lincoln: His Youth and Early Manhood*, 94.
118. Horace White, "Abraham Lincoln in 1854," *Transactions of the Illinois State Historical Society*, 1908, 31.
119. Nicolay and Hay, *Abraham Lincoln: A History*, Volume I, 210.
120. Based on a memorandum from Samuel S. Gilbert. George Fort Milton, *The Eve of Conflict: Stephen A. Douglas and the Needless War*, 184.
121. Angle, *Abraham Lincoln by Some Men Who Knew Him*, 103–4.
122. White, "Abraham Lincoln in 1854," 33. White wrote that "Mr. Lincoln did not use a scrap of paper" at either Springfield or Peoria. We know the substance of his speech from the newspaper reports and from Lincoln's printed text of his Peoria speech on October 16.
123. Milton, *The Eve of Conflict*, 180.
124. Horace White, New York *Evening Post*, February 12, 1909, in Wilson, *Lincoln Among His Friends*, 170. In White's recollections of Lincoln's speeches, he often urges the very same metaphors and analogies Lincoln deployed against Douglas.
125. White, "Abraham Lincoln in 1854," Address before Illinois State Historical Society, January 1908, 10.
126. Herndon and Weik, *Herndon's Life of Lincoln*, 333. See Donald, *Lincoln*, 249.
127. Horace White, "Abraham Lincoln in 1854," Address before Illinois State Historical Society, January 1908, 10.

128. Herndon and Weik, *Herndon's Life of Lincoln*, 248–49.
129. *Illinois State Journal*, October 5, 1854, in CWAL, Volume II, 247.
130. Illinois State *Register*, October 6, 1854, in Herbert Mitgang, ed., *Lincoln as They Saw Him*, 71–72.
131. Noah Brooks, *Abraham Lincoln and the Downfall of American Slavery*, 137–38.
132. *Illinois State Journal*, October 5, 1854, in Mitgang, *Lincoln as They Saw Him*, 71.
133. Stoddard, *Abraham Lincoln: The True Story of a Great Life*, 137.
134. Illinois State *Register*, October 6, 1854, in Mitgang, *Lincoln as They Saw Him*, 72.
135. Illinois *State Journal*, October 5, 1854, in Edwin L. Sparks, ed., *The Lincoln-Douglas Debates of 1858*, 13.
136. Isaac N. Arnold, *The Life of Abraham Lincoln*, 118.
137. Beveridge, *Abraham Lincoln, 1809–1858*, Volume II, 262.
138. Milton, *The Eve of Conflict*, 182.
139. Horace White, New York *Evening Post*, February 12, 1909, in Wilson, ed., *Lincoln Among His Friends*, 170.
140. Nicolay and Hay, *Abraham Lincoln: A History*, Volume I, 379–80.
141. Letter from Benjamin F. Irwin to William H. Herndon, February 8, 1866, in Douglas L. Wilson and Rodney O. Davis, eds., *Herndon's Informants*, 198.
142. David McCullough, ed., *Historical Encyclopedia of Illinois and History of Peoria County*, 149.
143. Nicolay and Hay, *Abraham Lincoln: A History*, Volume I, 208.
144. *Illinois State Register*, October 12, 1854, in Mark M. Krug, *Lyman Trumbull: Conservative Radical*, 89.
145. Charles A. Church, *History of the Republican Party in Illinois, 1854–1912*, 20–21.
146. Herndon and Weik, *Herndon's Life of Lincoln*, 229. Historian Don E. Fehrenbacher doubted Herndon's story: "Lincoln declined to become involved in the movement, however, and it soon fell apart. This is about the substance of this well-known incident, but some colorful embellishments were added by William H. Herndon, whose retentive memory yielded at times to his lively imagination." Fehrenbacher, *Prelude to Greatness: Lincoln in the 1850s*, 35. David H. Donald wrote that Herndon's story "is open to grave suspicion. There is absolutely no evidence to link Herndon with the Republican radicals at this time. The newspaper reports of the abolitionist convention make no mention of Herndon." David H. Donald, *Lincoln's Herndon*, 77.
147. Edgar Lee Masters, *Lincoln the Man*, 216.
148. Herndon and Weik, *Herndon's Life of Lincoln*, 229.
149. Debate at Ottawa, Illinois, August 21, 1858, in CWAL, Volume III, 13.
150. William Gienapp, *Origins of the Republican Party, 1852–1856*, 123.
151. Paul Selby, "Genesis of the Republican Party in Illinois," *Transactions of the Illinois State Historical Society for the Year 1906*, 277.
152. Selby, "Genesis of the Republican Party in Illinois," 277, 280.
153. Letter from Abraham Lincoln to Ichabod Codding, November 27, 1854, in CWAL, Volume II, 288.
154. Debate at Ottawa, Illinois, August 21, 1858, in CWAL, Volume III, 13.
155. Beveridge, *Abraham Lincoln, 1809–1858*, Volume II, 266.
156. Peoria *Gazetteer* reported in the Earnest E. East Collection, Abraham Presidential Library and Museum.
157. Byron C. Bryner, *Abraham Lincoln in Peoria, Illinois*, 18.
158. Peoria *Republican*, October 19, 1854, in ibid., 27–28.

159. McCullough, *Historical Encyclopedia of Illinois*, 147.
160. Peoria *Republican*, October 19, 1854, in Bryner, *Abraham Lincoln in Peoria, Illinois*, 28.
161. Letter from Benjamin F. Irwin to William H. Herndon, February 14, 1866, in Wilson and Davis, *Herndon's Informants*, 199.
162. Letter from Abner Y. Ellis to William H. Herndon, ca. January 1866, in ibid., 161.
163. Four years later during the 1858 Senate campaign, both Lincoln and Douglas stayed at this hotel on separate visits—both staying in Room 16. Peoria *Daily Transcript*, September 1, 1874, Earnest E. East Collection, Abraham Lincoln Presidential Library, Springfield, Illinois.
164. Bryner, *Abraham Lincoln in Peoria, Illinois*, 31–32.
165. Letter from Abner Y. Ellis to William H. Herndon, ca. January 1866, in Wilson and Davis, *Herndon's Informants*, 162.
166. Letter from Elihi N. Powell to William H. Herndon, February 10, 1866, in ibid., 199–200.
167. James M. Rice, *History of Peoria County*, Volume I, 113
168. McCullough, *Historical Encyclopedia of Illinois*, 300.
169. William H. Pierce Papers, April 25, 1915, Manuscript Division, Library of Congress, unprocessed collection.
170. Bryner, *Abraham Lincoln in Peoria, Illinois*, 86.
171. Peoria *Daily Union*, October 21, 1854, in ibid., *Abraham Lincoln in Peoria, Illinois*, 143–44.
172. Rice, *History of Peoria County*, Volume I, 369.
173. Illinois *Journal*, October 21, 1854, in CWAL, Volume II, 247.
174. Speech at Peoria, October 16, 1854, in CWAL, Volume II, 248.
175. Rice, *History of Peoria County*, Volume I, 369.
176. McCullough, *Historical Encyclopedia of Illinois*, 148.
177. Rice, *History of Peoria County*, Volume I, 369.
178. The Peoria Gas-Light and Coke Company had been authorized by the Illinois State Legislature in January 1853. According to local historian Charles Ballance, "Soon afterward, a company was organized in pursuance to that charter. They commenced supplying the central parts of the city first, and, as they progressed in laying down the gaspipes, they superseded all other kinds of light. . . ." (Charles Ballance, *The History of Peoria, Illinois*, 153.) Another later historian, Ernest E. East, wrote: "Manufactured gas was introduced for street lighting in 1856." (Ernest E. East, "History of Peoria," 5.)
179. Bryner, *Abraham Lincoln in Peoria, Illinois*, 33–34.
180. Speech at Peoria, October 16, 1854, in CWAL, Volume II, 266.
181. William H. Pierce Papers, April 25, 1915, Manuscript Division, Library of Congress, unprocessed collection.
182. Ibid.
183. Stoddard, *Abraham Lincoln: The True Story of a Great Life*, 139.
184. Letter from Elihu N. Powell to William H. Herndon, February 10, 1866, in Wilson and Davis, *Herndon's Informants*, 200.
185. Speech at Peoria, October 16, 1854, in CWAL, Volume II, 248. In 1866, William H. Herndon wrote Lincoln biographer Josiah G. Holland, a Massachusetts journalist and writer, that after the Peoria debate: "Mr. Lincoln was here writing out his Speech some [week] or more after the Peoria debate. This I Know,

because I assisted him to gather facts. The Speech is published in the weekly Journal—Octo 21 & 29th concluded." Letter from William H. Herndon to Josiah G. Holland, February 24, 1866, in Allen C. Guelzo, "Holland's Informants: The Construction of Josiah Holland's 'Life of Abraham Lincoln,'" *Journal of the Abraham Lincoln Association*, Winter 2002, 49.

186. Rice, *History of Peoria County*, Volume I, 369.
187. McCullough, *Historical Encyclopedia of Illinois*, 147.
188. Ernest E. East, "The 'Peoria Truce' Did Douglas Ask for Quarter?" Peoria *Republican*, October 20, 1854, in *Journal of the Illinois State Historical Association*, Volume XXIX, No. 1, April 1936, 71.
189. Letter from Benjamin F. Irwin to William H. Herndon, February 14, 1866, in Wilson and Davis, *Herndon's Informants*, 211. Another version stated that William Herndon, P. L. Harrison, and Isaac Cogdale were present in Lincoln's law office when he discussed what transpired at Lacon. (Ward Hill Lamon, *The Life of Abraham Lincoln*, 358).
190. Bryner, *Abraham Lincoln in Peoria, Illinois*, 34.
191. Wilson and Davis, *Herndon's Informants*, 200 (Letter from Elihu N. Powell to William H. Herndon, February 10, 1866).
192. East, "The 'Peoria Truce' Did Douglas Ask for Quarter?" 72.
193. Scripps, *Life of Abraham Lincoln*, 51.
194. Beveridge, *Abraham Lincoln, 1809–1858*, Volume II, 271.
195. Letter from John H. Bryant to Robert Boal, March 15, 1866, in Wilson and Davis, *Herndon's Informants*, 232.
196. Herndon and Weik, *Herndon's Life of Lincoln*, 230.
197. Ibid. In 1866, William H. Herndon published a broadside on the "Peoria Debates." Herndon recalled that Lincoln "good-naturedly" told friends after the Lacon accord: "Senator Douglas flattered me into the arrangement, and you must not blame me." Herndon incorrectly maintained that Lincoln did not speak after this accord. (Facsimile printed by H. E. Barker in 1917, courtesy of Douglas L. Wilson.)
198. Paul M. Angle, editor, Henry Clay Whitney, *Life on the Circuit with Abraham Lincoln*, 24.
199. Johannsen, *Stephen A. Douglas*, 458.
200. East, "The 'Peoria Truce': Did Douglas Ask for Quarter?" 73. Although Stephen Douglas did not debate Frederick Douglass on this occasion, it did not stop the Illinois senator in the 1858 Senate campaign from trying to tie the black abolitionist to Lincoln in order to stir up racist reactions. See James Oakes, *The Radical and the Republican, Frederick Douglas, Abraham Lincoln and the Triumph of Antislavery*, xiv.
201. Johannsen, *Stephen A. Douglas*, 458.
202. Letter from Richard L. Wilson to Abraham Lincoln, October 20, 1854, in David C. Mearns, ed., *The Lincoln Papers*, 189.
203. Chicago *Times*, October 20, 1854, in Paul M. Angle, "The Peoria Truce," *Journal of the Illinois State Historical Association*, January 1929, Volume XXI, No. 4, 503.
204. Henry Clay Whitney, *Life on the Circuit with Abraham Lincoln*, 53.
205. Ibid., 210–11.
206. Ibid., 230.
207. Paul M. Angle, editor, Henry Clay Whitney, *Life on the Circuit with Abraham Lincoln*, 24. Whitney's reputation as an observer is sullied in the opinion of Lin-

coln biographers and historians because years after the fact Whitney fabricated his own version of Lincoln's "Lost Speech" at the 1856 Republican state convention in Bloomington.

208. Whitney, *Life on the Circuit with Abraham Lincoln*, 230.
209. Letter from Abraham Jonas to Abraham Lincoln, September 16, 1854, in Mearns, *The Lincoln Papers*, 188. Letter from Richard L. Wilson to Abraham Lincoln, October 20, 1854, in Abraham Lincoln Papers at the Library of Congress, transcribed and annotated by the Lincoln Studies Center, Knox College, Galesburg, Illinois.
210. Letter from Horace White to Abraham Lincoln, October 25, in ibid.
211. Allan G. Bogue, *The Earnest Men: Republicans of the Civil War Senate*, 41.
212. Leonard Wells Volk, *Century Magazine*, December 1881, in Wilson, *Intimate Memories of Lincoln*, 243.
213. Letter from Abraham Lincoln to Richard Yates, October 30, 1854, in CWAL, Volume II, 284.
214. Speech at Quincy, Illinois, November 1, 1854, Quincy Whig, November 3, 1854, in CWAL, Volume II, 285.
215. Theodore Calvin Pease, ed., *The Diary of Orville H. Browning* Volume I, 160 (November 1, 1854).
216. In 1860, Lincoln recalled his Quincy visit in a letter to Jonas: "It was in 1854 when I spoke in some Hall there, and after the speaking, you, with others, took me to an oyster saloon, passed an hour there, and you walked with me to, and parted with me at the Quincy House, quite late at night. I left by stage for Naples before day-light in the morning, having come in by the same route, after dark, the evening previous to the speaking, when I found you waiting at the Quincy House to meet me. . . ." He went on to recall that it was this visit that led to a charge circulated by Congressman William A. Richardson that Lincoln had attended a Know-Nothing lodge in Quincy. Lincoln wanted to refute the allegation but without his personal involvement. Letter from Abraham Lincoln to Abraham Jonas, July 21, 1860, in CWAL, Volume IV, 85–86.
217. Speech at Chicago, October 27, 1854, Chicago *Daily Journal*, October 30, 1854, in CWAL, Volume II, 283.
218. *Chicago Daily Journal* October 30, 1854, in William E. Baringer, ed. *Lincoln Day by Day: A Chronology*, Volume II, 130.
219. Chicago *Journal*, reprinted in the *Illinois State Journal*, November 3, 1854, in Beveridge, *Abraham Lincoln, 1809–1858*, Volume II, 272.
220. Southern legislators began to use "peculiar institution" as a euphemism for slavery in the early nineteenth century.
221. Speech at Quincy, Illinois, November 1, 1854, Quincy *Whig*, November 3, 1854, in CWAL, Volume II, 286.

CHAPTER III
222. First Annual Message to Congress, December 5, 1853, in James D. Richardson, ed., *A Compilation of the Messages and Papers of the Presidents, 1789–1908*, Volume V, 222.
223. Inaugural Message, March 4, 1853, in ibid., 202.
224. Glyndon Van Deusen, *Horace Greeley: Nineteenth-Century Crusader*, 178.
225. Walter A. McDougall, *Freedom Just Around the Corner: A New American History, 1585–1828*, 453–54. See Woodrow Wilson, *A History of the American People*, Volume IV, 168.

226.   For a brief summary of the "Natural Limits thesis" see James M. McPherson, "The Fight for Slavery in California," *New York Review of Books*, October 2007, 13.

227.   Robert W. Fogel and Stanley L. Engerman, *Time on the Cross: The Economics of American Negro Slavery*, 4–6.

228.   Roy F. Nichols, *Blueprints for Leviathan: American Style*, 95; Eric Foner, *Politics and Ideology in the Age of the Civil War*, 45.

229.   Nichols, *Blueprints for Leviathan*, 93.

230.   William Earl Parrish, *David Rice Atchison of Missouri, Border Politician*, 143.

231.   Cole, *The Era of the Civil War*, 114.

232.   McCormack, *Memoirs of Gustave Koerner, 1809-1896: Life-sketches written at the Suggestion of His Children*, Volume I, 616.

233.   Don E. Fehrenbacher, *The Slaveholding Republic: An Account of the United States Government's Relations to Slavery*, completed and edited by Ward M. McAfee, 273.

234.   Roy F. Nichols and Eugene H. Berwanger, *The Stakes of Power, 1845–1877*, 49–50.

235.   Ludwell H. Johnson, *Division and Reunion: America 1848–1877*, 31–32.

236.   William J. Cooper Jr., *Jefferson Davis, American*, 246.

237.   Johannsen, *The Frontier, the Union and Stephen A. Douglas*, 91–92.

238.   John Niven *The Coming of the Civil War, 1837–1861*, 77–78.

239.   Louis Filler, *The Crusade Against Slavery, 1830–1860*, 272.

240.   Henry H. Simms, *A Decade of Sectional Controversy, 1851–1861*, 58.

241.   *Illinois State Journal*, January 15, 1854.

242.   Horace White, *The Life of Lyman Trumbull*, 36–37.

243.   P. Orman Ray, for example, argued that conflict between Missouri political rivals David Rice Atchison and Thomas Hart Benton was the proximate cause of the repeal of the Missouri Compromise. Both Atchison and Benton were maneuvering for political advantage and sought to develop positions on Kansas-Nebraska that would hurt the other. Atchison's position in the Senate gave him decisive leverage there. Biographer William E. Parrish noted that "many in the South looked to Atchison for leadership" on Kansas-Nebraska legislation. The pugnacious Missourian indeed provided some. See William Earl Parrish, *David Rice Atchison of Missouri, Border Politician*, 141.

244.   Elbert B. Smith, *The Death of Slavery: The United States, 1837–65*, 126–27.

245.   To extinguish Indian titles in the Kansas-Nebraska territory was necessary in order to transfer clear titles to new owners.

246.   David M. Potter, *The Impending Crisis*, 171.

247.   Johannsen, *The Frontier, the Union and Stephen A. Douglas*, 98.

248.   Albert Bushnell Hart, ed., *Documents Relating to the Kansas-Nebraska Act, 1854*, 2–3.

249.   Potter, *The Impending Crisis*, 158.

250.   James Schouler, *History of the United States of America, Under the Constitution*, Volume V 1847–1861, 280.

251.   John Niven, *The Coming of the Civil War, 1837–1861*, 80.

252.   James A. Rawley, *Secession: The Disruption of the American Republic, 1844–1861*, 60.

253.   Perley Orman Ray, *The Repeal of the Missouri Compromise, its Origin and Authorship*, 217.

254.   Gerald W. Wolf, *The Kansas-Nebraska Bill: Party, Section, and the Coming of the Civil War*, 164.

255.   Niven, *The Coming of the Civil War*, 81.

256.   Jefferson Davis, *The Rise and Fall of the Confederate Government*, Volume I, 28.

257. William C. Davis, *Jefferson Davis: The Man and His Hour*, 248.
258. Henry Wilson, *History of the Rise and Fall of the Slave Power*, Volume II, 384.
259. John Niven, *Salmon P. Chase: a Biography*, 149.
260. Frederick J. Blue, *Salmon P. Chase: A Life in Politics*, 94.
261. Richard H. Sewell, *Ballots for Freedom*, 255–56.
262. Albert Bushnell Hart, *Salmon P. Chase*, 139–40.
263. Theodore Clarke Smith, *Parties and Slavery, 1850–1859*, 100–101.
264. Hart, *Salmon P. Chase*, 142.
265. David Donald, *Charles Sumner and the Coming of the Civil War*, 253.
266. Niven, *Salmon P. Chase: a Biography*, 150–51.
267. Fehrenbacher, *The Dred Scott Case*, 186.
268. Smith, *Parties and Slavery, 1850–1859*, 100–101.
269. Nicolay and Hay, *Abraham Lincoln: A History*, Volume I, 335. See Niven, *Salmon P. Chase*, 151.
270. Speech by Salmon P. Chase, "Maintain Plighted Faith," February 3, 1854, in *The Nebraska Question: Comprising Speeches in the U.S. Senate by Mr. Douglas, Mr. Chase, Mr. Smith, Mr. Everett, Mr. Wade, Mr. Seward Mr. Badger, and Mr. Sumner Together with a History of the Missouri Compromise*, 60.
271. Henry Wilson, *History of the Rise and Fall of the Slave Power*, Volume II, 386.
272. William Lee Miller. *Lincoln's Virtues, An Ethical Biography*, 246.
273. Speech of Charles Sumner, February 21, 1854, in *The Nebraska Question*, 117.
274. Frederick J. Blue, *Charles Sumner and the Conscience of the North*, 78–79.
275. Blue, *Salmon P. Chase*, 95.
276. Wilson, *History of the Rise and Fall of the Slave Power*, Volume II, 393.
277. Letter from Stephen A. Douglas to the editor of the Concord *State Capitol Reporter*, February 16, 1854, in Johannsen, *The Letters of Stephen A. Douglas*, 288.
278. William Garrott Brown, *Stephen Arnold Douglas*, 91. See Johannsen, *Stephen A. Douglas*, 439.
279. Letter from Abraham Lincoln to Joshua F. Speed, August 24, 1855, in CWAL, Volume II, 320–23. See John L. Myers, *Henry Wilson and the Coming of the Civil War*, 234.
280. Sewell, *Ballots for Freedom*, 261–62.
281. Van Deusen, *Horace Greeley*, 179, 180.
282. Michael F. Holt, *Political Parties and American Political Development: from the Age of Jackson to the Age of Lincoln*, 812.
283. Donald, *Charles Sumner and the Coming of the Civil War*, 258.
284. Wilson, *History of the Rise and Fall of the Slave Power*, Volume II, 388–389.
285. Glyndon Van Deusen, *William Henry Seward*, 153.
286. Letter from Stephen A. Douglas to Ninian W. Edwards, April 13, 1854, in Johannsen, *The Letters of Stephen A. Douglas*, 322.
287. Arthur Charles Cole, *The Era of the Civil War, 1848–1870*, 123.
288. Smith, *The Death of Slavery*, 139.
289. Robert R. Russell, "The Issues in the Congressional Struggle over the Kansas-Nebraska Bill, 1854," *The Journal of Southern History*, May 1963, 200.
290. Letter from Stephen A. Douglas to Howell Cobb, April 2, 1854, in Johannsen, *The Letters of Stephen A. Douglas*, 300.
291. Smith, *The Death of Slavery*, 129.
292. Arnold, *The History of Abraham Lincoln*, 55–56.

293. Johannsen, *Stephen A. Douglas*, 424. See Nichols, *Blueprints for Leviathan*, 100; Larry Gara, *The Presidency of Franklin Pierce*, 94.
294. Roy F. Nichols, *Franklin Pierce: Young Hickory of the Granite Hills*, 334.
295. Hart, *Salmon P. Chase*, 145.
296. John M. Taylor, *William Henry Seward*, 94.
297. Johnson, *Stephen A. Douglas*, 250–51.
298. Cole, *The Era of the Civil War*, 117–18.
299. Johnson, *Stephen A. Douglas*, 251–52.
300. Van Deusen, *William Henry Seward*, 153.
301. Nichols, *Blueprints for Leviathan*, 94–95.
302. Arnold, *The History of Abraham Lincoln*, 57.
303. Ibid., 62.
304. Emil Ludwig, *Lincoln*, 464.
305. Rudolph Von Abele, *Alexander H. Stephens: A Biography*, 142.
306. Wilson, *History of the Rise and Fall of the Slave Power*, Volume II, 394–95.
307. Thomas E. Schott, *Alexander H. Stephens of Georgia: A Biography*, 168–69.
308. Richard Striner, *Father Abraham: Lincoln's Relentless Struggle to End Slavery*, 36.
309. Letter from Alexander Stephens, May 9, 1854, in Richard Malcolm Johnston and William Hand Browne, *Life of Alexander H. Stephens*, 276–77.
310. Potter, *The Impending Crisis*, 166.
311. McCormack, *Memoirs of Gustave Koerner*, Volume I, 615.
312. William Nisbet Chambers, *Old Bullion Benton, Senator from the New West: Thomas Hart Benton, 1782–1858*, 402.
313. Von Abele, *Alexander H. Stephens*, 144.
314. Schott, *Alexander H. Stephens of Georgia*, 172.
315. Sewell, *Ballots for Freedom*, 263.
316. Richard Malcolm Johnston and William Hand Browne, *Life of Alexander H. Stephens*, 277. See Schott, *Alexander H. Stephens of Georgia*, 173. (Letter from Alexander Hamilton Stephens to James Thomas, May 23, 1854).
317. William H. Seward, "Speech of William H. Seward on the Kansas and Nebraska Bill," May 26, 1854, 1.
318. Arnold, *The History of Abraham Lincoln*, 62.
319. Thurlow Weed, *The Life of Thurlow Weed*, Volume II, Memoir, 221.
320. J. Madison Cutts, *Constitutional and Party Questions*, 96.
321. Harry V. Jaffa, *Crisis of the House Divided*, 105.
322. Sewell, *Ballots for Freemen*, 257.
323. McCullough, *Historical Encyclopedia of Illinois*, 145–46.
324. David Zarefsky, *Lincoln Douglas and Slavery: In the Crucible of Public Debate*, 7.
325. Johannsen, *The Frontier, the Union and Stephen A. Douglas*, 230.
326. Letter from Stephen Douglas to Twenty-five Chicago Clergymen, April 6, 1854, in Johannsen, *The Letters of Stephen A. Douglas*, 320.

CHAPTER IV
327. Arnold, *The Life of Abraham Lincoln*, 121.
328. Nathaniel Wright Stephenson, *Lincoln*, 82.
329. Gabor Boritt, *Lincoln and the Economics of the American Dream*, passim.
330. Letter from Abraham Lincoln to George Shaw, July 27, 1854, in CWAL, Second Supplement, 8.
331. Fehrenbacher, *Prelude to Greatness*, 34.

332. Richard J. Carwardine, *Lincoln: Profiles in Power*, 28.
333. Speech at Peoria, Illinois, October 16, 1854, in CWAL, Volume II, 266–67. Communication to the People of Sangamon County, March 9, 1832, in CWAL, Volume I, 8.
334. Orville Vernon Burton, *The Age of Lincoln*, 21. James Oliver Horton noted: "Throughout New England and in New York, New Jersey, and Pennsylvania, an antislavery spirit pressured government to move against the institution. In these states, constitutions, court rulings or legislation brought slavery to an end or set it on the road to eventual extinction." Harold Holzer, editor, *Lincoln and Freedom: Slavery, Emancipation and the Thirteenth Amendment*, 7–8.
335. Max Farrand, *The Records of the Federal Constitution of 1787*, Volume III., 161 (November 30, 1787). See Clark Forsythe, *The Greatest Good Possible*, 49.
336. Max Farrand, *The Records of the Federal Constitution of 1787*, Volume III, 254–55 (January 16, 1788). See Paul Finkelman, *Slavery and the Founders: Race and Liberty in the Age of Jefferson*, 10.
337. See also Robert Forbes, *The Missouri Compromise*, passim, for a review of the nation's handling of the slavery issue between 1776 and the passage of the Missouri Compromise in 1820.
338. Speech at Peoria, Illinois, October 16, 1854, in CWAL, Volume II, 275.
339. Nicolay and Hay, *Abraham Lincoln*, Volume I, 211.
340. Speech at Peoria, Illinois, October 16, 1854, in CWAL, Volume II, 275.
341. In two letters—one to John L. Scripps on June 16, 1860 and one to James O. Putnam, on September 13, 1860—Lincoln admitted he was in error here. Virginia ceded the territory but without the deed restriction. The Northwest Ordinance of 1787 did provide the restriction on slavery.
342. Speech at Peoria, Illinois, October 16, 1854, in CWAL, Volume II, 249. Lincoln would later correct a partial error in his narrative here. William H. Herndon contended Lincoln did not like "Jefferson's moral character" after reading a book by Theodore Dwight which was critical of Jefferson. The 1839 book by the brother of Yale President Timothy Dwight had a "powerful" impact on Lincoln, according to Herndon. (Letter from William H. Herndon to T. Dwight, December 30, 1866 courtesy of Douglas L. Wilson).
343. Guelzo, *Abraham Lincoln, Redeemer President*, 193.
344. Ibid., 196.
345. William E. Gienapp, *Abraham Lincoln and Civil War America*, 61. See Fehrenbacher, *Slaveholding Republic*, passim.
346. Finkelman: *Slavery and the Founders*, ix–x.
347. Speech at Peoria, October 16, 1854, in CWAL, Volume II, 276.
348. Miller: *Lincoln's Virtues*, 267.
349. Jaffa, *A New Birth of Freedom*, 329.
350. See Robert Bray, "What Lincoln Read—An Evaluative and Annotative List, " *Journal of the Abraham Lincoln Association*, Summer, 2007, 28–81.
351. Guelzo, *Abraham Lincoln, Redeemer President*, 197.
352. Arnold, *The Life of Abraham Lincoln*, 119.
353. Speech at Peoria, October 16, 1854, in CWAL, Volume II, 277. Peoria *Daily Union*, October 21, 1854, in Bryner, *Abraham Lincoln in Peoria, Illinois*, 146.
354. Speech at Peoria, Illinois, October 16, 1854, in CWAL, Volume II, 251–252.
355. Ibid., 250.
356. Ibid., 274–75.

357. Debate at Ottawa, August 21, 1858, in CWAL, Volume III, 29.
358. Speech at Peoria, Illinois, October 16, 1854, in CWAL, Volume II, 251–52.
359. Ibid., 254.
360. Ibid., 254–55.
361. Ibid., 254.
362. Ibid.
363. Ibid., 257.
364. Fehrenbacher, *The Slaveholding Republic*, 267.
365. Speech at Peoria, Illinois, October 16, 1854, in CWAL, Volume II, 252.
366. Ibid., 258. The original text apparently said "Missouri" by mistake.
367. Fehrenbacher, *Lincoln in Text and Context*, 48.
368. Speech at Peoria, Illinois, October 16, 1854, in CWAL, Volume II, 257.
369. Ibid.
370. Ibid., 258.
371. Ibid.
372. Ibid., 258–59.
373. Peoria *Daily Union*, October 21, 1854, in Bryner, *Abraham Lincoln in Peoria, Illinois*, 146.
374. Speech at Peoria, Illinois, October 16, 1854, in CWAL, Volume II, 259.
375. Ibid.
376. Speech at Bloomington, Illinois, September 26, 1854, in CWAL, Volume II, 238.
377. Speech at Peoria, Illinois, October 16, 1854, in CWAL, Volume II, 253.
378. Holt, *The Fate of Their Country*, 93.
379. Leonard Richards, *Slave Power: The Free North and Southern Domination, 1780–1860*, passim.
380. Speech at Peoria, Illinois, October 16, 1854, in CWAL, Volume II, 253–54.
381. Ibid., 261.
382. Ibid., 259–60.
383. Ibid., 260.
384. Ibid.
385. Ibid., 261.
386. Ibid., 261–62.
387. Ibid., 272.
388. Ibid.
389. Ibid., 254.
390. Nichols, *Blueprints for Leviathan*, 101. The legislation of 1854 altered Douglas's original position and overturned settled national policy. The bill renounced congressional authority for organizing the territories, as specified in the Constitution, and turned the power over to a small group of early territorial settlers to determine the status of slavery for the future.
391. Peoria *Daily Union*, October 21, 1854, in Bryner, *Abraham Lincoln in Peoria, Illinois*, 146.
392. Ibid., 155–56.
393. Speech at Peoria, Illinois, October 16, 1854, in CWAL, Volume II, 267.
394. Ibid., 267–68.
395. Ibid., 268.
396. Ibid.
397. Ibid., 255.

398. Striner, *Father Abraham*, 49.
399. Speech at Peoria, Illinois, October 16, 1854, in CWAL, Volume II, 255–56.
400. Ibid., 262.
401. Ibid., 262–63.
402. Robert Fogel and Stanley Engerman, *Time on the Cross*, passim.
403. Jaffa, *Crisis of the House Divided*, 395.
404. Speech at Peoria, Illinois, October 16, 1854, in CWAL, Volume II, 273.
405. Ibid., 263.
406. Ibid., 264.
407. Ibid., 265.
408. Richardson, ed. *A Compilation of the Messages and Papers of the Presidents, 1789–1908*, Volume I, 6.
409. Speech at Peoria, Illinois, October 16, 1854, in CWAL, Volume II, 265–66.
410. Jaffa, *Crisis of the House Divided*, 347.
411. Speech at Peoria, Illinois, October 16, 1854, in CWAL, Volume II, 278–79.
412. Carwardine, *Lincoln*, 27.
413. Speech at Peoria, Illinois, October 16, 1854, in CWAL, Volume II, 264.
414. Ibid., 265.
415. Gienapp, *Abraham Lincoln and Civil War America*, 52.
416. Address Before the Young Men's Lyceum of Springfield, January 27, 1838, in CWAL, Volume I, 108–11.
417. Speech at Peoria, Illinois, October 16, 1854, in CWAL, Volume II, 266. For an early discussion of the pervasive antiblack prejudice in the North, see Leon Litwack, *North of Slavery: The Negro in the Free States, 1790–1860*, passim.
418. Jaffa, *A New Birth of Freedom*, 341.
419. Gienapp, *Abraham Lincoln and Civil War America*, 51.
420. Temperance Address before the Springfield Washington Temperance Society, February, 22, 1842, in CWAL, Volume I, 273. See Doris Kearns Goodwin, *Team of Rivals: The Political Genius of Abraham Lincoln*, 168.
421. Speech at a Republican Banquet, Chicago, Illinois, December 10, 1856, in CWAL, Volume II, 385.
422. Peoria *Daily Union*, October 21, 1854, in Bryner, *Abraham Lincoln in Peoria, Illinois*, 144.
423. Speech at Peoria, Illinois, October 16, 1854, in CWAL, Volume II, 248.
424. Ibid., 270–71.
425. James Daniel Richardson, ed., *A Compilation of the Messages and Papers of the President, 1789–1908*, Volume V, 222.
426. Speech at Peoria, Illinois, October 16, 1854, in CWAL, Volume II, 270.
427. Ibid. Jaffa, *A New Birth of Freedom*, 76.
428. Speech at Peoria, Illinois, October 16, 1854, in CWAL, Volume II, 270.
429. Ibid., 271–72.
430. Ibid., 271.
431. David Brion Davis, *Inhuman Bondage: The Rise and Fall of Slavery in the New World*, passim.
432. James Oliver Horton, "Naturally Antislavery: Lincoln, Race, and the Complexity of American Liberty," *Lincoln Lore*, Fall 2007, 21.
433. Hans L. Trefousse, *Benjamin Franklin Wade: Radical Republican from Ohio*, 311–12.
434. Cullom Davis, Charles B. Strozier, Rebecca Monroe Veach, and Geoffrey C. Ward, eds., *The Public and the Private Lincoln: Contemporary Perspectives*, 57–70 (Gabor Boritt, "The Right to Rise").

435. Speech at Peoria, Illinois, October 16, 1854, in CWAL, Volume II, 274.
436. Ibid.
437. Ibid.
438. Speech at Hartford, Connecticut, March 5, 1860, in CWAL, Volume IV, 5–6.
439. Letter from Abraham Lincoln to Albert G. Hodges April 4, 1864, in CWAL, Volume VII, 281. Lincoln wrote: "By general law life *and* limb must be protected; yet often a limb must be amputated to save a life; but a life is never wisely given to save a limb." He used the tumor metaphor as well in his speech at New Haven in 1860 (Speech at New Haven, March 6, 1860, in CWAL, Volume IV, 15). In 1862, he used the metaphor again in a conversation with the Rev. Elbert S. Porter in Fehrenbacher and Fehrenbacher, *The Recollected Words of Abraham Lincoln*, 368). He also used the metaphor in remarks to the Presbyterians (Remarks to Committee of Reformed Presbyterian Synod, July 17, 1862, in CWAL, Volume V, 327).
440. Speech at Peoria, Illinois, October 16, 1854, in CWAL, Volume II, 271.
441. Ibid., 281–82.
442. Allan Nevins, *Ordeal of Union*, Volume II, 107–8. See Allan Nevins, "Stephen A. Douglas: His Weaknesses and his Greatness," *Journal of the Illinois State Historical Society*, December 1949.
443. Foner, *Politics and Ideology in the Age of the Civil War*, 46.
444. Speech at Cooper Union, February 27, 1860, in CWAL, Volume IV, 550.
445. Graham A. Peck, "Was Stephen A. Douglas Antislavery?" *Journal of the Abraham Lincoln Association*, Volume 26, No. 2, Summer 2005, 1–2.
446. Ibid., 19–20.
447. Donald, *Lincoln*, 177.
448. Speech at Peoria, Illinois, October 16, 1854, in CWAL, Volume II, 276. Douglas L. Wilson has identified the "warning of friends" in a *New York Times* article from 1854 quoting a Spanish newspaper.
449. Eulogy of Henry Clay, July 6, 1852, in CWAL, Volume II, 130–31.
450. Carwardine, *Lincoln*, 66.
451. Nathaniel Wright Stephenson, *Lincoln*, 79.
452. Speech at Peoria, Illinois, October 16, 1854, in CWAL, Volume II, 283.
453. Ibid., 278.
454. Beveridge, *Abraham Lincoln, 1809–1858*, Volume II, 245.
455. Letter from Joseph Gillespie to William H. Herndon, December 8, 1866, in Wilson and Davis, *Herndon's Informants*, 507.
456. Fehrenbacher, *Prelude to Greatness: Lincoln the 1850s*, 34–35.
457. Wilson and Davis, *Herndon's Informants: Letters, Interviews, and Statements about Abraham Lincoln*, 507 (letter from Joseph Gillespie to William H. Herndon, December 8, 1866).
458. Beveridge, *Abraham Lincoln, 1809–1858*, Volume II, 237.
459. Speech at Peoria, Illinois, October 16, 1854, in CWAL, Volume II, 248 .

CHAPTER V
460. Larry Gara, *The Presidency of Franklin Pierce*, 95.
461. David M. Potter, *The Impending Crisis*, 167.
462. Speech at Peoria, Illinois, October 16, 1854, in CWAL, Volume II, 282.
463. Potter, *The Impending Crisis*, 173.
464. John S. Wright, *Lincoln & the Politics of Slavery*, 52–53.

465. Van Deusen, *Horace Greeley: Nineteenth-Century Crusader*, 178.
466. Gerald W. Wolf, *The Kansas-Nebraska Bill: Party, Section, and the Coming of the Civil War*, 162.
467. William H. Seward, "Speech of William H. Seward on the Kansas and Nebraska Bill," May 26, 1854, 7.
468. Blue, *Charles Sumner and the Conscience of the North*, 93 (letter from Salmon P. Chase to Charles Sumner, September 13, 1854).
469. Fehrenbacher, *Sectional Crisis and Southern Constitutionalism*, 49.
470. William H. Seward, "Speech of William H. Seward on the Kansas and Nebraska Bill," May 26, 1854, 5.
471. Rawley, *Secession*, 61.
472. Cole, *The Era of the Civil War*, 133.
473. Jaffa, *A New Birth of Freedom*, 305.
474. Potter, *The Impending Crisis*, 174.
475. Kenneth J. Winkle, *The Young Eagle*, 292.
476. Holt, *The Fate of Their Country*, 112.
477. Potter, *The Impending Crisis*, 175.
478. Letter from Stephen Douglas to James W. Sheahan, September 14, 1854, in Johannsen, *Letters of Stephen A. Douglas*, 330.
479. Cole, *The Era of the Civil War*, 137.
480. Holt, *Political Parties and American Political Development*, 75.
481. Wright, *Lincoln & the Politics of Slavery*, 52–53, and David H. Donald, *Liberty and Union*, 61.
482. George T. McJimsey, *The Dividing and Reuniting of America: 1848–1877*, 13.
483. Niven, *Salmon P. Chase*, 152.
484. Cole, *The Era of the Civil War*, 111–13; Wright, *Lincoln & the Politics of Slavery*, 69; Fehrenbacher, *The Slaveholding Republic*, 277; William J. Cooper and Thomas E. Terrill, *The American South: A History*, 297.
485. Fehrenbacher, *The Slaveholding Republic*, 276.
486. Potter, *The Impending Crisis*, 176.
487. Potter, *Division and the Stresses of Reunion, 1845–1876*, 70.
488. Johannsen, *Stephen A. Douglas*, 461.
489. Cole, *The Era of the Civil War*, 131.
490. Johannsen, *Stephen A. Douglas*, 461.
491. Illinois *State Register*, November 23, 1854, in Milton, *The Eve of Conflict*, 186.
492. Johannsen, *Stephen A. Douglas*, 465.
493. Beveridge, *Abraham Lincoln, 1809–1858*, Volume II, 272.
494. William C. Harris argued that Lincoln was more involved in politics during this period than many biographers have acknowledged. William C. Harris, *Lincoln's Rise to the Presidency*, 494.
495. Letter from Lyman Trumbull to John Trumbull, December 4, 1854, in Krug, *Lyman Trumbull*, 90–91.
496. Letter from Lyman Trumbull to John M. Palmer, November 23, 1854, in George Thomas Palmer, ed., *Letters from Lyman Trumbull to John M. Palmer, 1854–1858*, 4–5.
497. J. Sean Callan, *Courage and Country: James Shields: More Than Irish Luck*, 195–96.
498. Letter from Stephen Douglas to Charles H. Lanphier, December 18, 1854, in Johannsen, *The Letters of Stephen A. Douglas*, 331.
499. Peoria *Daily Union*, October 21, 1854, in Bryner, *Abraham Lincoln in Peoria, Illinois*, 155–56.

500. Stephen Hansen and Paul Nygaard, "Stephen A. Douglas, the Know-Nothings, and the Democratic Party in Illinois, 1854–1858," *Illinois Historical Journal*, Volume I7, Number 2, Summer 1994, 110.
501. Callan, *Courage and Country*, 195–96.
502. Letter from Lyman Trumbull to John M. Palmer, November 23, 1854, in Palmer, *Letters from Lyman Trumbull to John M. Palmer*, 3–4.
503. Palmer, *A Conscientious Turncoat*, 31.
504. Letter from John M. Palmer to his wife, January 31, 1855, in Palmer, *A Conscientious Turncoat*, 33.
505. Nicolay and Hay, *Abraham Lincoln: A History*, Volume I, 212.
506. Letter from Jesse O. Norton to Abraham Lincoln, January 20, 1855, in the Abraham Lincoln Papers at the Library of Congress, transcribed and annotated by the Lincoln Studies Center, Knox College, Galesburg, Illinois.
507. Letter from Richard Yates to Abraham Lincoln, January 8, 1855, in ibid.
508. Holt, *The Rise and Fall of the American Whig Party*, 270.
509. Letter from John Palmer to his wife, January 31, 1855, in Palmer, *A Conscientious Turncoat*, 34.
510. Callan, *Courage and Country*, 195–98.
511. Cole, *The Era of the Civil War*, 132.
512. Goodwin, *Team of Rivals*, 172.
513. Horace White, *Transactions Illinois State Historical Society*, 1903, 42.
514. Letter from Abraham Lincoln to Jesse O. Norton, February 16, 1855, in CWAL, Second Supplement, 9–11.
515. Letter Abraham Lincoln to Elihu B. Washburne, February 9, 1855, in the Abraham Lincoln Papers at the Library of Congress, transcribed and annotated by the Lincoln Studies Center, Knox College, Galesburg, Illinois.
516. Letter from Abraham Lincoln to William H. Henderson, February. 21, 1855, in CWAL, Volume II, 306–7.
517. Letter from Abraham Lincoln to George W. Dole, G. S. Hubbard, and W. H. Brown, December 14, 1859, in CWAL, Volume III, 507–8.
518. Robert Pierce Forbes, *The Missouri Compromise and its Aftermath*, 284.
519. Letter from Lyman Trumbull to John Trumbull, December 4, 1854, in Krug, *Lyman Trumbull*, 90–91.
520. McCormack, *Memoirs of Gustave Koerner*, Volume I, 625.
521. Wright, *Lincoln & the Politics of Slavery*, 64–65.
522. David Grimsted, *The Mobbing of America, 1828–1861*, 247.
523. Letter from Abraham Lincoln to Thaddeus Stevens, September 3, 1849, in CWAL, Volume II, 1. Lincoln wrote Pennsylvania Whig Thaddeus Stevens: "You may possibly remember seeing me at the Philadelphia Convention—introduced to you as the lone whig star of Illinois."
524. Letter from Lyman Trumbull to Abraham Lincoln, February 24, 1855, in the Abraham Lincoln Papers at the Library of Congress, transcribed and annotated by the Lincoln Studies Center, Knox College. Galesburg, Illinois.
525. Abraham Lincoln, Draft Resolutions for the Illinois General Assembly concerning Repeal of the Kansas-Nebraska Act, January 4, 1855, in ibid.
526. Reinhard H. Luthin, "Abraham Lincoln Becomes a Republican," *Political Science Quarterly*, September 1944, 424.
527. Nichols and Berwanger, *The Stakes of Power*, 49–50.

528. Fehrenbacher, *Sectional Crisis and Southern Constitutionalism*, 47–48; Nichols and Berwanger, *The Stakes of Power*, 49–50; Cooper and Terrill, *The American South*, 297.

529. Holt, *The Rise and Fall of the American Whig Party*, 835.

530. Frederick J. Blue, The *Free Soilers: Third Party Politics, 1848–54*, 283–284.

531. Wright, *Lincoln & the Politics of Slavery*, 58.

532. Sewell, *Ballots for Freedom*, 264–65.

533. Cole, *The Irrepressible Conflict*, 272–73.

534. Letter from Abraham Lincoln to Joshua F. Speed, August 24, 1855, in CWAL, Volume II, 320–23.

535. Henry Wilson, *History of the Rise and Fall of Slavery*, Volume II, 408.

536. Fehrenbacher, *Lincoln in Text and Context: Collected Essays*, 49.

537. Fehrenbacher, *The Dred Scott Case: Its Significance in American Law and Politics*, 189.

538. Whitney, *Life on the Circuit with Lincoln*, 339.

539. *Transactions of the McLean County Historical Society*, 1900, www.adena.com/adena/usa/cw/cw107.htm.

540. White, "Abraham Lincoln in 1854,", 6.

541. Fehrenbacher, *Lincoln in Text and Context*, 49.

542. Ludwell H. Johnson, *Division and Reunion: America 1848–1877*, 34.

543. William H. Seward, "Speech of William H. Seward on the Kansas and Nebraska Bill," May 26, 1854, 3.

544. Holt, *The Political Crisis of the 1850s*, 147.

545. William H. Hale, *Horace Greeley: Voice of the People*, 161.

546. McJimsey, *The Dividing and Reuniting of America*, 14.

547. Speech at Peoria, Illinois, October 16, 1854, CWAL, Volume II, 271–72.

548. Smith, *The Death of Slavery*, 129–30; Nichols, *Franklin Pierce*, 408, 410.

549. Ross Drake, "The Law That Ripped America in Two," *Smithsonian*, May 2004, 66.

550. Smith, *The Death of Slavery*, 130.

551. Letter from Abraham Lincoln to Joshua F. Speed, August 24, 1855, in CWAL, Volume II, 320–23.

552. Otto R. Kyle, *Abraham Lincoln in Decatur*, 68.

553. Ibid., 69.

554. Luthin, "Abraham Lincoln Becomes a Republican," 430.

555. Paul Selby, "The Editorial Convention of 1856," *Journal of the Illinois State Historical Society*, Spring 1955, 346.

556. Otto R. Kyle, "Mr. Lincoln Steps Out: The Anti-Nebraska Editors' Convention," *Abraham Lincoln Quarterly*, March 1941, 30, 32.

557. Herndon and Weik. *Herndon's Life of Lincoln*, 236.

558. William E. Lilly, *Set My People Free*, 197–98.

559. Eugene F. Baldwin, Peoria *Sunday Star*, March 1, 1908, in East, *Abraham Lincoln Sees Peoria*, 27.

560. Robert S. Harper, *Lincoln and the Press*, 17.

561. Pratt, "Abraham Lincoln in Bloomington, Illinois," 54.

562. Reuben M. Benjamin and Walter B. Stevens (edited by Michael Burlingame), *A Reporter's Lincoln*, 54.

563. Ibid., 54.

564. Ibid., 45.

565. Harper, *Lincoln and the Press*, 17.

566. Paul M. Angle, ed., "The Recollections of William Pitt Kellogg," *The Abraham Lincoln Quarterly*, Volume III, No. 7, September 1945, 323.

567. White, "Abraham Lincoln in 1854," 11.

568. Elwell Crissey, *Lincoln's Lost Speech*, 238.

569. Henry C. Whitney, *Life with Lincoln on the Circuit*, 76–77.

570. Illinois *State Journal*, June 11, 1856, in Earl Schenck Miers, ed., *Lincoln Day by Day*, Volume II, 171.

571. Earl Wellington Wiley, "Lincoln in the Campaign of 1856," Illinois *State Journal*, June 11, 1856, in *Journal of the Illinois State Historical Society*, January 1930, 584.

572. Cole, *The Era of the Civil War*, 145.

573. Guelzo, *Redeemer President*, 206.

574. Fragment on Stephen A. Douglas, ca. December, 1856, in CWAL, Volume II, 383.

575. Thomas F. Schwartz, "Lincoln, Form Letters, and Fillmore Men," *Illinois Historical Journal*, Spring 1985, 68.

576. Wiley, "Lincoln in the Campaign of 1856," 588.

577. Kenneth M. Stampp, *America in 1857: A Nation on the Brink*, 133. This observation came from the path-breaking author of *The Peculiar Institution* which appeared in 1956, two years after the momentous Supreme Court ruling, *Brown v. Board of Education*.

578. Speech at a Republican Banquet, Chicago, Illinois, December 10, 1856, in CWAL, Volume II, 383–85.

579. Fehrenbacher, *The Slaveholding Republic*, 284.

580. Zarefsky, *Lincoln Douglas and Slavery*, 17.

581. Holt, *The Fate of Their Country*, 121.

582. Paul Finkelman, "Slavery, the 'More Perfect Union,' and the Prairie State," *Illinois Historical Journal*, Winter 1987, 249, 267.

583. Benjamin Quarles, *Lincoln and the Negro*, 36.

584. Ibid., 37.

585. Carl F. Wieck: *Lincoln's Quest for Equality: The Road to Gettysburg*, 129.

586. Speech at Kalamazoo, Michigan, August 27, 1856, in CWAL, Volume II, 361, 364.

587. Speech at Peoria, October 9, 1856, in CWAL, Volume II, 379.

588. In endorsing Lincoln for governor in February 1856, Peoria *Weekly Republican* editor Thomas J. Pickett wrote that Lincoln had "earned a debt of gratitude from the 'Anti-Nebraska' party, by his unwearied efforts in favor of their cause, that can never be fully repaid. Let it be remembered that Mr. Lincoln has successfully met Judge Douglas upon the Nebraska issue; and let it be remembered that it was Mr. Lincoln who gave the Little Giant his final worsting, which occur[r]ed in our own city, and was the finishing stroke of that memorable struggle, in which, although the little champion of Nebraska bore himself with courage and vigor, yet the brave realities and unflinching stand for PRINCIPLE maintained by his noble antagonist, proved too much for him." Peoria *Weekly Republican*, February 22, 1856 (Earnest East Collection, Abraham Lincoln Presidential Library, Springfield, Illinois).

589. Robert W. Johannsen, "The Lincoln-Douglas Campaign of 1858: Background and Perspective," *Journal of the Illinois State Historical Society*, Winter 1980, 247.

590. Alexander H. Stephens, "Speech of Hon. Alexander H. Stephens, of Georgia on The Presidential Election of 1856; the Compromise of 1850; and the Kansas-Nebraska Act of 1854," January 6, 1857.

CHAPTER VI

591. Letter from James Buchanan to John Y. Mason, December 29, 1856, in Johannsen, "The Lincoln-Douglas Campaign of 1858: Background and Perspective," 248.
592. Jaffa, *A New Birth of Freedom*, 304.
593. Allan Nevins, *The Emergence of Lincoln*, Volume I, 109–10. From 1789 until the Civil War, the U.S. Supreme Court was dominated by a southern majority.
594. Damon Wells, *Stephen Douglas: The Last Years, 1857–1861*, 61–62.
595. Fehrenbacher, *The Dred Scott Case*, 190.
596. Potter, *The Impending Crisis*, 293.
597. McJimsey, *The Dividing and Reuniting of America*, 14.
598. Fehrenbacher, *The Slaveholding Republic*, 281.
599. Fehrenbacher, *The Dred Scott Case*, 444–45.
600. Ibid., 4–5.
601. Quarles, *Lincoln and the Negro*, 37.
602. Speech at Springfield, Illinois, June 26, 1857, in CWAL, Volume II, 404–5.
603. Ibid., 405–6.
604. Ibid., 406.
605. Ibid., 406–7.
606. Ibid., 407.
607. Jaffa, *A New Birth of Freedom*, 298.
608. Harry V. Jaffa and Robert W. Johannsen, eds., *In the Name of the People: Speeches and Writings of Lincoln and Douglas in the Ohio Campaign of 1859*, 48.
609. Letter from Thomas Jefferson to William Charles Jarvis, September 28, 1820, in Albert Ellery Bergh, ed., *The Writings of Thomas Jefferson*, Volume XV.
610. Speech at Springfield, June 26, 187, in CWAL, Volume II, 402.
611. Horace White, New York *Evening Post*, February 12, 1909, in Wilson, *Lincoln Among His Friends*, 171.
612. John W. Forney, *Anecdotes of Public Men*, Volume II, 179.
613. Herndon and Weik, *Herndon's Life of Lincoln*, 249.
614. Johannsen, "The Lincoln-Douglas Campaign of 1858: Background and Perspective," 251.
615. *Illinois State Journal*, June 18, 1858.
616. Bonham, *Fifty Years' Recollections*, 164.
617. Speech at Springfield, June 16, 1858, CWAL, Volume II, 461–62.
618. *Political Debates between Hon. Abraham Lincoln and Hon. Stephen A. Douglas in the Celebrated Campaign of 1858*, 51.
619. Allen Thorndike Rice, ed., *Reminiscences of Abraham Lincoln*, 205 (Lawrence Weldon).
620. Milton, *The Eve of Conflict*, 333.
621. Nevins, *The Emergence of Lincoln*, Volume II, 372.
622. Allen Thorndike Rice, ed., *Reminiscences of Abraham Lincoln*, 206 (Lawrence Weldon).
623. Bonham, *Fifty Years' Recollections*, 173.
624. Speech at Lewiston, August 21, 1858, in CWAL, Volume II, 546–47. When White presented this text to Lincoln, he said: "Well, those are my views, and if I said anything on the subject, I must have said substantially that, but not nearly so well as that is said." White maintains that this text was actually delivered at Beardstown, but Roy P. Basler noted that "in none of the reports of the Beard-

stown speech which have been found, is there any reference to the peroration on the Declaration of Independence. . . ." CWAL, Volume II, 544.

625. Letter from Stephen Douglas to Charles H. Lanphier, (August 15, 1858), in Johannsen, *The Letters of Stephen A. Douglas*, 426.

626. Zarefsky, *Lincoln Douglas and Slavery*, 53.

627. Hickey, "Lincolniana," 137.

628. White, "Abraham Lincoln in 1854," 13.

629. Debate at Ottawa, August 21, 1858, in CWAL, Volume III, 14–15.

630. Ibid., 15–16.

631. Thomas J. Pickett, Lincoln, Nebraska *Daily State Journal*, April 12, 1881, in Wilson, *Intimate Memories of Lincoln*, 195.

632. Rawley, *Abraham Lincoln and a Nation Worth Fighting For*, 25.

633. Speech at Carlinville, Illinois, August 31, 1858, in CWAL, Volume II, 79.

634. Speech at Clinton, Illinois, September 2, 1858, in CWAL, Volume II, 82. Speech at Bloomington, Illinois, September 4, 1858, in CWAL, Volume II, 88.

635. Weik, *The Real Lincoln*, 10–12.

636. Bryner, *Abraham Lincoln in Peoria, Illinois*, 97–99.

637. Milton, *The Eve of Conflict*, 341.

638. Smith, *Parties and Slavery*, 232.

639. Fehrenbacher, *The Slaveholding Republic*, 286.

640. Zarefsky, *Lincoln Douglas and Slavery*, 53.

641. Alton debate, October 15, 1858, in CWAL, Volume III, 315–16.

642. Article IV, Section 3 of the U.S. Constitution states: "The Congress shall have Power to dispose of and make all needful Rules and Regulations respecting the Territory or other Property belonging to the United States; and nothing in this Constitution shall be so construed as to Prejudice any Claims of the United States, or of any particular State."

643. Fehrenbacher, *The Slaveholding Republic*, 286–87.

644. Boritt, *Lincoln and the Economics of the American Dream*, 171.

645. Speech at Dayton, Ohio, September 17, 1859, in CWAL, Volume III, 460.

646. Seventh and Last Debate with Stephen A. Douglas at Alton, Illinois, October 15, 1858, in ibid., 312.

647. William Garrott Brown, "Lincoln's Rival," *The Atlantic Monthly*, February 1902, 232–33.

648. Debate at Galesburg, October 7, 1858, in CWAL, Volume III, 226. Lincoln used this language three times in 1858—at the debates at Quincy, Galesburg, and Alton.

649. Letter from Abraham Lincoln to Anson Miller, November 19, 1858, in CWAL, Volume III, 340.

650. Osborn H. Oldroyd, editor, *The Lincoln Memorial: Album-Immortelles*, 40.

651. Isaac N. Arnold, *Abraham Lincoln: A Paper Read Before the Royal Historical Society, London,* June 16, 1881, 9.

652. Hugh McCullough, quoted in Rice, *Reminiscences of Abraham Lincoln*, 414.

653. Speech at Chicago, March 1, 1859, in CWAL, Volume III, 369.

654. Speech in Colombus, Ohio, September 16, 1859, in ibid., 410.

655. Definition of Democracy, circa August 1, 1858, in CWAL, Volume II, 532.

656. Jaffa and Johannsen, *In the Name of the People*, 44.

657. Speech in Colombus, Ohio, September 16, 1859, in CWAL, Volume III, 417–18.

658. Speech at Leavenworth, Kansas, probably November 30, 1859, in ibid., 495–96.
659. Charles Arthur Hawley, "Lincoln in Kansas," *Journal of the Illinois State Historical Society,* June 1949, 189.
660. Speech at Leavenworth, Kansas, December 3, 1859, in CWAL, Volume III, 500–1.
661. Herbert Mitgang, *The Fiery Trial: A Life of Abraham Lincoln,* 166.
662. Letter from Abraham Lincoln to Thomas J. Pickett, April 16, 1859, in CWAL, Volume III, 377.
663. Letter from Abraham Lincoln to James O. Putnam, September 13, 1860, in CWAL, Volume IV, 115.
664. Letter from Abraham Lincoln to John L. Scripps, June 16, 1860, in ibid., 115.
665. Cooper Union Speech, February 27, 1860, in CWAL, Volume III, 550.
666. Harold Holzer, *Lincoln at Cooper Union: The Speech That Made Abraham Lincoln President,* 144.
667. Fehrenbacher, *The Slaveholding Republic,* 291.
668. Letter from Abraham Lincoln to Lyman Trumbull, April 29, 1860, in CWAL, Volume IV, 45.

CHAPTER VII
669. Mary A. Livermore, *My Story of the War: Four Years Personal Experience in The Sanitary Service of the Rebellion,* 552–53.
670. Nicolay and Hay, *The Complete Works of Abraham Lincoln,* Volume II, 190.
671. Beveridge, *Abraham Lincoln,* Volume II, 286.
672. Ida Tarbell, *The Life of Abraham Lincoln,* Volume I, 284.
673. Ronald C. White Jr., *The Eloquent President: A Portrait of Lincoln through His Words,* 235.
674. Carwardine, *Lincoln,* 39–40.
675. Joseph R. Fornieri: *The Language of Liberty: The Political Speeches and Writings of Abraham Lincoln,* 151.
676. Stoddard: *Abraham Lincoln,* 139.
677. July 18, 1864, in CWAL, Volume VII, 451.
678. Letter from Abraham Lincoln to Lyman Trumbull, December 10, 1860, in CWAL, Volume IV, 149.
679. Letter from Abraham Lincoln to William Kellogg, December 11, 1860, in CWAL, Volume IV, 150.
680. "Recollections of Judge Franklin Blades," in Angle, *Abraham Lincoln by Some Men who Knew Him,* 87, 89.
681. Speech in Independence Hall, Philadelphia, Pennsylvania, February 22, 1861, in CWAL, Volume IV, 240. Lincoln, according to political scientist Joseph Fornieri, "interprets American history as the unfolding of implications within the Declaration. The document is foundational in the following ways: (1) it commemorates the birth of the nation; (2) it defines the creed of collective American identity; (3) it represents a moral covenant; (4) it guides the nation's political institutions; (5) it constitutes a bulwark against despotism." Frank J. Williams, William D. Pederson, and Vincent J. Marsala, eds., *Abraham Lincoln: Sources and Style of Leadership,* 52.
682. Gettysburg Address, November 19, 1863, in CWAL, Volume VII, 22.
683. John Patrick Diggins, *On Hallowed Ground: Abraham Lincoln and the Foundations of American History,* 23.

684. Letter from William H. Herndon to Edward L. Pierce, February 18, 1861, in Harry Pratt, *Concerning Mr. Lincoln*, 52.

685. First Inaugural Address, March 4, 1861, in CWAL, Volume IV, 265.

686. Message to Congress in Special Session, July 4, 1861, in CWAL, Volume IV, 440.

687. Kenneth L. Deutsch and Joseph R. Fornieri, *Lincoln's American Dream: Clashing Political Perspectives*, 15.

688. Order Retiring Winfield Scott from Command, November 1, 1861, in CWAL, Volume V, 10.

689. Message to Congress, July 4, 1861, in CWAL, Volume IV, 426.

690. Reply to Committee Notifying Lincoln of His Renomination, June 9, 1864, in CWAL, Volume VII, 380.

691. Special Message to Congress, July 4, 1861, in CWAL, Volume IV, 436–37.

692. Fehrenbacher, *The Slaveholding Republic*, 312.

693. Goodwin, *Team of Rivals*, 749.

694. Letter to Horace Greeley, August 22, 1862, in CWAL, Volume V, 388–89.

695. Letter from Abraham Lincoln to Erastus Corning & others [June 12], 1863, in CWAL, Volume VI, 263.

696. Ibid., 264.

697. See Mark E. Neely Jr., *The Fate of Liberty: Abraham Lincoln and Civil Liberties*, and Mark Grimsley, *The Hard Hand of War: Union Military Policy toward Southern Civilians, 1861–1865*, passim.

698. Letter to James C. Conkling, August 26, 1863, in CWAL, Volume VI, 408–9.

699. Douglas L. Wilson, *Lincoln's Sword*, passim.

700. Annual Message to Congress, December 6, 1864, in CWAL, Volume VIII, 149–50.

701. Second Inaugural Message, March 4, 1865, in ibid., 332.

702. Ibid.

703. Jaffa, *A New Birth of Freedom*, 338.

704. Michael Davis, *The Image of Lincoln in the South*, 21.

705. Letter from Alexander Stephens to J. Henly Smith, July 10, 1860, in ibid., 24.

706. Myrta L. Avery, ed., *Recollections of Alexander H. Stephens: His Diary Kept When a Prisoner at Fort Warren, Boston Harbour, 1865*, 276.

707. Richard Malcolm Johnson, *Life of Alexander H. Stephens*, 581–82.

708. Letter from Abraham Lincoln to Alexander H. Stephens, December 22, 1860, in CWAL, Volume IV, 160.

709. Fehrenbacher, *The Slaveholding Republic*, 307.

710. Alexander H. Stephens, March 21, 1861, "Cornerstone" Speech in Savannah, Georgia.

711. Alexander H. Stephens, *A Constitutional View of the Late War Between the States; Causes, Character, Conduct and Results Presented in a Series of Colloquies at Liberty Hall*, Volume I, 29–30.

712. Second Inaugural Address, March 4, 1865, in CWAL, Volume VIII, 332.

713. Address at Sanitary Fair, Baltimore, Maryland, April 18, 1864, in CWAL, Volume VII, 301–2.

714. Ibid., 302.

715. Fourth Message to Congress, December 6, 1864, in CWAL, Volume VIII, 151.

716. Emancipation Proclamation, January 1, 1863, in CWAL, Volume VI, 30.

717. Letter to Horace Greeley, August 22, 1862, in CWAL, Volume V, 389.

718. Letter to Stephen A. Hurlburt, July 31, 1863, in CWAL, Volume VI, 358.

719. Letter from Abraham Lincoln to James C. Conkling, August 26, 1863, in ibid., 409.
720. Ibid.
721. Letter from Abraham Lincoln to Albert G. Hodges, April 4, 1864, in CWAL, Volume VII, 281.
722. James Oliver Horton and Lois E. Horton, *Slavery and the Making of America*, 207.
723. Annual Message to Congress, December 6, 1864, in CWAL, Volume VIII, 152.
724. Address to the New Jersey Senate at Trenton, New Jersey, February 21, 1861, in CWAL, Volume IV, 236.
725. Proclamation of Amnesty and Reconstruction, December 8, 1863, in CWAL, Volume VII, 55.
726. William Lee Miller, "Lincoln's Profound and Benign Americanism, or Nationalism Without Malice," *Journal of the Abraham Lincoln Association*, Volume 22, No. 2001, 1.
727. Jaffa, *Crisis of the House Divided*, 371.
728. Diggins, *On Hallowed Ground*, 37.
729. Last Public Address, April 11, 1865, in CWAL, Volume VIII, 405.
730. Speech at Hartford, Connecticut, March 5, 1860, in CWAL, Volume IV, 3.
731. Ibid., 3–4.
732. Speech at New Haven, Connecticut, March 6, 1860, in ibid., 17.
733. First Inaugural Address, March 4,1861, in ibid., 268–69.
734. Fehrenbacher and Fehrenbacher, *Recollected Words of Abraham Lincoln*, 508.
735. Letter from Abraham Lincoln to Nathaniel Banks, August 5, 1863, in CWAL, Volume, VI, 365–66.
736. Bloomington Weekly Pantagraph, September 20, 1854, in Sherman D. Wakefield, *How Lincoln Became President*, 41–42.
737. Speech at Hartford, Connecticut, March 5, 1860, in CWAL, Volume IV, 3.
738. Boritt, *Lincoln and the Economics of the American Dream*, 158–59.
739. Message to Congress in Special Session, July 4, 1861, in CWAL, Volume IV, 423.
740. Cooper Union Address, February 27, 1860, in CWAL, Volume III, 543.
741. Fehrenbacher and Fehrenbacher, *The Recollected Words of Abraham Lincoln*, 368.
742. Davis, *Inhuman Bondage*, passim.
743. Message to Congress in Special Session, July 4, 1861, in CWAL, Volume IV, 432–33.
744. Annual Message to Congress, December 6, 1864, in CWAL, Volume VIII, 151.
745. First Inaugural Address, March 4, 1861, in CWAL, Volume IV, 271.
746. Second Inaugural Address, March 4, 1865, in CWAL, Volume VIII, 332–33.
747. Ibid.
748. Last Public Address, April 11, 1865, in ibid., 405.
749. Robert Gerald McMutry, *Lincoln's Friend, Douglas*, 5.
750. Joseph R. Fornieri, *Abraham Lincoln's Political Faith*, 107.
751. McMurtry, *Lincoln's Friend, Douglas*, 5.
752. Weik, *The Real Lincoln*, 230–31.
753. Letter from Stephen Douglas to Ninety-six New Orleans Citizens, November 13, 1860, in Johannsen, *The Letters of Stephen A. Douglas*, 499–500.
754. April 14, 1861, in ibid., 509–10.
755. Brown, "Lincoln's Rival," 235.
756. Johannsen, *Stephen A. Douglas*, 868.
757. Letter from Stephen Douglas to Abraham Lincoln, April 29, 1861, in Johannsen, *The Letters of Stephen A. Douglas*, 511.

758. Speech at Peoria, Illinois, October 16, 1854, in CWAL, Volume II, 278.
759. William E. Barton, *The Soul of Abraham Lincoln*, 116.
760. Mark A. Noll, *A History of Christianity in the United States and Canada*, 322.
761. Garry Wills, *Inventing America: Jefferson's Declaration of Independence*, xvi.
762. Fornieri, *Abraham Lincoln's Political Faith*, 108–9.
763. Speech at Peoria, October 16, 1854, in CWAL, Volume II, 276.
764. Guelzo, *Abraham Lincoln, Redeemer President*, 193.
765. Second Inaugural, March 4, 1864, in CWAL, Volume VIII, 333.
766. White Jr., *The Eloquent President*, 282.
767. Speech at Peoria, October 16, 1854, in CWAL, Volume II, 255.
768. Speech at Springfield, June 26, 1857, in CWAL, Volume II, 406.
769. Boritt, *Lincoln and the Economics of the American Dream*, 283.
770. Lord Godfrey Charnwood, *Abraham Lincoln*, 455.
771. Reply to the Workingmen of Manchester, England, January 19, 1863, in CWAL, Volume VI, 64.
772. Message to Congress in Special Session, July 4, 1861, in CWAL, Volume IV, 426.
773. Message to Congress in Special Session, July 4, 1861, in ibid., 438.
774. Appeal to Border State Representatives, July 12, 1862, in CWAL, Volume V, 319.
775. Letter from Charles Sumner to John Bright, April 15, 1863, in CWAL, Volume VI, 176.
776. Draft Resolution on Slavery, (April 15, 1863), in ibid., 176.
777. Speech to 148th Ohio, August 31, 1864, in CWAL, Volume VII, 528.
778. Richard N. Current, "Lincoln and Multiculturalism, " quoted in James M. McPherson, ed., *"We Cannot Escape History": Lincoln and the Last Best Hope of Earth*, 129.
779. Ibid., 134.
780. Response to Serenade, November 8, 1864, in CWAL, Volume VIII, 96.
781. Ibid., 101.
782. Eulogy for Henry Clay, July 6, 1852, in CWAL, Volume II, 126.
783. Annual Message to Congress, December 6, 1864, in CWAL, Volume VIII, 150.
784. Response to a Serenade, February 1, 1865, from New York *Tribune*, February 3, 1865, in ibid., 254.
785. Ibid., 254.
786. Speech at Peoria, October 16, 1854, in CWAL, Volume II, 276.
787. Second Annual Message to Congress, December 1, 1862, in CWAL, Volume V, 537.

CHAPTER VIII

788. Horace White, New York *Evening Post*, February 12, 1909, in Rockwell, *Lincoln Among His Friends*, 168–69.
789. The Lincoln Legal Papers Project has demonstrated the breadth and depth of Lincoln's legal practice.
790. John Todd Stuart interview with William H. Herndon, ca. 1865–1866, in Wilson and Davis, *Herndon's Informants*, 482. While Stuart's memory might not be exact, there is little reason to doubt the sentiment.
791. Speech at Hartford, Connecticut, March 5, 1860, in CWAL Volume IV, 3.
792. Harry V. Jaffa, "The Emancipation Proclamation," quoted in Robert Goldwin, ed., *One Hundred Years of Emancipation*, 23.
793. Debate at Alton, October 15, 1858, in CWAL, Volume III, 311.

794. Speech at Republican Banquet, Chicago, December 10, 1856, in CWAL, Volume II, 385.

795. Fragments on Slavery, (July 1, 1854), in ibid., 222. See also Lewis E. Lehrman, "To Give all a Chance—Lincoln, Abolition, and Economic Freedom," New York: Gilder Lehrman Institute of American History, 2004.

796. Definition of Democracy, August 1, 1858, in CWAL, Volume II, 532.

797. Speech at Chicago, Illinois, July 10, 1858, in CWAL, Volume II, 492, 500–501.

798. Ida Tarbell, *The Life of Lincoln*, Volume 1, 33. See David J. Bodenhamer and Randall T. Shepard, *The History of Indiana Law*, 36.

799. Letter from Abraham Lincoln to William H. Seward, February 1, 1861, in CWAL, Volume IV, 183.

800. Speech at Chicago, Illinois, July 10, 1858, in CWAL, Volume II, 500–501.

801. "The Heroic Age in Washington," quoted in Michael Burlingame, ed., *At Lincoln's Side: John Hay's Civil War Correspondence and Selected Writings*, 115–16.

802. Fourth Message to Congress, December 6, 1864, in CWAL, Volume VIII, 405.

803. Kenneth M. Stampp, "Lincoln's History," quoted in McPherson, *"We Cannot Escape History,"* 18.

804. Letter from Abraham Lincoln to George Robertson, August 15, 1855, in CWAL, Volume II, 318.

805. Ibid., 317–18.

806. James M. McPherson, *Drawn with the Sword*, 196.

807. Speech at Peoria, October 16, 1854, in CWAL, Volume II, 271.

808. Letter from Joseph Gillespie to William H. Herndon, January 31, 1866, in Wilson and Davis, *Herndon's Informants*, 183.

809. First Annual Message to Congress, December 3, 1861, in CWAL, Volume V, 52. Lincoln scholar Robert Bray has exhaustively reviewed the books Lincoln is thought to have read. Based on the testimony of William H. Herndon, Bray rated the likelihood of Llincoln having read Francis Wayland's *Elements of Political Economy* (1837) with an A. Herndon had noted that "Lincoln liked the book, except the *free trade doctrines*." Robert Bray, "What Abraham Lincoln Read: An Evaluative and Annotated List," *Journal of the Abraham Lincoln Association*, Summer 2007, 78.

810. William H. Smith, New York *Herald Tribune*, February 7, 1932, in Wilson, *Intimate Memories of Lincoln*, 269.

811. Lyceum Address, January 27, 1838, in CWAL, Volume I, 112.

812. Lamon, *The Life of Abraham Lincoln*, 354. James M. McPherson, "Lincoln Freed the Slaves," quoted in William Dudley, ed., *The Civil War: Opposing Viewpoints*, 265.

813. Debate at Freeport, August 27, 1858, in CWAL, Volume II, 40.

814. Herndon and Weik, *Herndon's Life of Lincoln*, 231.

815. Wilson, *Lincoln Among His Friends*, 130–135.

816. Burlingame, *The Inner World of Abraham Lincoln*, 247.

817. *Illinois Gazette*, November 4, 1858, in Bonham, *Fifty Years' Recollections*, 158–59.

818. Speech in Columbus, Ohio, September 16, 1859, in CWAL, Volume III, 404.

819. "House Divided" Speech, June 16, 1858, in CWAL, Volume II, 468.

820. Speech in Columbus, Ohio, September 16, 1859, in CWAL, Volume III, 423.

821. David R. Locke, quoted in Rice, *Reminiscences of Abraham Lincoln*, 447.

822. William H. Smith, New York *Herald Tribune*, February 7, 1932, in Wilson, *Intimate Memories of Lincoln*, 269.

823. Albert D. Richardson in ibid., 213.

CHAPTER IX

824. Letter from Samuel C. Parks to William H. Herndon, March 25, 1866, in Wilson and Davis, *Herndon's Informants*, 239.
825. Selby, "Genesis of the Republican Party," 272.
826. White, "Abraham Lincoln in 1854," 11. My first reading of the speech cast the same spell over me.
827. Scripps, *Life of Abraham Lincoln*, 49–50.
828. Illinois *State Journal*, October 5, 1854, in Herndon and Weik. *Herndon's Life of Lincoln*, 227.
829. Arnold, *The Life of Abraham Lincoln*, 118.
830. Arnold, *The History of Abraham Lincoln*, 90.
831. Henry J. Raymond, *Lincoln, His Life and Times Being the Life and Public Services of Abraham Lincoln*, Volume I, 44.
832. Brooks, *Abraham Lincoln and the Downfall of American Slavery*, 141.
833. Nicolay and Hay, *Abraham Lincoln: A History*, Volume I, 211.
834. Josiah G. Holland, *Holland's Life of Abraham Lincoln*, 142.
835. Stoddard, *Abraham Lincoln*, 144.
836. Church, *History of the Republican Party in Illinois*, 27.
837. Tarbell, *The Life of Abraham Lincoln*, Volume I, 281–82.
838. Stephenson, *Lincoln*, 78.
839. Beveridge, *Abraham Lincoln*, Volume II, 218.
840. Paul M. Angle, "Lincoln's Power with Words," *Journal of Abraham Lincoln Association*, 1981, 16–17.
841. Sandburg, *Abraham Lincoln: The Prairie Years*, Volume II, 18.
842. Benjamin P. Thomas, "Abe Lincoln, Country Lawyer," *The Atlantic*, February 1954.
843. T. Harry Williams, "The Cause of the Civil War," O. Fritiof Ander, ed., *Lincoln Images: Augustana College Centennial Essays*, quoted in Fehrenbacher, *The Leadership of Abraham Lincoln*, 13.
844. Masters, *Lincoln the Man*, 214–21.
845. Milton, *The Eve of Conflict*, 184.
846. Thomas, *Abraham Lincoln*, 152.
847. Randall, *Lincoln the President*, Volume I, 99.
848. Ibid., 105.
849. Donald, *Lincoln*, 176–77.
850. Nevins, *The Emergence of Lincoln*, Volume I, 359.
851. Nevins, *Ordeal of the Union*, 341.
852. Neely Jr., *The Last Best Hope of Earth*, 37, 36, 39.
853. Richard Hoftstadter, *The American Political Tradition*, 110.
854. Fehrenbacher, *Prelude to Greatness*, 24–25.
855. Riddle, *Congressman Abraham Lincoln*, 249.
856. Brooks D. Simpson, *Think Anew, Act Anew: Abraham Lincoln on Slavery, Freedom, and Union*, 8.
857. Riddle, *Congressman Abe Lincoln*, 248.
858. Ibid.
859. Johannsen, *Lincoln, the South, and Slavery*, 28.
860. Ibid., 29.
861. Ibid., 31.
862. First Political Announcement, March 9, 1832, in CWAL, Volume I, 8.

863. Letter to Joseph Hooker, January 26, 1863, in CWAL, Volume VI, 78–79.

864. Fornieri, *The Language of Liberty*, 154.

865. Carwardine, *Lincoln*, 57.

866. Miller, *Lincoln's Virtues*, 69.

867. Niven, *The Coming of the Civil War*, 85–86.

868. Stephen B. Oates, *With Malice Toward None: A Life of Abraham Lincoln*, 118.

869. Stephen B. Oates, *Abraham Lincoln: The Man Behind the Myths*, 67.

870. Fehrenbacher, *Prelude to Greatness*, 85.

871. Carwardine, *Lincoln*, 24–25.

872. Wright, *Lincoln & the Politics of Slavery*, 65.

873. Lincoln's Eulogy for Henry Clay, July 6, 1852, in CWAL, Volume II, 123.

874. Ibid., 126.

875. Goodwin, *Team of Rivals*, 166.

876. Matthew Pinsker, *Abraham Lincoln*, 60.

877. John Channing Briggs, *Lincoln's Speeches Reconsidered*, 135.

878. Boritt, *Lincoln and the Economics of the American Dream*, 155–56.

879. Ibid., 276.

880. Courtesy of Michael Burlingame.

881. Guelzo, *Lincoln's Emancipation Proclamation*, 24.

882. Wilson, *Lincoln's Sword*, 20, 37.

883. Striner, *Father Abraham*, 46.

884. Rawley, *Abraham Lincoln and a Nation Worth Fighting For*, 17.

885. Ibid., 18.

886. Gienapp, *This Fiery Trial*, 28.

887. Speech at Peoria, Illinois, October 16, 1854, in CWAL, Volume II, 266.

888. Ibid.

889. First Annual Message to Congress, December 3, 1861, in CWAL, Volume V, 52.

890. Ibid.

891. Clayborne Carson and Kris Shepard, eds., *A Call to Conscience: The Landmark Speeches of Dr. Martin Luther King, Jr.*, 182.

892. Letter from Abraham Lincoln to John M. Brockman, September 25, 1860, in CWAL, Volume IV, 121.

893. See Boritt, *Lincoln and the Economics of the American Dream*, passim.

894. Speech at New Haven, Connecticut, March 6, 1860, in CWAL, Volume IV, 24–25.

895. Rice, *Reminiscences of Abraham Lincoln*, 193.

896. Fourth Annual Message to Congress, December 6, 1864, in CWAL, Volume VIII, 151.

897. Fragment on slavery, ca July 1, 1854, CWAL, Volume II, 222.

FULL TEXT OF SPEECH AT PEORIA, ILLINOIS

898. Speech at Peoria, in CWAL, Volume II, 247–83.

BIBLIOGRAPHY

PRIMARY PRINTED SOURCES

Angle, Paul M. *Abraham Lincoln by Some Men Who Knew Him.* Freeport, NY: Books for Libraries Press, 1969.

Avery, Myrta L., ed. *Recollections of Alexander H. Stephens: His Diary Kept When a Prisoner at Fort Warren, Boston Harbour.* New York: Doubleday, Page & Company, 1910.

Basler, Roy P., Marion Dolores Pratt, and Lloyd A. Dunlap. *The Collected Works of Abraham Lincoln.* New Brunswick, NJ: Rutgers University Press, 1953.

Bonham, Jeriah. *Fifty Years' Recollections with Observations and Reflections on Historical Events Giving Sketches of Eminent Citizens—Their Lives and Public Services.* Peoria, IL: J. W. Franks & Sons, 1883.

Bryner, B. C. *Abraham Lincoln in Peoria, Illinois.* Peoria, IL: Friends of the G. A. R. Hall, 2001.

Burlingame, Michael, ed. *An Oral History of Abraham Lincoln: John G. Nicolay's Interviews and Essays.* Carbondale: Southern Illinois University Press, 1996.

———. *Lincoln's Journalist: John Hay's Anonymous Writings for the Press, 1860–1864.* Carbondale: Southern Illinois University Press, 1998.

———. *At Lincoln's Side: John Hay's Civil War Correspondence and Selected Writings.* Carbondale: Southern Illinois University Press, 2000.

———. *Inside the White House in War Times: Memoirs and Reports of Lincoln's Secretary: William O. Stoddard.* Lincoln: University of Nebraska Press, 2000.

———. *With Lincoln in the White House: Letters, Memoranda, and Other Writings of John G. Nicolay, 1860–1865.* Carbondale: Southern Illinois University Press, 2000.

———. *Dispatches from Lincoln's White House: The Anonymous Civil War Journalism of Presidential Secretary William O. Stoddard.* Lincoln: University of Nebraska Press, 2002.

Burlingame, Michael, and John R. Turner Ettlinger, ed. *Inside Lincoln's White House: The Complete Civil War Diary of John Hay.* Carbondale: Southern Illinois University Press, 1997.

Brooks, Noah. *Washington, D.C., in Lincoln's Time.* Athens: University of Georgia Press, 1989.

Chase, Salmon P. "The Nebraska Question: Comprising Speeches in the U.S. Senate by Mr. Douglas, Mr. Chase, Mr. Smith, Mr. Everett, Mr. Wade, Mr. Seward, Mr. Badger, and Mr. Sumner Together with a History of the Missouri Compromise." Maintain *Plighted Faith*, February 3, 1854.

Fehrenbacher, Don E., and Virginia Fehrenbacher. *Recollected Words of Abraham Lincoln.* Stanford: Stanford University Press, 1996.

Forney, John W. *Anecdotes of Public Men.* New York: Harper & Brothers, 1873.

French, Benjamin Brown. *Witness to the Young Republic: A Yankee's Journal, 1828–1870.* Hanover, NH: University Press of New England, 1989.

Johannsen, Robert W., ed. *The Letters of Stephen A. Douglas.* Urbana: University of Illinois Press, 1961.

Livermore, Mary A. *My Story of the War: Four Years Personal Experience in the Sanitary Service of the Rebellion.* Hartford, CT: A. D. Worthington and Co., 1887.

McCormack, Thomas J., ed. *Memoirs of Gustave Koerner, 1809–1896: Life-sketches Written at the Suggestion of His Children.* Cedar Rapids, IA: The Torch Press, 1909.

Mearns, David C., ed. *The Lincoln Papers.* Garden City, NY: Doubleday, 1948.

Mitgang, Herbert, ed. *Lincoln as They Saw Him.* Athens: University of Georgia Press, 1956.

Oldroyd, Osborne H. *The Lincoln Memorial: Album Immortelles.* Chicago: Gem Publishing House, 1883.

Palmer, George Thomas, ed. "Letters from Lyman Trumbull to John M. Palmer, 1854–1858." *Journal of the Illinois State Historical Society,* April–July 1923.

Palmer, George Thomas, ed. *Letters to John M. Palmer.* Springfield, IL, 1924.

Palmer, John M. *Personal Recollections of John M. Palmer: The Story of an Earnest Life.* Cincinnati: Robert Clarke Company, 1901.

Pease, Theodore Calvin, ed. *The Diary of Orville H. Browning.* Volume I. Springfield: Illinois State Historical Library, 1925.

Pickett, Thomas J. "Reminiscences of Abraham Lincoln by Thomas J. Pickett." *Lincoln Herald,* December 1943.

Rice, Allen Thorndike, ed. *Reminiscences of Abraham Lincoln by Distinguished Men of His Time.* New York: North American Publishing Co, 1866.

Selby, Paul. "Republican State Convention, Springfield, Illinois, October 4–5, 1854." *Transactions of the McLean County Historical Society,* Volume 3, 1900.

———. "Genesis of the Republican Party in Illinois." *Transactions of the Illinois State Historical Society,* Volume 11, 1906.

———. "The Editorial Convention of 1856." *Journal of the Illinois State Historical Society,* Spring 1955.

Stephens, Alexander H. "Speech of Hon. Alexander H. Stephens, of Georgia on The Presidential Election of 1856; the Compromise of 1850; and the Kansas-Nebraska Act of 1854." Washington *Congressional Globe,* January 6, 1857.

———. *In Public and Private, With Letters and Speeches, Before During, and Since the War.* Edited by Henry Cleveland. Philadelphia, 1866.

———. *A Constitutional View of the Late War Between the States; Causes, Character, Conduct and Results Presented in a Series of Colloquies at Liberty Hall.* Volume I. Philadelphia: National Publishing Co., 1868.

Stevens, Walter B. *A Reporter's Lincoln.* Michael Burlingame, ed. Lincoln: University of Nebraska Press, 1998.

Weed, Thurlow. *The Life of Thurlow Weed including His Autobiography and a Memoir.* Boston: Houghton, Mifflin and Company, 1884.

White, Horace. "Abraham Lincoln in 1854." *Journal of the Illinois State Historical Society,* January 1908.

Whitney, Henry Clay. *Life on the Circuit with Abraham Lincoln.* Caldwell, ID: Caxton Printers, 1940.

Wilson, Douglas L., and Rodney O. Davis, eds. *Herndon's Informants.* Urbana: University of Illinois Press, 1998.

Wilson, Rufus Rockwell, ed. *Lincoln Among His Friends.* Caldwell, ID: Caxton Printers, 1942.

———. *Intimate Memories of Lincoln.* Elmira, NY: The Primavera Press, 1945.

Yates, Richard, "Speech of Richard Yates, Delivered in the Wigwam, at the Springfield Jubilee." November 20, 1860.

SECONDARY SOURCES

Abzug, Robert H., and Stephen E. Maizlish, eds. *New Perspectives on Race and Slavery in America: Essays in Honor of Kenneth M. Stamp.* Lexington: University Press of Kentucky, 1986.

Alger, Horatio. *Abraham Lincoln, the Young Backwoods Boy; or, How a Young Rail Splitter Became President.* New York: American Publishers, 1883.

Anderson, Dwight. *Abraham Lincoln: The Quest for Immortality.* New York: Knopf, 1982.

Angle, Paul M. "The Peoria Truce." *Journal of the Illinois State Historical Association,* January 1929, Volume 21, No. 4.

———. *"Here I Have Lived"; A History of Lincoln's Springfield.* Springfield, IL: Abraham Lincoln Association, 1935.

Angle, Paul M., and Earl Schenck Miers. *The Living Lincoln.* New York: Barnes & Noble Books, 1992.

Arnold, Isaac N. *The History of Abraham Lincoln, and the Overthrow of Slavery.* Chicago: Clark & Co., 1866.

———. Abraham Lincoln: A Paper Read Before the Royal Historical Society, London, June 16, 1881.

———. *The Life of Abraham Lincoln.* Lincoln: University of Nebraska Press, 1994.

Baker, Jean H. *Mary Todd Lincoln: A Biography.* New York: W. W. Norton, 1987.

———. *"Not Much of Me": Abraham Lincoln as a Typical American.* Fort Wayne, IN: Louis A. Warren Lincoln Library, 1987.

Balance, Charles. *History of Peoria, Illinois.* Peoria, IL: N. C. Nason, 1870.

Baringer, William E., ed. *Lincoln Day by Day: A Chronology 1809–1865.* 3 Volumes, Washington, D.C.: Lincoln Sesquicentennial Commission, 1960.

Barnes, Gilbert Hobbs. *The Antislavery Impulse, 1830–1844.* Gloucester, MA: Peter Smith, 1957.

Barton, William E. *The Soul of Abraham Lincoln.* Urbana: University of Illinois Press, 2005.

Belz, Herman. *Abraham Lincoln, Constitutionalism, and Equal Rights in the Civil War Era.* New York: Fordham University Press, 1998.

———. *Reconstructing the Union: Theory and Policy During the Civil War.* Ithaca, NY: Cornell University Press, 1969.

Bennett, Lerone, Jr. *Forced into Glory.* Chicago: Johnson Publishing Co., 2000.

Benson, T. Lloyd. *The Caning of Senator Sumner.* Belmont, CA: Thomson/Wadsworth, 2004.

Berlin, Ira, Leslie S. Rowland, et al, editors. *Freedom: A Documentary History of Emancipation.* New York: Cambridge University Press, 1982.

Beveridge, Albert. *Abraham Lincoln, 1809–1858.* Volume II. Boston: Houghton Mifflin Co., 1928.

Blight, David W. *Frederick Douglass's Civil War: Keeping Faith in Jubilee.* Baton Rouge: University of Louisiana Press, 1989.

———. *Race and Reunion: The Civil War in American Memory.* Cambridge, MA: Belknap Press, 2001.

———. *Beyond the Battlefield: Race, Memory, and the American Civil War.* Amherst, MA: University of Massachusetts Press, 2002.

Blue, Frederick J. *The Free Soilers: Third Party Politics.* Urbana: University of Illinois Press, 1973.

———. *Salmon P. Chase: A Life in Politics.* Kent, OH: Kent State University Press, 1987.

———. *Charles Sumner and the Conscience of the North.* Arlington Heights, IL: Harlan Davidson, 1994.

Bogue, Allan G. *The Earnest Men: Republicans of the Civil War Senate.* Ithaca, NY: Cornell University Press, 1981.

Boritt, Gabor S. *Lincoln and the Economics of the American Dream.* Memphis, TN: Memphis State University Press, 1978.

Bray, Robert. "What Lincoln Read—An Evaluative and Annotative List." *Journal of the Abraham Lincoln Association,* Summer 2007.

Briggs, John Channing. *Lincoln's Speeches Reconsidered.* Baltimore: John Hopkins University Press, 2005.

Brooks, Noah. *Abraham Lincoln and the Downfall of Slavery.* New York: G. P Putnam & Sons, 1894.

———. *Abraham Lincoln: His Youth and Early Manhood.* New York: G. P. Putnam & Sons, 1901.

Brown, William Garrott. "Lincoln's Rival." *The Atlantic Monthly,* February 1902.

Burlingame, Michael. *The Inner World of Abraham Lincoln.* Urbana, IL: University of Illinois Press, 1994.

———, ed. *"Lincoln's Humor" and Other Essays of Benjamin Thomas.* Urbana: University of Illinois Press, 2006.

Burton, Orville Vernon. *The Age of Lincoln.* New York: Hill and Wang, 2007.

Callan, J. Sean. *Courage and Country: James Shields: More than Irish Luck.* Lake Forest, IL: 1st Books Library, 2004.

Capers, Gerald Mortimer. *Stephen A. Douglas, Defender of the Union.* Edited by Oscar Handlin. Boston: Little, Brown, 1959.

Carr, Clark Ezra. *The Illini: A Story of the Prairies.* Chicago: A. C. McClurg & Co., 1904.

Carsmon, Clayborne, and Kris Shepard, eds. *A Call to Conscience: The Landmark Speeches of Dr. Martin Luther King, Jr.* New York: Warner Books, 2001.

Carwardine, Richard J. *Lincoln.* London: Pearson, 2003.

Chambers, William Nisbet. *Old Bullion Benton, Senator from the New West: Thomas Hart Benton, 1782–1858.* New York: Russell & Russell, 1970.

Charnwood, Lord Godfrey. *Abraham Lincoln.* Garden City, NY: Garden City Publishing Co., 1970.

Church, Charles A. *History of the Republican Party in Illinois, 1854–1912.* Rockford, IL: Wilson Brothers Co., 1918.

Cole, Arthur Charles. *The Era of the Civil War, 1848–1870.* Freeport, NY: Books for Libraries Press, 1971.

Condon, William Henry. *Life of Major-General James Shields, Hero of Three Wars and Senator from Three States.* Chicago: Press of the Blakely Printing Co., 1900.

Cooper, William J. *Jefferson Davis, American.* New York: Alfred A. Knopf, 2000.

Cooper, William J., and Thomas E. Terrill. *The American South: A History.* Boston: McGraw-Hill, 2002.

Cox, LaWanda F. *Lincoln and Black Freedom: A Study in Presidential Leadership.* Urbana: University of Illinois Press, 1985.

Crandall, Andrew W. *The Early History of the Republican Party, 1854–1856*. Boston: R. D. Badger, 1930.

Crissey, Elwell. *Lincoln's Lost Speech*. New York: Hawthorn Books, 1967.

Davis, Cullom, Charles B. Strozier, Rebecca Monroe Veach, and Geoffrey C. Ward, eds. *The Public and the Private Lincoln: Contemporary Perspectives*. Carbondale: Southern Illinois University Press, 1979.

Davis, David Brion. *The Problem of Slavery in the Age of Revolution*. Ithaca, NY: Cornell University Press, 1975.

———. *Inhuman Bondage: The Rise and Fall of Slavery in the New World*. New York: Oxford Press, 2006.

Davis, David Brion, and Stephen Mintz. *The Boisterous Sea of Liberty: A Documentary History of America from Discovery Through the Civil War*. New York: Oxford University Press, 1998.

Davis, Granville. "Douglas and the Chicago Mob." *The American Historical Review*, April 1949.

Davis, Jefferson. *The Rise and Fall of the Confederate Government*. Volume I. New York: Thomas Yoseloff, 1958.

Davis, Michael. *The Image of Lincoln in the South*. Knoxville: University of Tennessee Press, 1971.

Davis, William C. *Jefferson Davis: The Man and His Hour*. New York: Harper Collins, 1991.

Dean, Eric T., Jr. "Stephen A. Douglas and Popular Sovereignty." *The Historian*. Volume 57, 1995.

Deutsch, Kenneth L., and Joseph R. Fornieri. *Lincoln's American Dream: Clashing Political Perspectives*. Washington, DC: Potomac Books, 2005.

Dew, Charles B. *Apostles of Disunion: Southern Secession Commissioners and the Causes of the Civil War*. Charlottesville, VA: University of Virginia Press, 2001.

Diggins, John P. *The Lost Soul of American Politics: Virtue, Self-Interest, and the Foundations of Liberalism*. New York: Basic Books, 1984.

Diggins, John Patrick. *On Hallowed Ground: Abraham Lincoln and The Foundations of American History*. New Haven: Yale University Press, 2000.

Dirck, Brian R. *Lincoln & Davis: Imagining America, 1809–1865*. Lawrence: University Press of Kansas, 2001.

Donald, David. *Lincoln's Herndon*. New York: Alfred A. Knopf, 1948.

Donald, David H. *Charles Sumner and the Coming of the Civil War*. New York: Alfred A. Knopf, 1960.

Donald, David Herbert. *Liberty and Union*. Lexington, MA: Heath, 1978.

———. *Charles Sumner and the Coming of the Civil War*. Chicago: University of Chicago Press, 1981, c1960.

———. *Lincoln*. New York: Simon & Schuster, 1995.

———. *Lincoln's Herndon*. New York: Da Capo Press, 1948.

Dorfman, Joseph. *The Economic Mind in American Civilization, 1606–1865*. New York: Viking Press, 1946.

Drake, Ross. "The Law That Ripped America in Two." *Smithsonian*. May 2004.

DuBois, W. E. B. *John Brown*. Philadelphia: G. W. Jacobs Co., 1909.

Duberman, Martin. *The Antislavery Vanguard: Essays on the Abolitionists*. Princeton: Princeton University Press, 1965.

———. *James Russell Lowell*. Boston: Houghton Mifflin, 1966.

———. *Charles Francis Adams, 1807–1886*. Stanford: Stanford University Press, 1968.

Dudley, William, ed. *The Civil War: Opposing Viewpoints.* San Diego: Greenhaven Press, 1999.

Duff, John J. *Abraham Lincoln, Prairie Lawyer.* New York: Bramwell House, 1960.

East, Ernest E. "The 'Peoria Truce' Did Douglas Ask for Quarter?" *Journal of the Illinois State Historical Association.* Volume 29, No. 1, April 1936.

———. *Abraham Lincoln Sees Peoria.* Peoria, IL: Record Publishing Company, 1939.

Edwards, Arthur. *Sketch of the Life of Norman B. Judd.* Chicago: Horton & Leonard, 1878.

Engs, Robert F., and Randall M. Miller. *The Birth of the Grand Old Party.* Philadelphia: University of Pennsylvania Press, 2002.

Farrand, Max, ed. *Records of the Federal Convention of 1787.* New Haven: Yale University Press, 1911.

Fehrenbacher, Don E. *Prelude to Greatness: Lincoln the 1850s.* Stanford: Stanford University Press, 1962.

———. *The Changing Image of Lincoln in American Historiography.* Oxford: Oxford University Press, 1968.

———. *The Leadership of Abraham Lincoln.* New York: John Wiley & Sons, 1970.

———. *The Dred Scott Case: Its Significance in America Law and Politics.* New York: Oxford University Press, 1978.

———. *Slavery, Law and Politics: The Dred Scott Case in Historical Perspective.* New York: Oxford University Press, 1978.

———. *Lincoln in Text and Context: Collected Essays.* Stanford: Stanford University Press, 1987.

———. *Sectional Crisis and Southern Constitutionalism.* Baton Rouge: Louisiana State University Press, 1995.

———. (completed by Ward M. McFee.) *The Slaveholding Republic: An Account of the United States Government's Relations to Slavery.* New York: Oxford University Press, 2001.

Filler, Louis. *The Crusade against Slavery, 1830–1860.* New York: Harper, 1960.

Findley, Paul. *A. Lincoln, The Crucible of Congress: The Years Which Forged His Greatness.* New York: Crown Publishers, 1979.

Finkelman, Paul. "Slavery, the 'More Perfect Union,' and the Prairie State." *Illinois Historical Journal,* Winter 1987.

Fogel, Robert W. *Without Consent or Contract: The Rise and Fall of American Slavery.* New York: Norton, 1989.

———. *Slavery and the Founders: Race and Liberty in the Age of Jefferson.* Armonk, NY: M. E. Sharpe, 2001.

———. *The Slavery Debates: 1952–1990: A Retrospective.* Baton Rouge: Louisiana State University Press, 2003.

Fogel, Robert William, and Stanley L. Engerman. *Time on the Cross: The Economics of American Slavery.* New York: W. W. Norton, 1989.

Foner, Eric. *Free Soil, Free Labor, Free Men: The Ideology of the Republican Party Before the Civil War.* New York, Oxford University Press, 1970.

———. *Politics and Ideology in the Age of the Civil War.* New York: Oxford University Press, 1980.

———. *Nothing But Freedom: Emancipation and Its Legacy.* Baton Rouge: Louisiana State University Press, 1983.

———. *Reconstruction.* New York: Oxford University Press, 1988.

Foner, Philip. *The Life and Writings of Frederick Douglass.* New York: International Publishers, 1950.

Foner, Philip S. *Business and Slavery: The New York Merchants and the Irrepressible Conflict.* Chapel Hill: University of North Carolina Press, 1941.

Forbes, Robert Pierce. *The Missouri Compromise and Its Aftermath: Slavery and the Meaning of America.* Chapel Hill: University of North Carolina Press, 2007.

Fornieri, Joseph R. *Abraham Lincoln's Political Faith.* DeKalb, IL: Northern Illinois University Press, 2003.

———. *The Language of Liberty: The Political Speeches and Writings of Abraham Lincoln.* Washington, DC: Regnery Gateway, 2004.

Forsythe, Clark. *The Greatest Good Possible.* Unpublished manuscript.

Fort, George Milton. *The Eve of Conflict: Stephen A. Douglas and the Needless War.* New York: Octagon Books, 1980.

Franklin, John Hope. *The Emancipation Proclamation.* Garden City, NY: Doubleday, 1963.

Franklin, John Hope, and Loren Schweninger. *Runaway Slaves: Rebels on the Plantation.* New York: Oxford University Press, 1999.

Frederickson, George M. *The Inner Civil War: Northern Intellectuals and the Crisis of the Union.* New York: Harper and Row, 1965.

———. *The Black Image in the White Mind: The Debate on Afro-American Character and Destiny.* New York: Harper & Row, 1971.

Gara, Larry. *The Presidency of Franklin Pierce.* Lawrence: University Press of Kansas, 1991.

Gienapp, William. *Origins of the Republican Party, 1852–1856.* New York: Oxford University Press, 1987.

———. *Abraham Lincoln and Civil War America.* New York: Oxford University Press, 2002.

Goodwin, Doris Kearns. *Team of Rivals.* New York: Simon & Schuster, 2005.

Grimsted, David. *American Mobbing, 1828–1861, Toward Civil War.* New York: Oxford University Press, 1998.

Guelzo, Allen C. *Abraham Lincoln, Redeemer President.* Grand Rapids, MI: William B. Eerdmans Publishing Co., 1999.

———. *Lincoln's Emancipation Proclamation: The End of Slavery in America.* New York: Simon & Schuster, 2004.

Hale, William H. *Horace Greeley: Voice of the People.* New York: Harper & Brothers, 1950.

Hammond, Bray. *Banks and Politics in America from the Revolution to the Civil War.* Princeton: Princeton University Press, 1957.

Hansen, Stephen, and Paul Nygaard. "Stephen A. Douglas, the Know-Nothings, and the Democratic Party in Illinois, 1854–1858." *Illinois Historical Journal,* Volume 17, Number 2, Summer 1994.

Harper, Robert S. *Lincoln and the Press.* New York: McGraw-Hill Book Co., 1951.

Harris, William C. *Lincoln's Rise to the Presidency.* Lawrence: University of Kansas, 2007.

Hart, Albert Bushnell, ed. *Documents Relating to the Kansas-Nebraska Act, 1854.* New York: A. Lovell & Company, 1894.

———. *Salmon P. Chase.* New York: Chelsea House, 1980.

Hassler, William W. "The Irrepressible James Shields." *Lincoln Herald,* Fall 1979.

Hawley, Charles Arthur. "Lincoln in Kansas." *Journal of the Illinois State Historical Society,* June 1949.

Heckman, Richard Allen. "Political Fortunes of Lincoln and Douglas in 1858–1859." *Lincoln Herald,* Winter 1964, Volume 67, No. 4.

———. "Some Impressions of Lincoln and Douglas during the Campaign of 1858." *Lincoln Herald,* Volume 66, No. 3, Fall 1964.

Herndon, William H., and Jesse W. Weik. *Herndon's Life of Lincoln*. Edited by Douglas L. Wilson and Rodney O. Davis. Urbana: Knox College Lincoln Studies Center and the University of Illinois Press, 2006.

Hickey, James T. "Lincolniana: Robert S. Todd Seeks a Job for His Son-in-Law, Abraham Lincoln." *Journal of the Illinois Historical Society*, 1979.

Hill, Frederick Trevor. *Lincoln the Lawyer*. Littleton, CO: F. B. Rothman, 1986.

Hofstadter, Richard. *The American Political Tradition and the Men Who Made It*. New York: Alfred A. Knopf, 1948.

Holland, Josiah G. *Holland's Life of Abraham Lincoln*. Lincoln: University of Nebraska Press, 1998.

Holt, Michael F. *The Political Crisis of the 1850s*. New York: Wiley, 1978.

———. *Political Parties and American Political Development: From the Age of Jackson to the Age of Lincoln*. Baton Rouge: Louisiana State University Press, 1992.

———. *The Rise and Fall of the American Whig Party: Jacksonian Politics and the Onset of the Civil War*. New York: Oxford, 1999.

———. *The Fate of Their Country: Politicians, Slavery Extension, and the Coming of the Civil War*. New York: Hill and Wang, 2004.

Holzer, Harold, ed. *Lincoln and Freedom: Slavery, Emancipation and the Thirteenth Amendment*. Carbondale: Southern Illinois University Press, 2007.

Horton, James Oliver, and Lois E. Horton. *Black Bostonians: Family Life and Community Struggle in the Antebellum North*. New York: Holmes & Meier, 1979.

———. *In Hope of Liberty: Culture, Community, and Protest Among Northern Free Blacks, 1700–1860*. New York: Oxford University Press, 1997.

———. *Slavery and the Making of America*. New York: Oxford University Press, 2005.

Howe, Daniel Walker. *The Political Culture of the American Whigs*. Chicago: University of Chicago Press, 1979.

Howells, William D. *Life of Abraham Lincoln*. Bloomington: Indiana University Press, 1960.

Hubbard, Charles M., ed. *Lincoln Reshapes the Presidency*. Macon, GA: Mercer University Press, 2003.

Huston, James L. *Calculating the Value of the Union: Slavery, Property Rights, and the Economic Origins of the Civil War*. Chapel Hill: University of North Carolina Press, 2003.

Hyman, Harold. *A More Perfect Union: The Impact of the Civil War and Reconstruction on the Constitution*. New York: Knopf, 1973.

Jaffa, Harry V. *Crisis in the House Divided*. Chicago: University of Chicago Press, 1959.

———. *A New Birth of Freedom: Abraham Lincoln and the Coming of the Civil War*. Lanham, MD: Rowman & Littlefield Publishers, Inc., 2000.

Jaffa, Harry V., and Robert W. Johannsen. *In The Name of the People: Speeches and Writings of Lincoln and Douglas in the Ohio Campaign of 1859*. Columbus: Ohio State University Press, 1959.

Johannsen, Robert Walter. *Stephen A. Douglas*. New York, Oxford University Press, 1973.

———. "The Lincoln-Douglas Campaign of 1858: Background and Perspective." *Journal of the Illinois State Historical Society*, Winter 1980.

———. *The Frontier, the Union and Stephen A. Douglas*. Urbana: University of Illinois Press, 1989.

———. *Lincoln, the South, and Slavery: The Political Dimension*. Baton Rouge: Louisiana State University Press, 1991.

Johnson, Allen. *Stephen A. Douglas: A Study in American Politics*. New York: Chelsea House, 1983.

Johnson, Ludwell H. *Division and Reunion: America, 1848–1877*. New York: Wiley, 1978.

Johnston, Richard M., and William Hand Browne. *Life of Alexander H. Stephens*. Freeport, NY: Books for Libraries Press, 1971.

Jordan, Winthrop D. *White Over Black: American Attitudes Toward the Negro, 1550–1812*. Chapel Hill: University of North Carolina Press, 1968.

Kimball, E. L. "Richard Yates: His Record as Civil War Governor of Illinois." *Journal of the Illinois State Historical Society*, Volume 23, No. 1, April 1930.

Kolchin, Peter. *Unfree Labor: American Slavery and Russian Serfdom*. Cambridge: Belknap Press, 1987.

———. *American Slavery, 1619–1877*. New York: Hill and Wang, 1993.

Krug, Mark M. *Lyman Trumbull, Conservative Radical*. New York: A. S. Barnes, 1965.

Kyle, Otto R. "Mr. Lincoln Steps Out: The Anti-Nebraska Editors' Convention." *Abraham Lincoln Quarterly*, March 1941.

———. *Abraham Lincoln in Decatur*. New York: Vantage Press, 1957.

Lamon, Ward Hill. *The Life of Abraham Lincoln from His Birth to His Inauguration as President*. Kila, MT: Kessenger Publishing Company, 2007.

Lindsey, Richard A. "Lincoln and Shields." *Lincoln Herald*, Volume 80, No. 2, Summer 1978.

Litwack, Leon. *North of Slavery: The Negro in the Free States, 1790–1860*. Chicago: University of Chicago Press, 1961.

Litwack, Leon F. *Been in the Storm So Long: The Aftermath of Slavery*. New York: Alfred A. Knopf, 1979.

Ludwig, Emil. *Lincoln*. Boston: Little Brown and Co., 1930.

Luthin, Reinhard H. "Abraham Lincoln Becomes a Republican." *Political Science Quarterly*, September 1944.

———. *The First Lincoln Campaign*. Cambridge, MA: Harvard University Press, 1944.

Maizlish, Stephen E., and John J. Kushma, eds. *Essays on American Antebellum Politics, 1840–1860*. College Station: Texas A&M University Press, 1982.

Malin, James C. "The Motives of Stephen A. Douglas in the Organization of Nebraska Territory: A Letter Dated December 17, 1863." *Kansas Historical Quarterly*, Volume 19, 1951.

———. *The Nebraska Question, 1852–1854*. Lawrence: University of Kansas Press, 1953.

Martin, Waldo E. *The Mind of Frederick Douglass*. Chapel Hill: University of North Carolina Press, 1984.

Masters, Edgar Lee. *Lincoln the Man*. London: Cassell, 1931.

Mayer, George H. *The Republican Party*. New York: Oxford University Press, 1964.

Mayfield, John. *Rehearsal for Republicanism: Free Soil and the Politics of Antislavery*. Port Washington, NY: Kennikat Press, 1980.

McCullough, David, ed. *Historical Encyclopedia of Illinois and History of Peoria County*. La Crosse, WI: Brookhaven Press, 2001.

McDougall, Walter A. *Freedom Just Around the Corner: A New American History, 1585–1828*. New York: HarperCollins Publishers, 2004.

McFeely, William S. *Frederick Douglass*. New York: Norton, 1991.

McJimsey, George T. *The Dividing and Reuniting of America, 1848–1877*. St. Louis: Forum Press, 1981.

McMurtry, Robert Gerald. *Lincoln's Friend Douglas*. Principia Corporation, 1946.

McPherson, James M. *Ordeal by Fire: The Civil War and Reconstruction.* New York: Alfred A. Knopf, 1982.

———. *Abraham Lincoln and the Second American Revolution.* New York: Oxford University Press, 1990.

———. *This Mighty Scourge: Perspectives on the Civil War.* New York: Oxford University Press, 2007.

———. "The Fight for Slavery in California." *New York Review of Books,* October 2007.

———, ed. *"We Cannot Escape History": Lincoln and the Last Best Hope of Earth.* Urbana: University of Illinois Press, 1995.

Meyer, Daniel. *Stephen A. Douglas & the American Union.* Chicago: University of Chicago Library, 1994.

Meyers, Marvin. *The Jacksonian Persuasion: Politics and Belief.* Stanford: Stanford University Press, 1957.

Miller, William Lee. *Lincoln's Virtues: An Ethical Biography.* New York: Alfred A. Knopf, 2002.

———. "Lincoln's Profound and Benign Americanism, or Nationalism Without Malice." *Journal of the Abraham Lincoln Association,* Winter 2001.

Milton, George Fort. *The Eve of Conflict: Stephen A. Douglas and the Needless War.* Boston: Houghton Mifflin Company, 1934.

Mintz, Steven. *Moralists and Modernizers: America's Pre-Civil War Reformers.* Baltimore: Johns Hopkins University Press, 1995.

Mitgang, Herbert. *The Fiery Trial: A Life of Abraham Lincoln.* New York: Viking Press, 1974.

Neely, Mark E., Jr. *The Fate of Liberty: Abraham Lincoln and Civil Liberties.* New York: Oxford University Press, 1991.

———. *The Last Best Hope of Earth: Abraham Lincoln and the Promise of America.* Cambridge: Harvard University Press, 1993.

Nevins, Allan, and Irving Stone, eds. *Lincoln: A Contemporary Portrait.* Garden City, NY: Doubleday, 1962.

Nevins, Allan. *The Emergence of Lincoln.* Volumes I and II. New York: Charles Scribner, 1950.

———. *The Ordeal of Union.* Volume II. New York: Charles Scribner's, 1975.

Nicolay, John G., and John Hay. *Abraham Lincoln: A History.* Volume I. New York: The Century Co., 1914.

Nichols, Roy F. *The Democratic Machine, 1850–1854.* New York: Columbia University, 1923.

———. *The Disruption of American Democracy.* New York: Macmillan Company, 1948.

———. "The Kansas-Nebraska Act: A Century of Historiography." *Mississippi Valley Historical Review,* Volume 43 (1956): 1887.

———. *Franklin Pierce: Young Hickory of the Granite Hills.* Philadelphia: University of Pennsylvania Press, 1958.

———. *Blueprints for Leviathan: American Style.* New York: Atheneum, 1963.

———. *The Invention of the American Political Parties.* New York: Macmillan, 1967.

Nichols, Roy F., and Eugene H. Berwanger. *The Stakes of Power, 1845–1877.* New York: Hill and Wang, 1982.

Niven, John. *The Coming of the Civil War, 1837–1861.* Arlington Heights, IL: Harlan Davidson, 1990.

———. *Salmon P. Chase: A Biography.* New York: Oxford University Press, 1995.

Noll, Mark A. *A History of Christianity in the United States and Canada.* Grand Rapids, MI: William B. Eerdmanns Publishing Co., 1992.

North, Douglass C. *The Economic Growth of the United States, 1790–1860.* New York: W. W. Norton. 1966.

Northrup, Jack. "Gov. Richard Yates and Pres. Lincoln." *Lincoln Herald,* Volume 70, No. 4, Winter 1968.

———. "Lincoln and Yates: The Climb to Power." *Lincoln Herald,* Volume 73, No. 4, Winter 1971.

Oakes, James. *The Radical and the Republican: Frederick Douglass, Abraham Lincoln, and the Triumph of Antislavery Politics.* New York: W. W. Norton, 2007.

Oates, Stephen B. *To Purge This Land With Blood: A Biography of John Brown.* New York: Harper & Row, 1970.

———. *Abraham Lincoln: The Man Behind the Myths.* New York: HarperPerennial, 1984.

———. *With Malice Toward None: A Life of Abraham Lincoln.* New York: Harper Perennial, 1984.

Palmer, George Thomas. *A Conscientious Turncoat: The Story of John M. Palmer, 1817–1900.* New Haven, CT: Yale University Press, 1941.

Paludan, Phillip Shaw. "Lincoln and the Greeley Letter: An Exposition." Charles M. Hubbard, ed. *Lincoln Reshapes the Presidency.* Macon, GA: Mercer University Press, 2003.

Parish, Peter J. *Slavery: History and Historians.* New York: Harper & Row, 1989.

Parrish, William Earl. *David Rice Atchison of Missouri, Border Politician.* Columbia: University of Missouri Press, 1961.

Peck, Graham A. "Was Stephen A. Douglas Antislavery?" *Journal of the Abraham Lincoln Association,* Volume 26, No. 2, Summer 2005.

Pendleton, Louis. *Alexander H. Stephens.* Philadelphia: G. W. Jacobs & Co., 1908.

Peterson, Merrill D. *The Great Triumvirate: Webster, Clay, and Calhoun.* New York: Oxford University Press, 1987.

———. *Lincoln in American Memory.* New York: Oxford University Press, 1994.

Phillips, Ulrich B. *American Negro Slavery: A Survey of the Supply, Employment, and Control of Negro Labor as Determined by the Plantation Regime.* New York: D. Appleton and Co. 1918.

Pinsker, Matthew. *Abraham Lincoln.* Washington, D.C.: CQ Press, 2002.

———. *Lincoln's Sanctuary: Abraham Lincoln and the Soldier's Home.* New York: Oxford University Press, 2003.

Potter, David M. *Lincoln and His Party in the Secession Crisis.* New Haven: Yale University Press, 1942.

———. *The Impending Crisis, 1848–1861.* New York: Harper & Row, 1976.

Potter, David Morris. *Division and the Stresses of Reunion, 1845–1876.* Glenview, IL: Scott, Foresman, 1973.

Pratt, Harry E. "Abraham Lincoln in Bloomington, Illinois." Bloomington *Weekly Pantagraph,* September 29, 1854. In *Journal of the Illinois State Historical Association,* Volume 29, No. 1, April 1936, 53.

———. *The Personal Finances of Abraham Lincoln.* Springfield, IL: Abraham Lincoln Association, 1943.

———. ed. *Concerning Mr. Lincoln.* Springfield, IL: Abraham Lincoln Association, 1944.

Quarles, Benjamin. *Frederick Douglass.* Washington, DC: Associated Publishers, 1948.

———. *Black Abolitionists.* New York: Oxford University Press, 1969.

————. *Lincoln and the Negro.* New York: Da Capo Press, 1991.

Randall, James G. *Lincoln the President: From Springfield to Gettysburg.* Volume I. New York: Dodd, Mead & Company, 1945.

Rawley, James A. *Secession: The Disruption of the American Republic, 1844–1861.* Malabar, FL: Robert E. Krieger Publishing Co., 1990.

————. *Abraham Lincoln and a Nation Worth Fighting For.* Wheeling, IL: Harland Davidson, 1996.

Ray, Perley Orman. *The Repeal of the Missouri Compromise, Its Origins and Authorship.* Cleveland: Arthur H. Clark Company, 1909.

Raymond, Henry J. *History of the Administration of President Lincoln Including His Speeches, Letters, Addresses, Proclamation, and Messages.* New York: J. C. Derby & N. C. Miller, 1864.

Rice, James M. *Peoria City and County, Illinois: A Record of Settlement, Organization, Progress and Achievement.* Volume I. Chicago: S. J. Clarke, 1912.

Richards, Leonel. *Slave Power: The Free North and Southern Domination, 1780–1860.* Baton Rouge: Louisiana State University Press, 2000.

Richardson, James D. *A Compilation of the Messages and Papers of the Presidents, 1789–1908.* Volume V. Washington, DC: Government Printing Office, 1897.

Riddle, Donald W. *Lincoln Runs for Congress.* New Brunswick, NJ: Rutgers University Press, 1948.

————. *Congressman Abraham Lincoln.* Urbana: University of Illinois Press, 1957.

Roske, Ralph Joseph. *His Own Counsel: The Life and Times of Lyman Trumbull.* Reno: University of Nevada Press, 1979.

Russell, Robert R. "The Issues in the Congressional Struggle over the Kansas-Nebraska Bill, 1854." *The Journal of Southern History,* May 1963.

Sandburg, Carl. *Abraham Lincoln: The Prairie Years.* Volume II. New York: Harcourt, Brace & World, 1926.

Schott, Thomas E. *Alexander H. Stephens of Georgia: A Biography.* Baton Rouge: Louisiana State University Press, 1988.

Schouler, James. *History of the United States of America: Under the Constitution.* Volume V, 1847–1861. New York: Kraus Reprint Co., 1970.

Schweninger, Loren. *Black Property Owners in the South, 1790–1915.* Urbana: University of Illinois Press, 1990.

Scripps, John Locke. *Life of Abraham Lincoln.* New York: Greenwood Press, 1968.

Sellers, Charles. *The Market Revolution: Jacksonian America 1815–1846.* New York: Oxford University Press, 1991.

Senning, John P. "The Know-Nothing Movement in Illinois." *The Journal of the Illinois State Historical Society,* April 1914.

Sewell, Richard H. *Ballots for Freedom: Antislavery Politics in the United States, 1837–1860.* New York: Norton, 1976.

————. *A House Divided: Sectionalism and Civil War, 1848–1865.* Baltimore: Johns Hopkins University Press, 1988.

Sheahan, James W. *The Life of Stephen A. Douglas.* New York: Harper & Brothers, 1860.

Silbey, Joel H. *The American Party Battle: Election Campaign Pamphlets, 1828–1876.* Cambridge, MA: Harvard University Press, 1999.

————, ed. *The Transformation of American Politics, 1840–1860.* Englewood Cliffs, NJ: Prentice-Hall, 1967.

Sigelschiffer, Saul. *The American Conscience: The Drama of the Lincoln-Douglas Debates.* New York: Horizon Press, 1973.

Simms, Henry Harrison. *A Decade of Sectional Controversy, 1851–1861.* Chapel Hill: The University of North Carolina Press, 1942.

Simon, John Y. *House Divided: Lincoln and His Father.* Fort Wayne, IN: Louis A. Warren Lincoln Library, 1987.

Simon, Paul. *Lincoln's Preparation for Greatness: The Illinois Legislative Years.* Urbana: University of Illinois Press, 1989.

Simpson, Brooks D. *Think Anew, Act Anew: Abraham Lincoln on Slavery, Freedom, and Union.* Wheeling, IL: Harlan Davidson, 1998.

Smith, Elbert B. *The Death of Slavery: The United States, 1837–65.* Chicago: University of Chicago Press, 1967.

Smith, Theodore Clarke. *Parties and Slavery, 1850–1859.* New York: Negro Universities Press, 1969.

Snay, Mitchell. "Abraham Lincoln, Owen Lovejoy, and the Emergence of the Republican Party in Illinois." *Journal of the Abraham Lincoln Association,* Winter 2001.

Stampp, Kenneth M. *And the War Came: The North and the Secession Crisis, 1860–61.* Baton Rouge: Louisiana State University Press, 1950.

———. *The Imperiled Union: Essays on the Background of the Civil War.* New York: Oxford University Press, 1980.

———. *The Peculiar Institution.* New York: Vintage Books, 1989.

———. *America in 1857: A Nation on the Brink.* New York: Oxford University Press, 1990.

Stephenson, Nathaniel Wright. *Lincoln.* Grosset & Dunlap, 1924.

Stoddard, William O. *Abraham Lincoln: The True Story of a Great Life.* New York: Fords, Howard & Hulbert, 1884.

Storey, Moorfield. *Charles Sumner.* Boston: Houghton, Mifflin and Company, 1900.

Striner, Richard. *Father Abraham: Lincoln's Relentless Struggle to End Slavery.* New York: Oxford University Press, 2006.

Tarbell, Ida. *The Life of Abraham Lincoln.* Volume I. New York: Lincoln Memorial Association, 1900.

Taylor, John M. *William Henry Seward.* Washington, DC: Brassey's, 1996.

Temple, Sunderine, and Wayne C. Temple. *Abraham Lincoln and Illinois' Fifth Capitol.* Mahomet, IL: Mayhaven Publishing, 2006.

Thomas, Benjamin. *Abraham Lincoln.* New York: Alfred K. Knopf, Inc., 1973.

Thomas, Benjamin P. *Lincoln's New Salem.* Springfield, IL: The Abraham Lincoln Association/The Lakeside Press, 1934.

Thomas, John L. *The Liberator, William Lloyd Garrison: A Biography.* Boston: Little, Brown, 1961.

Van Deusen, Glyndon. *Horace Greeley: Nineteenth-Century Crusader.* Philadelphia: University of Pennsylvania Press, 1953.

———. *William Henry Seward.* New York: Oxford University Press, 1967.

Von Abele, Rudolph. *Alexander H. Stephens: A Biography.* New York: Alfred A. Knopf, 1946.

Wakefield, Sherman D. *How Lincoln Became President.* New York: Wilson-Erikson, 1936.

Warren, Louis A. *A. Lincoln's Parentage and Childhood.* New York: Century Company, 1929.

———. *A. Lincoln's Youth: Indiana Years, Seven to Twenty-one, 1816–1830.* Indianapolis: Indiana Historical Society, 1959.

Watkins, Albert. "Douglas, Lincoln and The Nebraska Bill." *American Historical Magazine,* May and June 1908.

Watson, Thomas Edward. *The Life and Times of Thomas Jefferson.* New York: D. Appleton and Company, 1903.

Weik, Jesse W. *The Real Lincoln: A Portrait.* Lincoln: University of Nebraska Press, 2002.

Wellman, Paul I. *The House Divides: The Age of Jackson and Lincoln, from the War of 1812 to the Civil War.* Garden City, NY: Doubleday & Company, 1966.

Wells, Damon. *Stephen Douglas: The Last Years, 1857–1861.* Austin: University of Texas Press, 1971.

Werstein, Irving. *Abraham Lincoln versus Jefferson Davis.* New York: T. Y. Crowell, 1959.

Wharton, Oliver P. "Lincoln and the Beginning of the Republican Party in Illinois." An Address Read before the Illinois Historical Society at its Annual Meeting, Evanston, Illinois, May 1911.

———. *The Life of Lyman Trumbull.* Boston: Houghton Mifflin Company, 1913.

White, Horace. *The Life of Lyman Trumbull.* Boston: Houghton Mifflin Co., 1913.

White, Ronald C., Jr. *The Eloquent President: A Portrait of Lincoln through His Words.* New York: Random House, 2005.

Wiecek, William M. *The Sources of Antislavery Constitutionalism in America, 1760–1848.* Ithaca: Cornell University Press, 1977.

Wieck, Carl F. *Lincoln's Quest for Equality: The Road to Gettysburg.* Dekalb: Northern Illinois University Press, 2002.

Wilentz, Sean. *The Rise of American Democracy: Jefferson to Lincoln.* New York: Norton, 2005.

Williams, Frank J., William D. Pederson, and Vincent J. Marsala, eds. *Abraham Lincoln: Sources and Style of Leadership.* Westport, CT: Greenwood Press, 1994.

Wills, Garry. *Lincoln at Gettysburg: The Words That Remade America.* New York: Simon and Schuster, 1992.

Wilson, Douglas L. *Lincoln before Washington.* Urbana: University of Illinois Press, 1997.

———. *Honor's Voice: The Transformation of Abraham Lincoln.* New York, Knopf, 1998.

———. *Lincoln's Sword.* New York: Alfred A. Knopf, 2006.

Wilson, Rufus Rockwell. *What Lincoln Read.* Washington, D.C.: 1932.

Wilson, Henry. *History of the Rise and Fall of the Slave Power.* Volume II. New York: Negro Universities Press, 1969.

Wilson, Woodrow. *A History of the American People.* Volume IV. New York: Harper & Brothers, 1902.

Winkle, Kenneth J. *The Young Eagle: The Rise of Abraham Lincoln.* Dallas, TX: Taylor Trade Publishing, 2001.

Wolf, Gerald W. *The Kansas-Nebraska Bill: Party, Section, and the Coming of the Civil War.* New York: Revisionist Press, 1977.

Woodward, C. Vann. *American Counterpoint.* Boston: Little, Brown, 1971.

Wright, John S. *Lincoln & the Politics of Slavery.* Reno: University of Nevada Press, 1970.

Zarefsky, David. *Lincoln Douglas and Slavery: In the Crucible of Public Debate.* Chicago: University of Chicago Press, 1990.

Zornow, William Frank. *Kansas: A History of the Jayhawk State.* Norman: University of Oklahoma Press, 1957.

INDEX

Page numbers in italics indicate photographs.